Political Economy in the Evolution of China's Urban–Rural Economic Relations

AF828924

This book investigates the trajectory and evolutionary mechanisms of China's urban–rural economic relationships, seeking to explore how a developing socialist country can attain sustainable development and common prosperity.

Grounded in a deep literature review and a practical analysis of real-world conditions in China, the study challenges the dual economy theory of development economics that has prevailed in discussion of Chinese urban–rural economic relationships and puts forward an alternative analytical framework based on political economy. Considering the role political and social factors have played in China's economic development since 1949, the author divides the evolution of China's urban–rural economic relationship into two stages. In the first stage, the relationship is seen to be a "separated" one, a situation that led to several repercussions; but the reform and opening-up of the late 1970s marked a turning point leading to a second stage featured by "imbalanced integration". Through empirical research, the book analyses the momentum, economic effects, and problems of this turn, thereby envisaging an upgraded stage marked out by "collaborative integration", integral to further economic development and a more prosperous society in all respects.

The title will appeal to scholars and student studying political economy, urban–rural economic relationships, development economics, and the Chinese economy.

Fan Gao is Professor of Economics in the Department of Economics at Fudan University in China. He specializes in urban–rural dual economic structure transformation, agricultural economics, political economics, and development economics.

China Perspectives

The *China Perspectives* series focuses on translating and publishing works by leading Chinese scholars, writing about both global topics and China-related themes. It covers Humanities & Social Sciences, Education, Media and Psychology, as well as many interdisciplinary themes.

This is the first time any of these books have been published in English for international readers. The series aims to put forward a Chinese perspective, give insights into cutting-edge academic thinking in China, and inspire researchers globally.

To submit proposals, please contact the Taylor & Francis Publisher for China Publishing Programme, Lian Sun (Lian.Sun@informa.com)

Titles in economics partly include:

Economics of the Pandemic
Weathering the Storm and Restoring Growth
Edited by Cai Fang

The Economics of Government Regulation
Fundamentals and Application in China
Wang Junhao

Macroeconomic Policy and Steady Growth in China
2020 Dancing with Black Swan
Edited by Zhang Xiaojing

Political and Economic Analysis of State-Owned Enterprise Reform
Huiming Zhang

Political Economy in the Evolution of China's Urban–Rural Economic Relations
Fan Gao

For more information, please visit https://www.routledge.com/China-Perspectives/book-series/CPH

Political Economy in the Evolution of China's Urban–Rural Economic Relations

Fan Gao

Routledge
Taylor & Francis Group
LONDON AND NEW YORK

First published in English 2022
by Routledge
2 Park Square, Milton Park, Abingdon, Oxon OX14 4RN

and by Routledge
605 Third Avenue, New York, NY 10158

Routledge is an imprint of the Taylor & Francis Group, an informa business

© 2022 Fan Gao

The right of Fan Gao to be identified as author of this work has been asserted by him in accordance with sections 77 and 78 of the Copyright, Designs and Patents Act 1988.

All rights reserved. No part of this book may be reprinted or reproduced or utilised in any form or by any electronic, mechanical, or other means, now known or hereafter invented, including photocopying and recording, or in any information storage or retrieval system, without permission in writing from the publishers.

Trademark notice: Product or corporate names may be trademarks or registered trademarks, and are used only for identification and explanation without intent to infringe.

Published in Chinese by Fudan University Press 2019
English Version by permission of Fudan University Press.

British Library Cataloguing-in-Publication Data
A catalogue record for this book is available from the British Library

Library of Congress Cataloging-in-Publication Data
Names: Gao, Fan, 1976- author.
Title: Political economy in the evolution of China's urban-rural economic relations / Fan Gao.
Description: Abingdon, Oxon; New York, NY: Routledge, 2021. | Series: China perspectives | Includes bibliographical references and index. | Identifiers: LCCN 2021002085 (print) | LCCN 2021002086 (ebook) | ISBN 9781032028378 (hardback) | ISBN 9781032029283 (paperback) | ISBN 9781003185857 (ebook)
Subjects: LCSH: Rural development--China. | Rural development--China. | Rural-urban relations--China. | Economic development--China. | China--Rural conditions. | China--Economic conditions.
Classification: LCC HN740.Z9 C63761125 2021 (print) | LCC HN740.Z9 (ebook) | DDC 307.1/4120951--dc23
LC record available at https://lccn.loc.gov/2021002085
LC ebook record available at https://lccn.loc.gov/2021002086

ISBN: 978-1-032-02837-8 (hbk)
ISBN: 978-1-032-02928-3 (pbk)
ISBN: 978-1-003-18585-7 (ebk)

DOI: 10.4324/9781003185857

Typeset in Times New Roman
by MPS Limited, Dehradun

Contents

Figures

Tables

Preface

Urban–rural duality is a common feature of economic system among developing countries. The Lewis-Fei-Ranis model is the classic dual economy theory of development economics. As the largest developing country in the world, China has also featured urban–rural duality all the time ever since 1949. Over time, its urban–rural economic relationship has differed from one period to another. In 1978, China embarked on the great cause of reform and opening up with rural management system reform as the cut-in point. Up to the present day, this monumental initiative has been going on for 40 years. The 40 years of reform and opening up has profoundly changed China's economic and social architecture, as well as its urban–rural economic relationship. Today, the socialism with Chinese characteristics is entering a new era, which both raises requirements and offers conditions for continuously improving China's urban–rural economic relationship. Based on this practical background, at a point of time when reform and opening up is advancing into the fortieth year, it is of great theoretical value and practical significance to make a systematic review and explanation on the evolutionary logic of China's urban–rural economic relationship after 1949, especially since the start of reform and opening up 40 years ago.

This book begins by defining the three core concepts covered in the research—urban and rural areas, urban–rural economic relationship, and separation and integration. It then reviews existing research literature along three clues: study on the contents and measurements of China's urban–rural economic relationship, study on the status quo and causes of China's urban–rural economic relationship, and study on potential ways and options for improving urban–rural economic relationship and points out that these studies are performed on the basis of the dual economy theory of development economics. Based on these studies, the book probes into the classic dual economy theory of development economics. In particular, it explains the theoretical essence and implied hypotheses of the Lewis-Fei-Ranis model and points out that this model contains implied hypotheses, such as dual economy results from endowment gap, the capital–labor ratio is constant, and the urban–rural factor market is perfect, which do not totally agree with the reality of China as a large developing country. On ground of this, the book maintains that the evolution of China's urban–rural economic relationship should be understood based on a fundamental proposition: how shall a large developing country with socialist system realize its goal of sustainable development and common prosperity? Next, it expounds on the major local characteristics of China—socialist system, a large developing country, and economic system transition, and puts forward a political economy analytical framework for urban–rural economic relationship, which is different from the Lewis-Fei-Ranis model of development economics but agrees with the local characteristics of China.

The analytical framework proposed herein holds that China's urban–rural economic relationship during different periods of time does not solely relate to the development of the urban and the rural sector themselves, but is the outcome of national development strategies and economic systems between the two sectors. Hence, China's urban–rural economic relationship should be understood in a broader institutional setting. That is, there has been an interaction chain among development strategy and constraints, choice of economic system, behavior of microeconomic subjects, and performance of economic development (transformation of urban–rural economic relationship) in China during different periods of time. In this sequential interaction, choice of economic system plays a critical role in urban–rural economic relationship, but choice of economic system itself derives from the way national development strategy is combined with constraints. When there is a change in the development strategy and constraints, and the way of their combination, urban–rural economic relationship is bound to change as an outcome of adjustments of the economic system and the change of the behavior of microeconomic subjects. Notably, in China, choice of economic system revolves around government–market relationship, whereas structural features exist inside the government and the market themselves. Hence, related intergovernmental and intermarket rules also constitute an important part of China's economic system. In other words, China's urban–rural economic relationship has formed and evolved under a series of economic systems (government–market relationship, intragovernmental economic systems, and intramarket economic systems), which is the most critical logical clue underlying the evolution of China's urban–rural economic relationship since 1949.

On the basis of the above-described theoretical construction work, in the empirical research section, the book first uses indicators such as urban and rural employment and population structure, urban–rural comparative labor productivity gap, and urban–rural resident consumption gap to depict the evolutionary trajectory of China's urban–rural economic relationship since the founding of the People's Republic of China (PRC) and separates it into two stages: a stage of separation before and a stage of transformation toward integration after 1978 when reform and opening up first started. Based on the results of this measurement, it explains the formation and dynamic evolution of China's urban–rural economic relationship during different periods of time. The book argues that in the planned economy era, the combination of China's heavy industry first strategy with given constraints led to a series of economic system arrangements: the people's commune in rural areas, unitary public ownership in urban areas, unified purchase and marketing of agricultural products, and urban and rural household registration. The core of these systems was implementing a planned economy with high power centralization to, and rigid control from, the central government, with hardly any differentiation among governments at different hierarchical levels and different markets. Under these economic system arrangements, China did manage to form an independent and fairly complete industrial system against the extremely unfavorable initial conditions, yet the entire economy was on the verge of collapse due to the low efficiency of resource allocation. Between urban and rural areas, microeconomic subjects were had no chance to trade products and allocate factors spontaneously. The gaps of labor productivity, income, and consumption stayed at a constantly high level. Urban–rural separation virtually characterized China's urban–rural economic relationship during this period.

The development of national industrialization and the continuation of low economic efficiency changed the country's development strategy and constraints. After 1978, China began to shift its development focus from heavy industry to economic growth. The new combination of development strategy and constraints led to unique government–market relationship and intragovernmental and intramarket institutional arrangements. Since reform and opening up, China's economic system reform has been advancing along the mainline of causing the government to relax its economic control over microeconomic subjects and constantly highlight the role of market in the optimal allocation of resources. Using market mechanism to improve the efficiency of resource allocation so as to realize rapid economic growth reflects the similarity of China's economic development to that of other countries. Being a large developing country with socialist system, however, China also began to see emerging intergovernmental and intermarket structural features—regionally decentralized authoritarianism and upstream-guided market expansion were shaped, which reflects the difference of China's market-oriented system transition from other economies. In other words, China's market-oriented system transition is unique in terms of pathway and mode. Subject to these economic systems, the behavioral choice of China's microeconomic subjects is bound to produce corresponding results: China's GDP has created a world "miracle" of growth, yet structural problems in the economic domain has kept accumulating and exacerbating at the same time; its urban–rural relationship is faced with the objective reality of overall integration but with a level of imbalance. In fact, imbalanced integration basically characterizes China's urban–rural economic relationship since reform and opening up.

After the entry into the 21st century, especially since the Eighteenth National Congress of the CPC in 2012, China has actively pushed forward the adaptive adjustment of development concept; its development strategy has also switched from economic growth to coordinated development. The report to the Nineteenth National Congress of the Communist Party of China (CPC) clearly declared that the socialism with Chinese characteristics has entered a new era that the main social contradiction has transformed and the economic development stage has changed. This signifies that the country has formally established a coordinated development strategy at the economic level. This new combination of development strategy and constraints implies the redirection of the country's urban–rural economic relationship from an imbalanced integration toward a collaborative one. Here, collaborative integration encompasses improved urban–rural factor fluidity and allocation efficiency, reduced urban–rural income and consumption gap, enhanced urban–rural equalization of basic public services, as well as structural optimization among different parts in a context of differentiation inside urban and rural areas. In terms of the realization mechanism, to achieve collaborative integration of urban–rural economic relationship in the context of the new era, China needs to reform its economic system continuously so as to make the market play a decisive role in the allocation of resources and give better play to the role of the government. The "market driven + government compensated combination policy" is a policy choice of China to achieve collaborative integration of urban–rural economic relationship. Furthermore, to achieve collaborative integration, China should also address the perfection of its intergovernmental and intermarket economic systems and highlight participation constraints and incentive compatibility constraints for related stakeholders as the base point for implementing policies in favor of the collaborative integration of urban–rural economic relationship.

In a nutshell, this book applies a political economy analytical framework with local characteristics to explain the evolutionary logic of China's urban–rural economic relationship. Such research work signifies that while the Lewis-Fei-Ranis model represents an important ideological source for understanding China's urban–rural duality, we cannot deduce the forming and evolutionary mechanism of the country's urban–rural economic relationship directly from this model. Rather, China's urban–rural economic relationship should be understood based on its local characteristics—socialist system, a large developing country, and economic system transition. Attention should be paid to the interaction chain among development strategy and constraints, choice of economic system, behavior of microeconomic subjects, and performance of economic development (transformation of urban–rural economic relationship). The research of economic system should account for multiple factors such as government–market relationship, intergovernmental structure, and intermarket structure. Since reform and opening up, regionally decentralized authoritarianism and upstream-guided market expansion have best characterized China's economic system. To understand the changes of urban–rural economic relationship, the generality and particularity of this system reform should be established, and government–market dichotomy should be extended to intragovernmental and intramarket structural features. Evidently, political economy is effective in understanding China's economic development; it is important to explain China's urban–rural economic relationship from the perspective of "political economy of development"; the proposition of establishing a political economy for socialism with Chinese characteristics has a strong practical basis. In that connection, this book not only tries to explain the evolutionary history of China's urban–rural economic relationship across a long-time span. It also tries to look at the generality and heterogeneity behind the evolution of China's urban–rural economic relationship. In selecting the analytical paradigm, it prefers to use a political economy perspective to explain the development economy issue of the changes of China's urban–rural economic relationship, thereby showing a more striking feature of a "political economy of development", and to present a response to the construction of a political economy of socialism with Chinese characteristics from the perspective of urban–rural economic relationship.

Gao Fan
December 2018

1 Introduction

The founding of the PRC in 1949 marked a monumental event in the development history of China and even in the development history of the human being. Since 1949, the fundamental proposition facing the country's modernization drive has been: how shall a large developing country with socialist system realize its goal of sustainable development and common prosperity? In response to this fundamental proposition, China has undergone two stages of economic development: a pre-1978 stage and a post-1978 stage. Particularly, compared to the pre-1978 stage of planned economy with emphasis on high power centralization to central government, in 1978, China embarked on a major strategy of market-oriented reform inside and global integration outside. Over the 40 years of reform and opening up, China's GDP has sustained continuous high-speed growth and created a world "miracle" of growth. Compared with the early days of the PRC or at the beginning of reform and opening up, the country's economic strength, comprehensive national strength, and international influence are remarkably greater; the income level and social well-being of its urban and rural residents have also upgraded rapidly. By longitudinal comparison, the reform and opening up since 1978 has indeed changed the overall image of China. It has brought about profound, fundamental changes in the Chinese society and will push the Chinese economy from a stage of high-speed growth up into a stage of high-quality development.

Notably, the 40 years of reform and opening up has not only affected China's overall economic and social architecture enormously but it has also made a great difference to the relevance and structural composition among different components of the Chinese economy. Alongside the continuous promotion of market-oriented reform and opening up to the outside world, continuous, systematic changes have also taken place in China's urban–rural economic relationship. In fact, as a large developing country with urban–rural duality, urban–rural economic relationship has always remained a major concern that China has to face up to on its road to modernization. The evolution of urban–rural economic relationship has also constituted an important part of China's modernization drive since 1949, especially after reform and opening up. It is embedded into the country's overall economic development and interacts with reforms in other segments. From a temporal point of view, China's urban–rural economic relationship today is already remarkably different from how it used to be in the early days of the PRC or at the beginning of reform and opening up. The change from separation toward integration and the enhanced degree of integration pinpoint the main trend of this relational evolution. Based on this practical reality, a question arises out of theoretical exploration: what is the evolutionary logic and mechanism of China's urban–rural economic relationship? Giving a systematic, in-depth answer to this question from an academic point of view becomes the core topic of this book.

1.1 Raising of the question

From international experience, urban–rural duality is a common issue among developing countries. Promoting the transformation of duality is also the common mission among developing countries to achieve economic development. Accordingly, the very influential dual economy theory has formed as part of development economics. Nevertheless, when it comes to China, a large developing country with socialist system, and at a particular point of time when reform and opening up is advancing into the 40th year, discussing the evolutionary logic and intrinsic mechanism of its urban–rural economic relationship does not simply involve direct application of existing theories or local testing on international experience. It obviously has a fairly unique theoretical concern and practical background.

1.1.1 A localized scrutiny into the classic theory of development economics

Research on China's urban–rural economic relationship involves a localized examination into the classic theory of development economics. Interests in urban–rural economic relationship can be traced back to as early as the classical political economy constructed by William Petty and Adam Smith. Marxist political economy also involves discussions and studies on the relationships between industry and agriculture and between urban and rural areas (Jiang Y.M., Xian R.S. & Zhang X.L., 2015; Liu, 2017). However, development economics, which emerged after the 1940s, is more interested in the intrinsic laws behind the prosperity of impoverished, backward agricultural countries or developing economies, and this interest has enabled the development of a systemic dual economy theory in light of the economic characteristics of these countries. Particularly, the Lewis–Fei-Ranis model, as the most representative dual economy theory, reveals that in developing countries there commonly coexist a traditional sector represented by agriculture and a modern sector represented by manufacture. It then demonstrates how the nonagricultural transfer of rural surplus labor as the core mechanism has caused these countries to evolve from urban–rural opposition to urban–rural integration. Over the 40 years of reform and opening up, as the role of the market in resource allocation grows more prominent, China has also seen its rural labor work in township enterprises or in cities as "rural migrant workers". This practice has prompted many authors to use the Lewis-Fei-Ranis model in theoretical research to examine China's urban–rural economic relationship. One point remains. The Lewis-Fei-Ranis model deals more with the important role of the nonagricultural transfer of rural labor, but it gives no detailed explanation on how urban–rural duality comes into being and in what way labor flows. More importantly, the implied hypothesis of a perfect factor market behind this model also disagrees with China's current economic system transition.

These realities signify that, to tie the dual economy theory of development economics with China's development practice, rather than presume that this theory can be directly transplanted and is able to interpret China's problems thoroughly, the first thing to do is make clear how well the implied hypotheses behind the theory agree with the local background. Only in this way can we better explain the general attribute and unique nature of the evolution of China's urban–rural economic relationship. In that connection, exploring the evolutionary logic of China's urban–rural economic relationship is crucial to theoretical research. It constitutes a necessary step for examining and discriminating the explanatory power of the classic theory of development economics based on local practice.

1.1.2 Building blocks for a political economy of socialism with Chinese characteristics

Research on China's urban–rural economic relationship involves the construction of a political economy of socialism with Chinese characteristics. Since 1949, China's economic development across different periods of time has been both successive and evolutionary. Particularly, remarkable achievements have been made in the country's economic development since reform and opening up. This development practice and performance calls for a theoretical explanation, which drives the modernization and Sinicization of Marxist political economy and the demand of constructing a political economy of socialism with Chinese characteristics on the academic dimension. Similar to other theories, the political economy of socialism with Chinese characteristics also consists of an understanding on the laws of economic issues. Different from other theories, the political economy of socialism with Chinese characteristics aims to, while maintaining the scientific kernel of political economy, distills out the systematic law for this large developing country with socialist system to realize economic prosperity, and forms a theoretical guide for China to realize its goal of sustainable economic growth and common prosperity. This systematic theory constitutes part of the discourse system of the Chinese philosophy and social sciences, as well as the Chinese contribution to the enrichment and development of existing economic theories. The political economy of socialism with Chinese characteristics is a logically consistent knowledge system composed of different components, for which the theoretical research on urban–rural economic relationship constitutes a strong support.

In terms of causes, China's urban–rural economic opposition is closely associated with the nation's heavy industry first strategy during the planned economy era, and it does not solely results from the allocation of labor resources between urban and rural areas. In terms of transformation pathway, China's urban–rural labor reallocation involves an occupational change and an identity transformation, and it does not solely relate to the nonagricultural transfer of rural labor. In terms of transformation mechanism, the evolution of China's urban–rural economic relationship has taken place in a context of market-oriented transition and unequal degree of marketization. It differs from the transformation of dual economy under the hypotheses of a perfect factor market. All these characteristics determine that the development issue of urban–rural economic relationship has to be investigated in light of the political and social systems, taking account of the local characteristics of China, that is, socialist system, a large developing country, and economic system transition. Obviously, exploring the evolutionary mechanism of China's urban–rural economic relationship constitutes an intrinsic requisite and constituent of constructing a political economy of socialism with Chinese characteristics.

1.1.3 Policy choice for urban–rural integrated development in the new era

Research on China's urban–rural economic relationship involves policy choice in favor of urban–rural integrated development in the context of the new era. Compared with the planned economy era, since reform and opening up, China's urban–rural economic relationship has changed from separation toward integration. However, at a point of time when socialism with Chinese characteristics is entering a new era, the country's integrated urban–rural economic development is standing at a new takeoff point with new missions and challenges. This is evidenced by the continued reduction of urban–rural income gap since 2009, although the sustainability of this reduction has to be observed across a longer time span and, by cross-country comparison, China's urban–rural income gap is still prominent at present. Against the narrowing urban–rural income gap, the "new duality" that emerged in urban China following the flow of rural labor has not been fundamentally resolved; income and consumption disparities among individual farmers in rural China are growing more prominent in recent years, too. This signifies that urban–rural dual contrast still remains an important structural problem for the country. In terms of development concept, after the entry into the new century, China began to advocate a scientific development outlook of people-oriented, overall coordinated, sustainable development. Recently, it has explicitly set forth the goal of implementing new development concepts of "innovation, coordination, green, openness, and sharing". In view of the fact that the socialism with Chinese characteristics has entered a new era, the report to the 19th National Congress of the CPC noted that China's main social contradiction has transformed into the contradiction between people's growing needs for a better life and imbalanced, inadequate development; that economic development has shifted from a stage of high-speed growth to a stage of high-quality development; and that China should, in addition to building a moderately prosperous society in all respects, basically realize modernization and become a great modern country. To respond to the new development concepts and resolve the new social contradiction, efforts have to be employed to boost the transformation of urban–rural duality so as to make China's urban–rural economic relationship an important pillar supporting the country's modern economic system and modernization drive.

In this practical reality, China's urban–rural economic relationship in the new era is more diverse in content and more important in function. It is not only a matter of economic relevance between the urban and rural sectors but also a matter of transformation of the country's overall economic development concept and mode. In its effort to bring into practice the new development concepts, since reform and opening up, especially after the entry into the 21st century, China has implemented a succession of policies intended to "support agriculture, benefit agriculture, and strengthen agriculture". At present, it is working hard to promote rural revitalization and agricultural and rural priority strategies. Accordingly, how to precisely evaluate the implementation effectiveness of these policies and find the right pathway for urban–rural integrated development in the new era becomes an important topic facing China. Logically speaking, to respond to this topic, the first thing to do is to gain a deep insight into the evolutionary logic of China's urban–rural economic relationship. Only by clarifying the "road bringing us here?, can we catch hold of the "road leading us to future" more accurately. In that connection, exploring the evolutionary logic of China's urban–rural economic relationship is a precondition for the country to effectively formulate and implement public policies for urban and rural development in the new era.

In a nutshell, this book focuses on the evolutionary logic and intrinsic mechanism of China's urban–rural economic relationship since the founding of the PRC, especially after reform and opening up. At the theoretical level, the book attempts to form a recomprehension of the dual economy theory based on the local practice of China, and then, from the political economy point of view, put forward a theoretical framework of urban–rural economic relationship that agrees with China's own characteristics. This analytical framework offers a new perspective for understanding the urban–rural economic issues of large developing countries and forms a strong support for the political economy of socialism with Chinese characteristics on the dimension of urban–rural relationship. At the practical level, the book attempts to respond to the changes of China's economic stage, development concept, and main social contradiction. After making clear the evolutionary logic of urban–rural economic relationship, it identifies the institutional conditions for China to push its urban–rural economic relationship up to a higher level of integration in the new era, and puts forward the evolutionary pathway and policy options for urban–rural relationship that agree with a stage of high-quality development. Obviously, the research topic of this book is very valuable both in theory and in practice.

1.2 Definition of important concepts

Theoretical research of economy is to grasp the intrinsic laws of economic activities by establishing concepts and analyzing the relevance among these concepts. This book focuses on the evolutionary logic of China's urban–rural economic relationship since the founding of the PRC, especially after reform and opening up, and summarizes this evolution as a change "from separation to integration". This research is also built on analyzing related concepts, which constitute the cut-in point for understanding China's urban–rural economic relationship. Hence by extension, before any concrete analysis is made, it is very necessary to define the few core concepts covered in this book.

1.2.1 Towns and villages

Towns and villages, also referred to as "urban" and "rural" for short, constitute the pair of core concepts covered by the research topic of this book. From human history, towns and villages did not exist from the birth of man. Over a long period of time after man bid farewell to ape, people had been mainly engaged in plant cultivation and animal rearing. These industrial activities were strictly dependent on land resources distributed on the earth's surface, resulting in the spatial dispersion of people's production and living. During this period, there was no rigid distinction between towns and villages. Following the three social divisions at the end of the primitive society, especially the gradual separation of handicraft and commerce from agriculture, the trading frequency throughout the human society began to rise and the trading scope began to broaden. The mode of production and way of life began to differentiate. Spatial agglomerations of population on account of falling trading costs began to emerge in succession. This way, towns became a new social form that was born out of, yet was different from, villages. Residents in the particular country also began to separate as town people and village people. The economic relationship between urban and rural areas, accordingly, became a major topic that has to be faced up to by the particular country over the course of modernization.

Theoretically speaking, urban and rural areas are two parts that jointly make up the overall national economic system of a particular country. These two parts are inevitably related by the exchange of commodities and factors, with a range of "disparities" or "heterogeneities" at the same time though. In fact, without these "heterogeneities", urban–rural duality, urban–rural economic relationship, and urban–rural structural transformation would all become a "pseudo-problem". Over the long period of social evolution, towns and villages have gradually evolved into a composite containing multiple dimensions such as economy, society, politics, culture, and ecology. While it is possible to describe, explain, and understand the differences between urban and rural areas from any dimension, comparison on the economic dimension is still the fundamental, decisive work for understanding urban–rural disparities. This is not only because urban–rural opposition originates from economic logic—they characterize different industrial and spatial conglomerations—but also because their disparities at the economic level have led to urban–rural gaps on other dimensions. That is, urban–rural disparities in society, politics, culture, economy and the like tend to stem from economic gaps; the reduction of urban–rural gaps on these dimensions is also highly dependent on the process of urban–rural economic integration. From an economic point of view, Gao F. (2016a) identified three perspectives from which urban–rural "heterogeneities" should be understood. First is the industrial perspective. That is, urban–rural disparity in economic nature originates from industrial form. Agriculture, primarily plant growing and animal rearing, is concentrated in rural areas, whereas industry, primarily manufacture, and service derived therefrom, are mainly concentrated in urban areas. While industry and service may exist in the rural sector, too, the prevalence of agriculture in rural areas still registers an important difference between urban and rural areas. Second is the spatial perspective. That is, urban–rural economic disparities are not solely manifested on the industrial dimension but also on the spatial dimension, for example, the way of economic organization and the process of commercialization and monetization. Compared with its rural counterpart, the urban sector has a higher degree of economic organization, commercialization, and monetization. These spatial disparities are typically reflected in the differentiated ways and efficiencies of factor allocation between the two sectors. Third is the resident perspective. That is, the economic activities in both the urban and rural sectors are driven by residents (and urban and rural labor). As such, attention should be paid to the economic objectives, constraints, and ways of behavior of urban and rural residents. Particularly, while urban residents and rural residents are in essence just two social groups with economic division of labor, they are very likely to be given the identity attributes for the allocation of different public goods and social security resources.

From the point of practice, the industry, spatial, and resident perspectives depict the different behaviors of urban–rural economic "heterogeneities", and they are important to understanding the urban and rural sectors and the relationship between them. Although these three perspectives do not strictly correspond to one another, namely, it is impossible to deduce disparities from the spatial or resident perspective directly from disparities from the industrial perspective, there still is a relevance among them. In a way, disparities from the industrial perspective combine with other factors to result in urban–rural disparities from the spatial or resident perspectives. This is mainly because, compared with industry and service, traditional agriculture tends to face higher natural risks, demand risks, and market pricing risks (industrial perspective). That is, compared with the second and the third industries, traditional agriculture tends to have an industrial vulnerability or lower comparative income. These industrial characteristics combine with other factors to make rural economic activities more inclined toward risk aversion and natural economy. Studies of peasant economics tend to emphasize the stronger risk aversion or "safety first" nature of agricultural producers (Ellis F., 2006) and the appreciable geographical decentralization of agricultural management, which is responsible for the lower level of commercialization and monetization of agricultural management (spatial perspective). The industrial characteristics and spatial decentralization of farmers determine the higher cost of organization. As a consequence, in the political structure of developing countries, rural residents are less influential to policies than their urban counterparts (Lipton M., 1977). This signifies that rural residents tend to be a disadvantaged social group in the formulation of public policies and the access to public resources (resident perspective).

In view of the difference and relevance among these three perspectives, this book attempts to understand urban–rural economic "heterogeneities" mainly from the spatial perspective. That is not only because the spatial perspective boils down urban–rural issues to the core economics topic of resource allocation but also because the spatial perspective constitutes a link between the industrial and resident perspectives. That is, urban–rural disparities in industrial characteristics are an important contributor to disparities in their spatial characteristics, which in turn constitute an important contributor to their disparities from the resident perspective. As such, analyzing urban and rural issues from the spatial perspective is of fatal importance. Based on this understanding, the book emphasizes that urban and rural areas are two sectors in a particular country formed in different geographical spaces and with differentiated ways of economic organization, different ways of factor allocation, and different levels of efficiency. Industrial disparities are one of the contributors to these inter-sectoral disparities, which in turn constitute one of the contributors to the disparities between urban and rural residents in economic rights and living status.

Notably, understanding the two key concepts of urban and rural from the spatial perspective can also be supported by the country's economic statistical practice. The "Provisions on Standards for Urban and Rural Division" adopted at the 20th plenary meeting of the State Council on November 7, 1955, marked the first systematic division between urban and rural China with respect to planning, statistics, business accounting, and social administration.

This document pointed out that "... Considering that urban and rural people are different in both economic conditions and way of life, all government work should be differentiated between urban and rural areas; the urban and rural populations should also be calculated separately". The concrete division scheme identified the three statistical categories of urban area, urban-type resident area, and rural area. The explanatory notes to these provisions wrote that "... As proposed, the standard for urban-rural division is basically related to the division between towns and villages. Towns are more centrally populated with more developed industry and commerce, and their residents are primarily non-agricultural population; villages are less centrally populated, and their residents mainly rely on agriculture for subsistence. This division is proposed not only because it is simple and clear, but also because it can reflect the basic aspects distinguishing between urban and rural areas". Following that, China has adjusted its statistical caliber for towns and villages from time to time to adapt to changes in the industrial structure and population structure in urban and rural areas, as well in the national establishment standard for cities and towns. For example, on December 6, 1999, the National Bureau of Statistics (NBS) issued the "Provisions on Statistical Division of Urban and Rural Areas (for Trial Implementation)". On March 10, 2006, the NBS issued the "Interim Provisions on Statistical Division of Urban and Rural Areas" (GT[2006]60). In July 2008, the State Council replied to approve the "Provisions on Statistical Division of Urban and Rural Areas" (GH[2008]60) jointly formulated by the NBS together with Ministry of Civil Affairs, Ministry of Housing and Urban-Rural Development, Ministry of Finance, Ministry of Land and Resources, and Ministry of Agriculture[1], effective from August 1, 2008. The provisions approved by the State Council in 2008 formally laid the policy basis and methodological foundation for statistical division of urban and rural areas. After establishing the standard distinguishing between urban and rural areas, the document further divided the country's urban areas into city areas and town areas and obtained the statistical data of urban China and rural China based on this division. Apparently, the Chinese statistical caliber for "urban" and "rural" tries to, despite practical changes, reflect the economic disparities between these two sectors, as are typically reflected by the differentiated ways of factor allocation and spatial structure between the urban sector and rural sectors. Considering the availability and convincingness of data, the urban and rural economic data used herein are consistent with the statistical caliber of the NBS and mainly come from the statistical results of the NBS.

1.2.2 Urban–rural economic relationship

The human society depends on the production and consumption of materials and service products for development. Economic activities refer to the production, distribution, exchange, and consumption activities formed by people around the supply of materials and service products. Particularly, for people to produce materials and service products in the context of scarce resources, the optimal allocation of resources or factors is always taken into consideration. Accordingly, urban–rural economic relationship is the connection and relevance between the urban and rural sectors of a particular country or region formed over the course of economic activities. In existing studies, people tend to understand urban–rural economic relationship from the perspective of urban–rural income gap, which reflects the relative relationship between the urban and rural sectors from result of economic activities. It is a part, and even a principal part, of urban–rural economic relationship, but does not cover every aspect of urban–rural economic relationship. Broadly speaking, urban–rural economic relationship can be understood from the following different dimensions:

First is the product and factor relevance between urban and rural areas. As two parts of the national economic system, urban and rural areas differ in terms of industrial characteristics. Plant cultivation and animal rearing are mainly concentrated in rural areas, hence the rural sector tends to provide agricultural products or foods that are closely related to the subsidence of the human being. The industrial sector, primarily manufacture, and the service sector are mainly concentrated in urban areas, hence the urban sector tends to provide industrial goods and service products that are closely related to the development and entertainment of the human being. Such an industrial distribution signifies that there is a need of reallocating products between urban and rural areas, and allocation of products takes place between the urban and rural sectors whether under a planned economy or a market economy. The difference, however, is that the former takes place between the two sectors under the mandatory government plan, and the latter takes place spontaneously among microeconomic subjects through price negotiation. In the former instance, what happens between the urban and rural sectors is the allocation of products due to the actual absence of a price mechanism and a demand–supply mechanism. In the latter instance, exchange takes place between the urban and rural sectors spontaneously according to the price signals, so the allocation of products is actually the exchange of commodities. It is the product relevance between urban and rural areas that enables people to understand why price "scissors" between urban and rural products should take place in China during the planned economy era and why the rural sector had a market contribution to the product production of the urban sector.

In addition to the above industrial characteristics, there usually is a gap in resource endowments or factor conditions between the urban and rural sectors, too. Compared with the urban sector, the rural sector tends to be more advantaged in possessing labor and land factors, whereas the scale effect, agglomeration effect, and network effect of the urban sector lead to higher efficiency of labor and land output, which usually leads the transfer of rural labor and land factors into the urban sector. Given that the urban sector is more advantaged in possessing capital, knowledge, and information, with changes in the demand–supply relationship of factors and marginal returns, there is still a possibility that some capital and knowledge information factors also flow from urban areas into rural areas. This signifies that there exists a reallocation of factors between the urban and rural sectors, which can also be realized through both a planned economic system and a market economic system. Particularly, market-oriented reallocation tends to improve the allocation efficiency of urban and rural factors as an outcome of the spontaneous choice of microeconomic subjects. Only when based on the factor relevance between urban and rural sectors can we understand why the dual economy theory emphasizes the transfer of rural labor as the core mechanism for promoting structural transformation and why the rural sector has a factor contribution to the development of overall national economy. These understandings signify that the product and factor relevance between urban and rural areas is an important behavior of urban–rural economic relationship; it is also an optional perspective for observing and analyzing urban–rural economic relationship and its dynamics.

Second is the income and consumption gap between urban and rural areas. The reallocation of commodities and factors between the urban and rural sectors always leads to corresponding results, as is typically reflected by the change of urban–rural resident income gap. Existing literature tends to address urban–rural income gap as the kernel of urban–rural economic relationship and analyze the basic characteristics, evolutionary trend, main causes, and possible improvements of urban–rural income gap in a particular country. Since reform and opening up, researches on China's urban–rural income gap have also built up a huge literature database. However, from a metric point of view, urban–rural income gap differs in result depending on whether the price factor is excluded and whether the population structure is included. Urban–rural income gap is a particular economic phenomenon associated with economic development, which involves how to determine the "optimal range" of this gap, namely, what kind of gap is favorable or unfavorable to economic development. This judgment also involves choosing the basis for the government to make policies and the way to implement these policies, namely, under what changes in urban–rural income gap are the policies implemented and what is the optimal policy option and implementation condition for alleviating urban–rural income gap. In a large developing country like China, urban–rural income gap is understood as the principle part of urban–rural economic relationship because this is better supported by relevant statistical data in empirical research, and urban–rural income gap is commonly accepted as an important determinant of a country's overall income distribution pattern.

Nevertheless, economic activities are intended to improve the living conditions and welfare level of social members. Income constitutes one, but not the only, determinant of people's living conditions and welfare level. Compared with income as an "instrument", consumption functions more as a "value" in understanding urban–rural economic relationship, since it is better able to reflect the access to welfare among individual groups. Existing literature also maintains that compared with urban–rural income gap, urban–rural consumption gap as a straightforward indicator of living status better reflects the welfare disparity between urban and rural residents (Lin Y.F. & Chen B.K., 2009), and it is a more ideal proxy variable for measuring urban–rural economic gap (Xu Z.Y., Guo Z.C. & Jing L.B., 2014). This signifies that urban–rural consumption gap is more able to reflect urban–rural economic relationship in the result sense rather than in the instrument sense.

Understanding urban–rural economic relationship from the perspective of consumption gap forms a complement to income gap in two aspects. First, according to the consumption function theory of macroeconomics, resident consumption level is determined by a number of variables such as income (immediate income and permanent income), income distribution, resident expectation, and economic policy. Consequently, the determinants of urban–rural consumption gap include, but are not limited to, urban–rural income gap. The disparity between urban and rural residents in access to public goods and social security resources can be included into the analytical framework for urban–rural consumption gap since it affects resident consumption expectation. Second, urban–rural consumption gap is directly relevant to the transformation of economic development mode. At present, China's economy is moving from a stage of high-speed growth to a stage of high-quality development, and economic growth requires giving a better play to the contributions of resident' consumption, innovation, and other factors. In a stage of economic development mode transformation, urban–rural income gap directly affects China's overall income distribution, yet its connection with economic development mode transformation is indirect. China's current high-quality economic development not only includes enabling individual social groups to share the fruits of development in a relatively equal manner but also includes extending domestic resident consumption, so as to form an effective replacement for government investment and product export. Evidently, urban–rural consumption gap is directly relevant to China's economic development mode transformation. Therefore, urban–rural consumption gap is also an important dimension to indicate urban–rural economic relationship. It combines with urban–rural income gap to reflect the economic opposition and convergence between urban and rural areas from the perspective of economic operation result.

Third is the economic status of individual parts of the urban and rural sectors. Among existing studies on urban–rural issues, a general trend is to directly equate urban–rural economic relationship to the duality between the urban and rural sectors and the transformation of this structure. That is, urban–rural relationship is a matter of urban–rural duality. Here an implied judgment is the urban and rural areas in a particular country are "homogenized" inside themselves. Consequently, their focus of research naturally falls on the allocation of commodities and factors between the urban and rural sectors, as well as urban–rural income and consumption gap associated with the allocation of factors. From social practice, the economic relevance between the urban and rural sectors constitutes the principal part of urban–rural economic relationship, but the economic relationship among different parts of the urban and rural sectors themselves is also worth attention. Urban–rural economic relationship is a complex concept encompassing the economic relationship between urban and rural areas and between different parts of urban and rural areas. With the development of economy and society, especially with the increasing fluidity of factors in different fields, there also exist remarkable economic disparities between different groups of the urban and rural sectors themselves. That is, there are also prominent "heterogeneities" inside the urban and rural sectors. For example, the inflow of rural labor into cities definitely involves urban employment and integration, which results in an economic relevance between urban and rural residents. Under increasing fluidity of commodities and factors between the urban and rural sectors, individual groups in the rural sector will also begin to differentiate in employment choice, income level, consumption structure, and living conditions due to the disparities in resource endowment and individual ability. For a large developing country like China, the economic development level differs among different levels and different regions of urban areas. In the transformation of urban and rural economic structure, the outflow of rural labor, as labeled by "rural migrant worker", reflects the spontaneous choice of microeconomic subjects. This choice, however, is accompanied by a "new duality" between the urban registered population and the migrant population. Inside rural areas, disparities also begin to emerge between small farmers and new business entities such as large specialized households, family farms, and professional cooperatives. Obviously, the contrast and structural opposition between urban and rural areas is a common phenomenon among developing countries. To understand urban–rural economic relationship, in addition to exploring the relationship between the urban and rural sectors, the economic relevance among individual parts of the two sectors themselves should also be taken into consideration.

In a nutshell, urban–rural economic relationship in a particular economy can be understood and discussed from more than one perspective. For example, urban–rural relevance in commodities and factors highlights the "process" of economic activities, whereas urban–rural income or consumption gap addresses the "result" of these activities. Both cast their analysis perspectives between the urban and rural sectors, which constitutes inter-sectoral structural analysis. The economic status among different parts of the urban and the rural sectors themselves incorporates the respective structural features of the two sectors, which constitutes intra-sectoral structural analysis. This book focuses on the evolutionary logic of China's urban–rural economic relationship since the founding of the PRC, especially after reform and opening up. So far, China is still a large developing country in the process of economic system transition, in which the allocation of factors represents the core issue throughout the whole investigation period, especially in the stage of market-oriented transition. Moreover, China's urban–rural issues are diverse in content and divergent in geography. Such an object of study intrinsically determines the conceptual definition of urban–rural economic relationship herein. In this book, urban–rural economic relationship is defined as an economic relevance between the urban and rural sectors of the particular large developing country of China and among the different parts of these sectors, formed around the optimal allocation of factors and also having an impact on the dynamics of urban–rural income and consumption gap. Obviously, this definition places the focus of analysis on the optimal allocation of factors as the base point, and regards urban–rural economic relationship as an outcome of this allocation. In the meantime, the book deals with the economic relationship between the urban and rural sectors as the subject of analysis, and it also addresses the structural features of the individual parts of these sectors themselves. This definition agrees better with the theoretical contents of urban–rural economic relationship as well the practical reality of China.

1.2.3 Separation and integration

Urban–rural economic relationship tends to behave differently in different temporal and spatial contexts. Separation and integration describe two different states of urban–rural economic relationship in different countries or within the same country during different periods of time.

In this book, "separation" does not mean that the urban and rural sectors carry out their respective activities in a "vacuum" without any economic exchanges between them. It means that the allocation of products and factors between the two sectors is not mainly carried out spontaneously by microeconomic subjects, and the two sectors are separated from each other under government economic interventions and mandatory plans. As a result of separated product and factor allocation, the urban and rural sectors are relatively solidified in their production and way of life and tend to be highly homogenized inside. In the meantime, there may exist income and consumption gap between urban and rural areas, but this gap tends to remain relatively stable with limited volatility. The little chance for microeconomic subjects to rely on urban–rural reallocation of factors has led to significant changes in urban–rural income gap and consumption gap.

"Integration", on the other side, is first of all manifested by the economic activities among microeconomic subjects of the urban and rural sectors based on their respective endowments. They mainly allocate products and factors between urban and rural areas spontaneously based on market price signals and depend on improved efficiency of this allocation to improve their economic gains, income level, and consumption. In other words, urban and rural microeconomic subjects are more tightly connected by the desire to maximize their own interests, and this connection takes place spontaneously under a given market, price, and competition mechanism. Government intervention as a separator between urban and rural areas has been gradually eliminated or even become nonexistent. As a result, the fluidity of commodities and factors between urban and rural areas is greatly enhanced. The breadth, depth, and frequency of the transaction of commodities and factors between urban and rural areas are significantly improved, too. Direct market docking among microeconomic subjects and enhanced fluidity of commodities and factors lead to changes in the urban–rural income gap and consumption gap. Particularly, under assimilating marginal returns on factors, urban–rural income and consumption gap are beginning to convergence, too. The same also happens to the relationship among individual parts of the urban and rural sectors.

Apparently, the above definition of "separation" and "integration" of urban–rural economic relationship is primarily based on how commodities are relevant and how factors are allocated. It also takes account of urban–rural income and consumption gap as an "outcome" of this factor allocation. Hence, it is intrinsically consistent with our conceptual understanding of urban–rural economic relationship described earlier.

This book uses "from separation to integration" to describe the evolutionary trajectory of China's urban–rural economic relationship since the founding of the PRC. Here, "separation" and "integration" depict the core features of China's urban–rural economic relationship during different periods of time. When using these two concepts to characterize individual stages, special emphasis should also be placed on the following four aspects:

1 Since the founding of the PRC, China has remained a country with ultra-large geographical and population sizes in the world. These features of a large country signify that in a particular period of time, there usually exists significant economic and social development gap among individual parts of the country. From this point of view, China's overall urban–rural economic relationship is characterized by "separation" or "integration" within a given period of investigation, but the state of separation and integration may not be totally consistent among all parts of the country. Compared with the difference in degree among individual regions, this book is more concerned about the basic evolutionary trend of China's overall urban–rural economic relationship during different periods of time.
2 For a big developing country like China, "separation" and "integration" of urban–rural economic relationship do not mean that they cannot be interwoven at all. Besides the dominant form of relevance, there may exist auxiliary or supplementary types of product and factor allocation between urban and rural areas. In the presence of state intervention, there can also be a small amount of spontaneous urban–rural allocation among microeconomic subjects and *vice versa*.

This signifies that the separation and integration of urban–rural economic relationship may be interwoven. This book attempts to present the basic characteristics and causes of China's urban–rural economic relationship during different periods of time, and the auxiliary or supplementary parts in these periods do not constitute the main content of our analysis herein.

3 As far as urban–rural economic relationship is concerned, "separation" and "integration" also feature dynamic variation. The separation and integration of China's urban–rural economic relationship during different periods of time are not characterized in a consistent manner. Even within the same period of time, the behavior and degree of separation and integration of urban–rural economic relationship are not completely the same. Particularly, the integration of urban–rural economic relationship is the basic goal of a country's modernization process. Over the 40 years of China's modernization since the start of reform and opening up, differences in development concepts, constraints, strategic objectives, and economic systems have also given rise to divergent contents and realization degrees of integration of urban–rural economic relationship. Currently, China is in the stage of implementing the new development concept and achieving high-quality economic development. This signifies that compared with the beginning of reform and opening up and even the early 21st century, China's urban–rural economic relationship today boasts more solid conditions, more abundant contents, and more ambitious objectives.

4 "Separation" and "integration" reveal two separate states of urban–rural economic relationship. To understand the urban–rural economic relationship in a particular country, the first thing to do is determine the state of its urban–rural economic relationship, and more importantly, to take a closer look into the background, driver, mode, and objective effect of the transformation of urban–rural economic relationship from separation to integration. It is more crucial to understand the change "process" of urban–rural economic relationship than to determine its "state", since only by catching hold of the exact internal logic and mechanism of these changes can people reveal the "story behind" such different "states" as separation and integration and, accordingly, work out public policies in favor of the sustainable transformation of urban and rural structure in the particular country more effectively.

Out of these considerations, this book applies the concepts "separation" and "integration" to analyze China's urban–rural economic relationship. The analysis not only includes a judgment on the state and characteristics of urban–rural economic relationship during a particular period of time but also supplies an explanation about how and why transformation takes place based on a reliable analytical framework so as to highlight the theoretical innovation and practical inspiration of our research in the systematic logical deduction.

1.3 Research thinking and framework

Our research on China's urban–rural economic relationship herein follows the analytical thinking of logical positivism. That is, argumentation is structured around the basic framework of "concept definition—logic construction—empirical research—policy implication", which seeks to envelop the research on urban–rural economic relationship within a reliable analytical procedure. In terms of research procedure, concept definition, theoretical construction, empirical research, and policy implication constitute the four links of analysis, which are intercomplementary and tightly relevant. In a nutshell, this procedure needs to define the core concepts covered in the research in the first place and then construct a theory by explaining the relationship among these concepts, namely, to form a logical explanatory framework for the theme of economic research. To test the convincingness of this explanatory framework, empirical analysis should be carried out based on the explanatory framework and using empirical data. Combining logic construction with empirical research will lead to an understanding of the laws of economic issues. That is, a theoretical construction is explanatory if it can pass the empirical test, and this theoretical construction can lead on to corresponding policy implication and trend analysis. Obviously, logical positivism seeks to show the consistency between the abstract "logic" of theory and the volatile "trajectory" of practice, and it can draw an understanding of the laws of China's urban–rural economic relationship out of the combination of theory with practice. This analytical thinking reflects the research feature of combing theory with practice and uniting logic with history, as well as the social sciences research method of from concrete to abstract, and then from abstract to concrete. From the methodological point of view, it is appropriate and desirable for this book to adopt the method of logical positivism to investigate China's urban–rural economic relationship.

According to the research thinking of logical positivism, the research thinking and analytical framework of this book can be illustrated by Figure 1.1. In the introduction section of Chapter 1, the book first describes the raising of the question and defines the three core concepts covered in the research: urban and rural areas, urban–rural economic relationship, and separation and integration. Chapter 2 reviews existing literature on urban–rural economic relationship and comments on the main contributions and shortcomings of these articles. Chapters 1 and 2 together provide the practical and theoretical background for the research herein, and they jointly make up the concept definition section of this research.

Following concept definition, Chapter 3 will focus on the theoretic core of the Lewis-Fei-Ranis model, using the dual economy theory of development economics as the cut-in point, and point out that the implied hypotheses of this theory do not totally agree with the economic development practice of China. On this ground, it emphasizes that, to analyze China's urban–rural

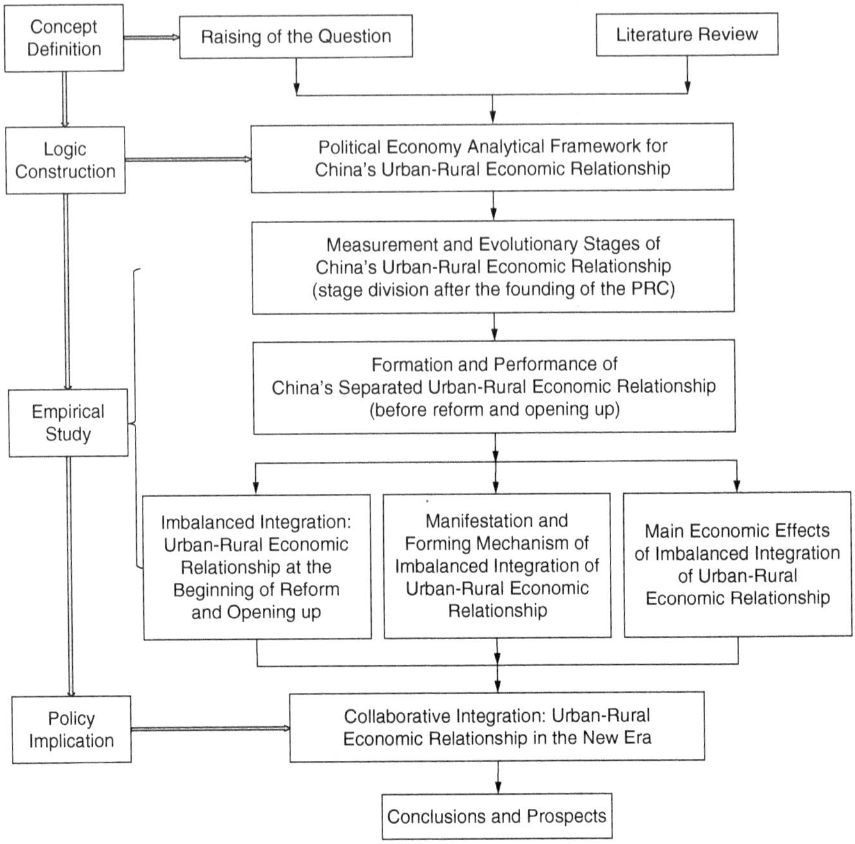

Figure 1.1 Schematics showing the research thinking and analytical framework of this book.

economic relationship, rather than directly apply or transplant the dual economy theory, a new analytical framework for China's urban–rural economic relationship should be developed in light of local practice. This analytical framework should agree with the important characteristics of China—socialist system, a large developing country, and economic system transition, and cover multiple dimensions—government-market relationship, inter-governmental structure, and inter-market structure in the economic system. As this analytical framework highlights the impact of political and social factors on economic development, as well as the generation and function of the economic systems with Chinese characteristics, it bears very striking features of political economy. This part of the book attempts to put forward a political economy analytical framework for China's urban–rural economic relationship which is different from the Lewis-Fei-Ranis model but consistent with local characteristics. Such research work constitutes the logic construction section of the book.

Using the political economy analytical framework consistent with local practice, Chapter 4 introduces a number of indicators for measuring urban–rural economic relationship and uses these indicators to measure China's urban–rural economic relationship since the founding of the PRC from multiple perspectives. It then separates China's urban–rural economic relationship by time sequence into different stages and describes the basic characteristics and typical behaviors of this relationship during different periods of time. As the investigation period of this book spans from the founding of the PRC to the present day, this part of the research features a long history and a large span, rendering a feeling of depth for understanding the urban–rural economic integration over the past 40 years of reform and opening up. Chapter 5 summarizes China's urban–rural economic relationship from the founding of the PRC to reform and opening up as being "separated" and uses the political economy analytical framework to explore the causes and economic effects of this separation. Chapter 6 summarizes the urban–rural economic relationship from reform and opening up to 2012 as imbalanced integration and then uses the political economy analytical framework to explore the internal causes of the transformation of urban–rural economic relationship from separation to imbalanced integration and the gradual manifestation of this imbalanced integration. Chapter 7 regards the imbalanced integration of urban–rural economic relationship at the beginning of reform and opening up as a characteristic fact and focuses on the main economic effects of this imbalanced integration, especially the performance of major indicators such as economic growth, income distribution, and resident consumption. Chapter 8 examines why imbalanced integration should persist in China for a long period of time. Its core is the use of the political economy analytical framework to investigate the impact of incentive compatibility on policy effectiveness amid integrated urban–rural economic relationship. This analysis also provides theoretical basis for China to continuously promote the integration of urban–rural economic relationship. Together, Chapters 4–8 make up the empirical research section of this book.

Following empirical research, Chapter 9 examines the changing tendency of China's urban–rural economic relationship under the new normal, in light of the changes in the economic and social architecture and the implementation of new development concepts. The book tends to summarize this change tendency as "collaborative integration". Hence, it is necessary to demonstrate the contents of collaborative integration, as well as the motivation, form, and institutional conditions of the change from imbalanced integration to collaborative integration with the help of the political economy analytical framework. This way, it is possible to put forward policy recommendations for China to achieve a higher level of integration of urban–rural economic relationship at the entry into the new era and a stage of high-quality economic development. Obviously, analysis on the collaborative integration of China's urban–rural economic relationship constitutes the policy implication section of this book. It reflects the ultimate purpose of this research project at the practical level and its policy inspirations in this respect.

Needless to say, this book attempts to examine the evolutionary mechanism of China's urban–rural economic relationship within a logically consistent research framework. As the pivot of this research is to construe urban–rural economic relationship as a matter of development economics from the political economy point of view, it bears a striking feature of a "political economy of development". Notably, the political economy as understood herein aims to highlight the local characteristics of China in the process of development—socialist system, a large developing country, and economic system transition, which are all the drivers behind government–market relationship and intergovernmental and intermarket structural arrangements. This way, our research not only attempts to extend the traditional thinking of government-market dichotomy but also strives to capture the most "characteristic" elements of China's economic development. Hence, this research reflects a positive response to constructing the discourse system of Chinese philosophy and social sciences and a political economy of socialism with Chinese characteristics.

As our research endeavors to put forward concepts and analyze them based on local practice, our policy recommendations resulted from empirical research are more pertinent and accurate. The transformation of urban–rural economic relationship from imbalanced integration to collaborative integration constitutes an integral part of building a moderately prosperous society in all respects, basically realizing modernization, and building a great modern country. The policy implication proposed herein based on theoretical and empirical research can provide inspiration and reference for promoting this transition.

In a nutshell, our localized political economy analytical framework for urban–rural economic relationship is innovative, and this research thinking is widely applicable and theoretically inspiring as it can be extended beyond urban–rural relationship to other fields of economics. This book demonstrates the transition of China's urban–rural economic relationship from separation to imbalanced integration and then to collaborative integration, providing theoretical basis for China to scientifically and effectively understand the stage characteristics of urban–rural economic relationship and policy choices. In a word, this book focuses on the evolutionary mechanism of China's urban–rural economic relationship. Its research thinking, demonstration process, and policy foothold constitute marginal improvements on existing research literature.

Note

1 The content of this policy document includes "1. These Provisions are formulated to give a scientific, genuine presentation of the current demographic, social, and economic development condition in urban and rural China and an accurate evaluation of the country's urbanization level. 2. These Provisions, as the basis for statistical division of urban and rural areas, do not change the existing administrative divisions, subordination, administrative authority, and organizational

establishment, or provisions concerning land planning and urban and rural planning. 3. Based on the country's administrative divisions, taking the jurisdictions of residents' committees and villagers' committees confirmed by the civil affairs department as the dividing objects, and actual constructions as the division basis, these Provisions divide the regions of China into urban areas and rural areas. Here, actual constructions are defined by public facilities, residential facilities, and other facilities that have been built or are under construction. 4. Urban areas include city areas and town areas. City areas are municipal districts or cities without districts, or residents' committees and other areas connected to the actual construction of the seat of a district or municipal government. Town areas include the seats of county people's governments or other towns other than a city area, or residents' committees and other areas connected to the actual construction of the seat of the government. Special areas like independent industrial and mining areas, development zones, research institutions, or institutions of higher education not connected to the seat of the government, and the seat of the headquarters of a farm or wood farm are regarded as town areas. 5. Villages are areas other than towns identified herein. 6. These Provisions are interpreted by the NBS. 7. These Provisions come into force as of August 1, 2008".

2 Literature review

In developing countries, there usually exists a contrast between the urban and rural sectors in terms of economic and social conditions. From a global perspective, urban–rural duality represents a common feature among developing countries, and this practical feature plays a critical role in economic theory research. In development economics, the dual economy theory occupies an important position, and it makes a considerable difference to the modernization of developing countries. As far as China is concerned, after the founding of the PRC, especially over the 40 years of reform and opening up, the country's GDP, comprehensive national strength, and people's living conditions have improved significantly from a temporal point of view. Despite this, however, China is still a developing country with world's largest population, in which urban–rural duality is still a major structural problem waiting to be resolved. Given this theoretical background and practical reality, academic workers have explored China's urban–rural economic relationship from different perspectives within the framework of the dual economy theory of development economics. In terms of research content, these articles are typically structured along the research clues such as the contents of urban–rural economic relationship, the *status quo* of China's urban–rural economic relationship, and possible ways promoting the improvement of urban–rural economic relationship. These research clues signify that the current research on China's urban–rural economic relationship is highly universal. Reviewing and commenting on existing literature following the research thinking of logical positivism constitutes the basic work of our research herein. Existing literature provides the ideological nutrients and methodological inspirations needed for our research. More importantly, the inadequacies and deficiencies of existing literature are very likely to favor our research with further room for expansion and new direction for innovation.

2.1 Studies on the contents and measurements of China's urban–rural economic relationship

Logically speaking, urban–rural economic relationship is a derivative of the concept of urban–rural relationship. Hence, urban–rural economic relationship can be understood in the broader spectrum of urban–rural relationship. In academic research, the mutual relevance between urban and rural areas is commonly expressed as "relationship", "connection", "interaction", "linkage", or "partnership", which, etymologically, all relate to connection, interrelation, and interaction. This signifies that the main meaning of urban–rural relationship is to regard urban and rural areas as two symbiotic systems closely linked and interrelated by the flow of population, commodities, and other factors. Urban–rural relationship is a state of factor fluidity and functional combination between urban and rural areas (Chen F., 2013). The disparities existent between urban and rural areas lead to the flow of products and factors, which in turn can give rise to functional complementation. This constitutes the core content underlined by the concept of urban–rural relationship. Urban–rural relationship can be classified from different perspectives. They encompass spatial relationship—the flow of population, goods, money, information, and waste between urban and rural areas, as well as inter-sectoral or interindustrial relationship—the cross-infiltration of production activities between urban and rural areas, which gives rise to the intersection and integration of the three major industries between urban and rural areas, such as urban agriculture and agricultural service industrialization (Venhuizen R., 2006; Overbek G. & Terluen I., 2006; Chen F., 2013). In addition to the spatial and intersectoral relationship between urban and rural areas, based on the way of cognition of urban and rural residents and their communication, Ye C. and Chen M.X. (2008) noted that urban–rural relationship is the relationship between urban and rural residents, formed and maintained through human activities. When people live in urban or rural areas and look at the connection between these areas with the way of life on either side, personal history, experience, and information will become important basis for judging urban–rural relationship.

Existing literature emphasizes that from a temporal point of view, according to the interdependence between the urban and rural sectors, urban–rural relationship in human society can be roughly divided into three stages: the early stage, the duality stage, and the post-1980s stage, which correspond to three different patterns of urban–rural relationship (Bengs C., 2000; Ye C. & Chen M.X., 2008; Zheng G. & Ye Y.M., 2009; Sun W.H. & Fang X.Q., 2014). Given the evolution of human history presented by urban–rural relationship, this division is intrinsically consistent with Marx and Engels's theories on urban–rural relationship (Jiang Y.M., Xian R.S. & Zhang X.L., 2015). Under this division, the urban–rural economic relationship in major developed countries is already in the third stage. There the industrial, spatial, and public service boundaries between urban and rural areas are becoming ambiguous, and the focus and goal of economic and social development has basically shifted from urban–rural separation to a network structure of people flow, material flow, information flow, capital flow, and technology flow between urban and rural areas. In contrast, in most developing countries, urban–rural relationship is still in the first or the second stage, namely, a stage of agriculture dominance or a stage of rural-to-urban attachment. There the economic and social contrast between urban and rural areas is more prominent, and industrialization and urbanization are being promoted. Although the development stage varies, from the evolution of urban–rural relationship in developed economies, current definitions of urban–rural relationship increasingly emphasize the following observations: urban–rural relationship is a symbiotic relationship between the two sectors arising out of their functional divergence and mutual complementation; urban–rural relationship should be examined across a regional network rather than within individual villages or cities; the intersectoral relationship between urban and rural areas has extended beyond the traditional division of labor between urban and rural areas; the interaction between agricultural and non-agricultural sectors also has a spatial dimension (Chen F., 2013).

The above review on the concept of urban–rural relationship is important for people to accurately grasp China's urban–rural economic relationship. The urban–rural relationship in particular countries is always manifested in more than one aspect, and it encompasses the relative state and relationship between these two sectors in economy, society, space, and even culture. Urban–rural economic relationship, on the other side, is more concerned with the relative economic state and relevance between the two sectors (and the individual parts of the two sectors themselves). This economic relevance is commonly manifested in the form of industry, way of factor allocation, and income and consumption gap. As economic activities play a fundamental and prepositive role in other fields, urban–rural relationship tends to present itself as urban–rural economic relationship in the first place, which usually constitutes the main content of the entire system of the urban–rural relationship in a particular country.

Logically speaking, the dual economy theory of development economics highlights the analysis of urban–rural economic relationship as the core topic. This theory emphasizes that, compared with developed countries, developing countries are faced with a more prominent labor productivity gap between urban and rural areas. Compared with the modern sector represented by nonagricultural industries or towns, in the traditional sector represented by agriculture and villages, the labor productivity and workers' wage level are lower. Therefore the duality has to be transformed through the flow and reallocation of factors between urban and rural areas. The transformation of dual economy is the process of industrialization, urbanization, and economic modernization in developing countries. In this regard, Lewis W.A. (1954) held that in developing countries, there exists urban–rural dual contrast, and the outflow of rural labor constitutes the key to transforming this duality. Fei J.C.H. and Ranis G. (1964) argued that the transfer of labor depends on population growth rate, agricultural technology progress, and industrial capital growth. Collectively, these theories can be referred to as the "Lewis-Fei-Ranis model", which lays the analytical foundation of the urban–rural dual economy theory of development economics. Subsequent studies on urban–rural relationship have basically been conducted by modifying, improving, or reflecting on this model. Examples include the use of the dual economy theory of development economics to investigate the causes of urban–rural duality and the determinants of rural labor transfer (Bardhan P. & Udry C., 1999; Fields G.S., 2005; Cherna E. et al. 2014), or the path choice of agricultural development (Hayami Y. & Rutan V.W, 1985; Fei J.C. & Ranis G., 1999; Cao K.H. & Birchenal J.A., 2013) under the neoclassic framework. Some authors have also presented empirical studies on the relative variation between the urban and rural sectors in the process of economic development (Shifa A.B., 2013).

As the largest developing country in the world, China has also been faced with the mission of transforming urban–rural duality for a long time. Urban–rural relationship, especially urban–rural economic relationship, has always played an important role in China's history. Since the founding of the PRC, China has seen different industry–agriculture relationship and urban–rural relationship over different periods of time (Zhang R.L., 2003; Wu L., 2007; Han J., 2009; Lin G., 2014). By cross-country comparison, apart from the general characteristics of other countries, the formation of urban–rural duality and the transformation urban–rural economic relationship in China also bear the heterogeneity of this particular economy (Bai Y.X, 2012; Lyu W. & Gao F., 2013; Sun W.H. & Fang X.Q., 2014). Particularly, after the entry into the 21st century, based on the new characteristics and new pattern of economic and social development, China explicitly declared that the country is now in the middle and late stage of industrialization as a whole, has entered a development stage of industry refeeding agriculture and cities supporting rural areas, and is facing the great mission of breaking urban–rural duality and forming a new pattern of integrated urban–rural economic and social development. In line with this judgment, for the purpose of building a moderately prosperous society in all respects, it is even more necessary to accelerate the process of urban–rural integration based on the five development concepts of "innovation, coordination, green, openness and sharing" and strive to form a new type of urban–rural relationship featuring industry refeeding agriculture, cities supporting rural areas, industry-agriculture reciprocity, and urban–rural integration.

In view of the above practical background, many authors have investigated the contents and process of urban–rural integration from the perspective of transforming urban–rural economic relationship. For example, Hong Y.X. & Chen W. (2003) suggested that China's "urban–rural integration" refers to the process in which cities and villages, as two economic-social units with different characters seek integrated development and harmonious coexistence within an interdependent area. Urban–rural integration means that urban and rural areas are an integrated whole inside which population, capital, information, material, and other factors flow freely between urban and rural areas and urban and rural areas penetrate, integrate, and are highly interdependent on each other in economy, society, and culture. Song H.Y. (2004) believed that to adjust the dynamics of China's urban–rural economic relationship is essentially to realize the transfer of agricultural population to nonagricultural industries through industrialization and urbanization, so as to foster the transformation of dual economy and dual society. Zheng Y.G. (2010) presented the exact contents and direction of the new type of industry–agriculture and urban–rural relationship and pointed out that to build a new type of industry–agriculture and urban–rural relationship, China must highlight harmonious and integrated industry–agriculture and urban–rural development as the main policy objective, stress coordinated agricultural modernization, industrialization, urbanization, and urban–rural integration as the strategic thinking, and implement major policies in favor of the harmonious, integrated development between industry and agriculture, between urban and rural areas, industry–agriculture and urban–rural development, and collaborative restructuring, such as those strengthening the position of farmers as the subject. Based on these understandings on the transformation of urban–rural economic relationship, Gu Y.K. & Xu Y.J. (2004) introduced evaluation indicators for urban–rural integration from the theoretical evolution point of view. Similar articles also measured the level of China's urban–rural integration with indicators (Jiao B.F., Lin D. & Peng J.N., 2011; Liu H.M., Zhang Z.J. & Wang K.Q., 2012).

2.2 Studies on the *status quo* and causes of China's urban–rural economic relationship

In the Lewis-Fei-Ranis model, the dual economy in developing countries is first of all reflected by the prominent gap between the urban and rural sectors in labor productivity and resident income level. To construct a new type of urban–rural economic relationship in the context of building a moderately prosperous society in all respects, the first thing for China to do is respond to its urban–rural income gap. As such, some authors have empirically examined China's urban–rural economic relationship from the perspective of urban–rural income gap. In this regard, existing literature shows that the absolute number of urban–rural income gap in China is too large. It is not only larger than that of developed countries but it is also larger than that of most developing countries (Chen B.K. & Lin Y.F., 2013). Cai F. (2003) compared the urban–rural income gap figures among 36 countries and discovered that China's figure has long stood at 2–3, whereas that of most other countries is smaller than 1.5. Through factorization analysis of income gap, Kanbur R. et al. (1999) and Gao F. (2012a) also detected that urban–rural income gap is the main constituent of China's overall income gap.

Since reform and opening up, China's urban–rural income gap has displayed differently across different periods of time. Around the chronological evolution of urban–rural income gap, there are three different descriptions: widening, narrowing, and "inverted U". For example, Cai F. (2003) discovered that over the 1978–2002 period, China's urban–rural income gap experienced a process of first narrowing, then widening, and gradual worsening and it was on the increase at large. His conclusion has been supported by other studies (Wang J.N. & Zhang Q.L., 2005; Wu X.M. & Perlof J.M., 2005; Cheng Y.H., 2006, 2007; Ravalion M. & Chen S., 2007; Wang Y.F., 2012; Li S. & Sicular T., 2014; Chen B.K. & Lin Y.F., 2013). On the contrary, Ding Huanfeng & Liu X.Y. (2017) discovered through research by exploratory spatial data analysis that since reform and opening up, China's urban–rural income gap has exhibited an evolutionary trajectory of first widening and then narrowing. Based on GMM estimation of maximum entropy density, using the income grouping data from 1985 to 2012, Zhang T. (2016) discovered that the evolution of China's urban–rural income gap was an inverted "U". Wang R. (2006) and Zhou Y.B. (2009) also provided support for the "inverted U" observation. As a large developing country, China's urban–rural income gap is not consistent across different regions. Shi L. & Gao F. (2006) used the spatial characteristics of dual economy and urban–rural income gap to explain the gap of economic growth among different provinces in China. Recently, using geographically weighted regression, Xu F. (2015) revealed that China's urban–rural income gap is characterized by a gradual increase from east to west and from south to north. Her discovery has also been verified by other authors (Lyu W. & Chu D.Y., 2011; Long H.M., Ling L., Tan C.J. & Wang Z.P., 2015; Ding H.F. & Liu X.Y., 2017). Besides, based on flexible Fourier function studies, Jiang C., Si D.K. & Su Z.W. (2016) also discovered that the urban–rural income gap in the Southwest Comprehensive Economic Zone of China is steadily converging, whereas that in the Northwest, Central South and Central North Comprehensive Economic Zones are trending toward divergence.

Urban–rural income gap constitutes an important determinant of constructing a new type of urban–rural relationship in China. Regarding the causes of China's urban–rural economic gap and its dynamics, there have been a range of explanations, such as urban-biased policies, economic development strategies, factor market distortion, household register discrimination, financial imbalance, and human capital disparity. For example, Lipton M. (1977), Krueger A. Maurice S. & Alberto V. (1992) noted that urban-biased polices in the economic development of developing countries will lead to or aggravate urban–rural income gap and play a critical role in the formation and transformation of dual economy. Many Chinese authors have also noticed that China's urban–rural dual economy is closely relevant to the formulation and implementation of economic policies, and urban-biased policies are the essential driver behind the continuously widening urban–rural income gap (Cai F. & Yang T., 2000; Cai F., Du Y. & Wang M.Y., 2003; Lu M. & Chen Z., 2004). Besides urban-biased policies, some authors have also explained China's urban–rural income gap from the perspective of development strategies. They suggested that a catch-up development strategy deflected from the country's endowment conditions, and comparative advantages constitute the key driver behind the aggravating urban–rural income gap in China (Lin Y.F. & Liu M.X., 2003; Lin Y.F. & Yu M.J., 2009; Chen B.K. & Lin Y.F., 2010; Chen B.K. & Lin Y.F., 2013).

In the Lewis-Fei-Ranis model of development economics, the non-agricultural flow of rural labor is the main approach and core driver for transforming urban–rural duality. This signifies that the free flow of rural labor can suppress urban–rural income gap, whereas labor market distortion is negative in reducing urban–rural income gap (Gu S.Z. & Li Z.Y., 1998; Hertel T. & Fan Z., 2004; Sun Z., Du Y. & Hong Y.M., 2009). Here the main point is that labor market distortion has affected the non-agricultural transfer of rural labor, thus delaying or blocking the continuous reduction of urban–rural income gap. By extension, the urban–rural duality cored around household registration is the most essential determinant of China's urban–rural income gap (Bourguignon F. & Morison C., 1998; Ravalion M. & Chen S.H., 2004; Au C.C. & Henderson J.V., 2006; Whaley J. & Zhang S.M., 2007; Wan H.Y. & Li S., 2013; Ning G.J. & Li R., 2016; Jiang C., Si D.K. & Su Z.W., 2016). For example, Wan H.Y. & Li S. (2013) used propensity score matching with difference in (PSM-DID) to construct counter facts. They revealed that China's household register discrimination has a significant negative impact on the country's urban–rural income gap, and reducing household register discrimination can effectively improve farmers' income. Yang N. & Ma C.X. (2014) used a nonparametric time-varying coefficient panel data model to investigate the relationship between financial development and urban–rural income gap. The empirical results presented a dynamic inverted "U" pattern of financial development on urban–rural income gap and significant interregional disparity. Similar empirical studies have also confirmed that imbalanced financial development **does** aggravate urban–rural income gap (Yao Y.J., 2005; Zhang L.J. & Zhan Y., 2006; Sun J. & Zhang Q.C., 2012; Qian L. & Ye J.T., 2017; Liu G.C., 2017). Besides, Guo J.X. (2005) assumed that human capital and fertility rate are important variables affecting urban–rural income gap. Chen B.K., Zhang P.F. & Yang R.D. (2010) concluded that educational inequality is the most important contributor to China's urban–rural income gap.

To construct a new type of urban–rural relationship in the context of building a moderately prosperous society in all respects, China not only needs to reduce its urban–rural income gap but also to respond to its urban–rural consumption gap. Among existing articles on China's urban–rural inequality, a considerable part have chosen to use income as a proxy variable, since income data are more easily accessible, are comparable over time, and have high overall quality (Liu J. & Li S., 2013). In recent years, however, more and more authors have suggested that urban–rural consumption gap is a more ideal indicator for measuring urban–rural inequality (Knight J., Song L. & Jia H.B., 1999; Wang D.W. & He Y.P., 2005; Zou H., Li A.L. & Yu K.Z., 2013). In the research on the urban–rural relationship in developing countries, the use of urban–rural consumption gap is emphasized because consumption indicators tend to smooth off over time and are relatively stable; they can better reflect changes in resident welfare, and are unlikely to incur misrepresentation or concealment (Liu X.L., 2008; Meyer B. & Sulivan J., 2011, 2013; Yang J.D., 2013; Xu Z.Y., Guo Z.C. & Jing L.B., 2014).

As far as China is concerned, existing articles have first of all empirically analyzed the evolutionary trend of urban–rural consumption gap. By using fold change and Theil index, we can find that despite the diversity of judgments about the timing of a turning point, overall, China's urban–rural consumption gap does display an inverted "U" (Gao F., 2014a; Xu Z.Y., Guo Z.C. & Jing L.B., 2014; Zhang W.J., Fang Z.R. & Huang J.X., 2015; Wang X.H. & Wen T., 2015). However, the inverted "U" hypothesis is not supported by the empirical study in Lin Y.F. & Chen B.K. (2009), who concluded that China's urban–rural consumption gap has been widening in the process of marketization and economic opening. Besides the inequality of consumption expenditure between urban and rural residents, some articles have also investigated the marginal propensity to consume (MPC) and the difference of consumption behavior between urban and rural residents in China. These studies argue that, compared with urban residents, rural residents' consumption is more prominently motivated by "precautionary saving", and rural residents tend to have a smaller MPC. The consumption disparities between urban and rural residents signify that urban and rural economic policies should be formulated and implemented by taking account of the pertinence of these policies, and different consumption policies should be implemented for urban and rural areas, respectively (Zhou J. & Yang X.Z., 2009; Pan W.X., 2010; Ling C. & Zhang A.Q., 2012; Wang X.H. & Wen T., 2015).

Regarding the determinants of urban–rural consumption gap, most authors hold that urban–rural income gap is the most important contributor to urban–rural consumption gap (Su L.J., He Y.F. & Jin S.N., 2006; Fang F.Q., 2009; Zhu X.K. & Luo C., 2011; Chen B.K., 2012; Gao F., 2014b). However, based on a vector error correction (VEC) model established for the income and consumption gap between urban and rural residents, Wu D. & Huo X.X. (2010) observed that the consumption gap between urban and rural residents leads to the income gap between urban and rural residents, but the income gap between urban and rural residents does not lead to the consumption gap between urban and rural residents. The study in Peng D.F. & Chen W.Y. (2014) suggested that there is no long-term equilibrium between urban–rural income gap and consumption gap, although the former is the Granger cause of the latter. Li J.Y. & Li H. (2016) tested the impact of urban–rural income gap on residents' consumption structure in China. The results showed that increasing urban–rural income gap greatly spurs human capital and social capital investment of rural households, but crowds out their living and entertainment consumption; for urban households, on the contrary, increasing urban–rural income gap has a negative impact on human capital investment, but it greatly promotes their consumption of entertainment commodities.

Apart from urban–rural income gap, the study in Zhang L.Y. (2007) revealed that the duality system and the supply discrimination by monopolistic manufacturers are the causes of urban–rural consumption gap. Lin Y.F. & Chen B.K.(2009) demonstrated that the heavy industry first strategy is closely relevant to urban–rural consumption inequality, and the greater the overtaking degree, the larger the urban–rural consumption gap. Based on life cycle hypothesis, Wu Ha.J., He L.X. & Zhang Z.G. (2014) found that in China, the ratio of urban–rural children dependency coefficient is negatively related to urban–urban resident consumption gap, whereas ratio of urban–rural elderly dependency coefficient is positively related to urban–rural resident consumption gap. Li Y.Y. & Zhong X.M. (2012) found that the application of fiscal policies has an asymmetric impact on the MPC between urban and rural residents, and this constitutes an important contributor to urban–rural consumption gap. Through empirical studies with a spatial econometric model, Xu M. & Jiang Y. (2015) revealed that urban–rural consumption gap is markedly provincially space-dependent; industrial structure upgrading can effectively narrow urban–rural consumption gap, but the effect is different over different periods of time and across different regions. Based on quantile regression model research, Liu H.P., Li Y. & Zhang G.Q. (2015) discovered that explicit factors (e.g., income, pension security, age, years of education) are the main influencing factors of China's urban–rural consumption disparity; as the consumption level differs, so does their influence on urban and rural households; urban–rural consumption disparity decreases with the increase of quantile, and the weakened influence of implicit factors (preference, habit, and development stage) is the main cause of this decrease.

The influencing factors of urban–rural consumption gap relate not only to urban–rural income gap but also to urban–rural disparity in access to public goods and social security resources. On this ground, some authors have pointed out that at present, China features not only an urban–rural dual economy but also an urban–rural dual society; its urban–rural gap is reflected not only in income gap but more importantly in the supply of public goods, such as infrastructure, education, medical care, health and social security, in rural areas (Chen X.J. & Yu X.H., 2011; Yu C.L., 2011). Sociologists even call urban–rural inequality in access to public goods as "urban–rural divide, one country two policies" (Lu X.Y., 2000, 2002). To build a moderately prosperous society in all respects, it is important to ensure that urban and rural residents share the fruits of economic and social development in a relatively equal manner. To construct a new type of urban–rural relationship and promote urban–rural integration, it is definitely necessary to minimize this gap, so that rural residents and urban residents can enjoy equal policies and opportunities in the supply of public goods (Hong Y.X. & Chen W., 2003; Wang W.T., 2009). Related academic studies have revealed that at this stage, the supply of public goods in rural China as a whole is suffering insufficient total supply, unitary source of funds, irrational product structure, and urba–rural imbalance (Zhang L.X. et al. 2005; Zhao Y. & Jiang H.C., 2007). For example, Wu Y.X. (2013) employed CGSS2008 data to examine the effects of school continuation opportunity at the junior high school, senior high school, and university stages in China and the trends of these effects. The results showed that there is no observable urban–rural disparity in school continuation opportunity at the junior high school stage, but the urban–rural inequality at the senior high school and university stages displays a rising trend. Wu's finding is supported by Li C.L. (2014) and some other authors. Based on the data of the China Health and Retirement Longitudinal Study (CHARLS), Liu X.L. (2017) applied the propensity matching score method to investigate the effect of medical insurance for urban and rural residents on the utilization level of outpatient and inpatient medical services. The results showed that the medical insurance for urban and rural residents in China has not significantly reduced the urban–rural disparity in actual compensation rate of medical insurance. Urban–rural dual society means that in order to comprehensively promote the urban–rural integration strategy, China has to deepen urban–rural comprehensive reform to equalize the quality of life between urban and rural residents, so that urban and rural residents can enjoy equal living standard and quality of life (Wei H.K., 2016).

2.3 Studies on potential ways and options for improving urban–rural economic relationship

In the dual economy theory of development economics, the Lewis-Fei-Ranis model addresses the nonagricultural transfer of rural labor as the core driver for transforming dual economy. From this point of view, some domestic and foreign researchers have validated China's strategies for promoting a new type of China's urban–rural relationship from the perspective of labor fluidity. As far as China is concerned, to construct a new type of urban–rural economic relationship in the context of building a moderately prosperous society in all respects, it is important to integrate urban–rural social and economic development based on the development concept of coordination and sharing, which requires the market to play a substantive role in urban–rural resource allocation to improve the efficiency of resource allocation (Qu F.T. & Tian G.M., 2011). Some authors emphasized that urban–rural integration is an important goal of urban–rural coordination; China needs to eliminate urban–rural duality, promote urban–rural collaborative development and form a new type of urban–rural relationship featuring "cities supporting rural areas, industry re-feeding agriculture", so as to allow rural residents to share the fruits of modernization with urban residents, accelerate urban–rural integration, and realize overall coordinated development between urban and rural areas (Liu H.M., Zhang Z.J. & Wang K.Q., 2012; Wei H.K., 2016). According to the Research Group of Rural Department of the Development Research Center of the State Council

(2014), China still has a prominent urban–rural duality, which represents the greatest structural problem of the country. In order to form a new type of urban–rural relationship and a new pattern of urban–rural integration, China must broaden its vision of urban–rural integrated development and promote urban–rural integrated development by releasing the potential of national economic growth. It must focus efforts on ensuring farmers' fair share of land value-added income and create a unified urban–rural construction land market with land use control, equal rights and functions, and sharing of value added. It must focus efforts on reducing the urban–rural disparity in labor productivity and accelerate the construction of a unified urban–rural employment market featuring freedom of job selection, equal pay for equal work, and the same rights in the same city. It must speed up the formation of a rural financial market system with moderate competition, convenient service, and universal benefits for agriculture, rural areas, and farmers. It must balance the allocation of public resources between urban and rural areas. It must establish a rural public service system with unified systems, unified standards, and accessible services. In this analysis of a new type of urban–rural relationship, the nonagricultural flow of rural labor (or urbanization process) plays a crucial role.

Since reform and opening up, along with the market-oriented economic system reform, China has seen large-scale, continuous nonagricultural transfer of rural labor. Corresponding to this transfer is the rapid advancement of urbanization. The nonagricultural transfer of rural labor has boosted economic growth and improved the well-being of urban and rural residents (Hayashi F. & Prescot C.E., 2008; Hsieh C.T. & Klenow P.J., 2009; Volrath D., 2009; Pan Y. & Du X.M., 2010; Zhang G.T., Jiang J. & Chen Y., 2010; Niu J.L., 2013; Li D.F. & Tang X.M., 2013; Hao D.M., 2016). For example, Zhang G.T., Jiang J. & Chen Y. (2010) built a labor allocation model to examine how the transfer of rural surplus labor has affected China's economic growth under urban–rural dual economy. The results showed that from 1997 to 2008, the contribution of the transfer of rural surplus labor to labor productivity increases and GDP growth is 16.3 percent and 1.72 percent, respectively. Vollrath D. (2009) revealed that the variation across countries in the degree of misallocation of labor factors accounts for 30–40 percent of the variation in income per capital and up to 80 percent of the variation in total factor productivity (TEP). These articles assume that effective flow of labor factors into urban areas will significantly drive the continuous, rapid economic growth in China. Some authors have also looked into the impact of rural labor transfer on savings rate in China (Li Y. & Yin J.F., 2007; Fan G. & Lyu Y, 2013; Zhang X., Liu X.G. & Fan G., 2014). For example, Fan G. & Lyu Y. (2013) noted that during the rapid economic development in China from 1978 to 2008, existence of rural surplus labor led to an increase in enterprise profit and enterprise savings rate, thus spurring the country's national savings rate. Zhang X., Liu X.G. & Fan G. (2014) decomposed savings rate into three types (urban residents, rural migrant workers, and farmers). The results revealed that during continuous transfer of rural surplus labor into the nonagricultural sector, rural migrant worker population has expanded constantly along with capital accumulation in the nonagricultural sector; the high savings rate of rural migrant workers has also increased farmers' savings rate and national savings rate.

Labor fluidity is of fatal significance to constructing a new type of urban–rural relationship in China, yet household registration restrains the flow of urban and rural labor (Au C.C. & Henderson J., 2006; Whaley J. & Zhang S.M., 2007; Wan H.Y & Li S., 2013; Ning G.J. & Li R., 2016). On ground of this, China's urbanization is characterized by the dominance of government preference and a divide between urban registered residents and migrant population (Luo X., Zhu P.F. & Xiang G.D., 2014; Chen Y.S. & Zhang Y., 2015). Household registration reform plays an important role in China's urban–rural integrated development (Sun W.K., Bai C.E. & Xie P.C., 2011; Yin H.P. & Liu Y.L., 2016). In terms of mechanism, household registration affects China's urban–rural integration and urban–rural coordinated development through three channels. First is population fluidity (Lu Y.L., 2008; Liang Q., Chen Q.Y. & Wang R.Y., 2013; Zhu J.L. & Li Z.L., 2016; Liu Z., 2005; Bosker M. et al. 2012). For example, Liang Q., Chen Q.Y. & Wang R.Y. (2013) discovered through numerical simulation that household registration can impede labor fluidity; liberalizing household registration in small cities and towns can guide the transfer of rural surplus labor and benefit the construction of new urbanization paradigm of urban agglomerations and metropolitan zones. Second is wage disparity (Meng F.Q. & Deng B.G., 2014; Zhang L. et al. 2014; Chang J.X. & Zhao H.T., 2016; Meng X. & Zhang J., 2001; Demurger S. et al. 2009, 2012). For example, Chang J.X. & Zhao H.T. (2016) used China Health and Nutrition Survey (CHNS) data to analyze the wage discrimination on labor with rural household register in China and found that the wage premium of labor with urban household register in state-owned enterprises (SOEs) is significantly higher than that of labor with rural household register. Research in Demurger S. et al. (2009) demonstrated that strict household registration control makes it difficult for Chinese farmers to flow into the urban public sector, leading to wage disparity between urban and rural residents; urban resident annual earnings are 1.3 times larger than long-term rural migrant earnings. The third is land circulation (Lu M. & Chen Z., 2009; Zhang M.L., 2014; Zhou W. et al. 2017; Lu M., Wan G. & Xiong J., 2014). For example, Zhou W. et al. (2017) built an endogenous urbanization model covering the two heterogeneous types of urban and rural labor and land. The results showed that household registration affects land circulation, whereas accelerated land circulation and loosened household registration can speed up urbanization. Lu M. & Wan G.H. (2014) revealed that rural land circulation has long been subject to rigid control, and household registration or *Hukou* largely restrains rural land transfer.

In the Lewis-Fei-Ranis model, the convergence of wages between the modern sector represented by manufacture and the traditional sector represented by agriculture has an important implication: when the transfer of rural labor causes a rise in the wage level of the rural sector, rural surplus labor disappears and the point at which labor wages are otherwise determined—the Lewisian turning point—is reached. The mass, continued nonagricultural transfer of rural labor in China has changed the country's urban–rural relationship and led to extensive discussions on China's Lewisian turning point. Among these discussions, some authors assumed that China's Lewisian turning point has arrived (Cai F., 2008, 2010; Wang D.W., 2009; Islam N. & Yokota K., 2008; Cai F. & Wang M., 2008). Others disagree that China's Lewisian turning point has yet to arrive (Knight J. & Li S., 2005; Meng X. & Bai N., 2007; Kwan F., 2009; Wang J & Zhong X.H., 2011; Mao X.F. & Liu J., 2011; Yu Y.X. & Zhang P., 2011; Gao F., 2012b). Among the former, Islam N. & Yokota K. (2008) used provincial panel data of China to measure the dynamic trend of agricultural wages and marginal productivity of labor force. The results showed that the marginal productivity of labor has been rising all the time, at a rate higher than that of wages, suggesting that the Lewisian turning point has arrived. Among the latter, Mao X.F. & Liu J. (2011) found that despite the substantially increased marginal productivity of rural labor, it has not caught up with the wages of the agricultural sector; despite increased nominal wages, real wages have experienced a rise and a fall and have never recovered to the previous maximum; the urban labor market expects to employ more skilled workers at lower wages, but unskilled workers may be undersupplied at given wages below the subsistence wages. These observations imply that China's Lewisian turning point has not arrived yet.

The Lewis-Fei-Ranis model assumes a close relevance between the non-agricultural transfer of rural labor and the development degree of the agricultural sector. Accordingly, to transform its urban–rural duality and construct a new type of urban–rural relationship, China needs to address agricultural development and matters concerning farmers' income growth. Regarding agricultural development, existing studies have demonstrated that, to achieve urban–rural integration, it is essential to adjust policies from time to time to improve agricultural productivity (Li M., Shao T. & Liu S.Y., 2014; Ouyang Z.G., 2014). Since the beginning of the new century, China has made remarkable achievements in agricultural development, especially grain production. Yet, its food production and agricultural development are subject to a range of constraints such as environmental changes (Ma J.L., Chen Y.F. & Qian X.P., 2012; Chen S., Xu J.T. & Zhang H.P., 2016; Kanwar S., 2006; Chen S., Chen X. & Xu J., 2016), labor outflow (Shi Z.L. & Yang Y.Y., 2011; Wang Y.M. et al. 2013; Gai Q.E., Zhu X. & Shi Q.H., 2014; Rozele S. et al.; Chang H. et al. 2011; Chiodi V. et al. 2012), and agricultural subsidies (Zhong C.P., Chen S.P. & Xu C.S., 2013; Wang O. & Yang J., 2014; Li J.Y., 2016; Fan S. et al. 2008; Just D.R., 2011). Under agricultural supply side structural reform and rural land and labor supply constraints, total factor productivity (TFP) plays an important role in China's endeavor to transform its agricultural development mode and change its industry–agriculture and urban–rural relationship. In this regard, researchers have applied growth accounting, data envelopment analysis (DEA), and stochastic frontier analysis (SFA) to examine the evolutionary trajectory and intrinsic mechanism of China's agricultural TFP (Zhou D.M., 2009; Xin X.F. & Qin F., 2011; Zhu X., Shi Q.H. & Gai Q.E., 2011; Gao F., 2015; Han H.B. & Zhang L., 2015; Fu M.H. & Qi C.J., 2016). For example, Zhu X., Shi Q.H. & Gai Q.E. (2011) noted that if capital and labor misallocation could be effectively eliminated, China's agricultural TFP would increase by more than 20 percent, and the agricultural TFP in Eastern and Western China would increase by more than 30 percent.

To transform China's urban–rural economic relationship also signifies to change the country's agricultural management mode. In fact, improving agricultural productivity is usually preceded by changing the management mode. In this regard, some authors have investigated the contents and functions of agricultural management (Guo Q.H., 2013; Liao Z.J. & Guo X.M., 2015; Han C.H., 2017; Brocfield H., 2008; Graeub B.E. et al. 2016). For example, Guo Q.H. (2013) suggested that the new agricultural management entities are large-scale, family-based agricultural economic organizations adapted to modern agriculture and market economy. At present, China's new agricultural management system is composed of family farms, farmers' cooperatives, and agricultural enterprises. Among them, family farms are the development direction of future agricultural management organizations. Graeub B.E. et al. (2016) also found that globally family farms constitute 98 percent of all farms, suggesting that family farming plays a crucial role in food production. Some authors have also looked at the benefit and efficiency of China's innovation on agricultural management mode (Kong X.Z., 2014; Lu Z.Y., 2016; Chavas J.P., 2001; Chaplin H. et al. 2014). For example, Lu Z.Y. (2016) discovered that the income effect and employment effect of the development of new agricultural management entities in China are significant; the welfare effect of the development of new agricultural management entities differs between minorities areas and non-minorities areas in Western China, with the non-minorities areas enjoying remarkably better income and employment benefits from the development of new agricultural management entities. Agricultural development and reform of agricultural management mode are closely relevant to land system. Qu F.T. & Tian G.M. (2011) believed that to achieve urban–rural coordinated development, it is essential to transform the land property right system. Huang J.K. et al. (2012) found that confirming farmland rights has stimulated farmers' long-term investment. China should speed up the construction of an urban–rural construction land market featuring equal rights and functions and sharing of value added (Research Group of Rural Department of the Development Research Center of the State Council, 2014) and form a three rights division pattern among ownership, contracting right, and management right of rural land (Sun X.Z., 2016). Apart from land system, based on the roles of finance in economic growth and structural change (Kumbhakar S.C. & Christopher F.P., 2009), some authors have also probed into the rural financial repression in China, its development direction, and its socioeconomic effects from the perspective of rural financial development (Hong Z., 2011; Dong

X.L. & Xu H., 2012; He Z.X. & Qu R.X., 2015; Su F. & Fang L., 2016). Overall, these changes in land and financial systems have contributed positively to scaling up agricultural management, increasing the number of new management entities, and integrating urban–rural development (Ni G.H. & Cai F., 2015).

Urban–rural income gap holds the balance in transforming urban–rural economic relationship. To improve China's urban–rural economic relationship, steps must be taken to contain urban–rural income gap. In this regard, existing literature has mainly examined farmers' income growth channels in China from three perspectives. First is land system (Xu Q. et al. 2008; Mao P.H. & Xu J., 2015; Luo Y.M. & Fan L.M., 2015; Jin S. & Deininger K., 2009; Winters P. et al. 2009; Gray C.I. & Bilsborow R.E., 2014). For example, Mao P.H. & Xu J. (2015) used farmer household micro survey data and counter factual analysis to investigate the impact of land management right transfer on household income. They concluded that land transfer can significantly improve the income level of rural households; land transfer can increase full-sample farmer household income by 19 percent and land-transferred farmer household income by 3 percent. Second is human capital (Xing C.B., Jia S.Y. & Li S., 2013; Luo Y.M. & Fan L.M., 2014; Yang D.T., 2004; Parman J., 2012). For example, Luo Y.M. & Fan L.M. (2014) presented an empirical study on the relationship between rural human capital and farmers' income growth in China. The results showed that rural human capital contributes positively to both wage income and nonwage income of farmers in the province. Third is agricultural technology (Xiao W. & Xiao L.Z., 2013; Zhou Z., Ma Q.C. & Kong X.Z., 2016). For example, following the transmission mechanism of "labor outputted from agricultural sector – demand for labor-saving technology generated – technology supplied by modern industrial sector – balanced factor allocation between two sectors", Xiao W. & Xiao L.Z. (2013) demonstrated the relationship between agricultural technology progress and farmers' income growth in China. The results showed that policy measures targeted at optimizing urban–rural factor allocation and enhancing technical support of modern departments for the agricultural sector are conducive to realizing the goal of sustainable income growth for farmers.

2.4 Review on existing relevant literature

In view of the practical reality that there still exists an urban–rural dual economy in China and the significance of the transformation of urban–rural economic relationship to the entire process of modernization, extensive studies have been carried out on China's urban–rural economic relationship. These studies deal with the definitions of the most typical behaviors of urban–rural economic relationship—urban–rural income gap and urban–rural consumption gap and possible ways and policies for improving urban–rural economic relationship. They are wide in coverage, divergent in perspective, and diverse in methodology. In terms of theoretical basis, most of the articles have relied on the classic dual economy theory of development economics—the Lewis-Fei-Ranis model—to examine urban–rural labor fluidity, agricultural development, and the effect of duality transformation. This avoids describing China's urban–rural relationship from the perspective of phenomena and renders the research efforts with the merits of logical deduction and theoretical exploration. Because of their extensive coverage and theoretical rationality, some existing studies have made undeniable contributions to China's economic development practice. For example, based on the Lewis-Fei-Ranis model, some authors noted that deepening the reform of the urban and rural household registration system helps encourage the substantial flow of urban and rural labor in China, which offers useful reference for the country to effectively formulate policies in favor of urban–rural integrated development. Moreover, the wide coverage and theoretical rationality also make it possible for individual studies to complement one another. For example, studies on urban–rural income gap are usually closely relevant with studies on urban–rural consumption gap, and they can therefore be mutually complemented and validated. In a nutshell, existing literature plays a significant role in deepening the research on China's urban–rural relationship. It also offers necessary theoretical reference for our research herein.

Nevertheless, this book aims to explore the evolutionary logic and intrinsic mechanism of China's urban–rural economic relationship since the founding of the PRC, especially after reform and opening up, and to provide potential policy options for continuously improving the country's urban–rural economic relationship in the new era on grounds of this evolutionary mechanism. To this end, although existing literature has responded to the topic in some aspects, it is still insufficient in terms of theoretical framework, demonstration process, and policy implication, and there is still considerable room for further improvement.

First of all, in terms of research purpose, existing literature tends to focus the urban–rural economic relationship "in a given period of time" after the founding of the PRC, particularly, the level, causes, effects, and possible ways to reduce, urban–rural income gap in a given period of time. After all, focusing on a particular period of time is necessary for characterizing China's dual economy. But this book attempts to analyze the overall and long-term dynamics of China's urban–rural economic relationship since the founding of the PRC, especially over the 40 years of reform and opening up. Addressing the characteristics and evolutionary mechanism of China's urban–rural economic relationship over different periods of time constitutes the core task of our research herein. In terms of logic layout, this book "segments" China's urban–rural economic relationship based on empirical data and uses core concepts such as separation and integration to characterize China's urban–rural economic relationship during these periods. Furthermore, an important task of this research is to explain how urban–rural economic relationship has evolved during different periods of time, how China's economic system arrangements have interacted with this evolution, and how corresponding policy implications are derived from the evolutionary mechanism of urban–rural economic relationship during different periods of time. Obviously, compared with existing literature, the research topic of this book is more prominently characterized by a long term and a large span, and it highlights the intrinsic law behind the evolution of urban–rural economic relationship across a long time spectrum.

Second, in terms of theoretical orientation, existing studies have commonly relied on the classic dual economy theory of development economics, namely, the Lewis-Fei-Ranis model, to investigate China's urban–rural relationship, as can be verified by their focus on the transfer of rural labor, the reform of urban–rural household registration, and the dynamics of urban–rural income gap and consumption gap. One point remains. To use dual economy theory, for example the Lewis-Fei-Ranis model, an implicit premise is that the causes of the urban–rural dual opposition in China are the same as those assumed by these models. The Lewis-Fei-Ranis model emphasizes that, between the modern sector represented by manufacture and the traditional sector represented by agriculture, there exists a disparity of labor productivity arising out of the totally different factor endowments between the two sectors: compared with the urban sector, the rural sector has a large amount of labor with extremely low or even zero marginal productivity; labor surplus in the rural sector in contrast to labor scarcity in the modern sector constitutes the economic driver of urban–rural economic contrast. Nevertheless, since 1949, China has remained a highly populous and geographically enormous developing country with socialist system. During different periods of time, the country would make institutional arrangements and policy measures according to its choice of development strategy, and such a strategy is bound to affect the behavior of urban–rural economic relationship. This signifies that, in terms of causes, China's urban–rural duality is relevant not only to inter-sectoral endowments but also to its overall development strategy and institutional arrangements. To investigate China's urban–rural economic relationship, we have to break through the implied hypotheses of the Lewis-Fei-Ranis model and respond to the local characteristics and complexities of the causes underlying the formation of urban–rural duality.

Third, existing literature relies on the Lewis-Fei-Ranis model of development economics to understand China's urban–rural economic problems. This understanding captures some important aspects of urban–rural economic relationship as it highlights the importance of labor transfer and urbanization to the transformation of urban–rural economic relationship. However, besides particular assumptions on the causes of duality, the Lewis-Fei-Ranis model also contains many implied hypotheses on how this duality is transformed. For example, it assumes a perfect urban–rural factor market so that urban–rural job transformation is possible for rural labor according to accurate price signals (wage levels) and at very low transaction costs; labor-intensive production in the modern sector (e.g., manufacture) so that the modern sector represented by manufacture can sustain an extraordinary attraction to rural labor; and unchanged capital/labor ratio so that the modern sector (e.g., manufacture) can maintain a remarkable capacity of capital accumulation to attract surplus labor from the rural sector. Unfortunately, however, all these hypotheses are gravely divergent from the local characteristics of China. For example, China launched and implemented the major strategy of reform and opening up in 1978. Up to the present-day China is still a developing economy in the stage of system transition, in which market-oriented system transition is ongoing and marketization is not fully synchronized among all fields. Overall, its marketization degree of factors is lagging behind that of commodities (Wang X.L., Fan G. & Yu J.W., 2017). This renders a unique array of marketization degree to the flow of factors, especially labor factors, between urban and rural China. The Lewis-Fei-Ranis model assumes an "efficient factor market", whereas a "perfecting factor market" agrees better with the basic background behind the evolution of China's urban–rural economic relationship. This signifies that the transformation of urban–rural duality and the evolution of urban–rural economic relationship in China have their own unique features.

Fourth, existing literature relies on the Lewis-Fei-Ranis model to understand China's urban–rural economic relationship. This model is related to the reallocation of productive factors such as urban and rural labor, and this reallocation logically requires giving full play to the role of the market in adjusting prices and of the government in supplying public goods. As such, most of the existing studies tend to examine the policy options in favor of urban–rural integration or a new type of urban–rural relationship within a framework of government–market dichotomy, under which the market plays a key role in resource allocation, and the government supplies public goods to offset market failure. An implied hypothesis behind these studies is that there are no internal structural features inside the government and the market. That is, the government and the market are homogenized inside themselves. One point remains. Since 1978, China has always been a developing country under economic system transition, with distinct structural features inside both the government and the market. For example, Xu C.G. (2011) noted that since reform and opening up, especially since the mid-1990s, China has formed a unique regionally decentralized authoritarianism (RDA), characterized by highly centralized political and personnel control at the central level, and highly decentralized economic and administrative authority at the local level. In light of the economic development practice in Taiwan, Wu Y.P. (2017) reminded that the process of economic development should be understood from the impact of political processes on economy and by addressing the structural features of the market (i.e., the interaction between the upper market and the lower market). Since 1978, China's market-oriented economic system reform has been advancing in an obviously progressive manner, suggesting that the intermarket structural feature is well worth attention. Both the government and the market have their own structural features. To discuss a new type of urban–rural relationship in the context of building a moderately prosperous society in all respects, it is essential to break through the government–market dichotomy and find out the roles of the intragovernmental and intramarket structure in the construction of a new type of urban–rural relationship.

Finally, at a time when China's economy is in the new normal and switching toward high-quality development, research on the evolutionary mechanism of its urban–rural economic relationship should be ultimately targeted at providing pertinent options for improving urban–rural economic relationship in the policy implication. Around the goal of transforming urban–rural duality and improving urban–rural economic relationship, some authors have proposed a series of improvements with respect to household registration, land system, financial system, agricultural subsidies, and allocation of public goods between urban and rural areas. However, most of these improvements are discussed as "what it ought to be" rather than as "actual". That is, they are basically analyzing what policies and measures ought to be taken to improve China's urban–rural economic relationship, but hardly give an answer to how these policy options are formulated and implemented or why certain logically perfect options are hard to implement effectively in practice. This compromises the practical value of existing literature and policy recommendations for improving urban–rural economic relationship. In the analysis of policy implication, we must shift from "what it ought to be" to "actual", examine the basic trend and intrinsic logic of the evolution of urban–rural economic relationship, and probe into the institutional background underlying the evolution of urban–rural economic relationship and the way of behavior among different subjects. In short, at a time when China is working hard to solve its imbalanced, inadequate development, to improve its urban–rural economic relationship in a sustainable manner, China should not only accurately understand the implementation effect of existing policies but also highlight the participation constraints and incentive compatibility constraints among different participants in the implementation mechanism of urban–rural economic relationship in light of mechanism design theory.

In a nutshell, extensive studies have been carried out and an abundance of findings have been reported on China's urban–rural economic relationship up to this day. In terms of practical background, these findings respond to the reality that there still exists an urban–rural duality in China. In terms of theoretical background, they reflect the application of the dual economy theory of development economics. Existing research literature covers the contents and measurements, *status quo* and causes of China's urban–rural economic relationship, as well as potential ways and options of improvement. It is extensive in content, divergent in perspective, and diverse in methodology. These articles are inspiring and referential for people to gain deeper insights on China's urban–rural economic relationship.

However, existing literature tends to confine their analyses on China's urban–rural economic relationship to a particular period of time, and they mainly rely on the Lewis-Fei-Ranis model of development economics, without careful consideration about whether the implied hypotheses of this model fits the local practice of China. Moreover, their logic argument and policy implication are more biased toward government–market dichotomy, with less attention paid to the structural features inside the government and the market themselves. This signifies that existing literature has not exhausted China's urban–rural economic relationship in their entirety, and there is still vast room for further improvement. This book attempts to construct a political economy analytical framework for urban–rural economic relationship based on local characteristics. Based on this framework, it explains the evolutionary logic behind China's urban–rural economic relationship since the founding of the PRC, especially over the 40 years of reform and opening up, and summarizes this evolutionary mechanism as a dynamic change from separation to imbalanced integration and then to collaborative integration. Its analytical mechanism highlights the institutional features inside the government and inside the market. This analytical perspective characterizes a long term, a large span, and the generation of argument logic from local characteristics. It seeks to complement existing findings in analysis purpose and argument perspective, thus deepening the theoretical understanding on China's urban–rural economic relationship and highlighting its inspirations to policy choice.

3 Political economy analytical framework for China's urban–rural economic relationship

Logically speaking, to understand the evolutionary mechanism of China's urban–rural economic relationship, an appropriate analytical framework is a prerequisite. In fact, development economics has already captured the reality that urban–rural contrast exists in almost all developing economies and formed the dual economy theory, typically the Lewis-Fei-Ranis model, based on this discovery. As demonstrated by our literature review earlier in this book, existing studies on China's urban–rural economic problems tend to rely on this model as the main theoretical source of research. The Lewis-Fei-Ranis model assumes an economic opposition between the urban and rural sectors in developing economies as a precondition and regards the nonagricultural transfer of rural surplus labor as the core driver of transforming urban–rural economic relationship. Admittedly, this line of analysis is inspiring for China's economic practice. But, similar to other economic theories, the Lewis-Fei-Ranis model also contains a number of implied hypotheses that do not fully agree with the local characteristics of China. Particularly, since 1949, China has remained a large developing country with socialist system, and its economic development has experienced two distinctly different stages: a pre-reform stage before and a post-reform stage after the late 1970s. While China's major strategy of reform and opening up has been promoted for 40 years so the country is still in the process of market-oriented economic system reform. Such a practical reality inevitably gives rise to corresponding development strategies, as well as economic systems that affect the formation, evolution, and performance of China's urban–rural economic relationship. In short, to analyze China's urban–rural economic relationship, we have to find out these economic systems and the development strategies, constraints, and social structures behind the economic systems. In this sense, political economy provides the ideological basis for exploring China's urban–rural economic relationship as a classic issue of "development". A "political economy of development" is therefore crucial to investigating China's urban–rural economic relationship.

3.1 The Lewis-Fei-Ranis model and its applicability in China

After the Second World War, developing countries were commonly faced with the urgent mission of economic development. Such a practical reality has shifted the focus of many researchers to the economic characteristics and social development of developing countries, among which "duality" is a famous summary by social scientists for the reality of developing countries. Etymologically, the term duality was initially coined for the particular social formation of developing countries. For example, Boeke J.B. (1953) introduced the terms "social dualism" and "dual society" and explored the economic–social disparities between colonial "enclaves" and local traditional sectors in Indonesia. Following him, many authors began extending their analyses on the duality of developing countries from society to economy, technology, and culture. Particularly, with the emergence of development economics, the dual economy theory has gradually became the theoretical basis for people to understand urban–rural economic relationship.

In development economics, the most representative model of the dual economy theory is the Lewis-Fei-Ranis model, which was introduced and gradually refined by Lewis W.A., Fei J.C.H., and Ranis G. in the 1950s and 1960s. As a response to the structural features of developing economies, Lewis W.A. (1954) examined how economies develop with unlimited supplies of labor and derived a logically consistent dual economy model at the theoretical level. The Lewis model emphasizes that in developing countries or underdeveloped economies, there commonly exist two distinct sectors: a traditional sector or subsistence sector and a modern sector or capitalist sector. The opposition and coexistence between these two sectors basically characterizes the economic systems of developing countries. The traditional sector is comprised primarily of the traditional agricultural sector, which mainly uses traditional factors such as land and labor for production and has a lower factor productivity and labor remuneration or wage level. The modern sector is comprised primarily of the nonagricultural sector or modern manufacture sector, which uses reproducible modern factors such as capital and other factors for economic activities, is quick to adopt scientific and technical innovations, and has a higher factor productivity and labor remuneration or wage level. In the traditional sector, there are laborers with zero marginal productivity, who seek subsistence wages determined by the minimum required for subsistence. Before the rural surplus labor is exhausted, the modern sector can get any amount of labor at constant wages slightly above subsistence wages. After the rural surplus labor is exhausted, however, the modern sector has to pay wages above subsistence wages to get any more labor from the rural sector. In this context, the changes in the dual economy in developing countries can be illustrated by Figure 3.1.

As illustrated, in developing countries, there coexist a traditional sector represented by agriculture (or villages) and a modern sector represented by

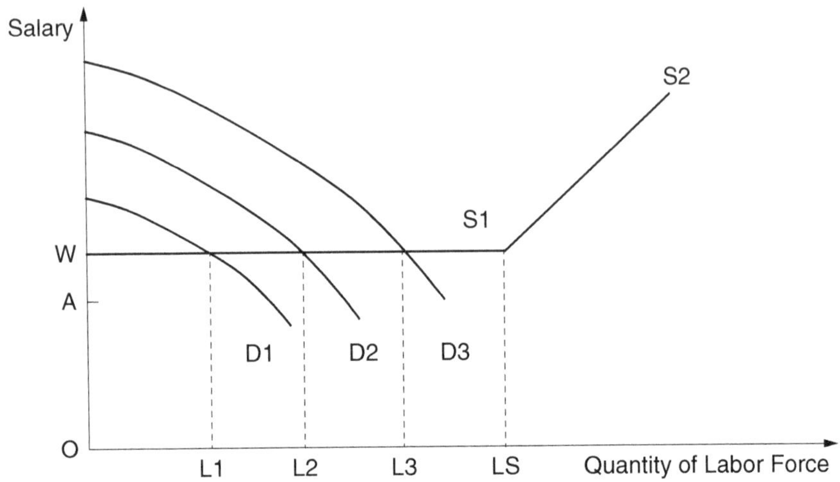

Figure 3.1 The Lewis model of urban–rural labor transfer.

nonagriculture (or towns), with labor endowment disparities and labor transfer between them. This intersectoral labor reallocation constitutes the core content of the dynamics of urban–rural economic relationship. In the labor transfer diagram, the horizontal axis represents the amount of labor withdrawn by the urban sector from the rural sector; the vertical axis represents the actual wage rates of the urban and rural sectors. Here, OA is the subsistence wage of the rural sector; OW is the constant wage at which the urban sector withdraws labor from the rural sector; and D1, D2, and D3 are the marginal productivity or amount of labor required by the urban sector for different capital inputs. From this diagram, according to the amount of labor transferred and the way wages are determined in the two sectors, there are two distinct dynamic phases of dual economy in developing countries:

Phase I is the time when an almost unlimited supply of labor is available in the rural sector, so that the manufacture sector can get any mount of labor factor from the rural sector at a constant wage OW, which is above the subsidence wage OA of the rural sector. In this phase, the urban sector first gets L1 amount of labor from the rural sector, whose marginal productivity is expressed by curve D1. As the constant wage is OW, the part of curve D1 above OW constitutes the production surplus (profit) for the urban sector, which immediately converts into capital accumulation. Next, the urban sector uses this capital accumulation to expand production and withdraws L2 amount of labor from the rural sector, still at the constant wage OW. This way, the balance between D2 and OW continues to constitute the production surplus or capital accumulation for the urban sector. This goes on until the amount of labor withdrawn from the rural sector reaches LS.

Phase II is the time when shortage of rural labor takes place under continuous outflow, its marginal productivity begins to rise and the wage level no longer remains the subsistence wage OA determined by the minimum required for subsidence. In this phase, if the urban sector wants to get more labor from the rural sector, it cannot always pay the constant wage OW slightly above the subsistence wage OA of the rural sector all the time. Instead, it has to pay the rural labor at a wage determined by the demand–supply relationship and the marginal productivity of labor, and this wage rises as the amount of labor withdrawn from the rural sector increases. As diagrammatically indicated to the right of LS, if the urban sector wants to get labor from the rural sector, it has to provide increasingly high wages according to the balanced point determined by the labor supply curve S1–S2, thus disabling the previous mechanism of getting rural labor at the constant wage OW.

Obviously, under the Lewis model, in the rural sector, there exists surplus labor with marginal productivity equal to zero, while in the urban sector, the marginal productivity of labor is higher than the constant wage at which it withdraws labor, and this difference results in the accumulation of capital in the urban sector and the continuous outflow of surplus labor from the rural sector. Existence of surplus labor in the rural sector signifies that economic activities in the urban sector are operated at low costs, and the high profits and high accumulations associated with these low costs constitute the precondition for the urban sector to continuously withdraw labor from the rural sector. When the urban sector continues to withdraw labor from the rural sector to such an extent as to change the wage determination mechanism, the Lewis turning point is reached for urban–rural economic relationship: the wage of rural labor is also determined by their marginal productivity; the urban and rural sectors begin to assimilate in the wage determination mechanism; urban–rural income gap begins to converge as a result of labor reallocation; the dual economy in developing countries begins to change toward unitary economy. This analytical thinking combines the capital formation and production capacity expansion in the urban sector with the labor transfer in the rural sector, thus validating the core mechanism behind the dual economy transformation in developing countries at the theoretical level, which is very instructive on the extension of economic theory and the economic practice in developing countries.

However, there is still room for further improving the Lewis model since its implied hypotheses are not all operative. Particularly, Ranis G. & Fei, J.C.H. (1961), Fei J.C.H., & Ranis G. (1964) noted that the Lewis model ignores the contribution of the rural sector to the development of the urban sector and fails to address the product surplus resulted from growing agricultural productivity as the precondition for the flow of rural labor. In other words, the Lewis model regards the rural sector as a dependent sector waiting to be reformed, and the expansion of the modern sector (e.g., urban sector) as the driver of eliminating dual economy and realizing economic modernization. Yet, this understanding does not agree with the practical transformation of dual economy, since economic development and productivity growth in the rural sector are also fatal to this transformation. In response to these deficiencies, Ranis G. and Fei J.C.H. introduced the disguised unemployment concept, which covers not only labor with marginal productivity equal to zero but also labor with marginal productivity above zero but below the constant wage level. To Fei and Ranis, the constant institutional wages in the traditional sector, namely, the average output or earnings of agricultural workers, are not primarily determined by market forces, but by institutional forces such as customs and moralities. Apparently, the disguised unemployment concept of Fei and Ranis is an extension of the zero marginal productivity hypothesis of the Lewis model, which makes the analysis of urban–rural economic relationship more diverse and practically pertinent.

According to the extended definition of the core concepts, Fei J.C.H. and Ranis G. separated the transformation of urban–rural duality in developing economies into three phases, as shown in Figure 3.2.

Phase I is the time when the marginal productivity in the rural sector equals zero, namely, from O to LS on the horizontal axis, during which labor transfer in the rural sector makes no difference to total agricultural output, and the urban sector can get labor from the rural sector at a constant wage (constant institutional wage OW). From the logic construction point of view, the labor transferred from the rural sector during this phase

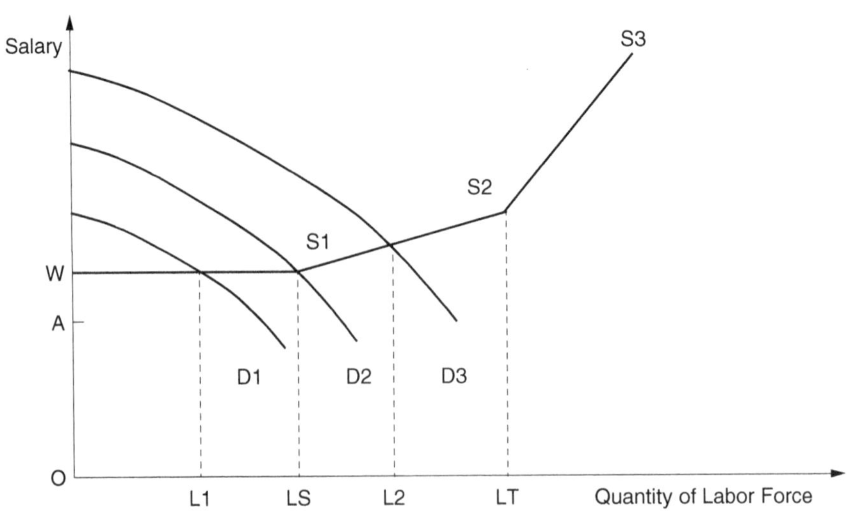

Figure 3.2 The Fei-Ranis model of urban–rural labor transfer.

marks off the first instance of disguised unemployment, which is fully identical to phase I of the Lewis model.

Phase II is a time when the marginal productivity of labor in the rural sector is above zero but below the constant institutional wages, namely, from LS to LT on the horizontal axis, during which the transfer of labor from the rural sector into the urban sector makes a difference to agricultural output—labor outflow leads to falling total agricultural output. The labor transferred from the rural sector during this phase marks off the second instance of disguised unemployment. Further, falling total agricultural output leads to rising prices of agricultural products and growing wage levels. That is, the urban sector has to raise the wage level a little to get labor from the rural sector, as reflected by the rise of the wage level from S1 to S2. This signifies that the labor supply curve of the urban sector begins to turn slightly up to the right.

Phase III is a time when all rural surplus labor is transferred into the urban sector, namely, the portion to the right of LT on the horizontal axis, during which the surplus labor in the rural sector is completely eliminated and the urban sector has to get labor from the rural sector at a wage determined by the marginal output of labor. This way, the wage of labor in the urban sector and in the rural sector is determined in completely the same way, and the flow of labor between the two sectors is dependent on changes and comparisons of marginal output. The wage determination mechanism during this period coincides with that in phase II of the Lewis model. Obviously, to achieve continuous transfer of rural labor during phase III, agricultural productivity growth has to remain at the level that accommodates a stable or even higher total agricultural output. Productivity growth in the rural sector is the precondition for the expansion of the urban sector and the continuous transfer of labor from the rural sector.

From the evolutionary histories and comparisons between these two models, the Fei-Ranis model extends the Lewis model from three dimensions. First, with regard to the understanding of rural surplus labor, the Fei-Ranis model addresses the portion of labor with marginal productivity above zero but below the constant institutional wages, which breaks through the limitation of the Lewis model to instances where the marginal productivity of rural labor equals zero. Second, concerning the transformation of urban–rural dual economy, the Fei-Ranis model underscores the importance of productivity growth in the rural sector to the expansion of the urban sector and to its own labor outflow. This way, the rural sector is no longer regarded as a passive sector waiting to be reformed, and productivity growth in the rural sector itself also becomes an important component of the transformation of dual economy. Third, in light of the outflow and wage determination of rural labor, the Fei-Ranis model discovers two turning points in the transformation of dual economy—a shortage point and a commercialization point. The former is the short supply of agricultural products caused by the transfer of rural labor at the transition from phase I to phase II; the latter the increasing commercialization in the traditional sector caused by the transition from phase II to phase III.

These extensions allow the Fei-Ranis model to depart from the Lewis model and dynamically examine dual economy by assuming a growth equilibrium between the urban and rural sectors, which is of fatal importance to accurately understanding the urban–rural economic relationship in developing countries, especially the positive roles of the development of the rural sector. Despite differences in implied hypotheses and assumed details, however, the two models are in essence intrinsically consistent and successive: both address the existence of urban–rural economic opposition in developing countries and emphasize the existence of surplus labor in the rural sector with negligible marginal productivity; both consider the reallocation of rural surplus labor as the core driver of the transformation of dual economy and believe that this reallocation will lead to urban–rural integration or a convergence of urban–rural income gap. As such, the models are usually collectively referred to as the "Lewis-Fei-Ranis model", which later became a typical representative of the dual economy theory and the theoretical basis for understanding urban–rural economic relationship.

The Lewis-Fei-Ranis model draws people's attention to the structural features of developing economies. It prompts people to look at the economic development issues in developing countries from the perspective of urban–rural structure and to pay attention to the important role of urban–rural allocation of labor factors on duality transformation. Hence, the model undoubtedly has great theoretical value and practical significance. However, like any other economic theory, the Lewis-Fei-Ranis model is built upon a number of implied hypotheses. For example, it assumes labor-intensive production in both the urban and rural sectors. That is, capital accumulation inevitably means vast labor demand to provide a continuous market pull for the transfer of surplus labor from the rural sector.

As far as China is concerned, urban–rural structural opposition has persisted throughout the long history of economic and social development. Urban–rural duality has existed since the founding of the PRC. To foster the transformation of urban–rural duality is a major issue that the country has to face up to in the process of modernization. Over the 40 years of reform and opening up, with fast growing economic strength and comprehensive national power, China has reiterated placing urban–rural integration in an important position of overall development during each period of time. Particularly, at a point of time when socialism with Chinese characteristics is entering a new era, the report to the 19th National Congress of the CPC noted that China's main social contradiction has transformed; imbalanced, inadequate development has become the main bottleneck to the country's modernization. This imbalanced, inadequate development is prominently embodied by the development gap between the urban and rural sectors, and a modern economic system highlights the implementation of rural revitalization strategies to establish and maintain a new mechanism of urban–rural integrate development. In response to this practical background, systematic, it is necessary to make in-depth investigation on the formation, *status quo*, and development trend of China's urban–rural economic relationship at the theoretical level. Academically, as the Lewis-Fei-Ranis model already supplies fairly mature theoretical resources which are influential to many developing countries, it would just be an easy choice to use this model to examine the local problems in China. However, we have to note here that China has remained a large developing country with socialist system since 1949, and after 1978, it embarked on a major strategy of market-oriented reform inside and global integration outside. These facts signify that China's urban–rural economic relationship is both theoretically generic and practically unique. Hence, rather than directly use the Lewis-Fei-Ranis model to explain China's urban–rural economic relationship, attention must be paid to several inconsistencies of this model from the local practice of China as described below.

First of all, in terms of the causes of urban–rural contrast, the dual economy theory, typically the Lewis-Fei-Ranis model, tends to ascribe urban–rural dual contrast to endowment disparities: there exists surplus labor in the traditional sector (or rural sector) relative to the modern sector (or urban sector), whose marginal productivity is near or equal to zero in the rural sector. Hence, the nonagricultural transfer of rural labor can eliminate the resource endowment disparities and improve the factor allocation efficiency by reallocating factors, which constitutes the core driver of duality transformation for developing countries. When it comes to China, however, over a lengthy period of time after the founding of the PRC, China was faced with not only factor endowment disparities between the urban and rural sectors but also the need to implement the heavy industry first strategy against grave capital scarcity. That was a major choice for the country to construct an independent industry system, resume the economic order, and ensure national strategic security during that time. This strategic choice, on the dimension of urban–rural relationship, led to a series of institutional arrangements: state monopoly of the purchase and marketing of agricultural products, people's commune, and household registration. Accordingly, these institutional arrangements became important drivers of urban–rural duality in China, as was reflected in the economic, social, and even cultural aspects. In terms of causes, China's dual contrast does not only relate to resource endowments between the urban and rural sectors but it is also related to the particular economic and social effects of development strategies and institutional choices between these two sectors. Hence, to transform urban–rural duality and to achieve urban–rural integration, China should also respond to these institutional arrangements.

Second, in terms of the pathway of urban–rural structural transformation, the Lewis-Fei-Ranis model underlines the nonagricultural transfer of rural labor as the core driver of duality transformation. That is, industrialization and urbanization are the basic evolutionary trend of urban–rural relationship in developing countries. China, however, as the largest developing economy in the world, has its own unique pathway of realizing this trend. According to the dual economy theory of development economics, the nonagricultural transfer of rural labor is a change of job opportunity or a transformation of farmers' identity. Hence, the nonagricultural transfer of rural labor will spur industrialization and urbanization simultaneously, and the increase of industrialization and urbanization rates will take place at roughly the same pace.

However, in 1978, China embarked on a great expedition of reform and opening up. Due to the progressive nature of market-oriented reform and the institutional combination among different fields, the nonagricultural transfer of rural labor in China mainly labels an occupational change instead of an identity transformation. In fact, the separation between occupational change and identify transformation marks a characteristic fact of the dynamics of China's urban–rural relationship. "Rural migrant worker" paints a vivid picture of this separation. According to statistics, as of the end of 2017, China had 286,520,000 rural migrant workers, including 114,670,000 locals and 171,850,000 working outside their home areas. Now that rural labor could not transform their identity in sync with the changed of their occupation, China recorded prominent divergence between industrialization rate and urbanization rate, between urbanization rate of registered permanent population and that of registered population. In 2017, the urbanization rate of permanent population and registered population were 58.52 percent and 42.35 percent. The share of secondary and tertiary industries in output value and the urbanization rate of permanent population were 92.09 percent and 58.52 percent. By horizontal comparison, China has its own characteristics whether in respect of industrialization and urbanization, or in respect of structural problems among different forms of urbanization. They are major issues that the country has to address when implementing supply-side structural reform and promoting the construction of a modern economic system. They also imply that China's urban–rural duality has its unique characteristics in the transformation pathway, and the country cannot expect to draw a formula of duality transformation directly from the Lew-Fei-Ranis model.

Last, in terms of the transformation mechanism of urban–rural relationship, duality transformation, as revealed by the Lewis-Fei-Ranis model, is highly demanding of a perfect labor market, and market mechanism is usually regarded as the key institutional element for transforming urban–rural duality. In the dual economy theory of development economics, an "efficient factor market" is a crucial implied hypothesis. That is, urban and rural labor forces are available for factor reallocation according to price signals from a perfect market. When it comes to China, however, after reform and opening up for 40 years, China is still a large developing country under economic system transition. By economic system transition, it means that China is still undergoing market-oriented system reform, during which its marketization degree of factors—land, labor, and capital—lags behind that of commercial products. Hence, a "perfecting factor market" pinpoints the realistic institutional background of the country's duality transformation. More notably, as an unmatched large developing country, China features structural relationship among different regions, among different residents, and among different levels of governments. To transform its economic system, China not only needs to promote for a positive government–market relationship but also address intragovernmental (central and local) and intramarket (upstream market, e.g., core factors, and downstream market, e.g., competitive products) structural features. Particularly, since the mid-1990s, China has implemented a power decentralization reform among governments at different levels, allowing the behavioral choice of local governments to affect economic and social development enormously. Given these structural features, governments at different levels and markets of different categories are usually not "homogenized". Intergovernmental and intermarket economic system arrangements are therefore important enough to affect changes in urban–rural relationship by influencing the behavioral choice of local governments and microeconomic subjects. Hence, the analysis of China's urban–rural economic relationship should be set in the context of economic system transition as well as the intragovernmental and intramarket structural features, which is particularly important for understanding the changes in China's urban–rural economic relationship over the 40 years of reform and opening up.

In a nutshell, urban–rural duality is a common structural feature among developing countries, and the Lewis-Fei-Ranis model is the classic dual economy theory of development economics. Yet as China's urban–rural economic relationship is both generic in evolutionary trend and unique in local background, the transformation of urban–rural duality has its "own story" distinctive from that of any other economy. This understanding of the evolution of China's urban–rural relationship as "heterogeneous" renders important economic implications. Urban–rural duality is a classic issue addressed by development economics. The dual economy theory, typically the Lewis-Fei-Ranis model, implicitly assumes the origination of urban–rural contrast from endowment conditions, the synchronicity between occupational change and identity transformation, and an efficient urban–rural factor market, which do not fully agree with China's practical reality. To explain China's urban–rural economic relationship, we should draw on, but not copy, the dual economy theory of development economics. We should create an analytical paradigm of urban–rural economic relationship that accords with the practical background of China based on local characteristics. This is the objective requisite for giving a profound explanation on the evolutionary logic of China's urban–rural economic relationship.

3.2 Social background of the evolution of China's urban–rural economic relationship

As a large developing country, China's urban–rural economic relationship does not exist by itself. Instead, it is embedded into the entire country's modernization process and subject to the country's overall development mission and social conditions. Hence, the understanding of China's urban–rural economic relationship has to be rooted in the social background of China as a particular economy. Since the 1920s, under the leadership of the CPC, China has won the Anti-Japanese War and the War of emancipation and founded the PRC in 1949. The founding of the PRC marked a monumental event in the development history of China and even of the human being. Ever since 1949, one subject matter has remained in China's economy all the time. That is, how shall a large developing country with socialist system realize its goal of sustainable development and common prosperity? In fact, socialist system, a large developing country, and the goal of sustainable development, together, make up the "keywords" of China's economic development. Gao F. (2016b) summarized this subject matter as the fundamental proposition of the country's economic development. To this subject matter, China has responded with two phases of practice: planned economy before and market-oriented system transition after, the start of reform and opening up in 1978. It was out of this grand proposition of economic development that China's urban–rural economic relationship emerged and has evolved over time. From this point of view, understanding the social background behind the evolution of China's urban–rural economic relationship is of fatal importance, and the core of this understanding is to make clear the principal content of the proposition of China's economic development. Broadly speaking, the fundamental proposition of China's economic development is composed of the following major concepts:

1 China is a country with socialist system. Socialism, as a doctrine and an ideological trend that advocates the ownership, administration, and distribution of products and productive factors by the whole society based on public interests, can be traced back to the utopian socialism in the 16th century. In the 1830s–1840s, Karl Marx and Friedrich Engels critically absorbed the ideological achievements of utopian socialism, summarized the experience of working class movements, analyzed the rules and trends of capitalist economy under the logical framework of the theory of surplus value, and founded scientific socialism. Very soon, scientific socialism became the ideological cradle to subsequent international communist movements and the emergence and development of socialist countries. Before the founding of the PRC, in leading the Chinese revolutionary cause, the CPC had identified socialism as the country's basic system. At the Second Plenary Session of the Seventh

> CPC Central Committee held in March 1949, it was set forth that "After the victory of the Chinese revolution, we should quickly resume and develop production, counteract foreign imperialism, and steadily transform China from an agricultural to an industrial economy, from a New Democratic into a socialist country". Article 1 of the "Common Program", adopted at the First Plenary Session of the Chinese People's Political Consultative Conference on September 29, 1949, explicitly stated that "the PRC is a New Democratic, namely, a people's democratic country with people's democratic dictatorship led by the working class, based on the alliance of workers and peasants, uniting all democratic classes and all ethnic groups nationwide, opposing imperialism, feudalism, and bureaucratic capitalism and struggling for an independent, democratic, peaceful, united, prosperous and strong China."

After the founding of the PRC, China immediately set about transforming from New Democracy to socialism. On September 25, 1953, the *People's Daily* officially released the general line and task of the CPC Central Committee for the transitional period: to gradually realize the country's socialist industrialization and gradually realize the country's socialist transformation of agriculture, handicraft, and capitalist industry and commerce in a long time to come. Under the general line and general task for the transitional period, China pushed through the agricultural cooperative movement in the mutual aid group–elementary cooperative–advanced cooperative sequence, the handicraft cooperative movement in the production cooperation group–supply and marketing cooperative–production cooperative sequence, as well as the transformation of capitalist industry and commerce by various means such as peaceful redemption, public–private partnership, and state capitalism. As of the end of 1956, the transformation of agriculture, handicraft, and capitalist industry and commerce had been virtually accomplished. This way, under the general deployment for the transitional period, China successful completed the transition from New Democracy to socialist system. The basic economic system of socialism also spread in full swing.

By horizontal comparison, on the economic dimension, China's socialist system is reflected in the following three aspects:

First, the CPC as leader of China's revolution and modernization causes. The PRC was created by the CPC after leading the people to victory in the revolution, and the CPC is the core leader of all China's undertakings. By nature, the CPC is a Marxist political party taking the realization of communism as its paramount ideal and ultimate goal. The paramount ideal of communism pursued by Chinese Communists can only be realized when socialist society is substantially developed and highly flourished. To emancipate and develop productivity and realize common prosperity on the basis of developed productivity is the basic goal for the CPC to lead the people of the country toward socialist modernization at the economic level.

Second, public ownership of means of production as a feature of China's economic system. For a long time after the founding of the PRC, under the influence of the Soviet system, China had understood socialist system as public ownership of means of production, planned economy, and distribution according to work, which views socialist system from the "instrument" point of view. After the late 1970s, the CPC made new explorations on the historical stage of socialism in China and came to the scientific conclusion that China still is, and will remain so for a long time, in the primary stage of socialism, during which the country needs to substantially emancipate and develop productivity through reform and opening up. Against this backdrop, China's ownership of means of production has gradually shifted from absolute dominance of public ownership to coexistence of public ownership with various other forms of ownership. Its economic operation mechanism has gradually switched from planned economy to socialist market economy. Its distribution system has gradually steered from distribution according to work to a combination of distribution according to work and distribution according to the contribution of productive factors. Even so, China's ownership of means of production, economic operation mechanism, and distribution system are still different from those of major capitalist countries. For example, Piketty T., Yang L. & Zucman G. (2017) compared the share of public property in national wealth between China and some capitalist countries. As shown in Figure 3.3, since 1978, China's share of public property in national wealth has stood higher than that in the United States,

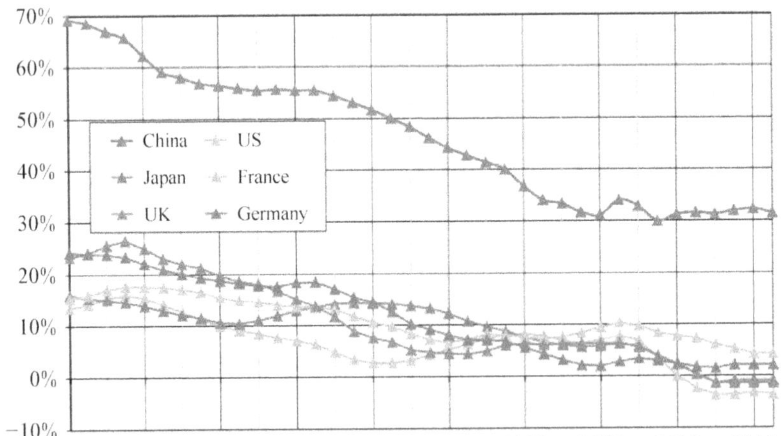

Figure 3.3 China's share of public property compared with other countries from 1978 to 2015.

Source: Piketty T., Yang L. & Zucman G. (2017).

Japan, France, the United Kingdom, and Germany. Even in 2015, its share of public property in national wealth was still higher than 30 percent, compared to 5 percent or less in major developed countries for the same year, and 15–25 percent for these countries back in the 1970s. Notably, after 2008, China's share of public property in national wealth began to change relative to major developed countries: China has been strengthening while major developed countries have been weakening. According to calculations by Chen Z.S. & Gao Y.W. (2015), in China's total assets, including operating assets, public and nonprofit assets, and resource assets, although public assets account for a little more than 50 percent of operating assets, they make up the overwhelming or absolute majority with a share of 81 percent. Hence, by horizontal comparison, the ownership of means of production, especially the share of public sector, is still an important cut-in point to understand China's socialist system.

Third, sustainable development and common prosperity as China's goals of economic development. The CPC, as the core leader of China's modernization cause, represents the fundamental interests of the vastest majority of the Chinese people. After the Third Plenary Session of the 11th CPC Central Committee, under the leadership of the CPC, China embarked on a major strategy of market-oriented reform and further opening to the outside world. Compared with the planned economy adopted in the past, this registered a widely influential and profound economic transformation. Since the inception of reform and opening up in 1978, beyond regarding socialist system as an "instrument", China has stressed understanding socialist system as a "function" and a "value" and reiterated that the greatest advantage of socialist system over capitalist system is its ability to drive the emancipation and development of productivity and to realize common prosperity on the basis of developed productivity. Particularly, the report to the 19th National Congress of the CPC explicitly established that China aims to build a moderately prosperous society in all respects by 2020, basically realize socialist modernization by 2035, and become a prosperous, democratic, civilized, harmonious, beautiful and great modern country in the middle of this century. Here, emphasis on the "common prosperity" goal is contained whether in building a moderately prosperous society in all respects, basically realizing modernization, or becoming a modern power. This signifies that China should not only substantially emancipate and develop productivity to achieve rapid growth of total GDP but also strive to resolve the current imbalanced, inadequate development on the basis of economic growth, so as to realize sustained, coordinated, and high-quality economic development, respond to the growing needs of urban and rural residents for a better life, and ensure that the fruits of economic development are shared among various groups of people in a relatively equal manner.

In a word, socialist system in China is typically reflected by the leadership of the CPC, the share of public sector, and the emphasis on the goal of sustainable development and common prosperity, which measure the Chinese socialist system on the dimensions of leadership, material base, and development goal. Socialist system has therefore become the institutional basis for understanding China's economic issues, and this institutional basis inevitably makes a difference to urban–rural economic relationship and its evolution.

2 China is a large developing country rarely found elsewhere in the world. Developing countries, as a category relative to developed countries by definition, are stagnant in economy, technology, and people's living standard. Although developing countries are different from their developed counterparts across many dimensions, economic growth, as measured by gross domestic product (GDP), represents the core dividing criterion between these two categories. GDP, and per capita GDP which accounts for population factor, thus become a principal metric for measuring the economic development level of a country. Since the founding of the PRC, China's economic development has lagged behind that of major capitalist countries in many respects, which partly explains why the country chose to give heavy industry the top priority and hastened to form an independent industry system in the planned economy era. In the late 1970s, stagnant productivity was still the basic reality facing the country's economic and social development. It also explains why China decided that the country is in the primary stage of socialism and began to push forward the major strategy of reform and opening up. Indeed, China has to rely on economic system reform to boost the emancipation and development of productivity, as reflected by the need of China's economy to sustain rapid growth.

Since the start of the great expedition of reform and opening up in 1978, driven by both economic system reform and integration into world economy, China's productivity level has been immensely emancipated and upgraded in the temporal sense. According to CEIC Data statistics, from 1978 to 2017, China's GDP had grown continuously from 367.87 billion yuan to 82.7 trillion yuan; its per capita GDP had grown continuously from 385 yuan to 59,660 yuan, with annual average GDP growth and per capita GDP growth of 9.59 percent and 8.55 percent, respectively, over the 40 years of reform and opening up. At the base value of 100 for 1978, China's GDP and per capita GDP indexes were 3,452.1 and 2,380.8, respectively. The figures show that, since 1978, China's GDP has sustained high-speed growth, creating a world "miracle" of growth and greatly enhancing the country's economic strength, comprehensive national power, residents' welfare, and international influence. With regard to emancipating and developing productivity, after the founding of the PRC, especially since reform and opening up, China as a balance holder in world's economy has made very remarkable achievements.

Even so, the high-speed economic growth over the 40 years of reform and opening up has not fundamentally changed the category to which China belongs. China still lags behind world's major developed countries and still ranks among developing countries defined by World Bank and other international organizations. Indeed, "China is still a developing country whether by the definition of international organizations or by the development of the country's economy itself" (Liu W. & Cai Z.Z., 2018). From a temporal point of time, economic growth takes place in almost any country over time. Hence, China's economic situation has to be understood by taking account of the changes in global economy and other major economies. That is, we need a good mastery of China's economic development by comparing relative status or development speed. According to World Bank data, as shown in Figure 3.4, at the nominal exchange rate, from 1978 to 2017, China's per capita GDP grew from 156.4 dollars to 8,827.0 dollars, compared to the per capita GDP growth from 10,587.3 dollars to 59,531.7 dollars for the United States over the same period. The share of China's per capita GDP in that of the United States increased from 1.48 percent to 14.83 percent. This shows that China' sustained high-speed growth has led to rapid "catch-up" of its per capita GDP with the United States and other major developed countries. It also shows that China is still remarkably stagnant in GDP relative to the United States and other major developed countries. Furthermore, World Bank divides world economies into four income groups according to per capita gross national income (GNI): low income, lower middle income, higher middle income, and high income, economies, defined as countries with per capita GNI of 1,036–4,085 dollars, 4,086–12,615 dollars, and more than 12,616 dollars, respectively. Economies of all the first three groups can be categorized as developing countries. At a particular point of time when reform and opening up is advancing into the 40th year, in 2017, China's per capita GDP was 8,827.0 dollars. This indicates that China is already an

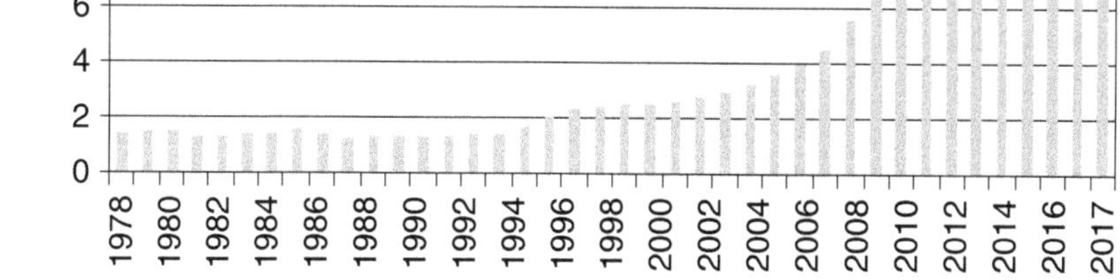

Figure 3.4 China's per capita GDP compared with the United States in current dollar terms from 1978 to 2015 (China/United States).

Source: World Bank Data.

economy of the upper middle income group defined by World Bank, but it still ranks among world's developing countries.

Since reform and opening up, China's continued high-speed economic growth has not fundamentally changed the basic reality that China is a developing country. Moreover, China is larger than other developing countries by both population and geographical sizes. According to World Bank data, in 2017, China had a total population of 1,386 million, compared to other developing countries like India (1,339 million), Brazil (209 million), Russia (144 million), and Pakistan (197 million). In 2017, the world had a total population of 7,530 million, and only 13 countries had a population exceeding 100 million. Yet, China makes up 18.41 percent of world's total population. By land area, China stands in the third place next only to Russia and Canada. Taken together, we can tell that China is still the largest developing country in the world. A large developing country in terms of both population and geographical sizes portraits the objective reality facing China's modernization drive. This judgment has multiple meanings in the economic, political, social, cultural, and ecological senses.

In the economic sense, a large developing country signifies that China's development is largely divergent across different groups and different regions. Viewing the different parts of China as a highly "homogenized" whole can lead to misunderstanding or grave misinterpretation of the country's local practice. A large developing country signifies that, besides emancipating and developing productivity, if China desires to achieve economic development, it also needs to address and flatten this structural development disparity. Imbalanced, uncoordinated, unsustainable development could be even worse in a country like China relative to other countries. A large developing country signifies that China needs to find a balance between driving internal development and integrating into world economy. China cannot expect to resolve its own economic development problems mainly by integrating into the world like a "small open economy" would do, but must create an economic development mode with its own characteristics according to its own basic national conditions, periodical characteristics, and goals. A large developing country also signifies that, to achieve economic development, China needs to find a balance between maintaining a steady order and pursuing development speed, since relying on radical reform can lead to pervasive social unrest inside the country. More importantly, from the social governance point of view, China as a large developing country cannot expect the central government to implement institutional supply to microeconomic subjects, but must cover the administrative process by coordinating governments at all levels. This inevitably expose economic development to intergovernmental interactions. That is, the central government needs to use particular institutional arrangements to cause local governments to fulfill the economic and social development goals of their respective jurisdictions. In a word, a large developing country is the objective reality facing China's economic development, and this reality will affect China's choice of economic system and the evolution of its urban–rural economic relationship through a number of channels.

3 China is currently a country under economic system transition. As a large developing country, under the leadership of the CPC, the country is faced with the great mission of achieving sustainable economic development and common prosperity. Since the founding of the PRC, in response to this great mission, China has undergone two development stages: planned economy and reform and opening up. From 1949 to 1956, China quickly completed the socialist transformation of agriculture, handicraft, and capitalist industry and commerce. On this basis, it promoted and implemented a catch-up strategy centering around heavy industry, which stemmed out of theoretical cognition and international environmental considerations (Gao F., 2016a). Theoretically, this strategic orientation bore the influence of Soviet textbooks and the social reproduction theory in Marxist political economy. Internationally, this strategic choice originated from comparison of economic structure with major developed countries like the United States and the United Kingdom, and the need of national defence and security following the outbreak of the Korean War. After the strategy was determined, however, the heavy industry first strategy was found to conflict with the country's endowments—capital shortage versus labor abundance—at the time. As a primary solution to this conflict, there appeared in China's economic system a macro policy environment characterized by distorted factor and product pricing, a highly centralized resource planning and allocation system, and a microeconomic mechanism lacking autonomy (Lin Y.F., Cai F. & Li Z., 2012). Accordingly, pursuit of sole public ownership of means of production, distribution according to work, and planned economy became the institutional feature of China's economic operation at that time (Gao F., 2018a).

From the implementation result of economic system, on the one hand, planned economy prompted China to form a fairly systematic and independent industrial system within a short time against the extremely unfavorable initial conditions. On the other hand, planned economy also led to a lack of vitality among microeconomic subjects due to excessive intervention of the government in economic activities. The entire economic system was challenged by grave mismatch of resources. The bulky public sector was commonly exposed soft budget constraint. The national economy was on the verge of collapse due to low efficiency. According to statistics, from 1956 to 1977, the average monetary wage of workers in China dropped from 601 yuan to 576 yuan, and per capita grain output over the same period dropped from 306.8 kg to 297.7 kg. This means that the income level and living of urban and rural residents in China were quite tough. Logically speaking, after 1949, China as a large developing country really needed to resort to industrialization to rebuild its economic order and tackle external challenges. Yet after the formation of an independent industrial system, it became an intrinsic requisite to improve economic efficiency and release the vitality of microeconomic subjects so as to achieve economic development. The austere economic reality resulted from planned economy also compelled China to give a reconsideration to its choice of economic operation mechanism.

That explains why China decided to adopt a reform and opening up strategy in the late 1970s. In fact, reform and opening up were ideologically inspired by the discussions on the standard of truth initiated in May 1978 and practically piloted by the all-round contract system of "distributing land to households and assuming own profits and losses" first implemented in Xiaogang Village of Anhui Province in November 1978. Under the joint effect of a number of preparatory campaigns, in December 1978, the 11th CPC Central Committee made a bold strategic move to implement reform and opening up. The communique of the Third Plenary Session of the 11th CPC Central Committee stated that "the focus of the Party's work and the attention of the whole nation should be shifted to the socialist modernization drive". It emphasized that "to realize the four modernizations, we need to significantly increase the productivity and, accordingly, we must change in many ways the relations of production and the superstructure that are not adaptable to the development of productivity, and change all ways of management, activity, and thinking that are not adaptable to them. It will therefore be an extensive, profound revolution". This statement signifies that reform and opening up is considered an intrinsic requisite for greatly enhancing social productivity and a profound reform involved in the self-improvement of socialist system.

Marked by the Third Plenary Session of the 11th CPC Central Committee, China immediately launched an economic system transition from planned economy to socialist market economy. As the core of this transformation was to change the subject of resource allocation from governments at various levels to microeconomic subjects—enterprises and residents, and to change the way of resource allocation from government mandatory orders to market prices resulted from equal intersubject negotiation, it can be summarized as a market-oriented economic system reform. The intrinsic logic underlying the reform is that, in a context of resource scarcity and as a large developing country, the core of long-term economic growth is to improve its resource allocation efficiency. To make this improvement happen, one precondition is to enhance the fluidity of resources at home and abroad according to price signals. To attain this fluidity at home, China must promote market-oriented economic system reform. To attain this fluidity abroad, it must raise the degree of integration into world economy. If opening to the outside world is considered a higher level of marketization toward the international community, the essence of reform and opening is to introduce and expand the resource allocation function of market mechanism. In other words, China has no other choice but transform its economic operation mode in the planned economy era into a macro policy environment with effective price signals, a resource allocation system featuring decentralized discretion among enterprises and residents, and a microeconomic system with the autonomy to make own choice. Only by this means will China be able to find the power engine for long-term economic development.

At the ideological level, after the Third Plenary Session of the 11th CPC Central Committee in 1978, China has gradually liberated its view on, deepened its recognition of, and clarified its insight into, market-oriented economic system reform. In 1982, the report to the 12th National Congress of the CPC suggested correctly carrying through the principle of taking planned economy as the main strategy and market economy as the supplement. In 1987, the report to the 12th National Congress of the CPC noted that socialist economy is a planned commodity economy based on public ownership. In 1992, the report to the 14th National Congress of the CPC stated that the goal of China's economic system reform is to establish a socialist market economic system. In 2013, the report to the Third Plenary Session of the 18th CPC Central Committee stated that the core of deepening economic system reform is to leverage government–market relationship to make the market play a decisive role in the allocation of resources and give better play to the role of the government. These changes, in theoretical cognition or policy texts, reflect market-oriented transition and the enhanced role of market mechanism. In social practice, around market-oriented economic system reform, China has promoted a succession of systematic reforms from rural-based management to urban-based enterprise management, from incremental adjustment of private enterprises to stock reform of state-owned enterprises (SOEs), from reform of various enterprises to reform of financial, taxation, and financial systems, from emancipation of product market prices to improvement of factor marketization, and from a "double-track" price system to gradual price integration. In the meantime, along the strategic line of coastal to inland, commodities to factors, and pilot-scale to full-scale implementation, China's opening to the outside world in the economic domain has been ramping up progressively. The accession to the WTO in 2001 registered a quantum leap of China's economy from limited opening to opening in all respects.

Compared with the planned economy era, over the 40 years of reform and opening up, the subject, way, and scope of resource allocation have all been changed profoundly. Microeconomic subjects—enterprises and residents—are enjoying greater autonomy over resource allocation. Market price mechanism is playing a more important role as a signal and an conditioner. The scope of market activity has also experienced a successive expansion from regionwide to nationwide and further to globewide. This signifies that, up to the present day, profound and extensive economic system reform has already taken place in China. According to economic theory and international experience, the degree of economic system transition is typically reflected by the change of the index of

Table 3.1 China's index of economic freedom from 1980 to 2015

Year	*1980*	*1990*	*2000*	*2005*	*2010*	*2013*	*2014*	*2015*
Composite Index (ranking)	3.64 (96)	4.09 (100)	5.75 (100)	6.05 (104)	6.24 (115)	6.37 (110)	6.38 (116)	6.40 (112)
Factorization Index 1: Government Volume	2.63	3.65	3.43	4.54	4.48	5.0	5.08	5.08
Factorization Index 2: Legal Structure and Property Right Protection	–	5.79	4.95	5.60	6.13	5.54	5.51	5.63
Factorization Index 3: Access to and Use of Sound Currencies	6.18	6.73	8.12	8.18	7.89	8.26	8.19	8.28
Factorization Index 4: Freedom to Trade Internationally	2.72	2.72	6.46	6.64	6.68	6.73	6.79	6.63
Factorization Index 5: Control of Credit, Labor and Commerce	3.04	1.58	5.79	5.31	6.04	6.34	6.31	6.37

Source: Fraser Institute, Economic Freedom of the World: 2017 Annual Report. The index ranges from 0 to 10. A total of 157 countries and regions are listed.

economic freedom. As shown in Table 3.1, according to the "Economic Freedom of the World: 2017 Annual Report" published by Fraser Institute, from 1980 to 2015, China's economic freedom rose from 3.64 to 6.40, suggesting that the country's economic system restructuring has achieved remarkable results since reform and opening up. In this report, economic freedom is subdivided into five subindices: government size, legal structure and property rights, access to and use of sound money, freedom to international trade, and regulation on credit, labor, and commerce. Since reform and opening up, these figures have also stayed in line with China's general trend of market-oriented transition and increasing economic freedom. For example, from 1980 to 2015, China's access to and use of sound money rose from 6.18 to 8.28; its freedom to international trade also rose from 2.72 to 6.63.

Although compared with the planned economy era, market-oriented economic system reform has taken place since the late 1970s, so far this transformation is still "on the way". China is still a country under economic system transition.

First of all, by cross-country comparison, there is still much room for further improving China's economic freedom. As shown in Table 3.1, although China's overall economic freedom has been rising in the temporal sense, it still ranks at the bottom of the world. In 2015, China's overall economic freedom ranked 112th among the 157 countries and regions listed. This suggests that China's economic system transition has yet to be completed, and the country still needs to further deepen market reform to release the potential of economic activity.

Second, by composition of marketization index, market-oriented system transition is a multidimensional, systematic, complex project. For China, the progressive nature of economic system transition determines that there is a significant disparity in marketization process among different fields, and this disparity is very likely to prevent economic sustainability by means of "institutional complementarity". As shown in Table 3.1, China's overall economic freedom in particular years differs largely among different subindices. For example, in 2015, China had a high access to and use of sound money, whereas its government size, legal structure and property rights, and regulation on factors were still on the low side.

Last, from a temporal point of view, China's market-oriented system transition has not proceeded with green light all the way, but has differentiated from one period to another. For example, through empirical studies, Wang X.L., Fan G. & Yu J.W. (2017) demonstrated that, from 2008 to 2010, China's marketization showed a level of slowdown, stagnation and even decline, and its marketization index did not begin to pick up until after around 2011. Obviously, China's economic system transition is still the present continuous tense instead of the simple past tense. To deepen economic system reform is still an important task facing China in its march toward the goal of modernization in the new era. Understanding China's urban–rural economic relationship since reform and opening up has to be set in the particular background of system transition.

In a nutshell, China's urban–rural economic relationship is not an isolated issue inside the urban–rural system. Nor is it solely a matter of urban–rural duality and the transformation thereof. In fact, it is a matter of economic development rooted in, and greatly affected by, the particular social background of China. Compared with other economies, China is a country with socialist system, is a large developing country, and is currently in the process of economic system transition. The coexistence and intersection of all these features are very unique in the world. The unique social background has rendered China's economic development with its own characteristics: a higher goal (the pursuit of sustainable development and common prosperity is contained in China's socialist system) against tougher conditions (a large developing country with population and geographical sizes rarely found elsewhere in the world), and the impossibility to directly apply economic theories for mature market economy given the particular practical conditions of the country (China currently is still under economic system transition). The perfect factor market hypothesis implied in the dual economy theory, for example, is markedly divergent from the practical reality of China. By extension, China's urban–rural economic relationship has emerged and evolved against these particular social realities. Hence, it is impractical to directly use the dual economy theory of development economics to generate a ready-made explanation of China's local problems.

Instead, a China-specific analytical framework for urban–rural economic relationship must be introduced based on these social realities, so as to respond to, and explain, the evolutionary logic of China's own urban–rural economic relationship during different periods of time.

3.3 China's urban–rural economic relationship from the perspective of political economy

To analyze China's urban–rural economic relationship based on its local realities—socialist system, a large developing country, and economic system transition, a cut-in point is to pay attention to how economic system came into being and how it influences urban–rural economic relationship. In other words, we should not simply deem urban–rural economic relationship as a matter of intersectoral factor endowment, especially the allocation of labor factor. Rather, we must take a closer look into the institutional causes behind the formation and variation of the particular patterns of factor allocation, since institutional aspects and their changes are the starting point for understanding the evolution of China's urban–rural economic relationship. In that connection, political economy should serve as the principal theoretical basis for understanding this relationship. Here the reason is: from the evolution of economic theory, classic political economy is characterized by social embeddedness, value judgment, and system reflection. The transition from political economy to mainstream economics, while enhancing the "scientific" nature of the doctrine, also weakened these characteristics. Current neo-institutional economics, neoclassic political economy, and neo-Marxist economics have reflected the "return of political economy" in respect of social embeddedness, value judgment, and system reflection (Gao F., 2016c).

In terms of economic practice, as a large developing country with socialist system and currently under economic system transition, the formation and evolution of China's urban–rural economic relationship is bound to be closely relevant to the particular economic system in effect. Economic system choice interacts with urban–rural economic relationship, and neither economic system choice nor urban–rural economic relationship is a constant. That is, economic system choice leads to corresponding urban–rural economic relationship, and changes in urban–rural economic relationship leads to changes in economic system and thus the dynamic adjustment of urban–rural economic relationship during different periods of time. By extension, understanding the evolutionary logic of urban–rural economic relationship has to involve exploration on economic system and its evolution. In a nutshell, China's urban–rural economic relationship is embedded in its overall development strategy and economic system transition; development strategy adjustment; and economic system transition are closely relevant to government behavior and system choice. As political and social aspects make up a large part of duality transformation, which is a classic issue of development economics, our analysis has to go farther than viewing problems simply based on urban–rural factor endowment. From the perspective of research thinking, political economy is the right choice for understanding the development issue of urban–rural economic relationship. "Political economy of development" is of high importance to explain China's urban–rural economic relationship across a long-time span.

Existing literature has attempted to use political economy to analyze China's local economic issues. For example, Gao F. (2016b) introduced a political economy analytical framework targeting China's coordinated development. Later on, Gao F. (2018b) used this framework to examine the connotational change of China's urban–rural gap during different periods of time. Extension and modification of this analytical thinking could generate a political economy analytical framework for China's urban–rural economic relationship, as shown in Figure 3.5. Under this framework, China's being a country with socialist system is not only reflected by the fact that its ultimate goal of economic development is to achieve sustainable development and common prosperity but also by the particular arrangements contained its economic operation mechanism—public ownership of means of production as the principal part and coexistence of multiple forms of ownership. China is a developing country with population and geographical sizes rarely found elsewhere in the world. This signifies that China needs to fulfill differentiated but temporally successive periodical tasks within different periods of time (e.g., to emancipate and develop productivity in the first place and then to achieve common prosperity) and pay close attention to the development disparity among different groups and the stability of the transformation and development process. Under the two local realities—socialist system and a

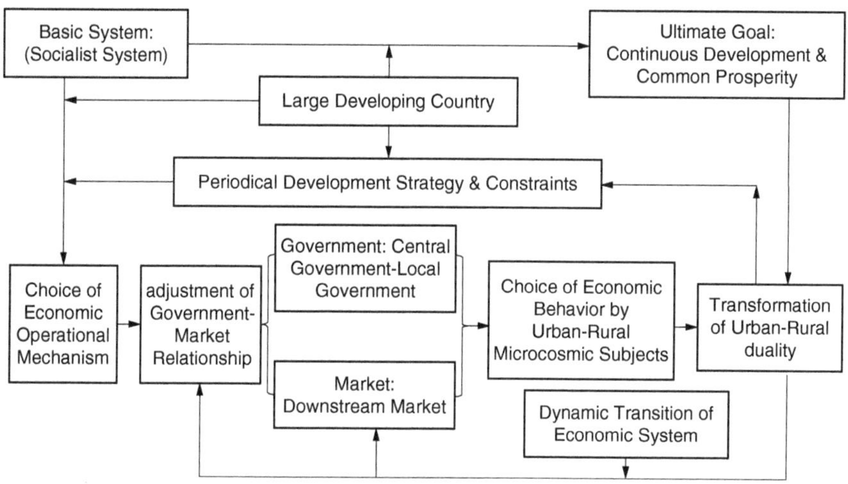

Figure 3.5 The political-economy analytical framework for China's urban–rural economic relationship.

large developing country—China will always form a relatively concrete economic development strategy in each individual period. The implementation of these strategies will always be exposed to a series of constraints. The continuation of economic development strategies across different periods of time essentially points to the ultimate goal of sustainable development and common prosperity.

From the economics point of view, trying to realize a development goal against particular constraints is bound to lead to given economic system arrangements. Economic system results from the attempt to resolve the "tension" between development strategy and constraints. This signifies that, in a particular period of time, China's development strategy and constraints will combine in a particular form to produce a corresponding economic operation mechanism, at the core of which is the adjustment of government–market relationship. Neo-institutional economics maintains that a system is a set of rules, law-abiding procedures, and moral codes of conduct established to restrict subjects' personal behavior of pursuing the maximal benefit of welfare or utility (North D., 1994). Hence, by extension, economic system is typically represented by a set of rules, procedures, and codes of conduct established by a country in a particular period of time to address government–market relationship. Economic system comprises arrangements for government–market relationship and adjustments thereof. Further, these institutional arrangements for government–market relationship affect the behavioral choice of microeconomic subjects—enterprises and governments, since the economic behaviors of microeconomic subjects are also made amid given economic system arrangements (government–market relationship). For example, if the government uses mandatory plans to allocate resources, the autonomy of urban and rural residents to allocate resources will be restrained; the freedom of microeconomic subjects to make their own choice will also be largely compressed. Conversely, if the government decentralizes discretion and benefits to microeconomic subjects and makes the market play a fundamental, or even a decisive role, in resource allocation, enterprises and residents will be able to carry out economic activity on their own according to market price signals. Consequently, the state of resource allocation and the economic benefits of individual groups will be affected. If a change from planned economy to market economy takes place in the government–market relationship or economic system arrangement, this change will be tied with the current economic system transition reality of China. That is, a third social reality facing China's urban–rural economic relationship will appear in this framework chart. In summary, the economic system targeting government–market relationship determines the choice of microeconomic subjects, and the behavioral choice of urban and rural microeconomic subjects always brings corresponding results. In urban–rural economic relationship, this performance is typically reflected by whether and to what extent duality has been transformed.

Obviously, subject to the particular realities of China—socialist system and a large developing country—its development strategy and constraints will combine in a particular form during each individual period of time, to determine or affect the country's economic system choice. The core of economic system is the operation mechanism centered around government–market relationship as the mainline. Economic system affects the behavioral choice of microeconomic subjects, which in turn makes a difference to urban–rural duality. Hence, without considering temporal changes, in China, there has been an interaction chain among development strategy and constraints, economic system, behavior of microeconomic subjects, and change of urban–rural duality, which is well able to explain the urban–rural economic relationship in particular periods of time and its typical characteristics.

From a dynamic point of view, changes in urban–rural duality over a particular period of time can be construed both as the result of implementing the economic system for this period and as the driver of changes in the economic system for the subsequent period. The performance evaluation of urban–rural economic relationship will bring about two forms of "feedback". First, people will compare the actual urban–rural economic relationship with the ultimate goal of common prosperity and further promote economic system reform by checking how well they agree with each other. Second, changes in urban–rural duality will lead to changes in the previous development strategy and constraints; consequently, changes in the way development strategy were combined with constraints. Objectively, this necessitates developing a new economic system based on the combination between new development strategy and constraints. As far as urban–rural economic relationship is concerned, both forms of feedback suggest that China's economic system choice (government–market relationship) is not a constant. It changes dynamically with the adjustment of development strategy and constraints, which inevitably leads to changes in the behavioral pattern and result of behavioral choice (state of urban–rural duality) of urban and rural microeconomic subjects. In the temporal sense, China's urban–rural economic relationship has shown different characteristics over each individual period and has changed dynamically across different periods. In that connection, Figure 3.5 well depicts the interaction between China's economic system choice and urban–rural economic relationship both in the static and dynamic sense.

More notably, as a large developing country with socialist system, China's economic system cored around adjusting government–market relationship is both generic and unique. It is generic in that, like other economies, China also underscores highlighting the role of market mechanism or adopting market-oriented system transition to boost economic growth. It is unique in that the government and the market themselves may not be completely "homogenized" inside, especially during post-reform economic system transition. For example, Gao F. (2018a) has understood the "heterogeneity" of China's economic development from other economies based on intergovernmental and intermarket structural features. From the founding of the PRC up to the late 1970s, China accomplished economic order restoration of a large socialist country mainly by means of a heavy industry first strategy and planned economy. But the pursuit of resource allocation efficiency and long-term development performance has promoted the country to embark on an economic transformation road of reform and opening up. Since the inception of reform and opening up in 1978, China's recognition of socialist system has gradually deepened from "instrumental reason" to "value reason". That is, socialist system does not directly equal sole public ownership, distribution according to work, or planned economy. In the functional sense, it is the emancipation and development of social productivity and the realization of the goal of common prosperity. As China construes both planned economy and market economy as an instrument for economic operation and optimal resource allocation rather than a benchmark distinguishing between socialist and capitalist systems, China was able to introduce market economy and adjust government–market relationship dynamically to promote economic development, and to better respond to the essence of socialist system in the value or functional sense.

Unlike other economies, China is a large developing country with socialist system, in which economic system transition cannot be promoted without a unique set of objective requirements and strategic arrangements. Here is our explanation:

First of all, China is strategic in fulfilling its ultimate goal of sustainable development and common prosperity in the economic aspect. In the first step, it tries to emancipate productivity by increasing economic growth and GDP so as to prepare the country for subsequent realization of the goal of sustainable development and common prosperity. That is, to improve economic growth and increase GDP first so as to emancipate and develop social productivity. Then, using this as the solid foundation for realizing the goal of sustainable development and common prosperity, it tries to resolve imbalanced, inadequate development problems to respond to the higher goal of common prosperity. In short, China has adopted a nonequilibrium, step-by-step approach to realize its goal of economic development: to step from the widespread poverty of planned economy toward sustainable, high-speed economic growth in the first step, and then toward sustainable development and common prosperity in the next step.

Second, China is also strategic in introducing market mechanism to improve resource allocation efficiency. That is, it chooses a progressive advancement from villages to towns, from pilot-scale to mass implementation, from increment to stock. Progressive reform is considered an important feature of China's market-oriented system transition. This progressive advancement gives substantial consideration to the disparities among different regions, sectors, and groups in market-oriented transition. Promoting market-oriented transition synchronously in all fields of a large developing country is very likely to cause economic and social disorder. Progressive advancement, on the contrary, can achieve system transition and improved resource allocation efficiency in a relatively steady order.

Last, China's system transition process involves the overall adjustment of government–market relationship. Yet, this adjustment has to address intragovernmental and intramarket structural features. That is, in a large developing country like China, neither government nor market is a concept with high uniformity and full homogeneity inside. Instead, intragovernmental and intramarket institutional arrangements constitute part of government–market relationship. They are also important determinants of the choices of microeconomic subjects and the performance of economic development. By cross-country comparison, intragovernmental and intramarket institutional arrangements immediately become a typical manifestation of China's "own characteristics" or "heterogeneity" of economic development (Gao F., 2018a).

Logically speaking, economic system is the product of a particular country's implementation of an economic development strategy under a given set of constraints. In the planned economy era, under the goals of developing heavy industry first and the constraints of a weak economic foundation, China adopted planned economy to resolve the problem of capital formation in the process of rapid industrialization. This choice led to the corresponding government–market relationship, and intergovernmental and intermarket institutional arrangements. The government used mandatory plans to allocate various factors; the government and the market themselves were highly homogenized inside as a result of "coordinating the activities of the country as a whole", and "concentrating resources on large undertakings". After reform and opening up, the core issue facing China's economy is China is a large developing country that has long implemented sole public ownership, distribution according to work, and planned economy. Now in what way can it introduce market mechanism to improve social productivity and boost the sustained, high-speed growth of its GDP, so as to lay a solid foundation for realizing the ultimate goal of sustainable development and common prosperity in terms of scale? This combination of goals and constraints is bound to lead to the redirection of government–market relationship, as well as unique intragovernmental and intramarket institutional arrangements. All these institutional arrangements, however, are subject to one same goal: to promote continued, high-speed GDP growth on the premise of ensuring the stability of the overall social order.

Inside the government, as a country with population and geographical sizes rarely found elsewhere in the world, China's state governance is performed through collaboration among governments at different levels with well-defined responsibility. Consequently, contest and interaction between central authority and local governance has always existed throughout the Chinese history (Zhou X.G., 2015). Hence by extension, the relationship among governments at different levels and the corresponding institutional arrangements are an important cut-in point for understanding China's economic and social development. Particularly, after reform and opening up, China has gradually developed a unique form of intergovernmental behavior and institutional arrangements. Existing literature has also noticed how the fiscal systems and objective functions facing local governments have affected the various aspects of China's economic development (Han L. & Kung J., 2015; Xie Z.F. & Zhang W., 2015). Xu C.G. (2011) defined China's post-reform intragovernmental institutional arrangements as regionally decentralized authoritarianism (RDA). He also argued that this system is typically characterized by highly centralized political and personnel control at the central level, and highly decentralized economic and administrative authority at the regional level. By economic system comparison, as indicated by Table 3.2, regionally decentralized authoritarianism distinguishes itself

Table 3.2 China's regionally decentralized authoritarianism compared with other systems

Comparative factor	Local decentralized government system in China	Soviet system	Federal system
National decision-making organ	Central, local, and ministry officials	Central & ministry officials	Federal legislature representing local voters
Decision-making process	Central-local negotiation; forming consensus; using local experiment as strategy	Top-down; SOE–ministry negotiation	Legislature voting; negotiation between federal & state governments
Incentives for local officials	Promotion; absolute and relative performance; responsible to superior; personnel control	Promotion; absolute performance; responsible to superior; personnel control	Through election; independent of federal government; responsible to voters
Regional competition	Yardstick competition; competition affects the promotion of local officials	Unimportant	Fiscal competition; competition affects reelection of officials
Local experiment	Local pilot projects constitute part of decision-making process at central level; result of pilot projects may become national policy	Unimportant	State is the "lab" of policies; experiment on voluntary basis

Source: Xu C.G. (2011).

from both the Soviet system and the federal system, whether in respect of national decision-maker, decision-making process, incentive for local officials, regional competition, or local experiment. In respect of regional competition, for example, China's regionally decentralized authoritarianism mainly involves a yardstick competition among local governments around economic growth. The result of this competition affects the promotion of local government officials in the longitudinal administrative hierarchy. Under the Soviet system which emphasizes high centralization of state power at the central level, competition among local governments is not important. This institutional background even lacks the social conditions in favor of intergovernmental competition, since all local governments merely serve as an executor of the mandatory plans of the central government. Under the federal system that emphasizes autonomy among different regions, competition among local governments tends to revolve around fiscal balance. The structure of this competition affects the reappointment or re-election of local government officials. Obviously, China's regionally decentralized authoritarianism is a unique intragovernmental economic system arrangement that is different from the central-local relationship under either the Soviet system or the federal system. Consequently, China's post-reform central-local relationship possesses a decision-making pattern and behavioral logic distinctive from other countries. This behavioral logic also makes a difference to the performance of economic development by affecting the institutional environment of microeconomic subjects. Now that intragovernmental institutional arrangements constitute an important part of government–market relationship, they are bound to play a part in China's urban–rural economic relationship by affecting the behavioral choice of microeconomic subjects.

Besides intragovernmental structural features, intramarket structural features are also an aspect to be included when investigating government–market relationship. In fact, in addition to the unique institutional arrangements among governments at different levels, China as a large developing country has also developed a unique set of intermarket structural arrangements during economic system transition. Between the intergovernmental and intermarket systems, while the intergovernmental regionally decentralized authoritarianism provides the possibility for the government, especially local governments, to affect economic activity, it has to rely on intermarket structural arrangements to bring this possibility into reality. The disparity of market-oriented transition among different fields after reform and opening up right provides these conditions. When explaining the economic takeoff in Taiwan over the 1960s–1980s, Wu Y.P. (2017) introduced the terms "market duality", "upstream markets", and "downstream markets". If these terms were used to interpret Mainland China's economic development and correlated with its regionally decentralized authoritarianism, we could say that, after reform and opening up, China has shaped an upstream-guided market expansion, which portraits the basic feature of the country's intermarket institutional arrangements during system transition. The connotation of upstream-guided market expansion is China initiated market-oriented economic system reform in 1978. Yet, this transformation is not advanced simultaneously at a uniform pace or in an identical way among all fields. During the rapid marketization of the downstream market (normally in connection with consumer goods and general productive factors), governments at various levels still exert quite a significant intervention or involvement in the upstream market (particularly in connection with core productive factors like land, capital, and important energy sources). In other words, China's marketization process since reform and opening up has not been consistent across different fields, as is evidenced by our analysis on China's economic freedom in the context of system transition earlier in this book. In terms of the way of system transition, this disparity of marketization among different fields also marks an important feature of China's progressive transition. It results from the attempt of a large developing country to balance economic system transition against social order stability.

By institutional comparison, upstream-guided market expansion is a unique intermarket institutional arrangement. Compared with strictly controlled planned economy and fully free market economy, China's upstream-guided market expansion distinguishes itself whether in respect of the subjects of resource allocation, the instrument of resource allocation, the characteristics of the upstream markets, the objective of the upstream markets, or the roles of the downstream markets. In respect of the subject of resource allocation, for example, under planned economy, the subjects of resource allocation are governments at all levels (especially the central government, since local governments are usually an executor of the mandatory plans of the central government). Under fully free market economy, the subjects of resource allocation are microeconomic subjects like enterprises and residents. Under upstream-guided market expansion, the subjects of resource allocation are governments at all levels (including the central government and local governments at different hierarchical levels), and microeconomic subjects like enterprises and residents. In respect of the characteristics of upstream enterprises, if SOEs, especially those under central management, were deemed as the organizational carriers by which the government influences or intervenes in economic activity, then under planned economy which emphasizes large scale, public ownership and sole socialist economy, SOEs exist in an enormous quantity. They make up the principal part of enterprises and are found in all parts of the industry chain from factor supply through commodity supply. Under fully free market economy, SOEs exist in a very small quantity or even does not exist at all. They are not advantaged at any part of the industry chain either in quantity or in function. Under China's upstream-guided market expansion, in contrast, despite their limited presence, SOEs (especially those under central management) are usually found in fields associated with core factors, upstream industries, or infrastructures. They dominate main trades and key fields concerning state security and national economy, playing the roles of a leader, a regulator, or executor of government development strategies in economic development. The share of the public sector in China's socialist system, as we have discussed in the previous section, right provides the material basis for the upstream enterprises to play these roles. This material basis is also contextually relevant to the reformation of agriculture, handicraft, and capitalist industry and commerce under the planned economy. In a word, since reforming and opening up, along with the progressive market-oriented system transition, an intergovernmental, upstream-guided market expansion regime was shaped in China, rendering the country with a prominent, unique intramarket structural feature that is markedly different from either planned economy or fully free market economy (Table 3.3).

As a large developing country with socialist system, if China desires to realize a higher goal against tougher conditions, a corresponding set of economic system arrangements will have to be produced. To understand China's economic system, one has to possess a systematic and holistic thinking. That is, besides government–market relationship, more attention should be paid to intragovernmental and intramarket institutional arrangements. Especially, after reform and opening up, China has developed a regionally decentralized authoritarianism and an upstream-guided market expansion on the economic dimension, which portrait the "heterogeneity" of the country's economic system from the perspective of intergovernmental and intermarket

Table 3.3 China's upstream-guided market expansion compared with other systems

Comparative factor	Upstream-guided market expansion in China	Planned economy	Complete free market economy
Subject of resource allocation	Governments at all levels; microeconomic subject	Governments at all levels	Microeconomic subject
Resource allocation tool	Price; government regulation; direct government intervention	Direct government intervention	Price
Characteristic of upstream enterprise	SOE-dominated, small number, distributed in core factors, upstream industries, infrastructures, etc.	SOEs are very large in number, constitute the principle part of enterprises, distributed in all parts of industry chain	SOEs are zero or very small in number, do not prevail in any part of industry chain
Goal of upstream enterprise	Economic objectives such as efficiency; social objectives such as stability	Economic objectives such as efficiency	Social objectives such as stability
Role of downstream enterprise	"Tugboat" effect, driving changes in upstream market	Embedded in mandatory plans	Develop separately from upstream enterprises

structural features, respectively. From a genealogical point of view, this heterogeneity originates from a tradeoff between the constraint of China's being a large developing country and its pursuit of the periodical goal of high-speed growth. Since China is a large developing country in which the stability of social foundation and system transition has to be highlighted and maintained, it is of crucial importance to ensure the central government's authority over economic development and its relative control over the upstream market. Moreover, since China desires to emancipate and develop social productivity, and the fulfillment of this desire is dependent on the vitality of microeconomic subjects and the efficiency of resource allocation, it is also of crucial importance to give autonomy to local governments and encourage them to "race for growth", while at the same time widely promote market-oriented reform of commodities and general productive factors.

More notably, while regionally decentralized authoritarianism and upstream-guided market expansion depict China's intergovernmental and intermarket structural features, respectively, from a functional point of view, they are not separated from each other, but are interdependent with "mirror complementation". For example, under regionally decentralized authoritarianism, one supporting condition for the central government to delegate economic discretion to local governments and for local governments to "race for growth" is that local governments still have the opportunity to exert influence on the allocation of core factors such as finance, land, and energy. Conversely, under upstream-guided market expansion, market-oriented economic system reform is guaranteed by the decisiveness and institutional choice of the central government. Marketization itself is also subject to the economic interaction between the central government and local governments. This observation signifies that regionally decentralized authoritarianism and upstream-guided market expansion are internested and mutually supported. They jointly make up an important feature of China's post-reform economic system choice, and enable its economic system to break away from the existing paradigm of sole government–market dichotomy.

From the system implementation result, any particular economic system will produce corresponding economic performance by affecting people's behavioral choice. Since reform and opening up, the combination of regionally decentralized authoritarianism and upstream-guided market expansion has, in the first place, brought along sustained rapid GDP growth. Accordingly, the long-lagging social productivity has also been strengthened enormously, as evidenced by the annual GDP growth of almost two digits and its per capita GDP catching up with the United States and other major developed economies since 1978. Here the core mechanism is both regionally decentralized authoritarianism and upstream-guided market expansion took place in the process of market-oriented transition. Market-oriented economic system reform offers favorable conditions for cross-regional, cross-sector, cross-time, and cross-border reallocation of various resources. Microeconomic subjects—such as enterprises and residents—are also enjoying greater economic autonomy, allowing them to make economic decisions for their own benefits. That is, microeconomic subjects have created extensive, lasting "self-motivation" in favor of economic growth. Optimizing resource allocation and rectifying incentive mechanism are precisely the main drivers behind China's sustained, high-speed economic growth. Moreover, regionally decentralized authoritarianism endows local governments with the important mission of boosting economic development. "Race for economic growth" prompts them to address economic growth as their key decision-making target, as evidenced by the local GDP growth above national average for the majority of provinces in any particular year. In the meantime, upstream-guided market expansion also offers conditions for local governments to boost economic growth. Local governments can also partly affect the allocation of core productive factors to enhance their short-run economic growth and become comparatively advantaged in the administrative yardstick competition. In fact, local governments' emphasis on inviting capital investment, on supporting and developing large projects, and on investing in fixed assets are all derivatives of this logic. In terms of emancipating and developing productivity, the economic system arrangements formed in China since reform and opening up have indeed harvested exceptionally remarkable performance of growth.

In the context of rapid GDP growth, the combination of regionally decentralized authoritarianism and upstream-guided market expansion has also induced or aggravated a series of economic system-related structural problems. Imbalanced, inadequate development has gradually become the main bottleneck to modernization. Here the core mechanism is market-oriented economic system reform itself brings about structural problems. For example, market economy emphasizes that microeconomic subjects—such as enterprises and residents—allocate resources according to price mechanism and receive corresponding returns therefrom. Yet the endowment disparities persisting among individual enterprises and residents are bound to produce a gap in economic income or wealth distribution. While market economy provides the mechanism for the substantial flow and optimal allocation of factors, it also highlights the endowment disparities among individual microeconomic subjects, inherently raising the bar for the government's ability and means to supply public goods. Furthermore, as a country of exceptionally large population and geographical sizes, China's market-oriented economic system reform is not proceeded uniformly across all fields. The progressive, imbalanced reform policy itself is also tied up with structural imbalance in economic development. Moreover, regionally decentralized authoritarianism motivates local governments to "race for growth". Upstream-guided market expansion also provides the basic conditions for this competition. Consequently, local governments are tempted to focus their efforts on increasing fixed asset investment, developing particular industries with limited varieties, or supporting large projects or large works that can bring growth effect in a short time, leaving the other dimensions of economic development less emphasized (e.g., energy utilization, ecological protection, adjustment of income distribution, and supply of livelihood public goods). Consequently, the input structure, industrial structure, structure between economic growth and energy environment, and structure between economic growth and social development has been accumulating and aggravating over time. China's economy, despite constant GDP growth, is challenged by imbalanced, uncoordinated, unsustainable development. Since reform and opening up, China's economic development has been trapped in an imbalance of "fast growing GDP against worsening structural problems". All these problems are the result of implementing particular economic systems and they make up the "two sides of the same one coin" of the institutional operation of regionally decentralized authoritarianism and upstream-guided market expansion. Hence they should, and also could, be explained within the same logic framework.

To sum up, China is a large developing country currently under economic system transition. To understand China's urban–rural economic relationship based on local reality, it is essential to grasp how economic system choice interacts with urban–rural economic architecture. To understand economic system choice, it is essential to grasp the main pulse of the adjustment of government–market relationship. Nevertheless, as the government and the market themselves are not fully homogenized inside, government–market dichotomy could easily lead to a narrow understanding on China's economic system. In fact, intragovernmental and intramarket structural arrangements also constitute an important part of economic system (government–market relationship). Both of them originate from the country's particular social realities—socialist system, a large developing country, and economic system transition, as evidenced by the inter-governmental regionally decentralized authoritarianism and intermarket upstream-guided market expansion in post-reform China. Yet, once the intragovernmental and intramarket institutional arrangements are in place, they become an important content of the economic system of government–market relationship. They also play a part in the behavioral choice of microeconomic subjects and in urban–rural duality, thus leading to changes in the country's economic system arrangements and urban–rural economic relationship from time to time.

In a word, the implied hypotheses of the dual economy theory—typically the Lewis-Fei-Ranis model—do not fully agree with China's local reality. Hence, it is impossible to generate a complete explanation on China's urban–rural economic relationship directly out of this theory. China's urban–rural economic relationship emerged under the particular realities of socialist system, a large developing country, and economic system transition. In this context, there has been an interaction chain among development strategy and constraints, choice of economic system, economic behavior of microeconomic subjects, and change of urban–rural duality. Economic system choice, in particular, contains government–market relationship and intragovernmental and intramarket structural arrangements. This framework attempts to capture the interaction between China's economic system choice and its urban–rural economic relationship. It also attempts to find out more elements of economic system, including intragovernmental and intramarket elements. Hence, this framework represents a marginal improvement on the Lewis-Fei-Ranis model based on local reality and incorporates political economy to explore the classic development issue of China's urban–rural economic relationship. This analytical framework or research perspective can be called the political economy analytical framework for China's urban–rural economic relationship, or the "political economy of development" targeting China's urban–rural economic relationship. In the remaining part of this book, we will apply this political economy analytical framework to make a systematic explanation on how China's urban–rural economic relationship in different periods has formed and evolved, and in what direction it will move in future.

4 Measurements and evolutionary stages of China's urban–rural economic relationship

From a global perspective, urban–rural economic relationship is not a particular issue found only in the country of China. From a temporal point of view, urban–rural economic relationship is not a short-lived issue found only in China at the current time, either. As population continued to gather into cities from an agrarian background, and with cities more than ready to play the role of an economic, political, and cultural center, China began to experience urban–rural opposition, as well as urban–rural economic relationship. In fact, urban–rural economic relationship is a historic phenomenon existent throughout the long history of China's economic and social development. It was not until after the founding of the PRC in 1949 that China's urban–rural economic relationship began to show up in the context of socialist system and a large developing country. Three decades later, the post-1978 reform and opening up set this relationship into a social background of economic system transition. If we placed our research in a time window from the founding of the PRC up to the present day, we would discover that China's urban–rural economic relationship has differed from one period to another. As this book deals with the evolutionary logic of China's urban–rural economic relationship after the founding of the PRC, especially since reform and opening up, the first thing to do is to use some measuring tool to depict how this relationship has changed over time, namely, to answer what stages China's urban–rural economic relationship has gone through, and how these stages should be divided. Notably, the initiation of reform and opening up in 1978 brought China into a stage of economic system transition. Over the 40 years of reform and opening, China's urban–rural economic relationship has not remained invariant. In the process of transforming the main social contradiction and constructing a modern economic system, the future trend of China's urban–rural economic relationship has to be studied and effectively realized. Indeed, evolving from the current urban–rural economic relationship into a more ideal one is of fatal significance for China to grow into a great modern country. As such, it becomes particularly important to make a careful analysis on the trajectory of China's urban–rural economic relationship since reform and opening up. From a logical positivism point of view, this part aims to describe and depict the "characteristic facts" of the evolution of China's urban–rural economic relationship, so as to provide preconditions for applying our new political economy analytical framework and for analyzing the evolutionary mechanism of China's urban–rural economic relationship.

4.1 Methodological basis for measuring China's urban–rural economic relationship

Ever since the founding of the PRC, urban–rural duality has always remained a major feature of China as a large developing country. In response to this practical background, existing literature tends to depict changes of this duality with indicators like urban–rural income gap. Yet, this measurement directly equates urban–rural income gap to urban–rural economic relationship, and its analysis tends to be more concentrated on the overall and province-wise urban–rural issues in China since reform and opening up. As discussed above, although urban–rural income gap does serve as an important signature of urban–rural economic relationship, and post-1978 statistics are available in even greater and accurate details, this choice of indicator and period still compromises the precise understanding on China's urban–rural economic relationship issues. The reason is urban–rural economic relationship itself covers far more contents than urban–rural income gap, and this book is concerned more with the long-run evolutionary mechanism of China's urban–rural economic relationship. When we try to measure and depict urban–rural economic relationship, the core is not exactly which indicators to choose, but why on earth to choose them. The criteria for choosing indicators are even more important than the application of these indicators after they are determined. In other words, to depict the trajectory of China's urban–rural economic relationship, we have to answer the methodological basis behind the measuring indicators.

To set forth the measuring indicators for urban–rural economic relationship, we have to respond to the essence of this concept. As has been reiterated in the concept definition section of this book, urban–rural economic relationship herein is an economic relevance between the urban and rural sectors of China as a particular large developing country and among the different parts of these sectors. This relevance originates from the optimal allocation of factors and it also influences the dynamics of urban–rural income and consumption gap. Apparently, this definition places the center of urban–rural economic relationship on the base point of optimal allocation of factors and looks at urban–rural income gap and urban–rural consumption gap as an outcome of this allocation. As such, urban–rural economic relationship should be measured around the mainline of allocation of productive factors between (and inside) the urban and rural sectors, taking into account also the result of this allocation from comparing income distribution and consumption. That is, changes in urban–rural income gap and urban–rural consumption gap should also be incorporated in the measurement. Urban–rural economic relationship covers, but does not equal to, urban–rural income gap. Also, in our new political economy analytical framework, urban–rural economic relationship is construed as the behavioral choice of urban and rural microeconomic subjects in a particular institutional context and the associated transformation of urban–rural duality. Here the behavioral choice of urban and rural microeconomic subjects comprises the mode of factor allocation, namely, the way in which enterprises and residents allocate various factors between the urban and rural sectors. The transformation of duality is the change of income and consumption gap between these two sectors. Evidently, whether from the definition of urban–rural economic relationship or from the logic sequence of the analytical framework, to depict China's urban–rural economic relationship, we have to highlight two dimensions: factor allocation and the result thereof. The former is even more important than the latter. Hence, it is questionable to attempt to directly use urban–rural income gap to measure and reflect China's urban–rural economic relationship.

In terms of research period, this book is concerned with the evolutionary logic and intrinsic mechanism of China's urban–rural economic relationship, especially the change of urban–rural economic relationship over the 40 years of reform and opening up. Even so, the time window of our research has to be extended to the early days of the PRC. That is, urban–rural economic relationship should be understood across a long-time span from 1949 up to the present day. A long term and a large span are the intrinsic requisite for analyzing the evolutionary logic of urban–rural economic relationship.

First of all, the founding of the PRC marked a fundamental change of the country's social nature. China was transformed from a semicolonial, semifeudal society into a socialist country under the leadership of the CPC. Socialist system represents an important social background underlying the evolution of China's urban–rural economic relationship. Although China embarked on the great expedition of reform and opening up in 1978, the pre- and post-reform periods have been the two stages of China's socialist modernization, during which urban–rural economic relationship has been revolving around the major theme of socialist modernization. Hence, it would inappropriate and not in line with the evolutionary logic of history if the two stages were investigated separately.

Second, even if people are concerned about the evolution of China's urban–rural economic relationship over the 40 years of reform and opening up, this evolution does not take place by itself beyond a particular temporal-spatial background. Instead, China's urban–rural economic relationship during different periods is highly path-dependent. That is, the post-reform urban–rural economic relationship was born out of the pre-reform urban–rural economic relationship, which provided the initial conditions for the post-reform urban–rural economic relationship. Our new political economy analytical framework has already addressed the relevance between these two stages, which is manifested by the feedback mechanism to the combination of development strategy and constraints, the economic system arrangements, the behavioral choice of microeconomic subjects, and the urban–rural duality transformation.

Last, to analyze China's urban–rural economic relationship, a key is to grasp the mechanism underlying the change of this relationship, although this mechanism has to be observed across a long-time window to obtain a reliable test result. A long-run analysis usually provides a more dependable conclusion than a short-run study. From a logical positivism point of view, conclusions of logical deduction can never become a convincing theory, and consequently the basis for predicting future development tendencies and proposing policy implications, until it is validated by historical process or data. In this sense, the 70 years' history of the PRC provides favorable conditions for people to obtain an accurate understanding of the "story behind" China's urban–rural economic relationship.

The above analysis indicates that China's urban–rural economic relationship should be measured in a way that highlights its feature of long term and large span. It is more valuable to address the country's urban–rural economic relationship since the founding of the PRC as the measurement and analysis object than to simply analyze the post-1978 urban–rural duality.

Obviously, China's urban–rural economic relationship should, to the furthest extent, be measured in line with two features: the comprehensive nature of its content and the long-term nature of its time. To this end, the measuring indicators used have to meet the following two requirements. First, the measuring indicators must be successive in time. They must cover all periods since the founding of the PRC. Indicators set forth in a given period (especially post-reform), if hardly able to accommodate cross-time comparison, should either be given up or placed in that period for analyzing the urban–rural economic relationship at that time. Here the most typical example is urban–rural income gap. This indicator is based on per capita income of urban residents and rural residents, yet existing statistics only include post-reform data, and the pre-1978 figures of per capita income of urban and rural residents are absent. Therefore, it is impractical to use this indicator to reflect China's urban–rural economic relationship since the founding of the PRC. For the post-reform period, however, it still serves as an important indicator for measuring urban–rural income gap. Second, the measuring indicators must be data available. They must be accessible from existing statistical records or survey databases that preferably have an official background to prove their reliability. In other words, indicators that are theoretically useful but are unavailable in existing statistical records have to be given up, too. For example, per capita physical capital stock in urban and rural areas is an important indicator of urban–rural economic relationship, but it is hardly usable due to the unavailability of prereform figures on, say, fixed asset investment. Considering technical processing, indicators that are not data-available cannot be used to depict China's urban–rural economic relationship since the founding of the PRC.

Under the criteria for measuring indicators, namely, being successive in time and data available, and based on the definition of urban–rural economic relationship, this book deems that the trajectory of China's urban–rural economic relationship should be measured with three concrete indicators. First, the change of population and employment structure between urban and rural areas, which reflects the urban–rural allocation of the factor of labor, and population structure closely relevant thereto. Now that physical capital data are unavailable, observing the change of population and employment structure will become an important perspective to understand urban–rural factor allocation from. In fact, urban–rural allocation of population and labor is also an indirect metric of how capital is distributed between urban and rural areas. After all, labor always tends to flow into areas with more capital to increase its productivity. Second, comparison of industry labor productivity between urban and rural areas, which reflects the relative state of the shares of output value and employment among different industries, and shows on the industry dimension whether the same share of "labor input" brings about the same share of "economic output" between urban and rural areas. Disparity of industry labor productivity is a major driver of urban–rural factor fluidity, whereas urban–rural factor reallocation is very likely to lead to a change in the comparative state of industry labor productivity. Third, comparison of per capita consumption level between urban and rural areas, which reflects whether residents' per capita consumption level is "convergent" between urban and rural areas. Now that income data are unavailable, urban–rural per capita consumption gap will become an important gauge of urban–rural economic relationship. It is better able to explain the living level and access to welfare between urban and rural residents. Logically speaking, these indicators are mutually progressive and complementary. Allocation of population and labor, and comparison of labor productivity examine urban–rural economic relationship from the perspective of factor allocation. Comparison of per capita consumption level looks at urban–rural economic relationship from the result of factor allocation. They all agree well with our definition of urban–rural economic relationship, fit in with the urban–rural duality under our new political economy analytical framework. Furthermore, these indicators are also temporally successive and data available. Hence, they can well qualify for the long-run depiction of China's urban–rural economic relationship.

4.2 Changes in China's urban–rural economic relationship since the founding of the PRC

Based on the comprehensive and long-run methodologies, the long-run dynamics of China's urban–rural economic relationship can be observed from the perspective of urban–rural population and employment structure, industry labor productivity, and per capital consumption level. From changes in these indicators, since the founding of the PRC, China's urban–rural economic relationship has not remained a constant, but has differentiated across different periods. Particularly, reform and opening up in 1978 marks a major turning point of China's urban–rural economic relationship. In fact, the country's urban–rural economic relationship is distinctly different before and after reform and opening up. These indicator-scale changes are undoubtedly an economic topic well worth explanation. Interestingly, the time-differentiated revelations of urban–rural economic relations by these three measuring indicators can validate and support one another among themselves.

4.2.1 Changes in urban–rural population and employment structure

Labor is an important productive factor for the urban and rural sectors to carry out economic activity. Compared with other productive factors (especially land), labor has a greater intersectoral and interregional fluidity. Without considering rigid government control, the flow of labor between sectors, industries, and regions based on economic income comparison is an intrinsic requisite for optimal resource allocation, and consequently a common phenomenon found in the economic operation of most countries. International experience shows that the economic development in a developing country is usually accompanied by the nonagricultural transfer of rural labor and the associated agglomeration of population into the urban sector. The Lewis-Fei-Ranis model described in the previous chapters, for example, assumes the transfer of rural labor as the core mechanism of dual economy transformation. Notably, changes in the urban–rural employment structure are usually accompanied by changes in the population structure. That is, the non-agricultural transfer of labor embodies a relative increase in the share of urban population. From this point of view, industrialization and urbanization are usually important characteristic realities of a country's economic development process. The former registers changes in employment structure; the latter changes in population structure. Conversely, if the industrialization or urbanization rate of a country stands at a constantly low level, that means its labor or population flow between urban and rural areas is gravely stagnant; its urban–rural economic relationship remains relatively separated as a consequence of this stagnation.

If we use this logic to examine China's urban–rural population and employment structure since the founding of the PRC, we can obtain Figure 4.1, which depicts changes in China's urban–rural population and employment structure from 1952 to 2018 with three indicators: share of rural population in total population, share of employment in the primary industry in total employment, and share of employment in the primary industry in rural employment. Among these indicators, share of employment in the primary

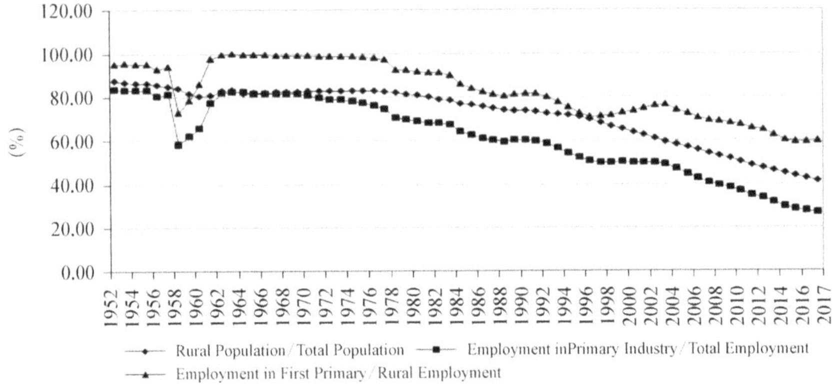

Figure 4.1 China's urban and rural population and employment structure from 1952 to 2017.

Source: CEIC Data

industry in rural employment reflects the distribution of labor resources inside the rural sector, namely, to what extent the labor forces engaged in agriculture, forestry, animal husbandry and fishery (the primary industry) can be transferred to other industries inside the rural sector (the secondary or tertiary industry inside the rural sector). Share of employment in the primary industry in total employment reflects the distribution of labor resources in the whole society, namely, to what extent the labor forces engaged in agriculture, forestry, animal husbandry and fishery (the primary industry) can be transferred to other industries inside the rural sector (the secondary or tertiary industry in the urban and rural sectors). Share of rural population in total population reflects the population between urban and rural areas, namely, to what extent rural population can become permanent urban population by job changes. These three indicators can be used to depict the trajectory of China's industrialization rate and urbanization rate. If we say that share of employment in the primary industry in rural employment reflects the urbanization process inside the rural sector, and share of employment in the primary industry in total employment reflects the industrialization process of the whole society, then share of rural population in total population reflects the urbanization process of the whole society. As far as population and employment structure is concerned, these three indicators can give a comprehensive description of changes in China's urban–rural economic relationship across the long-time window from 1952 up to the present day.

As illustrated by Figure 4.1, the year 1978 marked an important turning point for China's urban–rural economic relationship across the whole investigation period. From 1952 to 1977, all three indicators were obviously operating stably at a high level throughout the years except only the 1958–1961 period, when the country suffered nationwide grain and non-staple food crisis caused by weather change, the "Great Leap Forward" movement, and a policy encouraging industry at the sacrifice of agriculture. The share of employment in the primary industry in total rural employment rose from 94.92 percent to 96.99 percent. Particularly, over the 1961–1977 period, it stayed either close to or higher than 97 percent. This suggests that over that period, employment in the primary industry made up the overwhelming majority of total rural employment. It was almost impossible for laborers in the primary industry to enter other industrial segments of the rural sector. Or in other words, no other non-agricultural job opportunities were available inside the rural sector except agriculture, forestry, animal husbandry, and fishery. The share of employment in the primary industry in total employment dropped from 83.54 percent to 74.51 percent, with a decrease of less than 10 percentage points in 26 years. Employment in the primary industry was the largest contributor to China's employment. It was extremely difficult for laborers in the primary industry to enter other segments of the society. Or in other words, no major progress was made in increasing non-agricultural job opportunities. Over the same period, the share of rural population in total population dropped from 87.54 percent to 82.45 percent, with a decrease of less than 5 percentage points in 26 years. Rural population still was the largest contributor to China's population. It was hard for the rural population to become urban population through urban–rural reallocation of labor forces. China distinguished itself as a country in which farmers made up the largest part of the population and rural employment occupied the dominant position in total employment. Obviously, before 1978, China's industrialization and urbanization were both in a "suppressed" or relatively "stagnant" state. Labor and population flow between urban and rural areas, although taking place now and then, was negligible both in terms of degree and extent. Urban–rural population and employment structure was strongly solidified or rigidified.

After 1978, rapid and noticeable changes have taken place in China's urban–rural population and employment structure, compared to the previous solidity and rigidity. As illustrated by Figure 4.1, since 1978, all three indicators measuring urban–rural population and employment structure dropped very obviously, reversing the previous high-level operation. From 1978 to 2017, the share of employment in the primary industry in total rural employment dropped from 92.43 percent to 59.54 percent, with a decrease of 32.89 percentage points in 40 years, contrasting strongly with the pre-1978 figures. The job availability for laborers inside the rural sector increased enormously. More laborers had the opportunity to engage in economic activity in the nonagricultural segments of the rural sector. The "dominance" of employment in the primary industry in total rural employment was halved. Diversified job opportunities and industry structure in the rural sector became an important characteristic fact of economic development over this period. The share of employment in the primary industry in total employment dropped from 70.53 percent to 26.98 percent, with a decrease of

43.5 percentage points in 40 years and an annual average decrease of 1 percentage point. Laborers in the primary industry are freer to enter the non-agricultural segments of the whole society. In other words, an enormous stock of non-agricultural job opportunities is already in place throughout the society. So far, China has transitioned from the dominance of employment in the primary industry to the dominance of non-agricultural employment. As industrialization inside the rural sector and between urban and rural areas pushes on at a fast pace, the urban–rural population structure has also changed greatly. From 1978 to 2017, the share of rural population in total population dropped from 82.08 percent to 41.48 percent. At the caliber of permanent population, China's urbanization rate has increased from 17.92 percent to 58.52 percent, with an increase of 40.6 percentage points and an annual average growth of more than 1 percentage point in 40 years. This means that the rural population are freer to enter the urban sector and become urban permanent population. China has changed from a country in which rural population made up the largest part to one in which urban population makes up the largest part. China has structurally transformed from a "rural China" to an "urban China". In a word, from the trajectory of the country's urban–rural population and employment structure, it can be seen that since reform and opening up in 1978, China's urban–rural economic relationship has undergone a profound transition. Industrialization and urbanization are speeding up. Urban–rural labor and population flow has turned from being suppressed and stagnant to being active and intensive.

4.2.2 Comparison of industry labor productivity between urban and rural areas

Population and employment structure reflects the allocation of factors between urban and rural areas, yet it does not reveal the causes of urban–rural factor allocation and the result thereof. Logically speaking, without considering rigid government control, urban–rural factor allocation primarily arises out of the comparison of economic benefits. That is, population and labor have a higher productivity, and consequently higher income and consumption generated by labor productivity, in the urban sector. The readiness of microeconomic subjects to effect factor flow among different sectors on an earnings comparison basis is the power engine for enhanced industrialization and urbanization. On ground of this, when measuring China's urban–rural economic relationship, we have to introduce urban–rural labor productivity disparity to depict this power engine. Considering that existing statistics do not contain direct figures on urban–rural economic output, we can use the labor productivity figures of the three industries to approximately fit the relative state of urban and rural labor productivity. This fitting should be more appropriate for the pre-1978 period, since during this time the employment in the primary industry almost equaled to the rural employment, and the primary industry was actually the principal part of rural economic activity. After reform and opening up, labor flow within the rural sector has also featured the outflow from the primary industry into the secondary and tertiary industries where the productivity is comparatively higher. Hence it would be appropriate to use the labor productivity level of the three industries to reflect the change of urban–rural economic relationship.

Theoretically speaking, labor productivity is the ratio of economic output to labor input of an industry in a particular year, which reflects the output efficiency of the factor of labor in this industry. To improve labor productivity is a key issue facing any economy or economic sector. In a particular economy, any industry has a share of economic output (e.g., GDP of the primary industry) in total economic output, referred to as the share of output value of this industry, as well as a share of labor input in total labor input, referred to as the share of employment of this industry. On this basis, we can define the comparative labor productivity of the primary industry—the comparative labor productivity of the primary industry is the ratio of its share of output value to its share of employment, which reflects how the output (share of output value) of the primary industry is combined with its input (share of employment). This way of definition also applies to the comparative labor productivity of the secondary and tertiary industries.

By definition, comparative labor productivity reflects the departure of the share of output value of an industry from its share of employment. If the comparative labor productivity of an industry is greater than one, that means that the industry has produced a greater share of economic output with a smaller share of labor input. Hence this industry is more attractive to labor inflow than its other counterparts, and vice versa. As far as urban–rural economic relationship is concerned, given that the secondary and tertiary industries (nonagricultural industries) are mostly concentrated in the urban sector, whereas the primary industry is mainly distributed in rural areas, we can use the gap between the comparative labor productivity of the nonagricultural industries and that of the primary industry to reflect the change of urban–rural economic relationship in respect of labor productivity. In fact, in existing studies on urban–rural economic issues, people also tend to use dual contrast coefficient, defined as the ratio of the labor productivity of the primary industry to that of the secondary and tertiary industries, to reflect the change of urban–rural duality. From a methodological point of view, dual contrast coefficient is intrinsically consistent with the gap of comparative labor productivity used herein to reflect urban–rural economic relationship.

By virtue of the value added and employment figures of individual industries, we can work out the comparative labor productivity of China's three major industries from 1952 to 2017, consequently the change of the comparative labor productivity of the secondary industry (as well as of the tertiary industry and of the secondary and tertiary industries) to that

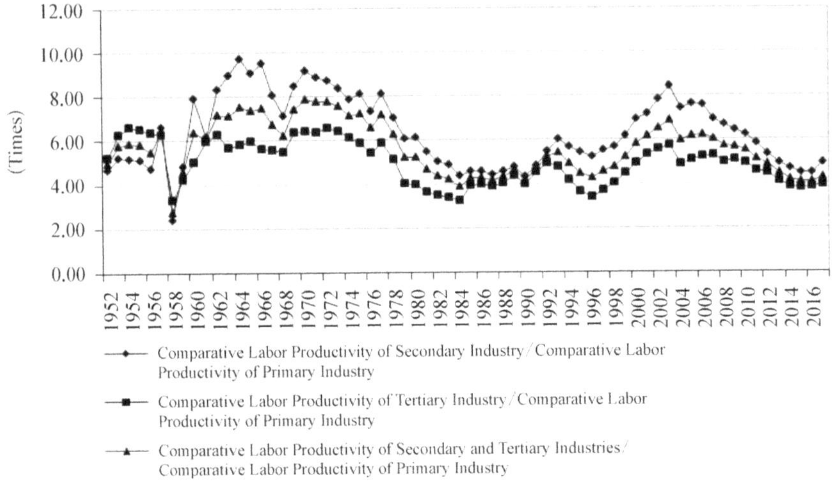

Figure 4.2 Comparative labor productivity disparity among China's three major industries from 1952 to 2017.

Source: CEIC Data

of the primary industry. As illustrated by Figure 4.2, compared to the pre-1978 period, profound changes have taken place in the relative state of comparative labor productivity among China's major three industries after 1978. Over the investigation period of 1952–1977, the comparative labor productivity of the nonagricultural industries and that of the primary industry, despite some ups and downs, did not fluctuate much and were both at a relatively high level, except only for the 1958–1961 interval. For example, from 1962 to 1977, the comparative labor productivity of the secondary industry to that of the primary industry stood at 7.10–9.52, with an annual average of 8.48; the comparative labor productivity of the tertiary industry to that of the primary industry stood at 5.44–6.57, with an annual average of 5.99; the comparative labor productivity of the secondary and tertiary industries to that of the primary industry stood at 6.24–7.87, with an annual average of 7.25. Overall, the comparative labor productivity of the nonagricultural industries was far higher than that of the primary industry overall this period. The nonagricultural industries produced a greater share of economic output with a smaller share of labor input. Their comparative labor productivity was markedly superior over the primary industry. The persistently high level of labor productivity gap indicates that, on the one hand, there was vast potential throughout the society for labor in the primary industry to enter the nonagricultural industries. On the other hand, institutional aspects beyond individuals' ability prevented labor in the primary industry from entering the nonagricultural segments where the comparative labor productivity was higher.

Since China launched reform and opening up in 1978, new changes have taken place in the interindustrial gap of comparative labor productivity. Typically, compared with the "relatively stable" state at a high level in the past, after 1978, all three indicators measuring the gap of comparative labor productivity have fluctuated remarkably. In the 40 years of reform and opening up, as marked by the years 1984 and 2003 as the dividing points, the fluctuation consisted of a fall, a rise, and another fall. Even so, compared with the prereform period, after 1978, all three gaps of comparative labor productivity have declined noticeably. By comparing between the starting year and the ending year, over the 1978–2017 period, the comparative labor productivity of the second industry to that of the primary industry dropped from 7.03 to 4.91, with an annual average of 5.75; the gap in any year of the investigation period was lower than the annual average of 8.48 over the 1961–1977 period. The comparative labor productivity of the third industry to that of the primary industry dropped from 5.15 to 3.92, with an annual average of 4.35; the gap in any year was lower than the annual average of 5.9 over the 1961–1977 period. The comparative labor productivity of the secondary and tertiary industries to that of the primary industry dropped from 6.25 to 4.30, with an annual average of 5.02; the gap in any year was lower than the annual average of 7.25 over the 1961–1977 period. These figures indicate that after 1978, the gap between the comparative labor productivity of the nonagricultural industries to that of the primary industry has been on the fall on the whole. Although comparative labor productivity may vary from one industry to another, the gaps are gradually converging at large. In terms of indicator changes, in China, the comparative labor productivity of the nonagricultural industries is still higher than that of the primary industry, suggesting that reallocation of labor factor will still exist between industries and between urban and rural areas. Since the late 1970s, China has seen increasing interindustrial and inter-sectoral flow of labor factor. This factor reallocation has played an important part in converging the comparative labor productivity between industries and between urban and rural areas.

4.2.3 Comparison of per capita consumption between urban and rural areas

Measurement of comparative labor productivity reflects the economic gap between urban and rural areas caused by industrial disparities. Yet comparative labor productivity does not directly equal to the income level and consumption state of different groups, nor is there a strict correlation between the urban and rural sectors and the three major industries, as evidenced by the rise of the secondary and tertiary industries in post-reform rural China. From this point of view, introducing the relative state of resident income and consumption between urban and rural areas is necessary for understanding urban–rural economic relationship. Considering the consistency and availability of data, we use urban–rural consumption gap to reflect the long-run changes in China's urban–rural economic relationship. The consumption figures used herein are the per capita consumption level of urban and rural residents released by the statistical department. The gap of per capita consumption can be defined as urban–rural consumption gap.

Urban–rural consumption gap can be measured by three indicators. First, nominal urban–rural consumption gap, which directly compares the per capita consumption between urban and rural areas without excluding the price factor or including the population structure factor. Second, real urban–rural consumption gap, which compares per capita consumption level between urban and rural areas that have been adjusted by consumption index. Third, the Theil index of urban–rural consumption gap, which includes the two groups of variables—urban and rural population structure and real urban and rural per capita consumption level—to calculate consumption gap[1]. Among these three indicators, real urban–rural consumption gap excludes the impact of the price factor on urban–rural consumption gap. The Theil index of urban–rural consumption gap includes the impact of population structure on urban–rural consumption gap. These two indicators, together with nominal urban–rural consumption gap, jointly make up the indicator system for measuring China's urban–rural economic relationship since the founding of the PRC.

Figure 4.3 compares the three indicators measuring China's urban–rural consumption gap from 1952 to 2017. Nominal, real, and Theil index of urban–rural consumption gap changed in almost the same fashion. They can verify one another and support the overall judgment on the dynamics of urban–rural consumption gap. Overall, before 1978, China's urban–rural consumption gap over the 1952–1977 period was prominently stable, especially when the 1958–1961 interval is excluded. Urban–rural consumption gap and its fluctuation both remained insignificant, especially over the

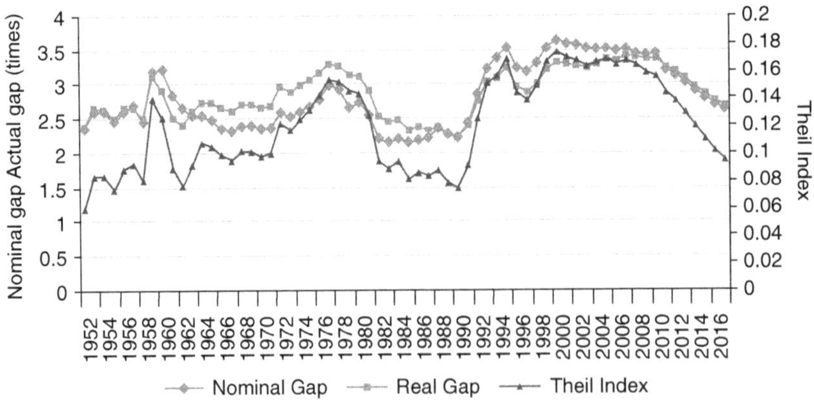

Figure 4.3 China's urban–rural resident consumption gap from 1952 to 2017.

Source: CEIC Data

1961–1971 period. For example, nominal urban–rural consumption gap lingered between 2.3 and 2.85, while real gap varied between 2.41 and 2.75. Over the 1971–1977 period, China recorded a rapid ramp-up in urban–rural consumption gap: nominal figure climbed up from 2.37 to 3.00; real figure rose from 2.69 to 3.30; and Theil index also grew from 0.10 to 0.15. In general, the overall stability of urban–rural consumption gap and its rise in the later stage portrait the basic features of China's planned economy. If we take into consideration the fact that during this period, China had gradually developed an allocation of social security resources featuring "urban–rural divide, one country two policies", under which rural residents were disadvantaged in access to public goods, then compared with urban–rural consumption gap, the welfare inequality between urban and rural residents would serve as an even better indicator. More notably, while urban–rural consumption gap can exist in many countries or in many periods of a particular country, whether microeconomic subjects are able to change this situation through factor flow and resource allocation remains the most critical point. The stability, solidity, and gradual rise of China's urban–rural consumption gap throughout the planned economy era signifies that urban–rural duality was gradually worsening, and it was extremely difficult for urban and rural microeconomic subjects—especially rural residents—to change this situation through reallocation of commodities and factors.

After the start of reform and opening up in 1978, China's urban–rural consumption gap has displayed a markedly different trend compared with the pre-1978 period. Typically, over this period, urban–rural consumption gap has not remained stable and on the rise like before, but has fluctuated and even declined noticeably. In general, over the 1978–1985 period, urban–rural consumption gap reduced markedly. Nominal figure dropped from 2.94 to 2.17; real figure dropped from 3.27 to 2.17; and Theil index also dropped from 0.15 to 0.08. After 1985, urban–rural consumption gap rose again and had remained at a fairly high level for quite a long time until 1997. However, after 2009, urban–rural consumption gap fell back again. Over the 2009–2017 period, nominal gap dropped from 3.47 to 2.65; real gap dropped from 3.37 to 2.69; and Theil index dropped from 0.16 to 0.10. By temporal comparison, China's current nominal gap, real gap, and Theil index of urban–rural consumption are already lower than the levels at the beginning of reform and opening up and are approaching the levels of 1952 when the PRC had just been founded.

From these changes, on the one hand, compared with the planned economy era, since reform and opening up, China's urban and rural microeconomic subjects, especially rural residents, have been enjoying substantial economic autonomy, and are able to seek higher economic returns through reallocation of commodities and factors. These economic returns constitute an important condition for improving their consumption level, thus contributing to the periodical shrinkage of urban–rural consumption gap amid fluctuation. On the other hand, the change of urban–rural consumption gap is a complex process subject to many constraints. Even the urban–rural factor reallocation among microeconomic subjects is exposed to fluctuation. As a result, China's urban–rural consumption gap has not sustained a continuous shrinkage, but has been narrowing and widening alternately throughout the 40 years of reform and opening up. In general, the change of urban–rural consumption gap after reform and opening up indicates that, compared with the previous planned economy era, microeconomic subjects have great autonomy in allocating factors and commodities between urban and rural areas, allowing urban–rural consumption gap to decline periodically.

If we used urban–rural population and employment structure, urban–rural industry labor productivity, and urban–rural per capita consumption together to measure China's urban rural economic relationship since the founding of the PRC, we would discover that China's urban–rural economic relationship has displayed different features before and after 1978 when reform and opening up was started. Before 1978, labor and population flow between urban and rural areas was almost stagnant. Industry comparative labor productivity and urban–rural resident consumption gap were also remarkably solidified. Urban and rural microeconomic subjects, especially rural residents, had no opportunity to relieve urban–rural economic gap through reallocation of factors. The urban and rural sectors were disconnected and separated from each other. After 1978, thanks to the market-oriented reform and further opening to the outside, China's urban–rural labor and population structure has changed remarkably. Its industrialization and urbanization have been greatly accelerated. The gap of industry comparative labor productivity has begun to fall. Urban–rural consumption gap has also recorded declines over a number of periods. This means that the urban and rural sectors have become more economically interactive, since microeconomic subjects have the autonomy to allocate resources. Widespread, frequent spontaneous economic connections occurred among microeconomic subjects based on market price signals. These connections have pulled the urban and rural sectors closer to each other and pushed urban–rural consumption gap out of the previous "solidity". In the conception definition section of this book, we have noted that the concepts "separation" and "integration" emphasize the factor relevance between the urban and rural sectors and the resulted change of income and consumption gap. Based on these definitions, and by combining the changes in the various indicators described above, we can conclude that the year 1978 marked a turning point at which China's urban–rural economic relationship began to transform from "separation" toward "integration".

4.3 Reexamination on changes of China's urban–rural economic relationship since reform and opening up

Since the founding of the PRC, China's urban–rural economic relationship has displayed a development trend of transforming from separation toward integration at large. From the perspective of theoretical research and practical inspiration, compared with the pre-reform period, a more detailed analysis on China's urban–rural economic relationship in the post-reform period seems to be particularly necessary. First of all, from the measuring indicators discussed earlier in this book, while China's urban–rural economic relationship has been transforming toward integration at large since 1978, the behavior of individual indicators appears to differ from one another, and even the same indicator may vary from one period to another across the long time spectrum from 1978 to 2017. Second, it is already 40 years since China started the reform and opening up initiative. One point remains. Although China's economic system transition in the past 40 years has targeted at establishing a socialist market economic system, throughout the investigation period this transformation has not been moving linearly at a constant speed. The fluctuation of economic system transition will inevitably make a difference to the behavior of urban–rural economic relationship. Next, China's urban–rural economic relationship over different periods tends to be path-dependent, and this path dependence seems to intensify with decreasing distance between two periods. In China's endeavor to spur high-quality economic development and build a modern economic system, its subsequent urban–rural economic relationship has arisen out of the post-reform economic architecture. As such, a focused analysis on the post-1978 urban–rural economic relationship would be more helpful to clarify future tendency of, and policy improvements on, urban–rural economic relationship. Last, from the perspective of data availability, after reform and opening up in 1978, China's statistical work on urban–rural economic relationship has also been greatly improved. Related data have become more accurate and abundant. The availability of urban–rural income gap data, in particular, allows people to trace the trajectory of urban–rural economic relationship in that period with a greater variety of empirical figures.

From the perspective of urban and rural population and employment, the post-1978 statistical data can help us get a better insight into the change of economic structure between urban and rural areas. Table 4.1 compares the indicator changes in China from 1978 to 2017 inside industrialization, inside urbanization, and between industrialization and urbanization. Inside urbanization, we can use the share of the secondary and tertiary industries in GDP, and the share of employment in the secondary and tertiary industries in total employment to express the industrialization rate of output value and industrialization rate of employment. Since 1978, both indicators have displayed a marked, continuous rise, suggesting that China's industrialization has been largely increased, and its GDP and employment are becoming more dependent on the secondary and tertiary industries. Compared with industrialization rate of output value, after reform and opening up, China's industrialization rate of employment has been growing even more rapidly. This indicates that laborers in the primary industry can largely change their

Table 4.1 China's industrialization and urbanization process from 1978 to 2017

Year	*Inside industrialization*		*Inside urbanization*		*Industrialization & urbanization*	
	Industrialization rate of output value (%)	*Industrialization rate of employment (%)*	*Urbanization rate of resident population (%)*	*Urbanization rate of registered population (%)*	*Industrialization rate of output value (%)*	*Urbanization rate of resident population (%)*
1978	72.31	29.48	17.92	–	72.31	17.92
1979	69.30	30.20	18.96	–	69.30	18.96
1980	70.37	31.25	19.39	16.64	70.37	19.39
1981	68.68	31.90	20.16	17.00	68.68	20.16
1982	67.21	31.87	21.13	18.26	67.21	21.13
1983	67.43	32.92	21.62	17.93	67.43	21.62
1984	68.46	35.95	23.01	19.02	68.46	23.01
1985	72.07	37.58	23.71	20.14	72.07	23.71
1986	73.36	39.05	24.52	19.77	73.36	24.52
1987	73.68	40.01	25.32	20.13	73.68	25.32
1988	74.76	40.65	25.81	20.69	74.76	25.81
1989	75.39	39.95	26.21	21.12	75.39	26.21
1990	73.42	39.90	26.41	20.86	73.42	26.41
1991	75.97	40.30	26.94	21.32	75.97	26.94
1992	78.67	41.50	27.46	21.89	78.67	27.46
1993	80.69	43.60	27.99	22.42	80.69	27.99
1994	80.53	45.70	28.51	23.28	80.53	28.51
1995	80.40	47.80	29.04	23.83	80.40	29.04
1996	80.67	49.50	30.48	24.37	80.67	30.48
1997	82.10	50.10	31.91	24.79	82.10	31.91
1998	82.84	50.20	33.35	25.07	82.84	33.35
1999	83.94	49.90	34.78	25.51	83.94	34.78
2000	85.32	50.00	36.22	26.08	85.32	36.22
2001	86.02	50.00	37.66	26.68	86.02	37.66

2002	86.70	50.00	39.09	27.89	86.70	39.09
2003	87.65	50.90	40.53	29.70	87.65	40.53
2004	87.08	53.10	41.76	30.81	87.08	41.76
2005	88.36	55.20	42.99	31.99	88.36	42.99
2006	89.37	57.40	44.34	32.53	89.37	44.34
2007	89.72	59.20	45.89	32.93	89.72	45.89
2008	89.75	60.40	46.99	33.28	89.75	46.99
2009	90.21	61.90	48.34	33.77	90.21	48.34
2010	90.47	63.30	49.95	34.17	90.47	49.95
2011	90.57	65.20	51.27	34.71	90.57	51.27
2012	90.58	66.40	52.57	35.33	90.58	52.57
2013	90.70	68.60	53.73	35.93	90.70	53.73
2014	90.94	70.50	54.77	36.63	90.94	54.77
2015	91.17	71.70	56.10	39.90	91.17	56.10
2016	91.44	72.30	57.35	41.20	91.44	57.35
2017	92.08	73.02	58.52	42.35	92.08	58.52

Source: The urbanization rates of registered population from 1980 to 2014 are calculated based on CIEC Data figures. The urbanization rates of registered population from 2015 to 2017 are sourced from the annual statistical communique of the PRC on national economic and development of individual years. The remaining original figures needed for calculation are sourced from CEIC Data.

own economic position through interindustrial labor flow. By temporal comparison, the degree of urban–rural integration has indeed been enhanced. Nevertheless, within the investigation period, China's industrialization rate of employment has lagged behind that of output value all the time. Compared with the primary industry, the secondary and tertiary industries are still holding a remarkably superior position in comparative labor productivity. The nonagricultural sector is still producing a greater share of output value with a smaller share of labor. The primary industry is still employing a greater share of labor and producing a smaller share of economic output.

Inside urbanization, we can use the share of urban permanent population in total population, and the share of registered nonagricultural population in total population to express the urbanization rate of permanent population and the urbanization rate of registered population. Observing the relationship between these two indicators can give us a better understanding on China's urbanization process. Within the investigation period, these two indicators have also been growing step by step. In particular, the urbanization rate of permanent population increased from 17.92 percent to 58.52 percent, with an annual average increase of more than 1 percentage point. This indicates that China's rural population is fairly free to work and live in town. However, so far, the urbanization rate of registered population is still significantly lower than that of permanent population. Over time, the gap between these two indicators is gradually widening, too. While the large armies of rural population are able to change the nature of their employment after entering town, they can hardly transform their identity at the same time and hence can hardly access the regular urban social security resources attached to this identify.

Between industrialization and urbanization, since reform and opening up, China's industrialization of output value and urbanization rate of permanent population have both been on the rise. The transfer of rural labor can help increase the output value of nonagricultural industries and allow rural labor to enter towns and become urban permanent population. Yet, the industrialization rate of output value has remained higher than the urbanization rate of permanent population and, of course, higher than the urbanization rate of registered population. Moreover, the urbanization rate of permanent population is also lower than the industrialization rate of employment. This indicates that China's modernization process has been characterized by the lag of urbanization behind industrialization, and changes in the urban–rural employment structure does not match changes in the urban–rural population structure. From changes inside industrialization, inside urbanization, and between industrialization and urbanization, over the 40 years of reform and opening up, the degree of factor flow and reallocation between urban and rural China has indeed been enhanced, as evidenced by the increase of all indicators. However, the imbalance inside industrialization, inside urbanization, and between industrialization and urbanization signifies that China's urban–rural economic relationship is not a relatively homogeneous integration, but rather, a structured, localized integration.

In measuring China's urban–rural economic relationship, besides population and employment structure, urban–rural income gap also represents a very important indicator. As data are also available for China's post-1978 urban–rural income gap, we can analyze changes in this indicator to form a supplement to changes in urban–rural consumption gap discussed earlier in this book. In the same way as was used to calculate urban–rural consumption gap, here we use three indicators again to reflect China's urban–rural income gap after reform and opening up. First, nominal urban–rural income gap, which directly compares the per capita disposable income between urban and rural areas without excluding the price factor or including the population structure factor. Second, real urban–rural income gap, which compares the per capita disposable income level between urban and rural areas that have been adjusted by income index. Third, Theil index of urban–rural income gap, which includes two groups of variables—urban–rural population structure and real urban and rural per capita income level—to calculate income gap. Among these three indicators, real urban–rural income gap and Theil index of urban–rural income gap either excludes the impact of the price factor or includes the change of population structure. Hence, they give a more convincing reflection of the change of China's urban–rural income gap. Based on these three indicators, Table 4.2 compares the indicator changes in China from 1978 to 2017. In order to provide a more intuitive depiction of the change of this gap, we can plot this table into Figure 4.4. By combining Table 4.2 and Figure 4.4, we can discover that over the 40 years of reform and opening up, along with changes in urban–rural population and employment structure, China's urban–rural income gap has changed remarkably, too. Urban–rural income gap has fluctuated with periodical declines, and all three indicators measuring urban–rural income gap have varied in roughly the same fashion. Besides, these changes also show a similar trajectory as the indicators measuring urban–rural consumption gap discussed above.

Table 4.2 and Figure 4.4 describe the evolution of China's urban–rural income gap from 1978 to 2017. From the evolutionary trend, over the 40 years of reform and opening up, China's urban– income gap has not been moving unilaterally in one same direction. Its rises and falls have been interweaving across different periods. According to direction of change, we can divide China's urban–rural income gap within the investigation period into five stages: continued decline over 1978–1985, continued increase over 1985–1994, a brief decline over 1994 to 1997, continued increase over 1997–2009, and continued decline from 2009 up to the present day. Table 4.3 compares the changes over these five stages. These changes not only demonstrate the increased degree of economic freedom and spontaneous factor allocation among microeconomic subjects in the context of marketization but also the exposure of urban–rural income gap to multiple

Table 4.2 China's urban–rural resident income gap from 1978 to 2017

Year	*Per capita disposable income of urban residents (yuan)*	*Per capita disposable income of rural residents (yuan)*	*Urban per capita income index (1978 = 10)*	*Rural per capita income index (1978 = 10)*	*Nominal urban–rural income gap (times)*	*Real urban–rural income gap (times)*	*Theil index of urban-rural income gap*
1978	343.400	133.600	100.0	100.0	2.570	—2.570	0.091
1979	405.000	160.200	115.7	119.2	2.528	2.495	0.087
1980	477.600	191.300	127.0	139.0	2.497	2.348	0.076
1981	500.400	223.400	129.9	160.4	2.240	2.082	0.055
1982	535.300	270.100	136.3	192.3	1.982	1.822	0.037
1983	564.600	309.80	141.5	219.6	1.822	1.656	0.026
1984	652.100	355.30	158.7	249.5	1.835	1.635	0.025
1985	739.080	397.600	160.4	268.9	1.859	1.533	0.019
1986	900.900	423.760	182.7	277.6	2.126	1.692	0.030
1987	1002.100	462.550	186.8	292.0	2.166	1.644	0.027
1988	1180.200	544.940	182.3	310.7	2.166	1.508	0.018
1989	1373.932	601.510	182.5	305.7	2.284	1.534	0.020
1990	1510.160	686.310	198.1	311.2	2.200	1.636	0.027
1991	1700.600	708.550	212.4	317.4	2.400	1.720	0.033
1992	2026.590	783.990	232.9	336.2	2.585	1.781	0.038
1993	2577.400	921.620	255.1	346.9	2.797	1.890	0.047
1994	3496.240	1220.980	276.8	364.3	2.863	1.953	0.053
1995	4282.950	1577.740	290.3	383.6	2.715	1.945	0.052
1996	4838.900	1926.070	301.6	418.1	2.512	1.854	0.045
1997	5160.320	2090.130	311.9	437.3	2.469	1.833	0.044
1998	5425.050	2161.980	329.9	456.1	2.509	1.859	0.047
1999	5854.020	2210.340	360.6	473.5	2.648	1.957	0.056
2000	6279.980	2253.420	383.7	483.4	2.787	2.040	0.063
2001	6859.580	2366.40	416.3	503.7	2.899	2.124	0.070
2002	7702.800	2475.630	472.1	527.9	3.111	2.299	0.086

2003	8472.200	2622.240	514.6	550.6	3.231	2.402	0.094
2004	9421.610	2936.40	554.2	588.0	3.209	2.423	0.095
2005	10493.030	3254.930	607.4	624.5	3.224	2.500	0.101
2006	11759.450	3587.040	670.7	670.7	3.278	2.570	0.106
2007	13785.810	4140.360	752.5	734.4	3.330	2.634	0.109
2008	15780.760	4760.620	815.7	793.2	3.315	2.643	0.109
2009	17174.650	5153.170	895.4	860.6	3.333	2.674	0.110
2010	19109.440	5919.010	965.2	954.4	3.228	2.599	0.102
2011	21809.780	6977.290	1046.3	1063.2	3.126	2.530	0.096
2012	24564.720	7916.580	1146.7	1176.9	3.103	2.504	0.092
2013	26467.004	9429.563	1227.0	1286.4	2.807	2.452	0.087
2014	28843.854	10488.83	1310.5	1404.7	2.750	2.398	0.082
2015	31194.828	11421.707	1397.0	1510.1	2.731	2.378	0.079
2016	33616.246	12363.409	1475.2	1603.7	2.719	2.364	0.077
2017	36396.194	13432.426	1571.1	1720.7	2.710	2.347	0.074

Source: Calculated based on CEIC Data figures on China's GDP and employment in three industries.

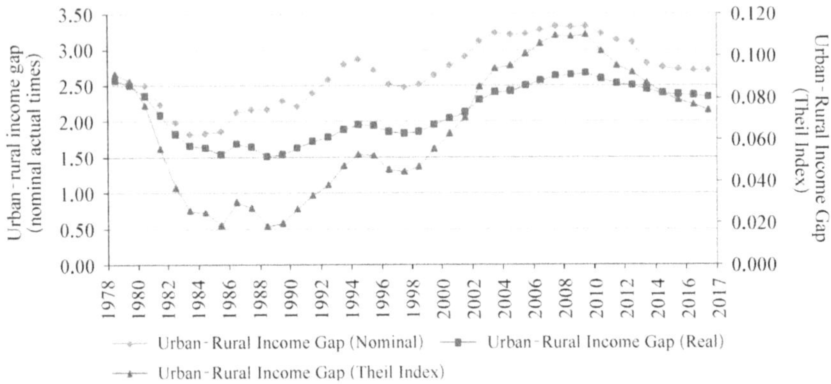

Figure 4.4 China's urban–rural resident consumption gap from 1978 to 2017.

Table 4.3 The five evolutionary stages of China's urban–rural income gap from 1978 to 2017

Stage SN	*Period*	*Indicator change*	*Duration (year)*	*Basic characteristics*
Stage 1	1978–1985	Nominal: 2.570–1.859 times; real: 2.570–1.53 times; Theil index: 0.091–0.019	7	Dropped continuously
Stage 2	1985–1994	Nominal: 1.859–2.863 times; real: 1.53–1.953 times; Theil index: 019–0.053	9	Rose continuously
Stage 3	1994–1997	Nominal: 2.863–2.469 times; real: 1.953–1.83 times; Theil index: 0.053–0.04	3	Dropped for a short time
Stage 4	1997–2009	Nominal: 2.469–3.33 times; real: 1.83–2.674 times; Theil index: 0.04 –0.10	12	Rose continuously
Stage 5	2009–2017	Nominal: 3.33–2.710 times; real: 2.674–2.347 times; Theil index: 0.10–0.074	8	Dropped continuously

constraints, and its fluctuation amid the interaction of these constraints. In particular, the year 2009 marked a turning point at which China's urban–rural income gap began to enter a stage of continued fall following two V-shaped fluctuations. If we observed the post-2009 continued decline across the whole investigation period, we would find that this fall has two important features. First, in terms of duration, the decline over this period lasted for eight years, compared with seven years for the first stage and three years for the third stage (both recording a decline), and it represents a more significant correction to the continued rise in the second and fourth stages. Second, in terms of degree of decline, although the decline of urban–rural income gap in this stage was not as great as that in the first stage, but it was greater than in the third stage. In 2017, China's nominal urban–rural income gap was 2.710, a figure very close to the initial level of 1978 when reform and opening up first started. Its real urban–rural income gap and Theil index of urban–rural income gap were already lower than the initial level of 1978.

From the economic gap between the urban and rural sectors, at this stage, China's urban–rural duality has indeed been transformed continuously and obviously. Its urban–rural coordinated development and urban–rural integration have indeed achieved remarkable results. An urban–rural income gap close to or lower than the initial level of 1978 signifies that China's urban–rural economic relationship has entered a new turning point. However, since reform and opening up, China's urban–rural income gap has been fluctuating remarkably. History has witnessed its continuous rise or persistence at a high level over the 1985–1994 and 1997–2009 periods. Hence, the reduction of urban–rural income gap after 2009 should be investigated across an even longer time spectrum. It is still early to derive urban–rural economic relationship straight from this reduction. Furthermore, existing literature also confirms that since reform and opening up, China's income gap inside urban areas and rural areas has been climbing up (Pikety T., Yang L. & Zucman G., 2017; Gao F., 2018b). This signifies that China's urban–rural economic relationship has a degree of deformation at present. Hence the exploration of urban–rural economic relationship should remain sensitive to these new trends. In a word, since reform and opening up, China's urban–rural income gap has been fluctuating across different periods and has been reducing for quite a long time after 2009. This suggests that the country's urban–rural economic relationship is indeed transforming from separation toward integration, although this transformation is not temporarily linear or continuous, but is punctuated by twists and turns.

To sum up, considering the comprehensiveness of contents and the continuity of time, China's urban–rural economic relationship can be measured by indicators like urban–rural population and employment structure, industry labor productivity, and urban–rural consumption gap. By observing changes in these indicators, we can discover that since the founding of the RPC, marked by 1978 as the dividing point, China's urban–rural economic relationship has been transforming from separation toward integration. Microeconomic subjects are enjoying more freedom to allocate factors spontaneously between urban and rural areas. Accompanying these changes are the changes in urban–rural labor productivity, urban–rural consumption gap, and urban–rural income gap. In particular, since reform and opening up, China has been pushing forward market-oriented economic system transition. Urban–rural intercourse over commodities and factors has been expanding both in frequency and scope. The role of urban and rural microeconomic subjects, especially—farmers—as the subject of resource allocation has been unprecedentedly prominent. Against this background, urban and rural areas are no longer separated from each other like before, but are tightly integrated by the economic intercourse among microeconomic subjects. However, over the 40 years of reform and opening up, China's urban–rural economic integration has differed from one aspect to another, as evidenced by the changes inside industrialization, inside urbanization, and between industrialization and urbanization. Its urban–rural economic integration has also differed from one period to another, as strongly evidenced by the changes in the three indicators measuring urban–rural income gap. In fact, rises and falls interweaving different periods depict the basic feature of these indicator changes. In summary, since reform and opening up, China's urban–rural economic integration has been structured and periodical. Hence, we can call this integration an "imbalanced integration", which depicts the basic orientation of the country's urban–rural economic relationship of transforming toward integration, and the complexity and fluctuation of this transformation. By extension, we have to answer these questions: How did the separated urban–rural economic relationship take form before 1978? Why did the "imbalanced integration" begin to transform from separation toward an "imbalanced integration" in the late 1970s? In what direction will the "imbalanced integration" develop and evolve in future?

Note

1 Let *Theil* represent the Theil index of China's urban–rural consumption gap in time t, we have:

Here, $j = 1,2$ stands for urban and rural areas, respectively; p_{jt} is the urban (j = 1) and rural (j = 2) population in time t; p_{1t} and p_{2t} are the total populations. Y_{jt} is the urban (j = 1) and rural (j = 2) consumption level; $y_t = y_{1t} + y_{2t}$ is the total consumption. In order to exclude the price factor, here total urban consumption is the real per capita consumption of urban residents multiplied by the population of urban residents. Total rural consumption is the real per capita consumption of rural residents multiplied by the population of rural residents. Real urban and rural per capita consumption levels are calculated according to their respective per capita consumption indexes (1952 = 100).

5 Formation and performance of China's separated urban–rural economic relationship

From the founding of the PRC to the late 1970s, China's urban–rural economic relationship was labeled with separation. This separation was not only reflected in the restraints on the spontaneous urban–rural factor allocation among microeconomic subjects but also in the persistently high level of urban–rural labor productivity gap and resident consumption gap. In view of the particular social background, separated urban–rural economic relationship in prereform China did not exist by itself. It was the product of the combination of development strategy and constraints and the choice of economic system. It also constituted the starting point for the subsequent dynamic evolution of urban–rural economic relationship. Hence, without understanding the forming mechanism of this starting point, we would not be able to get a deeper insight into the evolution of urban–rural economic relationship in post-reform China. Conversely, to make a systematic explanation of the long-run evolutionary logic of China's urban–rural economic relationship, the first thing to do is use our new political economy analytical framework to explain how separated urban–rural economic relationship in the early days of the PRC took form and what results were produced. In effect, the performance analysis herein also constitutes the practical background of the subsequent evolution of urban–rural economic relationship. From a logical positivist point of view, theoretical analyses around the prereform urban–rural economic relationship also forms a test on our political economy analytical framework introduced earlier in this book.

5.1 National development strategy and constraints during the early days of the PRC

In 1949, under the leadership of the CPC, China won the War of Resistance against Japan and the War of Liberation and founded the PRC with socialist system. The founding of the PRC provided China with a new social system and prepared it for sustainable development. However, economic state is largely a continuation from the past. As nature cannot fly, economy can never change dramatically overnight. Before the founding of the PRC, China had long remained a semi-colonial and semi-feudal society. Its national economy had also suffered tremendous damage by protracted wars. Stagnant productivity and post-"cold war" international economic relationship made up the initial conditions facing the country's economic development. The outbreak of the Korean War in 1950 also constituted a particular external environment for China to promote its modernization drive. It was against this background that China embarked on the modernization drive of a large developing socialist country. Since then, China has been faced with such a fundamental proposition on the economic dimension: how shall a large developing country with socialist system realize its goal of sustainable development and common prosperity? All efforts made in the economic domain can be considered a response to this fundamental proposition. In commenting on China's national economy when the PRC was first founded, Nicholas R. Lardy (1992) so described, "When the CPC took over the control of China from Kuomintang in 1949, the economy was on the verge of collapse. Appearing with the long-term structural problems unique to the premodern economy—low per capita income, short life, low savings and investment ratio, and prevailing traditional production methods—were material and manpower losses accompanying domestic and international wars and extreme inflation"[1] (MacFarquhar R. and Fairbank K., 1992a). In the face of these internal and external situations, China had to choose and determine a development strategy more prudently so as to restore the order of national economy and lay a solid foundation for the subsequent socialist modernization drive. In fact, after the founding of the PRC, following only a brief period of New Democracy, China was already beginning to explore, establish, and practice a development strategy in 1953, which was to rely on mobilizing national resources to realize industrialization, especially the implementation of a heavy industry first strategy, so as to form a relatively independent and complete industrial system and meet the challenges both inside and outside.

The determination and choice of China's development strategies is typically reflected in the central government's statement of development strategies. Table 5.1 lists China's policy statements regarding economic development strategies from the founding of the PRC up to reform and opening up. In 1953, China established the general line for the socialist transitional period, which emphasized relying on socialist transformation to realize rapid national industrialization. In fact, promoting national industrialization was the "main body", whereas the socialist transformation of agriculture, handicraft, and capitalist industry and commerce was the wings. The "three transformations" were intended to serve the country's strategic goal of promoting national economy. Following that, the first Five-Year Plan (FYP) not only continued to highlight the importance of socialist industrialization but also explicitly put forward the heavy industry first strategy and underline the development of heavy industry as the country's key task for that period. In addition to setting forth the distribution of investment among different industries and the growth target of industrial

Table 5.1 Policy statements of China's national development strategies during the planned economy era

Time SN	*Document Name*	*Issued Date*	*Core Contents*
1953	General line for the transition period of socialism	Sept 25, 1953, *People's Daily*	In a long historical period, we should basically realize national industrialization and the socialist transformation of agriculture, handicraft industry and capitalist industry and commerce. This is the basic requirement of national economic development and the material basis for realizing the three major transformations. The realization of socialist transformation of agriculture, handicraft industry and capitalist industry and commerce, in turn, is a necessary condition for realizing national industrialization.
First FYP (1953–1957)	The First FYP For the Development of the National Economy of the People's Republic of China	Adopted on Jul 30, 1955 at the second meeting of the First National People's Congress	We should carry out a positive policy of socialist industrialization to improve the level of China's productive forces; we should adopt a positive policy of industrialization, that is, the policy of giving priority to the development of heavy industry. Its purpose is to derive the material basis for establishing a solid national defence, meeting the needs of the people and realizing the socialist transformation of the national economy. We should regard the infrastructure of heavy industry as the keystone for formulating the First FYP for the development of national economy and first of all concentrate our efforts on the construction of 156 industrial units designed by the Soviet Union.
Second FYP (1958–1962)	Report on the Recommendations of the Second FYP for National Economic Development	Adopted in Sept 1956 at the Eighth National Congress of the CPC	We should continue industrial construction with heavy industry as the center, promote the technological transformation of national economy, and establish a solid foundation for China's socialist industrialization; The main requirement of China's socialist industrialization is to basically build a complete industrial system within about three FYP periods.

(*Continued*)

Table 5.1 (Continued)

Time SN	*Document Name*	*Issued Date*	*Core Contents*
1958	General line for socialist construction	Adopted in May 1958 at the second meeting of the Eighth National Congress of the CPC	The general line of socialist construction is to go all out, aim high and achieve greater, faster, better and more economic results in building socialism; under the condition of giving priority to the development of heavy industry, industry and agriculture should be developed simultaneously; we should strive to catch up with and surpass Britain in terms of the output of major industrial products within in 15 years, or in a shorter period of time.
Third FYP (1966–1970)	Outline of the Report on the Arrangement of the Third FYP	Drafted by State Development Planning Commission in Sept 1965 & basically agreed by the Central Government after discussion	The Third FYP is essentially a war preparation plan with national defence construction at the center. We should race against time to get together the main things of national defence and the third front line; we should consider various construction arrangements from the needs of war preparation.
Fourth FYP (1971–1975)	Outline of the Fourth FYP (Draft)	Discussed and formulated in Feb and March 1970 at a National Planning Work Conference	We should concentrate our efforts on building a strong strategic rear of the third line, accelerate the process of agricultural mechanization, strengthen the construction of iron and steel, military industry, basic industry and transportation, and vigorously develop new technologies to catch up with and surpass the world's advanced level.

goods production, the plan also included a detailed blueprint on the development of individual segments of heavy industry—iron and steel, non-ferrous metals, electric power, coal, petroleum, machine manufacture, chemicals, construction material, and timber. Following the roadmap of the first FYP, the second FYP explicitly resolved to continue to promote heavy industry and underscored the need to further expand metallurgy, vigorously promote machine manufacture, strengthen electricity, coal, and construction material, and actively promote the backward segments of industry—petroleum, chemicals, and radio. In 1958, China put forward the general line for socialist construction. Although it did address the development structure among different sectors and emphasized the importance of coordinated and simultaneous development between industry and agriculture, this coordinated development was still conditional upon giving priority to heavy industry. After that, the third and fourth FYPs began to underline national defence and three-line construction. As heavy industry is closely associated with national defence and third-line construction, both plans were a continuation of the strategic idea of industrialization, especially the heavy industry first policy. For example, in the third FYP, the projected investment on national defence was 8.7 billion yuan, while that on heavy industry was 40.8 billion yuan, which included 5.7 billion yuan mainly for making the variety of steel needed for building third-line iron and steel industrial bases and national defence.

In the early days of the PRC, China established the strategic orientation of industrialization, especially the development of heavy industry, at the policy-making level. This strategic orientation can not only be observed by reviewing policy texts but also be understood by analyzing the amount of investment in the planned economy era. Table 5.2 compares the infrastructure investment among different sectors, especially in the industrial sector, from 1953 up to the end of the fifth FYP period. Within the investigation period, industry remained the largest recipient of infrastructure investment all the time, with infrastructure investment accounting for more than 50 percent of the country's total in the second, third, fourth, and fifth FYP periods. That was consistent with the country's attempt to quickly complete socialist industrialization and build a relatively complete, independent industrial system at that time. Within the infrastructure investment in industry, heavy industry was the absolute apply of the eye, while light industry has remained in a marginal and auxiliary position of investment throughout the investigation period. For example, in the second FYP period, infrastructure investment in industry accounted for 60.4 percent of the country's total, with light industry contributing 6.4 percent and heavy industry contributing 54 percent. The same story repeated in the other periods too. This suggests that in the planned economy era, China's national industrialization was mainly reflected by giving priority to heavy industry. Compared with industry, especially heavy industry, the share of infrastructure investment was quite small in other sectors, especially in agriculture and agriculture-related forestry, water conservancy & meteorology,

Table 5.2 China's share of infrastructure investment in different sectors in different periods from 1953 to 1980

Description	*First FYP (1953–1957)*	*Second FYP (1958–1962)*	*1963–1965*	*Third FYP (1966–1970)*	*Fourth FYP (1971–1975)*	*Fifth FYP (1976–1980)*
Industry	42.5	60.4	49.8	55.5	55.4	52.6
Light Industry	6.4	6.4	3.9	4.4	5.8	6.7
Heavy Industry	36.1	54.0	45.9	51.1	49.6	45.9
Construction & Geological Resource Exploration	6.1	2.5	2.5	2.2	2.3	3.2
Agriculture, Forestry, Water Conservancy & Meteorology	7.1	11.3	17.7	10.7	9.8	10.5
Transpot, Post & Telecommunications	15.3	13.5	12.7	15.4	18.0	12.9
Commercial Catering, Service, Supply, & Marketing	3.6	2.0	2.5	2.1	2.9	3.7
Science Research, Culture, Education, Health, & Social Welfare	7.6	3.8	5.7	2.8	3.1	5.4
Urban Public Utility	2.5	2.3	2.9	1.8	1.9	4.1
Others	15.3	4.2	6.2	9.5	6.6	7.6

Source: *China Statistical Yearbook 1983*, p.324–328.

with a minimum share of 7.1 percent and a maximum of 17.7 percent. Within the investigation period, from 1963 to 1965, the share of investment in industry dropped a little compared with the second FYP period. Regarding this change, Dwight H. Perkins so explained: Investment in means of production over 1963–1965 reduced, but this reduction was more ascribable to the need to resume work following the 1959–1961 crisis than to changes in the long-term strategy[2] (MacFarquhar R. and Fairbank K., 1992b). This investment structure clearly shows that industrialization—especially the heavy industry first strategy—as the development strategy of the early days of the PRC, can be well validated both at the policy-making level and the concrete operation level.

In the early days of the PRC, China's decision to give priority to heavy industry so as to support the country's goal of rapid industrialization was made under a mix of theoretical, practical, and international environment considerations. These considerations signify that the choice of a development strategy at that time was too complicated to be interpreted and commented from one single perspective. On the theoretical dimension, Marxist political economy forms an important source of theory for China to formulate its economic policies. Marxist social reproduction theory deems that the material production in a particular country can be divided into two categories: the means of production category (generally heavy industry) and the means of subsistence category (generally light industry). While social reproduction requires that these two categories complete material compensation and value compensation at the same time, one of the prerequisite for realizing expanded reproduction is giving priority to the growth of means of production to accommodate the need of both categories for expanded input in means of production. The "Political Economy Textbook" by Institute of Economics, Soviet Academy of Sciences also holds that means of production should grow first. It also maintains that "let means of production grow first implies that industrial develops faster than agriculture". As remarked by Nicholas R. Lardy (1992), the strategy of China's first FYP is firmly based on Marxist belief of expanded reproduction. That is, it determines industry which produces means of production as the main source of growth[3] (MacFarquhar R. and Fairbank K., 1992a).

On the practical dimension, after the founding of the RPC, the economic growth mode of the Soviet Union was much a prototype for China to copy, and China's choice of development strategy was inevitably inspired by the Soviet Union's practice. The "Selected Important Articles since the Founding of China" published by the Central Party Literature Press (1993) commented that, "In the capitalist countries, starting with light industry, it generally took 50 to 100 years to realize industrialization. But in the Soviet Union that adopts the guideline of socialist industrialization, starting with heavy industry, it took only ten-plus years (from 1921 to 1932 when the first FYP was completed) to realize national industrialization. The road that has been taken by the Soviet Union in the past is exactly what we must learn from today…Our national socialist industrialization starts with establishing heavy industry as did by the Soviet Union." Nicholas R. Lardy (1992) also noted that China's industrialization industry is similar to the Soviet Union's strategy in the 1930s with respect to manufacture, where priority development features very large priority scale and dense capital. Its industrialization program is cored around 156 Soviet Union-aided projects, which together take in around a half of total industrial investment[4] (MacFarquhar R. and Fairbank K., 1992a).

Furthermore, in the early days of the PRC, China was in an era of "cold war" between the capitalist and socialist blocs following World War II. The outbreak of the Korean War in 1950 also brought impact on the country's national security. The international environment facing China at that time was indeed very austere. In this context, it was just natural that national security and defence industry were placed in the paramount position. China's first FYP provides an explanation of national security for the adoption of a heavy industry first strategy: "The purpose of adopting a proactive industrialization policy, namely, a heavy industry first policy, is to seek the material basis for establishing consolidated national defence, meeting people's needs and realizing socialist transformation of national economy". Obviously, in the early days of the PRC, China's choice of a heavy industry first strategy was the result of a combination of multiple factors. This combination of multiple factors was underlined by Bo Y.B. (1991) when explaining the basis on which the first FYP was compiled: "After repeatedly weighing and in-depth discussion on the pros and cons of politics, economy, and international environment, everyone agreed that we must start with heavy industry—raw material, energy, machine manufacture etc."

After the heavy industry strategy was determined, the next thing to consider was whether the initial conditions of the PRC could support the development strategy, namely, in what way was the development strategy going to combine with existing constraints. By nature of industry, compared with agriculture and light industry, heavy industry is characterized by an enormous capital demand and a limited labor demand or ability to create jobs. Besides, heavy industry also implies a long construction investment period, and it is hardly possible to form the capital sources for expanded reproduction with its own proceeds within a short term. Unfortunately, in the early days of the PRC, the constraints on national economy did not agree with these characteristics of heavy industry. Indeed, in a context of extremely difficult national economy, China's stock of capital was far too small to meet the enormous capital demand of the heavy industry first strategy. In 1952, China's total capital formation was 15.3 billion yuan, with total fixed capital formation of 8.07 billion yuan, an amount far too little compared with the projected investment of 76.64 billion yuan for economic construction and culture and education (the projected investment for the industrial sector was 31.32 billion yuan) under the first FYP. Besides a short stock of capital at home, to make things worse, it was impossible to solve the gap of capital supply through external aids. The reason is that although the means of production provided by the Soviet Union are very important for establishing the few key segments of industry, most of the Soviet Union machines are received either by spot payment or shorter-term loans rather than by unilateral transfer or long-term concessional loans[5] (MacFarquhar R. and Fairbank K., 1992a).

Moreover, China had an extremely large stock of labor force, which also contradicts the limited job demand of heavy industry. In 1952, China's total employment was 207.29 million, including 24.86 million in urban areas and 182.43 million in rural areas. Obviously, if labor factors were allowed to be allocated spontaneously according to market signals, the enormous armies of rural laborers would pour into the capital-rich sectors. That way, "equal share" of capita would give a hard time to the heavy industry first strategy. Evidently, the heavy industry first strategy did not agree with China's endowments in the early days of the PRC. In particular, the endowment of capital shortage versus labor abundance did not support giving priority to heavy industry. This signifies that China initiated its heavy industry first strategy against extremely unfavorable initial conditions. Subject to this combination of development strategy and constraints necessitated, the only way out was to adjust government–market relationship and make appropriate economic system arrangements to resolve the supply of capital needed for heavy industry and the associated labor allocation control.

5.2 Economic system under the heavy industry first strategy

For China to implement a heavy industry first strategy in a context of capital shortage versus labor abundance, it had to make the corresponding economic system choice. In any economy, economic system revolves around the core issue of resource allocation. Given that government and market are the predominant forces in the realization of resource allocation, to choose an economic system is essentially to change the government–market relationship. Economic system arrangements are a series of rules, procedures, and practices formed by the state around government-market relationship. In the early days of the PRC, given the disagreement between the development strategy and factor endowments, it was impractical to rely on market forces to achieve the spontaneous allocation of resources. Hence, governments, especially the central government, became the subject of resource allocation, and mandatory plans replaced price as the tool of resource allocation. Lin Y.F., Cai F. & Li Z. (2012) suggested that, due to the internal conflicts between development strategy and resource endowments, China formed a macro policy environment supporting a catch-up strategy, a highly centralized resource planning and allocation system, and a micro-management mechanism lacking autonomy. From the perspective of urban–rural economic relationship, due to the development strategy and constraints at that time, China's economic system choice had given rise to a series of institutional arrangements, which were all closely associated with the behavioral choice of urban and rural microeconomic subjects and the characteristics of urban–rural duality.

5.2.1 People's communes in the rural sector

For China to implement a heavy industry first strategy in a context of capital shortage versus labor abundance, it not only needed to transform the industrial characteristics and ownership nature of urban industry but also the production and management mode of rural economy. The "Common Program" adopted at the CPPCC in September 1949 clearly stated that, in areas where land reform has been implemented, the ownership of the land acquired by farmers must be protected; in areas where land reform has not been reformed, farmers must be mobilized and farm organizations must be set up to realize land to the tillers. "Land to the tillers" was the basic orientation of China's land system reform and management mode reform in the early days of the PRC. Later, on June 30, 1950, the "Land Reform Act" issued by the Central People's Government further emphasized that "we must abolish the land ownership system of feudal exploitation by the landlord class and implement a land ownership system of farmers so as emancipate rural productivity, develop agricultural production, and open up a road for the industrialization of the new China", and that "after the completion of land reform, the people's government will issue land ownership certificates and recognize the right of all land owners to manage, trade, and lease their land freely". In accordance with these policy texts, land reform was carried out in the vast rural China from 1950 to 1952. Following the "land to the tillers" guideline, the reform provided the 300 million Chinese farmers with approximately 700 million mu of land and turned them holder of full land property right, namely the right to own and manage land. Compared with the previous land ownership by landlords, this new land property right system registered a large step forward, greatly emancipating rural productivity and laying solid foundation for restoring the order national economy.

In 1953, in its endeavor to carry through the general line for the socialist transition period, China began to promote the socialist transformation of agriculture along the pathway of mutual aid groups–elementary cooperatives–advanced cooperatives. The transformation, in essence, was to turn individual agricultural economy based on private ownership of means of production into agricultural cooperation economy based on the public ownership of means of production, under the leadership of the CPC. From a temporal point of view, China's agricultural cooperative movement went through the following three stages.

The first stage was from 1949 to 1953, when agricultural production was carried out mainly in the form of mutual aid groups and pilot-scale

Table 5.3 Share of farmer households participating in agricultural cooperative organizations in China from 1950 to 1957 (%)

Year	*Household-based Operation*	*Mutual Aid Group*	*Elementary Cooperative*	*Advanced Cooperative*
1950	89.09	10.91	0.000 2	0.000 03
1951	82.46	17.54	0.001 5	0.000 03
1952	60.10	39.86	0.05	0.002
1953	60.53	39.23	0.235	0.002
1954	39.68	58.37	1.948	0.01
1955	35.14	50.66	14.162	0.033
1956	1.33	0.086	8.64	89.17
1957	–	–	1.3	96.5

Source: Wu L. (2007).

cooperatives in elementary form were operated. On December 15, 1951, the CPC Central Committee issued a "Draft Resolution on Mutual Aid and Cooperation in Agricultural Production", which underlined the importance to advocate "unite together" and develop the enthusiasm of farmers for mutual aid in labor under the principle of voluntariness and mutual benefit. Guided by the cooperative policy, China's agricultural mutual aid groups sprouted very rapidly. As indicated by Table 5.3, from 1950 to 1953, the share of farmer households participating in mutual aid groups rose from 10.91 percent to 39.23 percent, whereas that of household-based operation dropped from 89.09 percent to 60.53 percent.

The second stage was from 1954 to 1955, when elementary cooperatives were widely established and developed in rural areas nationwide. The "Resolution on Mutual Aid and Cooperation in Agricultural Production" adopted by the CPC Central Committee on December 16, 1953, explicitly pointed out that the country's individual economy of farmers was "becoming very contradictory with socialist industrialization"; and China's road of socialist transformation of agriculture was "from temporary mutual aid groups involving simple joint labor and additional constant mutual groups involving some small amount of public property resulted from some work and business division, to agricultural production cooperatives involving a considerable amount of public property resulted from land pooling and unified management, to more advanced agricultural production cooperatives implementing full socialist collective farmer ownership (i.e., collective farms)". Guided and requested by this transformation pathway, the number of households engaged in household-based operation dived swiftly. Mutual aid groups quickly became the prevailing form of agricultural management. Advanced cooperatives also entered a booming stage. As indicated by Table 5.3, in 1954 and 1955, the share of farmer households participating in mutual aid groups rocketed to 58.37 percent and 50.66

percent, whereas those engaged in household-based operation dropped to 39.68 percent and 35.14 percent.

The third period was the post-1956 period, when agricultural cooperatives boomed, as marked by the prevalence of people's communes, a form of advanced cooperative, in agricultural management. On October 11, 1955, the Sixth Plenary Session of the seventh CPC Central Committee adopted the "Resolution on Mutual Aid and Cooperation in Agricultural Production", which stated that: in places where the mutual aid and cooperative movement are more advanced, the cooperative degree already reached 30–40 percent of the local total number of farmer households in the summer of 1955. Approximately in the spring of 1958, this figure will grow to 70–80 percent of local total number of farmer households. That is, semi-socialist cooperative will have been realized by then. In most parts of China, the cooperative degree is already around 10 percent or 20 percent of local total number of farmer households in the spring of 1955. Semi-socialist cooperative will have been realized roughly by the spring of 1958. Guided and requested by this policy, China's agricultural cooperative made a sharp turn from elementary cooperatives to advanced cooperatives. The latter soon became the basic organizational form of rural management. As indicated by Table 5.3, in 1956 and 1957, the share of farmer households participating in advanced cooperatives grew to 89.17 percent and 96.5 percent. On August 29, 1958, the CPC Central Committee issued the "Resolution on Establishing People's Communes in Rural Areas", which decided to upgrade all newly-established advanced agricultural production cooperatives into large-scale administration-economy integrated people's communes. This formally declared the establishment of people's commune system in rural China, marking the basic realization of socialist transformation of agriculture and the completion of the transition from individual farmer ownership to socialist collective ownership across the vast rural areas.

From the stage-by-stage review above, we can discover that in the planned economy era, China's socialist transformation of agriculture was built upon cooperative movement as the primary form of development, which in turn was built upon people's commune system as the paramount form of development. In terms of motivation, cooperative movement and the resulted people's commune system were both intended to serve the heavy industry first strategy. The policy texts of that period, for example, contained an awareness that small-scale farming was beginning to contradict socialist industrialization. In the eyes of the decision makers, this contradiction mainly lay in the fact that small-scale farming went against the capital accumulation for heavy industry development, the marketing of industrial products, and the state's unified administration of rural economy.

In terms of the implementation results, the people's commune system, first of all, led to remarkable changes in the ownership of means of production in rural areas. For example, the "Model Regulations for Advanced Agricultural Production Cooperatives" adopted by the First National

People's Congress on June 30, 1956, explicitly stated that "farmers who join in the cooperatives must transfer their private land, farming animals, large agricultural tools and other major means of production into collective ownership by cooperatives". In the meantime, the people's commune system also led to noticeable changes in the form of economic and social organization in rural China. For example, on December 10, 1958, the Sixth Plenary Session of the Eighth CPC Central Committee adopted the "Resolution on Several Issues concerning the people's Commune", which explicitly noted that "people's communes are the grassroots units of the country's socialist structure combining industry, agriculture, commerce, schooling, and military. They are also the grassroots units of socialist political power organization". This endorsed people's communes with multiple functions—they were both an economic organization and a social administrative organization. Accordingly, "administration-economy integration" became the basic organizational feature of people's communes. Although the previous model regulations for cooperatives had granted commune members the freedom to withdraw from a cooperative, the superposition between an economic organization and a social administrative organization, and the interweaving between economic function and social governance function, still brought the organizational degree of the vast population of farmers up to an unprecedented high. Individual rural residents became increasingly dependent on this two-in-one organization". It was even more difficult for rural microeconomic subjects to allocate goods and factors spontaneously outside this organization.

5.2.2 Public ownership in the urban sector

In the early days of the PRC, China's heavy industry first strategy was not only closely associated with the socialist transformation of agriculture (and the people's commune system formed therefrom) but also with the socialist transformation of handicraft and capitalist industry and commerce. Similar to the socialist transformation of agriculture, the transformation of handicraft and capitalist industry and commerce also targeted causing a change in the ownership of means of production, with a view to transforming the previous private ownership into ownership by the whole people (i.e., SOEs) or collective ownership (i.e., collective enterprises) through peaceful redemption or public–private joint venture. In the early years of the PRC, as handicraft and capitalist industry and commerce were mostly concentrated in urban areas, their socialist transformation also represented a change to the economic subjects and economic operation mode in urban China, which, together with the socialist transformation of agriculture, collaborated to reshape the economic organizational mode of the urban and rural sectors.

From the perspective of the heavy industry first strategy, the transformation of handicraft and capitalist industry and commerce made it possible to bring the human, financial and material resources and production, supply and marketing activities under the control of the government through mandatory plans, so that enterprise development at the micro level would remain coincident and fully synchronous with national development strategy at the macro level. Otherwise, the resource allocation of separate enterprises would have preferred to develop the light industry sector that consumes less capital and more labor along the factor endowment conditions. Obviously, to promote a heavy industry first strategy against unfavorable resource endowments, the government had no other choice but to directly intervene in enterprise behavior and to implement public ownership of means of production of enterprises. Government–market relationship also had to highlight the decisive role of governments at all levels (especially the central government) in resource allocation. In this sense, the ownership transformation in the urban industrial sector originated from the heavy industry first strategy, and at the same time provided preconditions for its implementation at the enterprise institutional level. Without the socialist transformation of handicraft and capitalist industry and commerce, the inherent conflicts between development strategy and endowment conditions would have made it hard to implement the heavy industry first strategy effectively.

To trace how handicraft and capitalist industry and commerce was transformed in the planned economy era, Table 5.4 compares the ownership system in the urban industrial sector from 1949 to 1977. Over the 1949–1958 interval, China recorded a steep change in the ownership of industrial enterprises, as marked by two important characteristic facts. One was the continuous rise in the share of output value of public enterprises (including both SOEs and collective enterprises), which ramped up from 26.8 percent to 100 percent. After a decade of socialist transformation, the ownership system in the industrial sector changed from multiple ownership to sole public ownership. Public–private joint ventures, private enterprises, individually owned enterprises, and any other type of industrial enterprises were no longer existent. Over 1958–1977, the share of public enterprises stood at a constant 100 percent, suggesting that public economy had become the only form of ownership in the urban industrial sector. The other was the particularly rapid increase in the share of enterprises owned by the whole people or SOEs, which rocketed from 26.3 percent to 89.2 percent. After 1958, this figure spanned from 77 percent (1977) to 90.6 percent (1960). Within the investigation period, the share of output value of collective enterprises remained far lower than that of SOEs. This suggests that China's industrial ownership transformation comprised a switch toward public ownership and more importantly a switch toward state ownership. Compared with collective enterprises, SOEs were usually larger in size, and government intervention was more convenient, direct, and effective. Hence "big, public, pure" would best describe the economic form of urban industry over this period.

In a word, in the early days of the PRC, China rapidly promoted the process of public ownership of industrial enterprises in the urban sector.

Table 5.4 Share of public sector in China's gross industrial output value from 1949 to 1977

Year	*Total Industrial Output Value (×10⁸ yuan)*	*SOE (×10⁸ yuan)*	*Collective Enterprise (×10⁸ yuan)*	*Share of SOEs (%)*	*Share of Collective Enterprises (%)*	*Total Share of Public Enterprises (%)*
1949	140.0	36.8	0.7	26.3	0.5	26.8
1950	191.0	62.4	1.5	32.7	0.8	33.5
1951	264.0	91.0	3.4	34.5	1.3	35.8
1952	349.0	145.0	11.4	41.5	3.3	44.8
1953	450.0	193.7	17.4	43.0	3.9	46.9
1954	515.0	242.7	27.5	47.1	5.3	52.5
1955	534.0	273.9	40.5	51.3	7.6	58.9
1956	642.0	350.2	109.6	54.5	17.1	71.6
1957	704.0	378.5	134.0	53.8	19.0	72.8
1958	1 083.0	965.7	17.3	89.2	10.8	100.0
1959	1 483.0	1313.2	169.8	88.6	11.4	100.0
1960	1 637.0	1483.1	153.9	90.6	9.4	100.0
1961	1 062.0	940.0	122.0	88.5	11.5	100.0
1962	920.0	807.8	112.2	87.8	12.2	100.0
1963	993.0	887.1	106.0	89.3	10.7	100.0
1964	1 164.0	1 042.3	121.8	89.5	10.5	100.0
1965	1 402.0	1 262.8	139.2	90.1	9.9	100.0
1966	1 624.0	1 461.5	159.5	90.0	9.8	99.8
1967	1 382.0	1 222.5	159.5	88.5	11.5	100.0
1968	1 285.0	1 136.2	148.8	88.4	11.6	100.0
1969	1 665.0	1 477.0	188.0	88.7	11.3	100.0
1970	2 117.0	1 854.7	262.3	87.6	12.4	100.0
1971	2 414.0	2 073.9	340.1	85.9	14.1	100.0
1972	2 565.0	2 177.2	387.8	84.9	15.1	100.0
1973	2 794.0	2 347.5	46.5	84.0	16.0	100.0
1974	2 792.0	2 300.9	491.1	82.4	17.6	100.0
1975	3 207.0	2 600.6	606.4	81.1	18.9	100.0
1976	3 278.0	2 567.7	710.3	78.3	21.7	100.0
1977	3 725.0	2 869.4	855.6	77.0	23.0	100.0

Source: *China Compendium of Statistics*, p.40.

Accordingly, public economy became the main, and even the only, economic form in the urban industrial sector. From the perspective of the heavy industry first strategy, a public economy in the urban sector would enable the resource allocation in the urban sector to better reflect the national development strategy, since it allows enterprises—as microeconomic subjects—to carry out economic activity spontaneously according to market signals. As far as urban–rural economic relationship is concerned, public economy in the urban sector also greatly restrained the spontaneous flow and allocation of rural factors. Even though rural labor was free to flow into the urban sector, the dominance of public economy would easily empower the state to exert strict control over the allocation of labor force.

5.2.3 Unified purchase and marketing of agricultural products

After the early 1950s, while China picked up an industrialization strategy biased toward heavy industry, different sectors had been interconnected by the input–output relationship all the time. Industrialization always needed to remain relevant with agricultural economy. In particular, the material source of industry, the need of agricultural products by industry laborers, and the capital accumulation for industrial development could never have been solved inside industry itself without the help of agriculture and the rural sector. Unfortunately, this function was obviously far beyond the ability of a decentralized agricultural product market, since decentralized market transaction around the allocation of agricultural products did not necessarily meet the needs of a heavy industry first strategy. Also, from the perspective of national resource allocation, such a market form would also face persistently high administrative costs. That is to say, it was important, and also necessary, for the government to allocate grain and other agricultural products through mandatory plans.

Under such a realistic background, the CPC Central Committee made the "Resolution on the Implementation of unified purchase and marketing of Grain" on October 16, 1953, and the State Council issued an "Order on the Implementation of unified purchase and marketing of Grain" on November 23 of the same year. These policy documents were cored around the planned purchase and planned supply of grain nationwide in a programmed, step-by-step manner. Particularly, both documents expressly prescribed that farmers producing grain were obliged to sell their surplus grain of the purchase varieties, at the purchase price and in the planned quantity prescribed by the state, that the grain market should be solely controlled by the state, and that no individual farmers or private dealers were allowed to trade grain themselves. From then on, planned purchase and supply by the government was implemented on oil plants, cotton, and cotton cloth, marking the beginning of unified purchase and marketing of agricultural products between urban and rural China.

Figure 5.1 compares total purchase and structure of agricultural and sideline products in China from 1952 to 1977. By sector, total purchase of agricultural and sideline products fell into three categories: purchase by commercial sector, purchase by industry and other sectors, and purchase by nonagricultural residents from farmers. In the socialist transformation of handicraft and capitalist industry and commerce, now that the commercial sector was increasingly more public and played the important role of executing mandatory government plans, purchase by nonagricultural residents from farmers can be seen as the degree of freedom for farmers to trade commodities. Within the investigation period, total purchase of agricultural

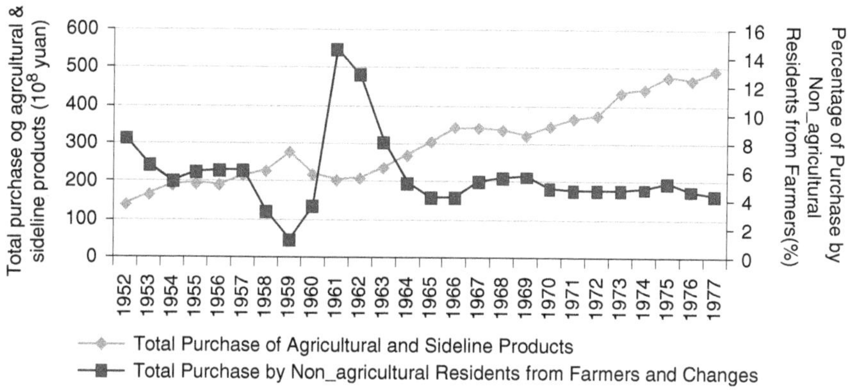

Figure 5.1 China's total purchase of agricultural and sideline products and its structure from 1952 to 1977.

Source: China Statistical Yearbook 1983, p387.

and sideline products gradually climbed up from 14.08 billion yuan to 49.46 billion yuan. Over this process, purchase by nonagricultural residents from farmers was quite volatile, especially over the 1961–1963 period, when its absolute value and share both increased considerably. These increases, however, were largely a response to the "three-year difficult period" from 1958 to 1961. That is, the size of spontaneous transaction between non-agricultural residents and farmers increased against the backdrop of grave shortage of grain and sideline products nationwide. If we do not consider this special period, from 1952 to 1954, the share of purchase by nonagricultural residents from farmers dropped from 8.38 percent to 5.34 percent; for a long time thereafter, this figure had stood at a constant low of 4–5 percent and did not rise until after the agricultural management system reform in 1978. The persistently low share of purchase by nonagricultural residents from farmers signifies that the spontaneous product transaction between urban and rural microeconomic subjects was actually restrained. Obviously, under unified purchase and marketing of agricultural products, the urban–rural allocation of agricultural products was mainly realized through government institutions and mandatory plans. It was extremely difficult for urban and rural residents to trade agricultural products directly or for rural residents to provide agricultural products to urban residents autonomously.

5.2.4 Urban and rural household registration

In the planned economy era, to implement a heavy industry first strategy, the government needed to function not only to control urban–rural product transaction but also urban–rural factor transaction, especially when it concerned population and labor since both are highly mobile. Without intervention, rural labor would very likely flow into urban areas along with capital accumulation, thus affecting the economic and social order of the urban sector, consequently the heavy industry first strategy by way of capital "dilution". So, controlling the free flow of population and labor between urban and rural areas became an important policy option for the young PRC, and accordingly, an objective need for the successful implementation of the heavy industry first strategy. In that connection, the "Regulations of the People's Republic of China on Household Registration" promulgated and enacted by the Chinese government in 1958 was undoubtedly of monumental significance. It marked the prelude to a household registration and management system characterized by urban–rural isolation. In Clause 4 of this act, it was so stipulated: "In cities, on waters, and in towns with a public security police station, a household register shall be issued to each household; in rural areas, a household register shall be issued to each co-operative, and no household register shall be issued to any household other than a cooperative". That means that the Chinese nationals were to be discriminated by household register (or hukou) into agricultural population and non-agricultural population. In Clause 10, it was stated: "Citizens moving from rural areas into cities shall apply to the household registration authority of their permanent residence for moving out with an employment certificate issued by the urban labor department, an admission certificate issued by the school, or a certificate of permission to move in issued by the target city's household registration authority". This set quite a high threshold for the rural population to become an urban resident.

More notably, in addition to social administrative functions such as population and labor registration, household registration also evolved into an important criterion for distributing public goods and social welfare between urban and rural residents (Gao F., 2016a). As Barry Naughton (2010) noted, starting from the mid-1960s, Chinese urban residents have generally been granted the following benefits: job security with guaranteed access to food and other rare commodities at low prices; medical care; post-retirement pension and other benefits, including medical care; elementary and secondary schooling for children; and employer-provided low-cost housing, which are noticeably superior to the benefits available for their rural counterparts. Household registration, once established and enacted, brought the population flow between urban and rural areas, especially the non-agricultural transfer of rural population and labor, under great restraint. For a prolonged time to come, the urban–rural population and labor structure also remained remarkably solidified.

To understand the effects of urban and rural household registration on China's economy and society, it would be helpful to examine the changes in the population structure between urban and rural areas. In our measurement of China's urban–rural economic relationship earlier in this book, we have already used share of rural population and other indicators to describe the solidification of urban–rural population and labor structure before the founding of the PRC.

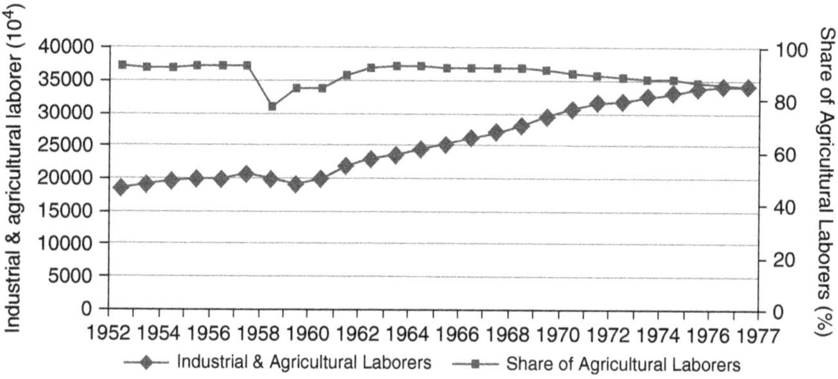

Figure 5.2 China's numbers of industrial and agricultural laborers and its structure from 1952 to 1977.

Source: China Statistical Yearbook 1983, p122.

As an addition, we can also use number of industrial/agricultural laborers and its structure to reflect the effects of urban and rural household registration on China's urban–rural economic relationship. As illustrated by Figure 5.2, from 1952 to 1977, the number of industrial/agricultural laborers increased progressively from 185.63 million to 344.35 million. Over this process, the share of agricultural laborers had stood in a very high position, well above 85 percent for all years except 1958. The share of industry laborers, in contrast, had remained below 15 percent and was even lower than 10 percent over the 1952–1970 period (except for the "three-year difficult period from 1958 to 1961). The structural figures of industrial and agricultural laborers demonstrate that, during the hastened industrialization, the urban–rural laborer structure was highly elastic and solidified. Industrialization did not incur a steep rise in industrial employment or a sharp decline in the share of agricultural employment, which concurred with the heavy industry first strategy and the modest job demand of heavy industry. From the perspective of labor flow mechanism, the persistently high share of agricultural employment in the planned economy era was not caused by the lack of a desire among rural laborers to flow freely between urban and rural areas. It was the rigorous urban and rural household registration system that prevented them from doing so.

To sum up, in the early days of the PRC, China sought to implement national industrialization, especially the heavy industry first strategy, against the endowment conditions of capital shortage versus labor abundance. This inevitably led to a tension between development strategy and constraints and forced the country to make the corresponding institutional arrangements on the government–market dimension and form a series of urban–rural economic systems in line with this strategic need: people's communes in rural areas, public economy in urban areas, unified purchase and marketing of agricultural products, and urban and rural household registration. Behind these systems, governments at various levels became the subject of resource allocation and ensured—by means of mandatory plans rather than price signals—that resources were allocated to meet the needs of the heavy industry first strategy. As market mechanism was actually replaced by government plans, intermarket structure simply did not count. In the planned economy era, as market mechanism was nonexistent, intermarket structural feature did not exist either. Through a package of efforts targeted at "one game of the whole country" and "concentrating efforts on major endeavors", and high power centralization to mobilize resources needed for meeting internal and external challenges, the central government became the ultimate decision maker over resource allocation, and local governments were, to a large extent, barely an executor of the ready-made policies. Intragovernmental structure was not a big issue at that time, either. In fact, there was a high level of homogeneity among different levels of governments in the planned economy era.

Now that market mechanism was replaced by government plans and there was a high level of homogeneity inside the government, this provided a reliable institutional basis for the heavy industry first strategy. As far as urban–rural economic relationship is concerned, once determined, these economic systems were bound to affect the behavioral choice of microeconomic subjects and urban–rural relationship. After commodity and factor market was replaced by mandatory government plans, urban–rural separation was an avoidable outcome. Particularly, these different economic systems were usually nested into each other and would compound to prevent and restrain the spontaneous economic behavior between urban and rural microeconomic subjects. For example, the combination of public economy in urban areas with people's communes in urban areas caused the urban–rural microeconomic subjects to be integrated into a particular economic and social organization. It became even harder for them to carry out economic activity and their economic activity, if any, was increasingly restrained by the collective organization. Furthermore, the combination of these two systems also provided important support for the effective implementation of unified purchase and marketing of agricultural products and household registration. The coupling of public economy in the industrial sector, people's communes in the rural sector, and unified purchase and marketing of agricultural products made it almost impossible for microeconomic subjects to carry out spontaneous commodity transaction between urban and rural areas. The coupling of public economy in the industrial sector, people's communes in the rural sector, and household registration also prevented the full flow of factors between urban and rural sectors. Once commodity and factor transaction was wholly banned, the urban and rural sectors were destined to be separated on the economic dimension.

5.3 Multiple effects of separated urban–rural economic relationship

Before reform and opening up, in order to implement the heavy industry first strategy against the endowment conditions of capital shortage versus labor abundance, China formed a whole set of economic system arrangements in respect of government-market relationship, which led to a separated urban–rural economic relationship. According to our political economy analytical framework for urban–rural economic relationship, the economic behavior of microeconomic subjects always takes place under a particular economic system. Subject to the conspiration of people's commune system in the rural sector, public economy in the urban sector, unified purchase and marketing of agricultural products, and urban and rural household registration, microeconomic subjects would inevitably make a behavioral choice and produce multidimensional economic effects. Separated urban–rural economic relationship affects China's economic and social development in multiple ways. When reviewing the performance of China's system operation in the planned economy era, some authors commented that "during the quarter century prior to the start of economic reform in the late 1970s, China's plan system delivered mixed results" (Brandt L. & Rawski T., 2009). Logically speaking, understanding the multiple effects of separated urban–rural economic relationship helps clarify the positive roles of economic strategy choice in the planned economy era. It also helps identify the practical background underlying China's decision to launch reform and opening up in 1978.

Now that in the early days of the PRC, China sought to realize national industrialization, especially the development of heavy industry, to evaluate the performance of economic system operation and the separated urban–rural economic relationship in this period, we need to start with how this strategy was implemented. In that connection, separated urban–rural economic relationship well supported China's national industrialization. It enabled the country to create a relatively independent and complete industrial system against extremely unfavorable initial conditions. In fact, such an industrial system worked as a positive respond to internal and external challenges, especially the needs of national security. Here the main mechanism is:

On the one hand, separated urban–rural relationship created capital accumulation sources for the development of heavy industry through multiple channels—agricultural taxes, price scissors of industrial-agricultural products, and outflow of rural savings. According to statistics, from 1950 to 1955, China's agricultural taxes totaled 79.94 billion yuan. In the planned economy era, there had always been a distinct gap in the exchange price parity between agricultural and industrial products. For example, in 1952, 1957, 1978, and 1983, 100 kg of wheat could exchange for 70, 62, 95, and 16 kg of salt; 11, 13, 17, and 21 kg of white sugar; 19, 21, 30, and 29 m of plain white cloth; and 15,

19, 38, and 46 kg of kerosene, respectively. If we say that the post-1978 market-oriented reform turned the price parity of industrial products an accurate signature of the degree of their rarity, the prices of agricultural products before reform were obviously "undervalued". Existing literature has demonstrated that, in the planned economy era, the Chinese government managed to transfer an estimated amount of 600 to 800 billion yuan's worth of rural resources into the industrial (or urban) sector through public taxes, price scissors of industrial/agricultural products, and net outflow of savings (Cai F. & Lin Y.F., 2003; Cai F., 2006), and this transfer of agricultural surplus made up an important capital source for the heavy industry first strategy.

On the other hand, separated urban–rural economic relationship also raised the barrier of nonagricultural transfer of rural labor through household registration, thus imprisoning the spontaneous flow of factors between urban and rural areas. More than that, government-guided one-dimensional population flow from urban areas to rural areas also took form (e.g., the "Going Rural" movement). At a time when public ownership prevailed throughout the urban sector, people's communes were implemented in the rural sector, and urban and rural residents were discriminated by household registration, the absolute majority of rural labor had no choice but engage in production activities in rural collective organizations, which were limited to agriculture, forestry, animal husbandry, and fishery. This way, the contradiction between limited demand of non-agricultural jobs and the enormous supply of jobs under the heavy industry first strategy, thus ensuring that capital factors were mostly allocated to the heavy industry sector, although the number of jobs created by this sector was fairly modest. In a word, separated urban–rural economic relationship provided quite a satisfactory solution to the two major problems facing the industrialization drive—capital source and employment exclusion, enabling the industrial sector of national system, especially heavy industry, to gain rapid development.

Regarding the economic output of the industrial sector, Table 5.5 compares China's output of major industrial products from 1949 to 1977. Within the investigation period, China gradually formed an independent, complete industrial system. Apart from the already existent industrial categories, other industrial segments that had used to be blank in the early days of the PRC also recorded very fast development. For example, in 1949, the output of automobiles was almost negligible; but in 1977, the figure was already 125400. The same thing happened to the output of sewing machines, which was already 4242000 in 1977. Among all the industrial segments, the development of heavy industry—capital source and employment exclusion—especially iron and steel, coal, petroleum, electric power, and machinery—capital source and employment exclusion—were particularly outstanding, as evidenced by the index of gross output value of different sectors in Table 5.6. Assuming a base value of 100 for 1952, from 1949 to 1977, China's index of gross output value of industry grew rapidly from

Table 5.5 China's output of major industrial products from 1949 to 1977

Description	*1949*	*1953*	*195*	*1960*	*1965*	*1970*	*1975*	*1977*
Steel (×10⁴ t)	15.8	177	285	1 866	1 223	1 779	2 390	2 374
Iron (×10⁴ t)	25	223	387	2 716	1 077	1 706	2 449	2 505
Power Generation (×10⁸ kWh)	43	92	123	594	676	1 159	1 958	2 234
Raw Coal (×10⁸ t)	0.32	0.70	0.98	3.97	2.32	3.54	4.82	5.50
Crude Oil (×10⁴ t)	12	62	97	520	1 131	3065	7 706	9364
Cement (×10⁴ t)	66	388	450	1 565	1 634	2 575	4 646	5 565
Chemical Fertilizer (×10⁴ t)	0.6	5.0	7.8	19.6	103.7	152.3	370.9	550.9
Machine Tool (×10⁴ piece)	0.16	2.05	1.37	15.35	3.96	13.89	17.49	19.87
Car (×10⁴ piece)	–	–	–	2.26	4.05	8.72	13.98	12.54
Cloth (×10⁸ m)	18.9	46.9	43.6	54.5	62.8	91.5	94.0	101.5
Sewing Machine (×10⁴ piece)	–	–	15.3	88.0	123.8	235.2	356.7	424.2
Bicycle (×10⁴ piece)	1.4	16.5	33.5	176.5	183.8	368.8	623.2	742.7
Timber (×10⁴ m²)	567	1 754	2 093	4 129	3 978	3 782	4 703	4 967

Source: *China Statistical Yearbook 1983*, p.242–248.

40.8 to 1408.4. Compared to that of agriculture which increased from 67.4 to 210.6, the growth rate of gross output value of industry was remarkably superior. Inside the industrial sector, the index of gross output value of light industry grew from 46.6 to 873.7, while that of heavy industry soared from 30.3 to 2402.9. In the planned economy era, the growth rate of heavy industry was remarkably superior over light industry.

In the planned economy era, industrialization, especially the rapid development of heavy industry, also led to remarkable changes in the structure of national economy. As indicated by Table 5.6, in the gross industrial/agricultural output value, the share of agricultural output value displayed a sharp decline. From 1949 to 1977, this figure dropped from 70.0 percent to 28.1 percent, compared to the share of industrial output value which rose from 30.0 percent to 71.9 percent. Inside the industrial sector, over 1949–1957, the share of output value of light industry remained larger than that of heavy industry all the time. But afterward, the share of output value of heavy industry began to outperform that of light industry (except only for 1965 and the 1967–1969 interval). In the planned economy era, China not only transformed from a country dominated by agricultural output value into one dominated by industrial output value, its industrial focus also shifted from light industry to heavy industry. Over this period, China's industrialization strategy, especially the heavy industry first strategy, achieved remarkable results.

From the above figures, due to the particular economic system arrangements and separated urban–rural economic relationship, in the planned

Table 5.6 China's index of gross industrial and agricultural output value and its structure from 1947 to 1977

Year	Index of Gross Industrial/Agricultural Output Value (1952=100)				Structure of Gross Industrial/Agricultural Output Value (%)			
	Agriculture	Industry	Light Industry	Heavy Industry	Agriculture	Industry	Light Industry	Heavy Industry
1949	67.4	40.8	46.6	30.3	70.0	30.0	22.1	7.9
1950	79.3	55.7	60.6	46.7	66.8	33.2	23.5	9.7
1951	86.8	76.8	81.0	69.7	61.4	38.6	26.2	12.4
1952	100.0	100.0	100.0	100.0	56.9	43.1	27.8	15.3
1953	103.1	130.3	126.7	136.9	53.1	46.9	29.4	17.5
1954	106.6	151.6	144.8	163.9	50.9	49.1	30.2	18.9
1955	114.7	160.0	144.8	187.7	51.8	48.2	28.5	19.7
1956	120.5	204.9	173.3	262.3	48.7	51.3	29.6	21.7
1957	124.8	228.6	183.2	310.7	43.3	56.7	31.2	25.5
1958	127.8	353.8	245.0	555.5	34.3	65.7	30.5	35.2
1959	110.4	481.8	298.8	822.7	25.1	74.9	31.1	43.8
1960	96.4	535.7	269.5	1 035.5	21.8	78.2	26.1	52.1
1961	94.1	330.7	211.1	553.6	34.5	65.5	27.8	37.7
1962	99.9	275.9	193.5	428.4	38.8	61.2	28.9	32.3
1963	111.6	299.4	197.9	487.8	39.3	60.7	27.2	3.5
1964	126.7	358.2	233.2	590.3	38.2	61.8	27.4	34.4
1965	137.1	452.6	344.5	650.6	37.3	62.7	32.3	30.4
1966	149.0	547.4	394.3	829.5	35.9	64.1	31.4	32.7
1967	151.2	471.8	366.4	663.6	40.1	59.9	31.8	28.1
1968	147.5	448.0	348.3	629.8	41.9	58.1	31.2	26.9
1969	149.2	601.6	436.1	906.6	36.3	63.7	32.0	31.7
1970	166.3	786.0	514.9	1 289.9	33.7	66.3	30.6	35.7
1971	171.4	903.3	548.2	1 565.5	31.8	68.2	29.3	38.9
1972	171.1	962.9	582.2	1 675.1	30.9	69.1	29.6	39.5
1973	185.5	1 054.2	643.6	1 820.7	30.9	69.1	30.0	39.1
1974	193.2	1 056.9	660.6	1 790.9	31.9	68.1	30.3	37.8
1975	202.1	1 216.4	746.5	2 091.8	30.1	69.9	30.8	39.1
1976	207.1	1 232.2	764.4	2 102.2	30.4	69.6	30.7	38.9
1977	210.6	1 408.4	873.7	2 402.9	28.1	71.9	31.6	40.3

economy era, China did form an independent and fairly complete industrial system, especially with respect to heavy industry. Its industrialization strategy biased toward heavy industry did achieve remarkable results. Unlike other smaller-sized economies, China is a large developing country with socialist system. Hence, it is neither possible nor desirable for the country rely mainly on other economies to establish and develop its own industrial sector. Hence, the industrial system formed in the planned economy era is of extraordinary significance to the national security of the young PRC. It also plays a fundamental role in the country's subsequent rapid economic development.

One point remains. As China relied on mandatory government plans to implement its heavy industry first strategy against the endowment conditions of capital shortage versus labor abundance, this led to a series of system arrangements and separated urban–rural economic relationship. Such a separated urban–rural economic relationship not only affected the heavy industry first strategy but could also affect overall resource allocation efficiency and urban–rural structure. Apart from providing support for the heavy industry first strategy, separated urban–rural economic relationship also brought about the following consequences:

First, imbalanced development among different sectors. Along with the net outflow of rural capital and the implementation of people's communes, the entire national economy was under a policy system and resource allocation architecture characterized by "agriculture supports industry, villages support towns". While this macro environment was conducive to industrialization, it inevitably hampered and delayed agricultural development. A striking evidence would be found from Table 5.6, which shows far smaller total output value figures of agriculture than industry, especially heavy industry, from 1949 to 1977. The urban–rural labor productivity and urban–rural consumption expenditure figures presented earlier in this book would serve as another striking evidence. In other words, a prominent urban–rural duality was shaped over the course of hastened industrialization. This duality was not solely the result of labor allocation between urban and rural areas, but was largely the byproduct of the economic systems under the combination of development strategy and constraints. Regarding the consequence, the series of system arrangements formed in the planned economy era aggravated China's urban–rural dual contrast, and supplied the soil for a separated urban–rural economic relationship to root and sprout.

Second, reduced marginal return on investment in the industrial sector. In the planned economy era, despite the implementation of the national industrialization strategy, especially the heavy industry first strategy, as a result of inadequate incentive to microeconomic subjects inside the industrial sector, the resource mismatch caused by planned economy, and demand–supply constraints caused by imbalanced industrial development, in the late 1960s and the early 1970s, many industrial segments (especially heavy industry segments such as electric power, metallurgy, petroleum, and coal) were reporting growing capital–output ratio, suggesting that the output growth caused by given industrial investment was beginning to fall[6] (MacFarquhar R. and Fairbank K., 1992b). In other words, China had to put in more investment in order to produce a given amount of industrial products. Its industrialization strategy was facing intensifying pressure of capital accumulation.

Third, persistently low output efficiency in the agricultural sector. While the heavy industry first strategy was being implemented, inside the urban sectors, people's communes, people's communes, unified purchase and marketing of agricultural products, and household registration also emerged. People's communes made it hard for agricultural management to solve the "supervision" over microeconomic subjects, and collective management would often choose to adopt an "equalitarian" distribution among the commune members. Unified purchase and marketing of agricultural products and household registration prevented microeconomic subjects from improving their economic positions through commodity transaction and labor reallocation. Rural labor had no other choice but to engage in economic activities within the collective organization of people's communes. Yet even these economic activities were also confined to agricultural productions and agriculture-related forestry, animal husbandry, and fishery. In the absence of sufficient supervision and self-motivation, trying to "goof off" would inevitably become a rational choice for the rural microeconomic subjects in the people's communes. Hampered commodity and factor transaction also made it hard to improve the factor allocation efficiency. These, together, were bound to result in low efficiency of agricultural production. Table 5.7 compares China's per capita output of major agricultural products from 1949 to 1977. Over this period, China's per capita output of agricultural products did not increase significantly. For example, in 1952, the per capita output of grain was 576 *jin*/person (1 *jin* equals to 0.5 kg); in 1977, it was 599 *jin*/person. Over some of the time intervals of the investigation period, many indicators even declined. In the late 1970s, the agricultural output of rural labor was even unable to sustain its own demand of agricultural products. Later, these hardships became the practical motive for the Xiaogang villagers in Anhui province to start an adventurous "big contracting" move.

More notably, the heavy industry first policy adopted in the young PRC conflicted with the constraints at that time. This forced the government to rely on mandatory plans of resource allocation so as to bring into practice the established industrialization strategy. Over this period, along with separated urban–rural economic relationship, governments at all levels (especially the central government) replaced enterprises and residents as the subject of resource allocation. Mandatory plans also replaced market price as the instrument of resource allocation. While this was conducive to realizing the short-term objectives set by the government—such as the heavy

Table 5.7 China's per capita output of major agricultural products from 1949 to 1977

Year	*Grain (jin/person)*	*Cotton (jin/person)*	*Oil (jin/person)*	*Fat Pig (head/person)*	*Pork, Beaf, Mutton (jin/person)*	*Aquatic Product (jin/person)*
1949	418	1.6	9.5	–	–	1.7
1952	576	4.6	14.7	0.12	11.9	5.9
1953	574	4.0	13.3	0.12	–	6.6
1954	570	3.6	14.5	0.13	–	7.6
1955	604	5.0	15.9	0.11	–	8.2
1956	620	4.7	16.4	0.10	–	8.6
1957	612	5.2	13.2	0.11	12.5	9.8
1958	612	6.0	14.6	0.13	–	8.6
1959	510	5.1	12.3	0.10	–	9.2
1960	430	3.2	5.8	0.07	–	9.2
1961	446	2.4	5.5	0.05	–	7.0
1962	481	2.3	6.0	0.06	5.8	6.8
1963	498	3.5	7.2	0.11	–	7.6
1964	538	4.8	9.6	0.15	–	8.0
1965	544	5.9	10.1	0.17	15.4	8.3
196	582	6.4	–	0.18	–	8.4
1967	579	6.3	–	0.18	–	8.2
1968	540	6.1	–	0.17	–	7.0
1969	530	5.2	–	0.16	–	7.3
1970	586	5.6	9.2	0.15	14.6	7.8
1971	595	5.0	9.8	0.18	–	8.3
1972	558	4.5	9.6	0.19	–	8.9
1973	601	5.8	9.5	0.19	–	8.9
1974	611	5.5	9.8	0.19	–	9.5
1975	621	5.2	9.9	0.18	17.4	9.6
1976	615	4.4	8.6	0.18	16.8	9.6
1977	599	4.3	8.5	0.18	16.5	10.0

Source: *China Statistical Yearbook 1983*, p.184.
Note: 1 *jin* equals to 0.5 kg.

industry first strategy—as the government was unable to be fully informed of the demand and supply of particular products and to create long-term incentives for microeconomic subjects, the resource allocation efficiency was bound to remain low. For example, with a separated urban–rural economic relationship, the spontaneous transaction of agricultural products between urban and rural microeconomic subjects was restrained. The reallocation of rural labor between urban and rural areas based on income comparison was also perplexed by a range of difficulties. In fact, the public economy inside the urban industry was also challenged by how to supervise and incentivize microeconomic subjects. This inevitably led to society-wide resource mismatch and persistently low efficiency of national economy.

Table 5.8 China's per capita GDP from 1960 to 1977 compared with the world, United States and Japan

Year	*China (USD)*	*World (USD)*	*U.S. (USD)*	*Japan (USD)*	*China/ World (%)*	*China/ U.S. (%)*	*China/ Japan (%)*
1960	89.52	446.47	3 007.12	479.00	18.69	2.98	20.05
1961	75.81	458.63	3 066.56	563.59	13.45	2.47	16.53
1962	70.91	482.65	3243.84	633.64	11.19	2.19	14.69
1963	74.31	510.67	3 374.52	717.87	10.35	2.20	14.55
1964	85.50	549.03	3 573.94	835.66	10.23	2.39	15.57
1965	98.49	585.90	3 827.53	919.78	10.71	2.57	16.81
1966	104.32	622.01	4 146.32	1 058.50	9.86	2.52	16.77
1967	96.59	650.45	4 336.43	1 228.91	7.86	2.23	14.85
1968	91.47	687.24	4 695.92	1 450.62	6.31	1.95	13.31
1969	100.13	740.18	5 032.14	1 669.10	6.00	1.99	13.53
1970	113.16	797.59	5 246.88	2 037.56	5.55	2.16	14.19
1971	118.65	863.00	5 623.44	2 272.08	5.22	2.11	13.75
1972	131.88	978.15	6 109.93	2 967.04	4.44	2.16	13.48
1973	157.09	1 167.27	6 741.33	3 997.84	3.93	2.33	13.46
1974	160.14	1 315.37	7 242.44	4 353.82	3.68	2.21	12.17
1975	178.34	1 437.86	7 820.07	4 659.12	3.83	2.28	12.40
1976	165.41	1 534.08	8 611.40	5 197.81	3.18	1.92	10.78
1977	185.42	1 703.98	9 471.31	6 335.79	2.93	1.96	10.88

Source: Absolute value figures are sourced from World Bank Database. Ratio figures are calculated based on absolute value figures.

Table 5.8 compares China's per capita GDP with the world, the United States, and Japan from 1960 to 1977. Over this period, although China's per capita GDP increased from 89.52 dollars to 185.42 dollars, the per capita GDP of the world, the United States, and Japan increased even more rapidly, widening the per capita GDP gap between China and the other economies. Over this period, relative to world average, the ratio of China's per capita GDP dropped from 18.69 percent to 2.93 percent, Relative to the United States, it dropped from 2.98 percent to 1.96 percent. Relative to Japan, it also dropped from 20.05 percent to 10.88 percent. These cross-country comparative figures show that, from the founding of the PRC up to reform and opening up, China's separated urban–rural economic relationship had been accompanied by persistently low efficiency of national economy. Compared with the rapid development of the other economies, China's national economy was indeed on the verge of collapse.

In a word, in the early days of the PRC, China chose a national industrialization strategy, especially a heavy industry first strategy, against the endowment conditions of capital shortage versus labor abundance. Such a combination of development strategy and constraints gave rise to the corresponding economic system arrangements, which were cored around how to solve the conflicts between development strategy and constraints. In terms of the performance of economic system, on the government–market dimension, the central government took the place of market mechanism as the subject of resource allocation. As neither the intragovernmental nor intramarket structural problems were prominent, market was even replaced by the government's economic interventions. To match the needs of the heavy industry first strategy, between urban and rural China also emerged people's communes, public economy in the urban sector, unified purchase and marketing of agricultural products in the rural sector, and urban and rural household registration. All these economic systems were intended to serve such a core goal: to provide capital accumulation for developing heavy industry and to furthest preclude the transfer of rural labor from diluting industrial capital. The combination of these systems brought about corresponding behavior choices among microeconomic subjects. For example, in the heat of agricultural cooperative movement and the implementation of people's commune system, "goofing off" became a common practice among rural laborers.

From the results of implementation, the combination of these systems did support the heavy industry first strategy, enabling China to form an independent and complete industrial system against the extreme unfavorable initial conditions. On the other side, however, this combination also accounted for imbalanced industrial structure, urban–rural duality, and low efficiency of overall national economy. Domestically, the constantly sluggish agriculture was even threatening the needs of urban and rural residents for basic means of subsistence. Internationally, the persistently low efficiency of national economy widened the economic gap between China and other countries, posing an austere challenge to its goal of sustainable development and common prosperity. Obviously, China's urban–rural duality did not solely originate from the reallocation of labor resources between urban and rural areas. It essentially stemmed from the combination of development strategy and constraints under the particular background and the series of economic system arrangements derived therefrom. The genetically complicated and diverse nature of China's urban–rural economic relationship makes it different from other developing nations and dual economy theory. Moreover, the performance of its urban–rural economic relationship also features a "double-edged sword". It leads to a change in both the previous development strategy and constraints, and this change is bound to bring along a dynamic adjustment of its economic system and urban–rural economic relationship.

Notes

1 Nicholas R. Lardy, *Economic Recovery and the 1st Five Year Plan,* cited from *The Cambridge History of China (Volume 14)*, MacFarquhar R. and Fairbank K. (eds). (1998). Beijing: China Social Science Press, p.131.

2 Dwight H. Perkins, *China's Economic Policy and Performance*, cited from The Cambridge History of China (*Volume* 15), MacFarquhar R. and Fairbank K. (eds). (1992). Beijing: China Social Science Press, p.493.
3 Nicholas R. Lardy, *Economic Recovery and the 1st Five Year Plan*, cited from *The Cambridge History of China (Volume 14)*, p.14.
4 Nicholas R. Lardy, *Economic Recovery and the 1st Five Year Plan*, cited from *The Cambridge History of China (Volume 14)*, p.143.
5 ibid, p.142.
6 Dwight H. Perkins, *China's Economic Policy and Performance*, cited from *The Cambridge History of China (Volume 15)*, p.493–495.

6 Imbalanced integration: urban–rural economic relationship at the beginning of reform and opening up

In the late 1970s, China formed an independent and complete industrial system by virtue of planned economy and separated urban–rural economic relationship. Yet the low efficiency of resource allocation and imbalanced urban–rural development were already challenging its economic and social sustainability. This practical background forced China to launch a market-oriented reform inside and to integrate into global economy outside. Accordingly, reform and opening up became the "keyword" labeling China's post-1978 economic reform. If we say that before reform and opening up, China had responded to the economic development of a socialist country in the sense of national industrialization, then after reform and opening up, China has been responding to the economic development of a large socialist country in the sense of high-speed economic development. They can be seen as two stages of the endeavor of China as a developing socialist country to realize its goal of sustainable development and common prosperity since 1949. As far as urban–rural economic relationship is concerned, compared with the early days of the PRC, in the late 1970s, the implementation performance of separated urban–rural economic relationship brought a change in the development strategy and constraints. Dynamic changes took place in both the heavy industry first strategy and the factor endowments. These changes intrinsically necessitated an adjustment of the economic system. That is, the government–market relationship had to catch up with the new development strategy choice. This set the scene for the generation and continuous advancement of market-oriented economic system transition. Over the course of market-oriented system reform emerged the intragovernmental and intramarket structural features and the associated economic system arrangements. These system arrangements worked on the economic choice and behavioral pattern of urban and rural residents, transforming the country's urban–rural economic relationship from separation toward integration. In the same way, under the conspiration of these economic systems, the integration of urban–rural economic relationship was also imbalanced in form and performance. Hence, it would be appropriate to use "imbalanced integration" to summarize China's urban–rural economic relationship at the beginning of reform and opening up.

6.1 China's development strategy and constraints at the beginning of reform and opening up

As a large developing country with socialist system, one precondition for China to realize its goal of sustainable development and common prosperity was to emancipate and develop productivity so as to form more abundant material and cultural products and greater economic strength. While the economic system arrangements in the planned economy era were intended in favor of the heavy industry first strategy, they did not match the goal of emancipating and developing social productivity. Instead, accompanying planned economy was the persistently low economic efficiency and imbalanced urban–rural structure. Separated urban–rural economic relationship was right the product of the economic system over that period. In the late 1970s, after an independent and complete industrial system had been established, China made a quick decision to adapt its national development strategy to the austere challenges facing national economy. Typically, these changes included shifting the focus of work of the Party and the country to socialist modernization, placing economic construction at the core of socialist modernization, listing emancipating and developing productivity as the central task of economic construction, and taking continuously increased economic growth rate as the main sign of emancipating and developing productivity. As such, after the late 1970s, China changed its heavy industry first strategy into an economic growth-oriented strategy. This adjustment of strategy set the scene for the subsequent changes in China's urban–rural economic relationship in the post-reform era.

The changes in China's national development strategy after the late 1970s can be observed and analyzed through a series of policy texts. Table 6.1 lists the policy statements of the central policymakers on national development strategies. The Third Plenary Session of the Eleventh CPC Central Committee held in 1978 raised the curtain on nationwide reform and opening up. The conference not only declared that the focus of work of the Party and the whole people should be shifted to socialist modernization. It also emphasized the importance of improving productivity to the four modernizations drive. This policy orientation was continued in the 1979 government work report, which underscored that our main task at present and for a long time to come was to carry out socialist modernization in a systematic and planned manner. In his speech at the Fifth Plenary Session of the Eleventh CPC Central Committee, Deng Xiaoping also reiterated that the Party's political line was to realize the four modernizations, and the main content of the four modernizations was to promote economic construction and develop national economy and social productivity.

If we say that these policy texts underlined the importance of economic construction and developing productivity, then the report to the Twelfth National Congress of the CPC in 1982 attached even greater importance to the speed of emancipating and developing productivity. Included in the

Table 6.1 Policy statements of China's national development strategies after 1978

Time SN	*Document name*	*Issued date*	*Core contents*
1978	Communique of the Third Plenary Session of the Eleventh Central Committee	Adopted on Dec 22, 1978, at the Third Plenary Session of the Eleventh Central Committee	We should shift the focus of work of the whole Party and the attention of the whole nation to the socialist modernization drive; to realize the four modernizations requires a substantial increase in productivity, which inevitably requires changing the relationship of production and superstructure that are not suited to the development of the productive forces, and changing all unsuitable management, activity and ideological modes and is therefore an extensive, profound revolution.
1979	Report on the Work of the Government 1979	Jun 18, 1979, at the second meeting of the Fifth National People's Congress	From this year on, we should shift the focus of national work to socialist modernization. This is a great historical change. At present and for a long period in the future, our main task is to carry out socialist modernization in a systematic and planned manner. Whether we can realize the four modernizations in the 20th century will determine the fate of our country and our nation.
1980	Adhere to the Party Line and Improve the Methods of Work	Speech of Comrade Deng Xiaping on Feb 29, 1980, at the third meeting of the Fifteenth Plenary Session of the Eleventh Central Committee	The political line of our Party at the present stage, in a nutshell, is to carry out the four modernizations wholeheartedly, which should not be interfered with at any time and must be carried on unswervingly and wholeheartedly. The Party's political line… in essence, is to carry out the four modernizations, most importantly, to carry out economic construction, develop national economy and develop socialist productive forces.
1982	Report at the Twelfth National People's CongressCreate A	Adopted on Sept 8, 1982, at the Twelfth National Congress of the CPC	The general task of the Party in the new historical period is to unite the people of all ethnic groups in the country, rely on ourselves, work hard, gradually realize the modernization of industry, agriculture,

(*Continued*)

Table 6.1 (Continued)

Time SN	*Document name*	*Issued date*	*Core contents*
	New Situation in All Fields of Socialist Modernization		national defence and science and technology, and build China into a highly civilized and highly democratic socialist country. Among the tasks of opening up a new situation in all respects, the primary task is to continue to push forward the economic construction of socialist modernization. Over the 20 years from 1981 to the end of the 20th century, the overall goal of China's economic construction is to, on the premise of continuously improving economic benefits, strive to quadruple the annual gross output value of industry and agriculture of the country, that is, from 71 billion yuan in 1980 to around 280 billion yuan in 2000.
1984	Communique of the Third Plenary Session of the Twelfth CPC Central Committee, the "Decision of the CPC Central Committee on Economic Restructuring"	Adopted on October 20, 1984, at the Third Plenary Session of the Twelfth CPC Central Committee.	The fundamental task of socialism is to develop social productive forces, that is, to make more and more social wealth emerge and constantly meet the people's growing material and cultural needs; socialism should eradicate poverty and we should not regard poverty as socialism; we should make up our minds and concentrate our efforts economic construction with the greatest perseverance, and realize the modernization of industry, agriculture, national defence and science and technology, which is the historical necessity and the aspiration of the people.
1987	Report to the Thirteenth National Congress of the CPC, "Advancing along the Socialist Road with Chinese Characteristics"	Adopted on December 25, 1987, at the Thirteenth National Congress of the CPC	The fundamental task of socialist society is to develop productive forces. At the primary stage, in order to get rid of poverty and backwardness, it is particularly important to make the development of productive forces the central task of all work. After the Third Plenary Session of the Eleventh Central Committee of the CPC, China's economic development strategy has been roughly divided into three steps. The first step is to double the GNP of 1980 and

r-

			solve the problem of food and clothing for the people. This task has been basically realized. The second step is to double the country's GNP by the end of the 20th century and raise the people's living standards to a well-off level. The third step is to raise the per capita GNP of the country to the level of moderately developed countries by the middle of the 21st century so that the people's lives will be relatively rich, and modernization will be basically realized. On this basis, we will continue to move on.
1992	Report to the Fourteenth National Congress of the CPC, "Accelerate the Pace of Reform, Opening up and Modernization, and Strive for Greater Victory in the Cause of Socialism with Chinese Characteristics"	Adopted on October 12, 1992, at the Fourteenth National Congress of the CPC	To push forward the great cause of socialism with Chinese characteristics in the 1990s, the most fundamental thing is to adhere to the Party's basic line, speed up reform and opening up, and concentrate on economic development. The growth rate of China's economy in the 1990s was originally set at an average annual GNP growth rate of 6 percent. Now, judging from the development of the international and domestic situation, it can be faster. According to preliminary estimates, it is possible to increase by 8–9 percent, and we should move towards this goal. On the basis of improving quality, optimizing structure, and increasing efficiency, we should try to realize such a development speed and, by the end of the 20th century, the overall quality and comprehensive national strength of China's national economy will step to a new level.

eport was the goal of doubling gross industrial and agricultural output value over the 1981–2000 period, which could not be realized without sustained high-speed economic growth. In 1987, the report to the Thirteenth National Congress of the CPC put forward a "three-step" strategic plan: to solve the problem of food and clothing, to become a moderately prosperous society, and to basically realize modernization. The precondition of this "three-step" strategy, however, was the sustained improvement of GNP and per capita GNP. In 1992, the report to the Fourteenth National Congress of the CPC not only emphasized the need to speed up reform and opening up and concentrate efforts on economic construction but also raised the previously established annual average GDP growth target from 6 percent to 8–9 percent. These policy statements clearly demonstrate that after 1978, emancipating and developing productivity, especially high-speed economic growth, became China's new strategic orientation. The heavy industry first strategy was beginning to give way to the economic growth-oriented strategy.

In the late 1970s, China began to shift its focus from the heavy industry to economic growth. This strategic redirection resulted from the conspiration of multiple factors described below.

First, the austere challenges facing domestic economy. While mandatory government plans and separated urban–rural economic relationship were intended in favor of the development of heavy industry, the persistently low efficiency of factor allocation had long restrained national economy, leaving the emancipation and development of social productivity under austere challenge. For example, from 1956 to 1977, average monetary wage of workers dropped from 601 yuan to 575 yuan; in 1978, the Engel coefficients of urban and rural residents were as high as 57.5 percent and 67.7 percent, respectively. From these figures, over that period, the consumption expenditure of urban and rural residents in China mainly revolved around food and other means of subsistence. The income level and livelihood improvement were very limited in the planned economy era.

Second, horizontal comparison with international economic development. China's development in the planned economy era should be examined in the global context. While China was implementing a heavy industry first strategy through planned economy, other countries were reporting sustained fast economic growth. The per capita GDP comparison between China and the world, the United States, and Japan from 1960 to 1977 described earlier can serve as a good evidence. The widening economic gap between China and major developed economies is a characteristic fact. This international comparison provided an external driver for China to change its development strategy.

Third, China's new understanding on socialist system. Before launching reform and opening up, China had used to equate socialist system to public ownership of means of production, planned economy, and distribution according to work based on the Soviet model and the Soviet Union's "Political Economy Textbook". Over time, its understanding on the nature of socialism deepened. It came to understand socialist system from the perspective of emancipating and developing productivity and achieving common prosperity. Both the Third Plenary Session of the Twelfth CPC Central Committee in 1984 and the Thirteenth National Congress of the CPC in 1987 underscored the importance of emancipating and developing productivity to socialist system. The Thirteenth National Congress even made systematic argumentation that China was in the primary stage of socialism. This enabled China to place emancipating and developing productivity at the core of its modernization drive based on the particular national conditions. It is well worth noting that, from the late 1980s to the early 1990s, the upheaval of Eastern Europe and the disintegration of the Soviet Union promoted China to place even more emphasis on emancipating and developing productivity and to regard the development speed and quality of productivity as an embodiment of its superiority over capitalist countries.

From this point of view, in the late 1970s, China's decision to adopt an economic growth-oriented strategy was driven by both the austere challenge of economic practice and a deepened ideological understanding. From any perspective, China's development strategy in the economic domain did change significantly. The previous heavy industry first strategy was being replaced by an economic growth-oriented strategy, which widely affected the subsequent economic system choice and urban–rural economic relationship.

Notably, in the late 1970s, the redirection of development strategy toward economic growth was also attributable to the previous separated urban–rural economic relationship. On the one hand, separated urban–rural economic relationship supported the country's pursuit to form an independent and complete industrial system, which was the prerequisite for achieving high-speed economic growth. With a weak industrial base or heavy dependence on overseas countries for industrial products, it would be unimaginable for China as a large developing country to achieve high-speed economic growth. On the other hand, the low efficiency of resource allocation and imbalanced urban–rural development resulted from separated urban–rural economic relationship also yelled for a new development strategy. In this sense, separated urban–rural economic relationship was both the implementation result of the heavy industry first strategy, and the starting point of the economic growth-oriented strategy.

In the late 1970s, the redirection of China's development strategy toward economic growth was also attributable to its preparedness for implementing such a strategy. In terms of ideological understanding, in May 1978, China launched a nationwide "discussion on the criterion of truth". The discussion reestablished the ideological line of freeing the mind and seeking truth from facts, thus providing a solid ideological basis for accelerating the socialist modernization drive. In terms of international relationship, the heavy industry first strategy greatly improved the country's national defence capacity. Compared with the early days of the PRC, in the late 1970s, China was faced with less external pressure. In particular, the establishment of formal diplomatic relationship between China and the United States greatly improved the international economic and political environment. In 1985, Deng Xiaoping made his famous remark about international environment: peace and development are the two major themes of the world today. This signifies that the external environment and international order had changed remarkably. China was able to promote economic construction and high-speed economic growth in a more relaxed international context. In terms of social practice, in the late 1970s, spontaneous economic reforms emerged in some parts of China. Microeconomic subjects began to explore ways of economic organization reform out of the desire to improve their own conditions. For example, in November 1978, Xiaogang villagers in Anhui province ventured to implement a "big contracting" move under a secret agreement. Later on, this way of agricultural management proved to have greatly emancipated agricultural productivity and improved agricultural production efficiency compared with the previous people's commune system. Spontaneous reform of rural economic system was immediately affirmed and more extensively promoted by the central policymakers. These reform attempts also provided practical basis for the China to redirect its development strategy toward economic growth.

One point remains. Now that the country's development strategy had shifted from heavy industry to economic growth, the implementation of the new strategy was confronted by a series of constraints. Typically, the long implementation of a heavy industry first strategy had already given rise to an economic operation mode and interest distribution pattern that matched the strategy. Particularly, under the conspiration of the series of urban–rural separating economic systems, rural residents had long been confined to economic activities inside the collective organization of people's communes. Their opportunity to carry out spontaneous economic activities and improve their living conditions was very remote. Their access to formal social security resources was also very limited. Compared with rural residents, urban residents were privileged in economic gains and access to social security resources. In that connection, the economic growth-oriented strategy marked a change to the original economic system, as well as an adjustment to the original interest distribution pattern. Furthermore, as China is a large developing country with socialist system, it was impossible to push forward the reform among all sectors at the same pace. Nor was it desirable to incur great surge in the economic and social system. Hence, a perfect implementation plan was needed. The strategy had to be implemented in a manner to ensure high-speed economic growth in a context of a calm overall social order. The concrete implementation plan of the economic growth-oriented strategy should start with the less volatile aspects and then spread to a broader spectrum. A progressive change from pilot scale to full scale and from local to global would be desirable.

More notably, in the late 1970s, China was still a country where farmers made up the majority of total population, rural employment made up the majority of total employment, and agriculture was badly compromised by the heavy industry first strategy. For example, in 1977, rural population and rural employment accounted for 82.45 percent and 76.82 percent of total population and total employment. With such a population and employment structure, it was extraordinary significance to improve rural social productivity. Associated with this population and employment structure was China's per capital output of grain of merely 297.7 kg/person in 1977, a figure even lower than the 306.8 kg/person at the end of the "three transformations" in 1956. The persistently low efficiency of agriculture can be detected by comparing per capita output of grain. Regarding this situation, in the opinions of the early 1980s Chinese leadership, the annual agricultural performance was unable to meet the need of the country itself, as a result of poor planning and management, and farmers' lack of motivation to work hard and play an economic role[1] (MacFarquhar R. & Fairbank K., 1992b). In a word, in the late 1970s, China was implementing the economic growth-oriented strategy against the background of extended planned economy, the dominance of farmers and rural employment, and the heavy obstruction on rural economy. Such a combination of development strategy and constraints was different from that in the early days of the PRC. It would inevitably affect the economic system choice and the adjustment of government–market relationship, consequently the behavioral choice of urban and rural microeconomic subjects and the result thereof.

6.2 China's economic system arrangements under the economic growth-oriented strategy

After 1978, China shifted its focus of economic development strategy from heavy industry to economic growth. However, this new strategy was faced with an unavoidable initial condition: the country's economic operation had long relied on a planned economy, and China was a country where farmers and rural employment made up the majority but agriculture had long been restrained. In such a context, the implementation of the new strategy was bound to prompt the adjustment of government–market relationship, namely, from traditional planned economy to market economy. The cut-in point for implementing the new strategy was to rely on management system reform to achieve economic growth in the agricultural sector first. From the perspective of strategic implementation, the following two features best describe the economic growth-oriented strategy implemented at the beginning of reform and opening up. First, in terms of the direction of system evolution. Along the mainline of adjusting government–market relationship, China emphasized delegating discretion to microeconomic subjects and giving full play to the role of market price. Accordingly, market-oriented became the basic trend of China's economic system evolution. Second, in terms of the domain of system evolution. China promoted economic system reform in the rural domain first, then triggered and accelerated changes in other sectors by virtue of demonstration effect, staring with rural reform and extending into other sectors. This shows the tactical nature of China's strategy implementation and its response to a steady economic and social order. Based on these two features, at the beginning of reform and opening up, China unfolded a series of system reforms concerning urban–rural economic relationship.

6.2.1 Economic organization in the rural sector: from people's commune to household contract responsibility system

From the perspective of institutional change, China's overall strategy of reform and opening up started with rural economy, and rural economic reform started with contracting production or work to households. Replacing people's communes with household contract responsibility system became the trigger of the entire market-oriented reform initiative. At the beginning of reform and opening up, China's decision to adopt rural economic system reform as the cut-in point for overall reform and opening was made under a profound practical background (Gao F., 2018e). The Third Plenary Session of the Eleventh CPC Central Committee emphasized the need to shift the focus of work of the Party to the socialist modernization drive. To achieve socialist modernization, the first thing to do was to solve the problem of food and clothing for urban and rural residents. The solution of this problem directly depended on the development level of rural economy, let alone the fact that the majority of the Chinese population and employment was concentrated in the rural sector at that time. Only with developed rural economy was it possible to promote reform and transition in other sectors. Rural economic reform is the basis and precondition form overall economic reform. Besides, under the prolonged planned economy, a public economy dominated by SOEs had already taken form in urban China. Different sectors of the urban economy crisscrossed with each other, involving multiple stakeholders. If reform started with urban economy and SOEs, it would very likely trigger a drastic shock. If it started with rural economy, the economic and social shock would be weaker. "The reform of household contract system, mainly in the form of contracting work to households, did not involve the vested interest of any group except that it may have conflicted with the traditional ideology, primarily the political requirement of adhering to collective ownership" (Cai F., 2008). As such, it becomes understandable why reform and opening up would start with rural economy and why the government remained tolerant toward farmers' spontaneous attempts to make reforms.

Now that an economic growth-oriented strategy was implemented, in the 1970s, in response to the persistent shortage of agricultural products in the planned economy era, the paramount goal of China's rural economic reform was to quickly enhance the production and supply capacity of agricultural products, so as to improve the production and living conditions of rural villagers who made up the majority of the country's population, and to prepare for its overall modernization drive and reform and opening up. In that connection, to enhance production and supply capacity of agricultural products is meant to emancipate and develop rural productivity. Yet the development of rural economy could not be achieved by tightening mandatory control over farmers or increasing financial investment in agriculture. The only way out was to update the management organization and improve the resource allocation efficiency inside the rural sector. This way, the institutional change was redirected from the previous communal system to contracting production and work to farmer households. In 1982, the first "No.1 Document" of the Central Committee in the course of socialist modernization explicitly noted that both contracting production to households and contracting work to households were production responsibility systems of socialist collective economy. Regarding the nature of production responsibility system, the document so declared, "All responsibility systems currently practiced, including small-section contract with fixed-rate remuneration, special contract responsibility with output-related remuneration, contracting work to laborers, contracting production to households or to production groups, and contracting work to households or groups, are production responsibility systems of socialist collective economy. Whatever the form, they should not be changed unless and until so requested by the masses." In addition, this "No.1 Document" also specifically underscored the superiority of production responsibility systems, obviously relative to the efficiency flaw of the previous people's commune system: "The application of the production contract system is able to properly coordinate between the collective interests and individual interests, and gives plays to the enthusiasm of both the collectives' unified management and laborers' independent management. Hence it is widely applied and warmly welcomed by the masses." On the basis of the post-1970s rural management mode reform, after the early 1980s, household responsibility system (HRS) immediately became a basic economic system for rural China.

In the planned economy era, as people's communes were an organizational form with both economic function and social administrative function, individual farmers or farmer households were highly dependent on this "administration-economy integrated organization". On the economic dimension, the core of people's commune system was the collective ownership of land factors, under which individual farmers engaged in economic activities on land collectively, and the collective results were shared among commune members in an equalitarian manner of distribution according to "workpoints". In contrast to people's communes, the core of HRS was to allow farmers to obtain the contractual right of land from the collective in units of households, together with the right to decide on the management of and profit from the land, without changing the collective ownership of the land. Having the right to decide on and profit from the contracted land signaled an expansion of farmers' economic rights, as well as a change in the way of agricultural production and distribution.

From the perspective of property right structure, the institutional change from people's communes to HRS reflected a subdivision and reallocation of land property rights (ownership and contractual right). From the perspective of income structure, this institutional change reflected the direct connection between rural resident income and their management efforts (delivering the mandatory amount of grain to the state, retaining the needed amount of grain for the collective, all that was left belonged to themselves). From the perspective of government–market relationship, this institutional change reflected the government's relaxation of control over land and agricultural management. Expanding farmers' autonomy over agricultural management and delegating discretion and benefits to farmers constituted the basic trend of adjusting government–market relationship at that time (Gao F., 2018e). In terms of practice, HRS succeeded in improving rural factor allocation and farmers' livelihood by adjusting government–market relationship, with almost no prejudice to the well-being of any group. Its shock to social order should have been modest, but its demonstrative inspiration to other sectors was marvelous. In terms of the concrete implementation of reform, as rural economic system reform started with the spontaneous initiation by villages in Anhui province, it was a bottom-up inductive institutional change. However, this institutional change immediately won support from the local and central governments and spread nationwide within a short time, as evidenced by the statements in the "No.1 Document" of the Central Committee in 1982 regarding the practice of contracting production and work to households. Obviously, rural economic system reform reflected the interaction between microeconomic subjects and the government authority in the market-oriented economic system transition.

Similar to the rapid advancement of the agricultural cooperative movement, the implementation of HRS in rural China was also completed within a very short time. Table 6.2 shows how HRS was implemented in rural China from 1983 to 1984. Backed up by the post-1978 practice of rural management system reform and the support from related central government policy documents, in the early 1980s, HRS quickly spread all over and replaced people's communes as the prevailing form of rural management. In 1983 and 1984, the share of teams implementing big contracting in the country's total rose to 97.9 percent and 99.0 percent. The share of households implementing big contracting in total number of farmer households soared from 94.2 percent and 96.6 percent, compared to that of non-HRS teams, which dropped to 27,000 and 2,000 in 1983 and 1984, respectively. This shows that within a very short time, HRS had already replaced people's communes, and the agricultural management of HRS was already in place in the vast majority of rural China. This quick replacement was associated with the policy support and navigation from the central government, but more importantly, it was the spontaneous choice of farmers as microeconomic subjects after economic comparison.

Table 6.2 HRS and administrative-economic organizations in rural China from 1983 to 1984

Description	*Unit*	*1983*	*1984*
I. Implementation of HRS			
1. Teams implementing HRS	$\times 10^4$	586.3	569.0
Incl. Teams implementing big contracting	$\times 10^4$	576.4	563.6
Share of teams implementing big contracting in national total	%	197.9	999.0
2 Households implementing HRS	$\times 10^4$	17985.4	18397.9
Incl. Households implementing big contracting	$\times 10^4$	17497.5	18145.5
Share of households implementing big contracting in total rural households	%	94.2	96.6
3 Teams not implementing HRS	$\times 10^4$	2.7	0.2
II. Rural Administrative-Economic Organizations			
1. Administration-economy separated		16,252	91,171
Village committee under township (town) government		1,99,657	9,26,439
People's commune of economic organization		11,866	28,218
2 Administration-economy not separated yet			
Rural people's commune		40,079	249
Production brigade		5,50,484	7,046
Production team	$\times 10^4$	457.5	12.8

Source: China *Statistical Yearbook 1984*, China S*tatistical Yearbook 1985*.

Associated with the rapid implementation of HRS were the profound change in the rural social administrative mode. As the previous people's communes were prominently characterized by administration-economy integration, when this form of organization was quickly replaced by HRS, the separation of government administration from economic management was but just an inevitable trend. Now that HRS had replaced the economic functions of people's communes, a new form and carrier was needed to play the social governance role of people's communes. On ground of this, it was imperative to reform the rural social organization and governance mode. On October 12, 1983, the CPC Central Committee and the State Council issued a "Notice on the Establishment of Township Government by Separating Government Administrative from Commune Management". It so read, "With the reform of rural economic system, the current rural system of integrating government administration with economic management is becoming very incompatible. The Constitution has stipulated that township governments must be established in rural areas and government administration must be separated from economic management". It also noted that administration-economy separation must have been completed and township governments must have been established by the end of 1984. As indicated by Table 6.2, in 1984, administration-economy separated township governments and villager committees were already making up the absolute majority. The administration-economy integrated functions of people's communes was also quickly replaced by a new mode of rural social administration. This created favorable conditions for improving the economic freedom of rural microeconomic subjects.

6.6.2 Ownership regime in the urban sector: from sole public ownership to multiple forms of ownership

The HRS-led rural economic system reform played a critical role in China's implementation of a broader range of economic growth-oriented strategy. On the one hand, rural economic system reform greatly raised the country's overall agricultural output level. Over 1978–1984, total grain output increased from 332 million tons to 407 million tons. Per capita grain production also increased from 316.6 kg/person to 390.3 kg/person. Rural productivity was emancipated and developed in the first place. This greatly solved the supply of means of subsistence for urban and rural residents and stabilized the social order of rural areas which made up the majority of population and employment, laying a more solid material and social basis for the modernization drive and reform and opening up. On the other hand, rural economic system reform also played a demonstrative and promotive role in the urban reform. With vivid examples and remarkable performances, it confirmed that economic system reform is able to release tremendous social productivity. The basic direction of economic system reform is to relax the government's excessive intervention in economy and rely on the spontaneous choice of microeconomic subjects to raise productivity. Against this background, urban economic system reform gradually took place. A variety of economic forms in urban China began to emerge and develop, which in turn provided the power engine for active commodity transaction and factor flow between urban and rural areas.

In the process of implementing the heavy industry first strategy, China's industrial economy was mainly concentrated in the urban sector. After socialist transformation of handicraft and capitalist industry and commerce, public ownership became the only form of ownership in the industrial sector. That is, SOEs and collective enterprises occupied all segments of industry, and their resource allocation, management, and product marketing were mainly reliant on mandatory government plans. To implement the economic growth-oriented strategy, one necessary step was to change this situation. At the beginning of reform and opening up, demonstrated and inspired by the reform of agricultural management mode, China had two reform options for its industrial sector. One was to implement reforms of a "stock" adjustment nature by introducing market mechanism. The other was to implement reforms of an "increment" extension nature by introducing other economic forms besides SOEs and collective enterprises. In the case of the former, as it involved the interests of the related administrative authorities, managers, and ordinary employees of enterprises, and even different viewpoints on the social nature of ownership reform, its economic and social shock could be enormous. In economic practice, although at the beginning of reform and opening up China had made attempts to streamline administration and delegate discretion in some of the public enterprises, these attempts were of pilot scale and the extent of reform was also confined to a small area. By comparison, the latter would be a better choice, since its core is to, without touching the existing public economy, develop individual economy, private economy, and foreign investment economy to form a multiownership economic pattern with public ownership at the core. This way, the productivity in the industrial sector could be emancipated and development by optimizing resource allocation efficiency.

In this sense, "double-track" would best describe China's industrial reform at the beginning of reform and opening up. While retaining the previous public economy, nonpublic economic forces would be introduced to spur marketization. Let us take a look at individual economy as an example. In August 1980, the CPC Central Committee forwarded a document titled "Better Improving the Work of Urban and Rural Labor and Employment". For purpose of solving the country's employment problem, the document emphasized the need to strongly encourage and support the development of urban individual economy. It pointed out that steps must be taken to foster individual economy since it is an indispensable supplement to the socialist public economy and will play a positive role for a long time to come. On July 7, 1981, the State Council issued the "Several Policy Provisions on Urban Non-agricultural Individual Economy", which elaborated on the nature and management scope of urban individual economy, and the way to support and protect the development of urban individual economy. It so explained, "To the extent that state-operated economy and collective economy remain dominant, restoring and developing urban non-agricultural individual economy is of great significance to developing production, activating market, and meeting the needs of people's life". Under this adjustment of reform idea and policy orientation, urban China began to see more forms of ownership. More and more other forms of economy appeared as an addition to public economy, a phenomenon remarkably different from the "large, public, pure" image of the previous urban economy.

Table 6.3 compares China's gross industrial output value and ownership structure in the industrial sector from 1978 to 1994. Within the investigation period, at the then-current price, China's gross industrial output value increased from 423.7 billion yuan to 7690.946 billion yuan. Accompanying the continued increase of gross output value was the remarkable change in the ownership structure inside industry. Particularly, the gross industrial output value of both 1978 and 1979 totally came from public economy, repeating the story of the post-1958 era when public economy was the only form of ownership in urban China. After 1979, however, the share of public economy began to drop continuously. From 1979 to 1994, this figure dropped from 100 percent to 74.94 percent. Accordingly, the shares of individual industry and other forms of economy continued to rise. In 1994, these figures rose to 11.51 percent and 13.55 percent, respectively. Together,

Table 6.3 China's gross industrial output value and its structure from 1978 to 1994

Year	*Total industrial output value ($\times 10^8$ yuan)*	*Share of state-owned industry (%)*	*Share of collective industry (%)*	*Urban–rural individual industry (%)*	*Other economic types of industry (%)*
1978	4237.00	77.63	22.37		
1979	4681.30	78.47	21.53		
1980	5154.26	75.97	23.54	0.02	0.48
1981	5399.78	74.76	24.62	0.04	0.58
1982	5811.22	74.44	24.82	0.06	0.68
1983	6460.44	73.36	25.74	0.12	0.78
1984	7617.30	69.09	29.71	0.19	1.01
1985	9716.47	64.86	32.08	1.85	1.21
1986	11194.26	62.27	33.51	2.76	1.46
1987	13812.99	59.73	34.62	3.64	2.02
1988	18224.58	56.80	36.15	4.34	2.72
1989	22017.06	56.06	35.69	4.80	3.44
1990	23924.36	54.60	35.62	5.39	4.38
1991	28248.01	52.94	35.70	5.70	5.66
1992	37065.71	48.09	38.04	6.76	7.11
1993	52691.99	43.13	38.36	8.35	10.16
1994	76909.46	34.07	40.87	11.51	13.55

Source: *China Statistical Yearbook 1991*, p394, 396; *China Statistical Yearbook 1995*, p377.

they already accounted for 25.06 percent. Inside public economy, the share of state-owned industry dropped year by year, while that of collective industry kept rising. Over 1978–1994, the former dropped from 77.63 percent to 34.07 percent, while the latter rose from 22.37 percent to 40.87 percent.

Compared with individual and other types of enterprises, public economy was more greatly affected by mandatory government plans. Compared with collective industrial enterprises, SOEs were also more heavily affected by mandatory government plans. These structural changes in the industrial sector demonstrate that, at the beginning of reform and opening up, China's economic form did begin to switch from unitary public ownership to multiownership. While the industrial sector was undergoing ownership diversification, microeconomic subjects in the urban sector were also enjoying greater economic autonomy. This created an internal pull for product transaction and factor flow between urban and rural areas, since only by frequent product transaction and factor flow was it possible to meet the additional demand of the various ownership forms of enterprises for agricultural products and labor factors.

6.2.4 *Circulation of agricultural products: from state monopoly of the purchase and marketing to market-oriented circulation*

Now that HRS was being implemented in the rural sector and the ownership structure of urban industry was beginning to diversify, it became imperative to adjust the previous unified purchase and marketing of agricultural products cored around rigid government control. In other words, the product docking regime between urban and rural areas had to change along with the inter-sectoral economic system reform. Such an adjustment was necessary because of three important characteristic facts. First, unified purchase and marketing of agricultural products was a derivative of the heavy industry first strategy. Although it was conducive to enhancing the state's intervention in urban–rural product and factor allocation, as it greatly restrained the spontaneous economic activities of urban and rural microeconomic subjects, it had negatively affected the efficiency of urban–rural product and factor allocation over time. In order to redirect the national development strategy from heavy industry to economic growth, it was also necessary to adjust the practice of unified purchase and marketing of agricultural products that matched the previous strategy. Second, unified purchase and marketing of agricultural products were the institutional arrangement in a context of undersupply of agricultural products. Now the implementation of HRS had greatly increased the country's agricultural productivity, and the supply capacity of agricultural products had been largely enhanced in a short time. This eliminated the product supply conditions in favor of unified purchase and marketing of agricultural products. Third, at the beginning of reform and opening up, the economic organization mode in both urban and rural China had changed remarkably. HRS had replaced the previous administration-economy integrated people's communes. Farmers were engaging in agricultural management activities on household basis. This greatly weakened the government's control over rural economy and the supply of agricultural products. In the meantime, the diversification of industrial ownership had also greatly reduced the government's control over the demand of the urban sector for agricultural products. Nonpublic enterprises in the industrial sector also had the objective need to be spontaneously connected to the agricultural sector. In this context, it was very hard for unified purchase and marketing of agricultural products to further sustain at the operational level. These three facts signify that, after the start of reform and opening up, especially after the early 1980s, China's reform on unified purchase and marketing of agricultural products was not only necessary but also feasible.

In response to this reality, after the start of reform and opening up in 1978, China continuously scaled down the coverage of unified purchase and marketing of agricultural products, reduced the government's right to price agricultural products, and gradually switched toward a market-oriented agricultural product circulation regime. From the perspective of reform strategy, China's switch toward a market-oriented agricultural product circulation system did not happen immediately at the inception of reform and opening up. Instead, in the early 1980, there was a "double-track" interval when both unified purchase and marketing and market regulation were practiced. Starting with the "double-track", China managed to switch from unified purchase and marketing to a market-oriented agricultural product circulation system by scaling up the coverage of market regulation. This transition pathway can be evidenced by related policy statements. On September 28, 1979, the Fourth Plenary Session of the Eleventh CPC Central Committee adopted the "Decisions on Several Issues concerning the Acceleration of Agricultural Development", which read: "The planned purchase price of grain will be increased by 20 percent in 1979 from the time summer grain becomes marketable. For the part beyond the purchase limit, an additional 50 percent will be charged. The purchase prices of cotton, oil plants, sugar crops, animal products, aquatic products, and wood products will also be gradually raised as appropriate." The document also noted that the grain purchase target should be reduced to relieve the burden on farmers and promote agricultural development. In 1982, the "No.1 Document" of the Central Committee, the "Summary of the National Rural Work Conference", specifically addressed the agricultural product circulation system: "Agricultural economy is an important part of national economy. We must implement planned economy supplemented by market regulation"; and "As to the purchase prices of products beyond the minimum limits are allowed to be fluctuated to a given extent according to market demand and supply condition".

In 1983, the "No.1 Document" of the Central Committee, the "Several Issues concerning Rural Economic Policy", explicitly emphasized the need to adjust the purchase and supply policy of agricultural and sideline products, suggesting that the reform on unified purchase and marketing of agricultural products was officially put on the agenda. The document so stated: "From now on, we will continue to implement unified purchase and fixed-state purchase of the few important agricultural products concerning national economy and the people's livelihood; for products beyond farmers' unified purchase and fixed-state purchase tasks (including grain but excluding cotton) or not listed for unified purchase and fixed-state purchase, we should allow them to be operated through multiple channels". In 1984, the "No.1 Document" of the Central Committee, the "Notice on Rural Work in 1984", further emphasized: "We must adhere to the principle of planned economy supplemented by market regulation, adhere to the policy of joint efforts among the state, collectives, and individuals, continue with the reform of rural commercial system, and further invigorate the rural economy"; and "We must continue to reduce the variety and quantity subject to unified purchase and fixed-state purchase along with the development of production and improvement of market supply". In the same year, the "Report on Doing a Good Job in Rural Commodity Circulation" forwarded by the State Council on August 7 explicitly stated: "We must continue to reduce the variety subject to unified purchase and fixed-state purchase, and reduce the variety of class I and II agricultural and sideline products currently under the management of the ministry of commerce system from 21 to 12". Finally, in 1985, China issued the "No.1 Document" titled "Ten Policies on Further Invigorating

Table 6.4 China's total purchase of agricultural and sideline products and its structure from 1978 to 1984 (Unit: 100 million yuan)

Description	*1978*	*1980*	*1981*	*1982*	*1983*	*1984*
Total Purchase of Agricultural & Sideline Products	557.9	842.2	955.0	1083.0	1265.0	1440.0
On basis of sector						
1 Commercial departments	459.9	677.0	764.7	855.6	980.6	1070.3
2 Industry & others	66.9	96.2	100.9	116.6	151.4	200.3
3 By non-agricultural residents from farmers	31.1	69.0	89.4	100.8	133.0	169.4
On basis of purchase price—Absolute Amount						
1 List price	472.4	542.2	555.6	622.2	607.0	487.8
2 Additional price for excess pur-	44.2	151.0	200.0	225.0	355.0	483.9
chase	10.2	80.0	110.0	125.0	170.0	207.0
3 Negotiated price	31.1	69.0	89.4	110.8	133.0	261.3
4 Market price						
—Share in Total Purchase						
1 List price	84.7	64.4	58.2	57.5	48.0	33.9
2 Additional price for excess pur-	7.9	17.9	20.9	20.8	28.1	33.6
chase	1.8	9.5	11.5	11.5	13.4	14.4
3 Negotiated price	5.6	8.2	9.4	10.2	10.5	18.1
4 Market price						

Source: *China Statistical Yearbook 1985*, p479.

Rural Economy", which read: "From this year on, except some particular varieties, the state will no longer assign tasks of planned purchase and state fixed purchase of agricultural products to farmers. Instead, contracted purchase or market purchase will be implemented according to different situations". This signifies that at the policy level, China was declaring the abolition of unified purchase and marketing of agricultural products that had been practiced for three decades. After the "double-track" interval, from the mid-1980s, China began to step into a stage of accelerated marketization of agricultural products.

Table 6.4 compares China's total purchase of agricultural and sideline products and its structure from 1978 to 1984. From these changes, we can see that unified purchase and marketing of agricultural products was fading out, while the degree of market regulation of agricultural product circulation was increasing constantly. From 1978 to 1984, total purchase of agricultural and sideline products soared from 55.79 billion yuan to 144 billion yuan. By sector, total purchase by non-agricultural residents from farmers increased from 3.11 billion yuan to 16.94 billion yuan; its share in national total rose from 5.57 percent to 11.76 percent. Given that this figure had persistently stood at 4–5 percent in the planned economy era, the increase in the 1980s should signify that urban and rural residents had much greater freedom to trade agricultural products spontaneously according to market mechanism. In terms of purchase price, over that period, total purchase at the state-set prices changed from 47.24 billion yuan to 48.78 billion yuan; its share in national total dropped steeply from 84.7 percent to 33.9 percent. In contrast, total purchase at market prices increased from 3.11 billion yuan to 26.13 billion yuan; its share in national total rose from 5.6 percent to 18.1 percent. The share of purchase at negotiated prices also grew from 1.8 percent to 14.4 percent. From the late 1970s to the mid-1980s, continued reduction of government control and remarkable growth of spontaneous market transaction did take place in the circulation of agricultural products. Unified purchase and marketing of agricultural products was gradually replaced by a market-based circulation system. This institutional change implies that, around the transaction and allocation of agricultural products, the government was no longer able to rely on unified purchase and marketing to maintain rigid control. Urban and rural residents had much more freedom to make their own choice and decisions.

6.2.4 Rural labor employment under household registration: from unitary to diverse

In the planned economy era, in order to implement the heavy industry first strategy against the particular mix of constraints, China's urban and rural household registration was actually serving two important functions. One was employment control—restrict rural labor from flowing into the urban industrial sector—so as to accord with the dense capital input and modest job creation of heavy industry. The other was social security resource allocation—to provide social security and other public goods for agricultural and nonagricultural population separately—so as to distribute the limited public goods available through a binary social security supply scheme. At the beginning of reform and opening up, household registration was still serving the function of social security resource allocation, but its employment control function was weakening enormously. With full-scale implementation of HRS, the supply capacity of agricultural products in rural China was commonly enhanced. The needs of urban and rural residents—especially rural residents—for grain (and other agricultural and sideline products) were substantially satisfied. For rural residents, enhanced supply capacity of agricultural products signifies that rural labor productivity was enhanced, and the rural sector dominated by grain production was able to release more labor outside. In a context where the constraint of household registration was still prominent, rural labor would first find a job in rural nonagricultural industries. This set the scene for the sudden rise of township enterprises in the 1980s, and spurred the sudden rise of a nonagricultural employment form of rural labor of "away from land but not away from home". With the relaxation of household registration control, rural labor began cross-regional and cross-sectoral flow as rural migrant workers, creating another form of nonagricultural employment of "away from both land and home". Notably, the diversification of industrial ownership in urban China at the beginning of reform and opening up also offered job opportunities for the nonagricultural of rural labor. That is, the labor demand of the urban sector also provided conditions for relaxing the employment control function of household registration.

Inside rural China, the relaxation of the employment control function of household registration was closely connected with the disintegration of people's communes. Now that people's communes were being replaced by HRS, rural residents were granted not only the autonomy to manage their contracted land but also the freedom to allocate their own labor factors. Even though urban and rural household registration still existed, once the collective management mode of people's communes was canceled and farmers became less dependent on this administration economy integrated organization, it was always possible for individual farmers to allocate labor among different industries inside the rural sector. After reform and opening up, the product shortage resulted from planned economy also provided a market pull for the development of nonagricultural industries (especially industrial sectors) inside rural China. That is, marketing was hardly a problem for products supplied by rural commune and brigade-run enterprises (i.e., township enterprises).

Besides, in view of the increase of agricultural products and the employment pressure for the vast population in rural China, the government also provided more freedom for the development of rural commune and brigade-run enterprises or township enterprises. For example, on September 28, 1979, the Fourth Plenary Session of the Eleventh CPC Central Committee adopted the "Decisions on Several Issues concerning the Acceleration of Agricultural Development", which explicitly stated: "It is important to make a great development in commune and brigade enterprises and gradually increase the share of their income in the three-level economic income of the communes. All agricultural and sideline products should gradually be processed by commune and brigade enterprises as long as they are economically proper and suitable to be processed in rural areas". The "Several Provisions on the Implementation of the Guidelines for National Economic Adjustment by Commune and Brigade Enterprises promulgated by the State Council on May 4, 1981, also noted stated: "Commune and brigade-run enterprises have achieved remarkable results in utilizing and developing local resources, arranging rural surplus labor, consolidating and strengthening collective economy and increasing the income of commune members. It has played a positive role in gradually changing the economic structure of rural areas and agriculture, supporting agricultural development and fostering the construction of small market towns. It has also made contribution to developing commodity production, invigorating the market, expanding export, and increasing state revenue. Commune and brigade-run enterprises have become an important part of rural economy and are in line with the overall development direction of rural economy.

After that, from 1982 to 1985, all "No.1 Documents" of the Central Committee reiterated the important role of commune and brigade-run enterprises in national economy. For example, in 1984, the "No.1 Document" of the Central Committee titled "Notice on Rural Work in 1984" so noted: "Collectives and farmers are encouraged to pool funds and jointly start up various enterprises under the principle of voluntary participation and mutual benefit"; and that "Existing commune and brigade enterprises are important pillar of rural economy; some of them are indispensable aids to large-scale urban industries". On March 1 of the same year, the CPC Central Committee and the State Council forwarded the "Report on Creating a New Situation for Commune and Brigade Enterprises", which agreed to officially rename commune and brigade-run enterprises "township enterprises", and set forth policy measures for promoting the development of township enterprises, pushing China's township enterprises up into a high-speed growth era. The spring-up of township enterprises effectively solved the needs of rural labor for carrying out nonagricultural production locally, thus providing an important channel for weakening the employment control function of household registration. From a deeper and broader perspective, "this rural industrialization tide and boom of township enterprises in China also eventually detonated in the late 1980s and early 1990s the first industrial revolution that had long been awaited and expected in the modern history of China" (Wen Y., 2016).

Table 6.5 shows the development of township enterprises in China from 1978 to 1994. After reform and opening up, China saw very rapid growth in both the number and gross output value of township enterprises. In 1994, these figures had soared to 24.945 million and 42588.85 billion yuan. The "spring-up" of township enterprises marked a major characteristic fact of national economy at that time. When township enterprises were booming, their job absorption capacity was also quickly strengthened. In 1978, the number of employees in township enterprises was 28.2656 million; in 1994, it already jumped to 120.182 million. Township enterprises became the primary form of employment for rural labor in local nonagricultural industries. This not only altered the employment structure of rural labor but also created more job options for rural labor to choose from. In the planned economy era, rural labor was highly locked inside people's communes and engaged in the production of the primary industry in the form of collective management. Individual farmers had almost no freedom to choose their production unit, industrial type, or production mode. Now with the "spring-up" of township enterprises, rural labor had the discretion to choose to work either in the rural primary industry or in rural township enterprises (primarily secondary industry). They had great more job options to choose from. As indicated by Table 6.5, from 1978 to 1994, the share of employees in township enterprises in total rural employment rose constantly from 9.23 percent to 24.63 percent. Over the same period, the share of employment in primary industry in total rural employment dropped from 92.43 percent to

Table 6.5 Development of township enterprises in rural China from 1978 to 1994

Year	*Qty of township enterprises (×10⁴)*	*Output value of township enterprises (× =10⁸ yuan)*	*Qty of on-the-job employees in township enterprises (×10⁴)*	*Qty of rural employment (×10⁴)*	*Qty of employment in first industry (×10⁴)*	*Qty of employees in township enterprises/Qty of rural employment (%)*	*Qty of employment in first industry/Qty of rural employment (%)*
1978	152.42	–	2826.56	30,638	28,318	9.23	92.43
1979	148.04	548.41	2909.34	31,025	28,634	9.38	92.29
1980	142.46	656.90	2999.67	31,836	29,122	9.42	91.48
1981	133.75	745.30	2969.56	32,672	29,777	9.09	91.14
1982	136.17	853.08	3112.91	33,867	30,859	9.19	91.12
1983	134.64	1016.83	3234.64	34,690	31,151	9.32	89.80
1984	606.52	1709.89	5208.11	35,968	30, 868	14.48	85.82
1985	1222.45	2728.39	6979.03	37,065	31,130	18.83	83.99
1986	1515.30	3540.87	7937.14	37,900	31,254	20.89	82.27
1987	1750.24	4764.26	8805.18	39,000	31,663	22.58	81.19
1988	1888.16	6495.6	9545.45	40,067	32,249	23.82	80.49
1989	1868.63	7428.38	9366.78	40,939	33,225	22.88	81.16
1990	1850.40	8461.64	9264.75	47,708	38,914	19.42	81.57
1991	1908.90	11621.70	9609.10	48,026	39,098	20.01	81.41
1992	2079.20	17975.40	10581.10	48,291	38,699	21.91	80.14
1993	2452.90	31540.7	12345.3	48,546	37,680	25.43	77.62
1994	2494.50	42588.5	12018.2	48,802	36,628	24.63	75.05

Source: The number of township enterprises, gross output value and employees figures are sourced from *China Statistical Yearbook 1991*, p377-378 and *China Statistical Yearbook 1995, p363-365*. The rural employment and employment in the first industry figures are sourced from *China Compendium of Statistics*, p7.

75.05 percent. This reflects the important influence of township enterprises to the employment structure of rural labor. Now that township enterprises were booming, the employment control function of urban and rural household registration began to weaken naturally.

When HRS was implemented in rural areas, the employment control function of household registration began to weaken, since farmers were free to pick up a job in a variety of segments inside the rural sector. More than that, as time went on, between the urban and rural sectors, the same story also happened to the employment control function of household registration. That is because ownership in urban industries became diversified. Even though public economy still maintained a fairly rigid threshold for employment, nonpublic economy was yelling for more sufficient and flexible labor flow between urban and rural areas. After the mid-1990s, with greatly relieved economic shortage compared with at the beginning of reform and opening up, rural township enterprises began to receive adjustment. Their ability to absorb rural labor began to decline. More importantly, in October 1992, the Fourteenth National Congress of the CPC explicitly declared that the goal of China's economic system reform was to establish a socialist market economy. In November 1993, the Third Plenary Session of the Fourteenth CPC Central Committee adopted the "Decision of the CPC Central Committee on Several Issues concerning the Establishment of a Socialist Market Economic System". This marked a new stage for China's reform and modernization drive when industrialization and urbanization began to gain speed. It also triggered the need for labor factors to flow between urban and rural areas and among industries and regions according to market price signals. In response to this new stage and new requirement of reform and opening up, it was just imperative to further relax the employment control function of urban and rural household registration.

From the trajectory of institutional change, to accord with the practical needs above, China also made adjustments to its rigorous household registration rules. For example, in October 1984, the State Council promulgated the "Notice on Farmers' Entering and Settling down in Market Towns", which emphasized: "Governments at all levels must actively support farmers with business ability and technical expertise to operate industries and businesses in market towns". Farmers were free to settle down in market towns with their own grain provisions and would enjoy equal rights and perform equal obligations as market town residents. This signifies that the previous rigid urban and rural household registration was beginning to relax. In July 1985, the Ministry of Public Security issued the "Interim Provisions on the Management of Urban Temporary Resident Population", which underlined the need to improve the management system of urban temporary population and establish a registration and management system of market town temporary population. This signifies that urban–rural population flow was becoming more frequent, and the management system of urban temporary population was beginning to refine. In November 1993, the

Third Plenary Session of the Fourteenth CPC Central Committee adopted the "Decision of the CPC Central Committee on Several Issues concerning the Establishment of a Socialist Market Economic System", which raised the idea of promoting household registration reform by category as to "gradually reform the household registration system of small towns, allow farmers to work or run business in small towns, develop rural tertiary industry, and foster the transfer of rural surplus labor". In June 1997, the State Council approved and forwarded the "Notice of the Ministry of Public Security on the Pilot Scheme for the Reform of the Household Registration System in Small Towns and Opinions on Improving the Rural Household Registration Management System", which stipulated that qualified rural population who were already working and living in small towns were allowed to apply for an urban permanent household register in the small towns. In February 2012, the General Office of the State Council issued the "Notice on Actively and Steadily Promoting the Reform of Household Registration Management System". In this document, the state expressed its determination to firmly promote the household registration management system reform, and bring into effect the policy of relaxing the qualification for settling down in small and medium-sized cities and small towns; to guide the orderly transfer of nonagricultural industries and rural population into small and medium-sized cities and organic towns, and gradually equalize the basic public services between urban and rural areas.

From these policy texts, after reform and opening up, China has been constantly reforming urban and rural household registration which was originally intended in favor of the heavy industry first strategy. The employment control function of household registration has been relaxing step and by step, and in a tactic manner. Along the evolutionary roadmap of non-agricultural industries inside rural areas–market towns–small towns–small and medium-sized cities, the household registration reform between urban and rural China gradually deepened. Rural laborer were free to work in different levels of urban nonagricultural sectors. The employment control effect of household registration on rural labor was largely weakened. In existing statistical data, outside migrant workers are defined as farmers working outside the towns or townships local to their place of household registration, which largely depicts the picture of rural laborers working in the urban sector. According to statistics, in 2008, the number of migrant workers totaled 113.9 million. In 2017, it rocketed to an astonishing 180.2 million. As is also verified by figures presented earlier, after reform and opening up, especially since the mid-1990s, urbanization has been speeding up whether by employment or population data. They all confirm that labor flow and reallocation between urban and areas have been enhanced.

In summary, since 1978, China has promoted an economic growth-oriented strategy against multiple constraints. This combination of development strategy and constraints has given rise to corresponding economic systems. For a large developing country that used to implement planned economy, to achieve sustainable economic growth, China has to resort to improving resource allocation efficiency. To improve the resource allocation efficiency, enterprises and residents must be made the subject of resource allocation. Price, demand and supply, and competition must replace mandatory government plans as the primary instrument of resource allocation. In short, market-oriented reform is an endogenous product of fulfilling the economic growth-oriented strategy. To ensure effective implementation of this strategy, the previous government–market relationship has to be changed. Out of this practical requirement, China initiated market-oriented system transition and further opening to the outside world. Accordingly, its government–market relationship also changed from the previous highly government-controlled economy to the delegation of discretion and benefits to microeconomic subjects—enterprises and residents. The resource allocation role of market mechanism was also continuously enhanced and highlighted. At the government–market relationship level, compared with the previous heavy industry era, great changes have taken place in the institutional arrangements since reform and opening up. These changes were very substantially and clearly manifested on the dimension of urban–rural economic relationship.

As far as urban–rural economic relationship is concerned, following the start of reform and opening up in 1978, people's communes in rural China were quickly replaced by HRS. The unitary public ownership in urban industries began to diversify. Unified purchase and marketing of agricultural products gradually switched toward market-oriented reform in the circulation system. The employment control function of urban and rural household registration also weakened remarkably. These changes signal that urban and rural areas were becoming integrated rather than separated. Dynamic evolution was taking place in China's urban–rural economic relationship as a result of a series of economic system changes. Since reform and opening up, China's microeconomic subjects have gained much more freedom to allocate products and factors spontaneously according to market price signals. Urban and rural residents, especially rural residents, have enjoyed unprecedented autonomy to allocate products and factors by themselves and could carry out product transaction and factor flow spontaneously according to market price signals. As a result, the capacity of product and factor reallocation between urban and rural areas has been greatly improved. The scope, size, and frequency of economic intercourse between urban and rural areas have all been enormously enhanced. The urban and rural sectors are already economically integrated across a greater scope and at a higher level, contrasting strongly to the previous separation in the planned economy era due to rigorous government control.

Notably, following the start of reform and opening up, the implementation of HRS enabled farmers to obtain the right to contract land and to decide on, and profit from, agricultural management on the contracted land, under the premise of collective ownership of the land. Farmers became more economically autonomous. The diversification of ownership in urban industries provided the demand pull for the autonomous transaction of rural products and the substantial flow of rural factor. The market-oriented reform of agricultural product circulation created institutional conditions for the spontaneous product transaction between urban and rural areas. The reform of urban and rural household registration led to the gradual relaxation of its employment control function, creating a solid basis for rural labor to allocate employment spontaneously both inside rural areas and between urban and rural areas. Undoubtedly, during the implementation of the economic growth-oriented strategy, the government's control over both products and factors between urban and rural areas was largely relaxed. Urban and rural products (especially agricultural products) and factors (especially rural labor factors) could be allocated by microeconomic subjects in a greater scope. This signifies that the marketization degree of both products and factors between urban and rural areas were improving. Market-oriented reform was also a logic mainline of the dynamics of urban-rural economic relationship. It changed the previous urban–rural separation into an integration with substantial flow and reallocation of products and factors.

6.3 Imbalanced integration of government–market relationship and urban–rural economic relationship

Compared with the early days of the PRC, in the late 1970s, China saw remarkable changes in both its development strategy and constraints. Particularly, its development focus was shifted from heavy industry to economic growth. The changes of development strategy, constraints, and the way of their combination objectively called for an adjustment to the country's economic system, since a new economic system was needed to solve the "tension" between development strategy and constraints in the new era. The mainline of this adjustment was to cause a change in government–market relationship. That is, governments at different levels (especially the central government) had to relax their economic control over various microeconomic subjects, so that market prices would accurately reflect the relative scarcity of commodities and factors; microeconomic subjects—enterprises and residents—would have greater autonomy over resource allocation; and the strategic goal of high-speed economic growth would be fulfilled with improved resource allocation efficiency. Despite twists and turns in ideological understanding and concrete policies, one thing is very clear. That is, after reform and opening up, marketization has served as the basic trend of China' economic system transition. Governments at different levels have been striving to delegating discretion and benefits to microeconomic subjects and relying on market price to optimize resource allocation.

From the perspective of policy texts, China has had different statements of its economic operation system in different periods. The intrinsic logic of these statements is to perform economic reform around government–market relationship and continuously highlight the role of market in optimizing resource allocation over time. In September 1982, the report to the Twelfth National Congress of the CPC stressed that China should correctly carry through the principle of planned economy supplemented by market economy. In 1983, the report to the Thirteenth National Congress of the CPC stated that socialist economy is a planned commodity economy based on public ownership. Overall, the new economic operation mechanism should be one in which "the state regulates the market and the market guides the enterprises". In November 1992, the Fourteenth National Congress of the CPC clearly pointed out that the goal of the country's economic system reform was to establish a socialist market economic system, which should cause the market to play a fundamental role in resource allocation under the macro control of socialist countries. In November 2013, the Third Plenary Session of the Eighteenth CPC Central Committee adopted the "Decision of the CPC Central Committee on Several Major Issues concerning Comprehensively Deepening Reform", which noted that the core of economic system reform was to leverage the government–market relationship so as to make the market play a decisive role in the allocation of resources and give better play to the role of the government. From planned economy supplemented by market economy to planned commodity economy and to socialist market economy, the evolution reflects China's continuous exploration and gradual finalization of its economic operation mechanism. From regarding market as an aid to resource allocation to recognizing its fundamental role in allocation and to affirming its decisive role in resource allocation, this ideological change reflects the continuous highlighting and emphasis of the importance of market in economic operation mechanism. Undoubtedly, the year 1978 marked China's entry into a market-oriented economic system transition. As urban–rural economic relationship was set in this background of institutional transition, it inevitably was affected by this transition and the characteristics thereof.

After reform and opening up, under an economic growth-oriented strategy, China's economic system reform unfolded in the direction of relaxing government control and highlighting market forces. On the dimension of urban–rural economic relationship, the reform can be described along the following line. First, HRS replaced people's communes, thus giving farmers greater autonomy to carry out agricultural management by themselves. Second, multiownership in urban areas replaced unitary public ownership, thus creating the driving force for the free allocation of commodities and factors between urban and rural areas. Third, market circulation of agricultural products replaced unified purchase and marketing, providing institutional conditions for the free transaction and flexible allocation of agricultural products between urban and rural areas. Fourth, the employment control function of household registration was greatly weakened, laying a solid foundation for the reallocation of labor both inside rural areas and between urban and rural areas. As a result of these changes, China's urban–rural economic relationship began to transform from the previous separation toward integration. Microeconomic subjects, especially rural residents, are free to carry out frequent product and factor transaction out of their own economic interest. The urban and rural sectors are more tightly connected due to this economic intercourse.

The evolution of China's urban–rural economic relationship has taken place in the particular context of socialist system and a large developing country. In a country with enormous population and geographical sizes like China, economic system transition is bound to be a system project involving multiple factors and lasting an extended time. In other words, the economic system transition underlying the evolution of urban–rural economic relationship has its own complexities. Economic system transition revolves around the adjustment of government–market relationship, whereas this adjustment is inevitably subject to the structural features of government and market themselves. In the planned economy era when high power centralization at the central government level was underscored, intragovernmental and intramarket structural problems were unimportant. Yet market-oriented reform has led to economic disparities among different segments of the market and the different levels of the government. In the face of market-oriented economic system transition, the way, as well as the outcome, of reaction is also different among different market subjects and different levels of governments. Economic system transition, in reality, is also accompanied by amplified intragovernmental and intramarket structural features. In China's market-oriented economic system transition, government and market cannot be simply assumed as highly homogenized inside themselves. Instead, research on China's urban–rural economic relationship has to account for the relationship between different parts inside government and inside market. This relationship will affect the way and process of the evolution of government–market relationship, thus affecting the behavioral choice of urban and rural microeconomic subjects and the results of thereof. Accordingly, urban–rural economic relationship will transform to integration, but with an imbalanced or a structural nature. In fact, imbalanced integration of urban–rural economic relationship took place immediately after reform and opening up. This imbalanced integration is the objective outcome of China's endeavor to cause an adjustment to government–market relationship.

Inside the government, China has always been a populous and geographically large country characterized by grand unity in history. Grand unity implies the need to emphasize the central government's control over economy, society, politics, military, and diplomacy. A large country implies the existence of significant disparities in the economic and social development among different regions and different groups. Hence, it is necessary to give relatively flexible dispositions to different regions over economic and social affairs. One question arises: how shall the country deal with the boundary and relationship between central control and local disposition? If excessive economic and social disposition were given to individual regions, central control would be easily weakened. Conversely, if the central department overstressed its control, it would compromise the flexible disposition and governance autonomy of individual regions. As such, over the long history of China, there has always existed an interaction between central jurisdiction and local governance. How to effectively deal with the central–local relationship has remained an important proposition throughout the long social evolution of China.

After 1949, China became a large developing country with socialist system. Socialist system implies that China is carrying out socialist construction under the leadership of the CPC. A large developing country implies that China has a population and geographical size rarely found in other parts of the world, and there are economic and social development gaps among different regions and groups. After the founding of the PRC, under the leadership of the PRC, China gradually formed a five-level administrative system inside the government: central, provincial (autonomous region, municipality), municipal (region, autonomous prefecture, league), county (district, banner, county-level city), and township (town, subdistrict). The first level is the central government, and all the remaining four levels can be seen as local governments. From the economics point of view, as all government institutions, regardless of the level, seek to maximize their interests against the constraints, although the central government and local governments are collectively called "government", it is uncertain whether their ways of behavior are synchronous. In view of this, on April 25, 1956, late chairman Mao Zedong made a report titled "On the Ten Major Relationships" at the expanded meeting of the Political Bureau of the Central Committee. In this report, he listed the central–local government relationship as one of the ten major relationships to be leveraged by China in promoting socialist construction. It also stated: "We should, under the premise of consolidating the unified leadership of the Central Committee, expand the discretion of local governments to a modest degree and give them more independence so that they will do more things. This will be more helpful for our endeavor to build a powerful socialist country. Given that our country is so large, so populous, and so complicated, it will be much better to have both central and local initiatives than to have only one initiative". Theoretically, as local governments are faced with particular constraints and goal functions, whether they have precisely the same goal pursuit as the central government depends on whether the economic system is designed to achieve the incentive compatibility between them, namely, whether local governments are able to attain the goal function of the central government while pursuing their own goals. If an incentive compatibility is not achieved, there may exist a remarkable structural feature among different levels of governments, which will inevitably affect the operation and development performance of the economic system.

From the founding of the PRC up to reform and opening up, while China was implementing the heavy industry first strategy, the economic relationship between the central government and local governments was characterized by the high power centralization over resource allocation at the central level. Local governments mainly served as an executor of the mandatory plans of the central government. The fiscal arrangements among different levels of governments also had the typical feature of unified collection and allocation. After reform and opening up, the economic regime between the central and local governments gradually broke the traditional regime. The central government delegating discretion to local governments and local governments possessing greater economic autonomy became an important content of market-oriented system transition. In February 1980, the State Council issued the "Notice on the Implementation of the Financial Management System of 'Dividing Revenue and Expenditure and Contracting by Levels'". The basic content of the notice was the scope of revenue and expenditure between central and local fiscal administrations will be clearly identified according to the subordination identified by the economic management system. Fiscal revenue will be divided into three categories: central fixed revenue, local fixed revenue, and central–local adjusted shared revenue. Fiscal expenditure will be divided according to the subordination of enterprises and institutions into the two categories: regular expenditure and special expenditure allocated by the central government. Based on these categories, the payout proportion, proportion of adjusted revenue, or central quota subsidies will be determined taking the amount of revenue and expenditure executed in fiscal year 1979 as the base value and will be contracted hierarchically and remain unchanged for five years. This means that the fiscal management at the central and local levels was beginning to "cook separately". Contracting by levels greatly motivated local governments' enthusiasm to promote economic growth. In March 1985, the State Council promulgated the "Provisions on the Implementation of the Financial Management System of 'Dividing Taxes, Verifying Revenues and Expenditures, and Contracting by Levels'." According to the tax setup and enterprise subordination after the tax-for-profits reform, this policy divided fiscal revenue into three categories: central fixed revenue, local fixed revenue, and central–local shared revenue. The fiscal expenditure remained roughly the same as the "revenue classification and contracting by levels" practiced at local levels in 1980. Afterwards, in addition to the original fiscal system, China also implemented a range of other forms of fiscal contracting, such as revenue incremental contracting, total amount sharing, total amount sharing plus proportionate sharing of increased revenue, payout amount incremental contracting, quota payout, and quota subsidies. Essentially, these methods were still a continuation of the "cook separately" mechanism. Their purpose and ultimate goal were both to fully motivate the enthusiasm of local governments to develop economy in the economic system reform.

Replacing unified collection and allocation with the "cook separately" fiscal system greatly motivated local governments' enthusiasm for economic growth at the beginning of reform and opening up. Yet, the system implementation also resulted in a prominent structural feature among different levels of governments. That is, the economical practice of local governments disagreed with the strategic goal of the central government. Typically, fiscal contracting intensified local governments' intervention in local economic activities and aggravated the economic separation among different regions. In the meantime, this system institutional arrangement also largely locked in the central fiscal revenue. Moreover, due to information asymmetry, regions with more abundant fiscal revenue and obligated to pay out revenue to the central government would very likely to make self choice, namely, to apply economic means to maximize their own revenue and minimize their revenue payout to the central government. This would lead to relative reduction of the central fiscal revenue and gradual weakening of the state's macroeconomic control. Now that China was striving to establish socialist market economic system, the central government was feeling the pressure of reduced access to, and control over, resources. As illustrated by Figure 6.1, since the start of reform and opening up in 1978, over the period of fiscal contracting, both the share of fiscal revenue in GDP and the share of central fiscal revenue in total fiscal revenue declined remarkably. From 1978 to 1993, the share of fiscal revenue in GDP dropped from 30.78 percent to 12.19 percent that of the central fiscal revenue in total fiscal revenue dropped from 40.51 percent to 22.02 percent.

In this context, China urgently needed to reform the previous fiscal contracting practice so as to adapt it to the reform goal of establishing socialist market economic system. In November 1993, the Third Plenary Session of the Fourteenth CPC Central Committee adopted the "Decision of the CPC Central Committee on Several Issues concerning the Establishment

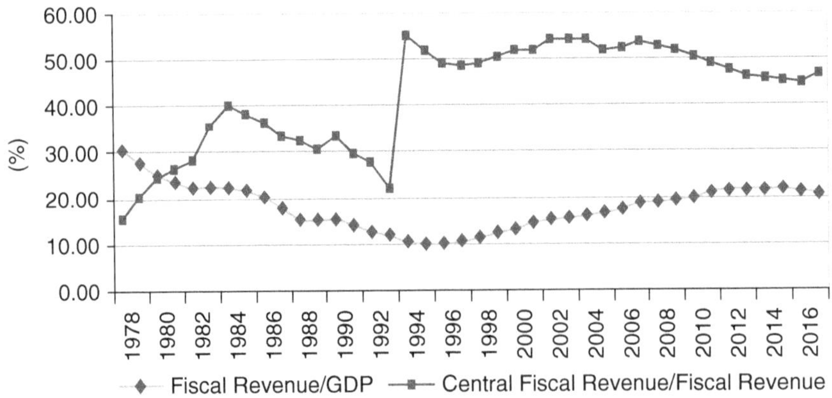

Figure 6.1 China's share of fiscal revenue and share of central fiscal revenue from 1978 to 2017.

Source: CEIC Data.

of a Socialist Market Economic System", which explicitly noted that socialist market system should have a sound macro control system, and China should actively promote fiscal and revenue system reform to change the current local fiscal contracting system into a tax sharing fiscal system based on a proper division between central and local administrative discretion and establish a central taxation system and a local taxation system. In December of the same year, the State Council issued the "Decision on the Implementation of Tax Sharing Fiscal Management System", which announced that starting from January 1, 1994, actions would be taken to reform the current local fiscal contracting system, and implement a tax sharing fiscal management system for provinces, autonomous regions, municipalities, and cities separately listed in the state plan. The tax sharing reform was intended to correctly leverage the distribution relationship between the central government and local governments, motivate the enthusiasm of both of them, and foster the proper growth of state fiscal revenue. The concrete implementation scheme was to, by combining administrative power with financial power, divide taxes into central taxes, local taxes, and central–local shared taxes, establish a central taxation system and a local taxation system, respectively, set up a central taxation organ and a local taxation organ to collect and manage tax resources separately, and ensure the scientific ratification of the amount of local revenue and expenditure, and gradually put into practice a relatively standard tax return and transfer payment system from central finance to local administrations. From the goal and implementation scheme above, tax sharing represented an important revolution to the previous local fiscal contracting practice. It marked a change in the economic system and way of association between the central government and local governments.

The tax sharing reform launched in 1994 was an important intergovernmental economic system revolution after reform and opening up. It greatly affected the intergovernmental economic relationship and overall economic development and made intergovernmental structure an important part of the adjustment of government–market relationship.

First of all, an important foothold of the tax sharing reform was to increase the share of central fiscal revenue, thus enhancing the state's macroeconomic control. In that connection, as illustrated by Figure 6.1, in 1994 when tax sharing was first implemented, the share of central fiscal revenue in total fiscal revenue quickly rose to 55.70 percent, and it stood above 45 percent all years afterwards. This implies that the central government's financial access and macroeconomic control had been greatly enhanced.

Second, under the tax sharing regime, business tax and local corporate income tax were listed as local fixed revenue, while value added tax and resource tax were included as central–local shared revenue, which greatly motivated local governments' enthusiasm to promote local economic growth. After 1994, all parts of China were reporting high-speed economic growth. This, at the local level, provided such a push for China to create the world "miracle" of growth, that some author even deemed local government behavior as an important cut-in point for explaining China's "ultranormal" economic growth. To him, a three-dimensional market system comprising a strategic central government, competitive local governments, and competitive businesses systems provided the power engine for the sustained high-speed economic growth in post-reform China (Shi Z.F., 2013).

Next, under tax sharing reform, the central government had the jurisdiction over local governments in personnel appointment. Local governments worked to spur economic growth out of the desire to increase local fiscal revenue or to obtain administrative promotion. Different local governments began to compete around economic growth and other targets. The behavior of local governments can be summarized as economic incentive (in pursuit of increasing local fiscal revenue) or administrative incentive (in pursuit of promoting administrative level). According to Xu C.G. (2011) and our political economy analytical framework described earlier in this book, a unique inter-governmental "regionally decentralized authoritarianism" took form in China.

Last, while local governments promoted local economic growth in the context of tax sharing reform, as the central government possessed more financial resources, the division of administrative power or financial power between the central and local governments became more and more ambiguous. Local governments were increasingly embarrassed by the disagreement between financial power and administrative power. For example, in 2017, the share of local governments' fiscal revenue at their respective levels in total fiscal revenue was 53.0 percent, but the share of their fiscal expenditure in total fiscal revenue was 85.3 percent. Besides highlighting the importance of the central government's fiscal transfer payment system to the national fiscal system, this regime also implies the possibility for local governments to offset their fiscal revenue-expenditure gap by intervening in the factor market (e.g., urban–rural land market) or delaying the supply of public goods (e.g., urban–rural equalization of basic public goods) so as to maximize their goal under the fiscal system in effect.

Logically speaking, the tax sharing reform strengthened the state's economic control through fiscal system reform and aroused local governments' motive for economic growth, which is very crucial for China to achieve sustainable high-speed GDP growth. However, the implementation of this reform also stimulated the economic behavioral choice of local governments. Under the economic growth-oriented strategy, local governments were faced with an economic growth-oriented performance assessment, propelling them to "race for growth" in an administrative yardstick competition. With unmatched financial and administrative powers, they tried to attain their goals by intervening in the factor market or affecting the supply of public goods. The intergovernmental structural feature began to show up in a new form and is destined to affect the evolution of government–market relationship and the change of urban–rural economic relationship.

Inside the market, since reform and opening up, while structural problems were emerging among different levels of governments, a remarkable structural feature also sprouted inside the market—another important concept of China's economic system arrangements. In 1978, China launched a market-oriented economic system transition, but this transition was not promoted homogeneously or synchronously at the same pace among all fields. Market is a system concept containing multiple components and can be classified by different criteria. For example, by scope of transaction, it can be classified as regional market, national market, or global market; by object of transaction, it can be classified as product market and factor market; by way of transaction, it can be classified as stock market and futures market. Regarding the object of transaction, after 1978, China's market-oriented reform started with the product segment first. Accordingly, the marketization of products was faster. A typical example is the "price breakthrough" campaign in the mid- and late 1980s. The year 1992 also witnessed largely liberalized state control over the purchase prices of agricultural products and the prices of most industrial products. In contrast, reform in the field of core productive factors (especially land, capital, and important energy sources) was not as fast. Governments at different levels still maintained considerable intervention in, and influence over, the allocation of these core factors. Given that in overall national economy, these core factors are usually in the upstream position of the production chain, China's market-oriented reform actually consisted of an "upstream-guided market expansion", as described earlier in this book. That is, there existed a deviation of transition process among the upstream and downstream markets.

The deviation of marketization among different market segments since reform and opening up can be described by marketization index. In addition to performances of economic freedom and its components discussed earlier in this book, Wang X.L., Fan G. & Yu J.W. (2017) also presented the distribution of marketization index at provincial level and national level. As indicated by Table 6.6, from 2008 to 2014, China's marketization index went up spirally, yet the performances in different parts were largely different. In particular, within the investigation period, the development degree of the product market remained higher than that of the factor market all the time. For example, in 2014, the development degree of the product market scored 7.77, while that of the factor market only scored 5.93. This demonstrates that governments at different levels were still maintaining greater intervention in finance, human resources, and technology. China's factor marketization is still stagnant compared with product marketization. Upstream-guided market expansion has also resulted in a heterogeneity and structural feature inside the market.

There are many reasons that explain why an upstream-guided market expansion should emerge inside the market when China is implementing market-oriented economic system transition. First of all, socialist system implies that China is carrying out modernization under the leadership of the

Table 6.6 China's national average score of marketization index and its changes from 2008 to 2014

Description	*2008*	*2010*	*2012*	*2014*
Total Score	5.48	5.44	5.98	6.56
1. Government–market relationship	6.83	6.20	5.40	5.62
1a Share of economic resources allocated by market	8.39	7.78	7.27	7.06
1b Reduce government intervention in businesses	4.28	3.60	2.31	3.52
1c Reduce government volume	7.82	7.23	6.63	6.29
2. Development of non-state-owned economy	5.40	5.77	6.54	7.33
2a Share of non-state-owned economy in primary operating income of industrial enterprises	5.47	5.83	6.16	6.66
2b Share of non-state-owned economy in total investment in fixed assets	6.38	6.16	7.06	7.28
2c Share of employment of non-state-owned economy in total urban employment	4.35	7.06	6.41	8.03
3. Development degree of product market	7.59	7.59	7.59	7.77
3a Extent to which price is determined by market	7.29	7.29	7.29	7.29
3b Reduce local protection in commodity market	7.90	7.90	7.90	8.26
4. Development degree of factor market	4.01	3.83	5.04	5.93
4a Marketization of financial industry	5.39	5.78	6.78	7.37
4b Human resources supply condition	5.25	3.87	5.79	6.91
4c Marketization of technical achievements	1.37	1.84	2.57	3.50
5. Development & legal institutional environment for market intermediaries	3.58	3.83	5.32	6.13
5a Development of market intermediaries	4.12	4.33	4.80	5.44
5b Legal environment for safeguarding market	4.75	2.86	4.71	6.11
5d IPR protection	1.86	4.30	6.45	6.85

Source: Wang X.L., Fian G. & Yu J. W. (2017).

CPC. The unitary state regime also forces China to highlight macro control in national economic development. In other words, China's economic system transition is effected by maintaining the stability of overall order. Pushing forward system reform at the same pace among all fields would induce great shock to the economic and social order. Second, China is a country with enormous population and geographical sizes. As development disparities tend to exist among different regions and groups, economic system reform has to account for the bearing capacity of different parts and adopt differentiated system reform schemes according to the intergroup and interregional disparities. Next, for purpose of maintaining a steady order and in view of the characteristics of a major economy, China's market-oriented system transition is bound to take a progressive form, namely, to start with segments less exposed to the shock effect and then gradually spread to full scale. As such, "market-oriented" and "progressive" depict the two aspects of China's economic system reform since the 1970s. As a result, compared with the factor market (especially the market of core factors like land, capital, and important energy sources), market-oriented reform in the product segment was less influential to overall national economy. In contrast, the large-amplitude marketization of land, capital, and important energy sources can make a difference to many downstream industries. As reform in these fields involves a broader range of industries, the shock must be even more prominent. In a large developing country like China, the suppliers of these core factors are generally regarded as the key departments concerning overall national security and the lifelines of national economy, it is therefore a fairly rational and pragmatic choice for market-oriented system reform to start in the product segment. Finally, when implementing the heavy industry first strategy, China has already formed an allocation regime or management mechanism for the upstream core factors in the economic domain—land ownership with collective nature and important banking institution with public nature, as well as SOEs and government management organizations controlling the supply of main energy sources. They also provide preconditions for the government to adjust the operation of national economy by controlling the upstream industries. As such, in pursuit of economic growth, it is both necessary and feasible for China to implement an upstream-guided market expansion inside the market.

Upstream-guided market expansion stemmed from a progressive system reform. Accompanying this marketization mode is the intramarket structural feature, which denotes a "heterogeneity" among different components of the market. From the perspective of institutional complementarity, upstream-guided market expansion is nested in, and complementary to, regionally decentralized authoritarianism. That is, local governments, with unmatched financial and administrative powers, need to resort to intervening in some market segments or affecting government–market relationship to improve local economic growth and fiscal revenue, so that they can remain competitive in the growth-oriented performance assessment race. Upstream-guided market expansion offers just the right conditions for fulfilling their pursuit. After all, governments at different levels are still able to pose an influence to the allocation of upstream core factors in the overall marketization process. Once it is shaped, this intragovernmental structural feature will definitely affect the behavioral choice of different levels of governments and of microeconomic subjects. For example, local governments will try to use their right to allocate core factors like land, capital, and important energy sources to affect the marketization process. The rural land expropriation by many local governments and the resulted "land finance" is an evident example of this practice. In the meantime, this intramarket structural features will also make a difference to urban–rural economic relationship. It affects the option of urban and rural microeconomic subjects to factor allocation, as well as the distribution of factor allocation gains between urban and rural areas, leading to fluctuations in urban–rural income gap and consumption gap across different periods of time.

In conclusion, since the founding of the PRC, China has had differentiated development strategies and constrains over different periods of time, which have resulted in different economic operation systems and government–market relationships. These systems have accounted for corresponding urban–rural economic relationship and its dynamic change. In the early days of the PRC, China implemented a heavy industry first strategy. The combination of this strategy with constraints gave rise to a highly centralized economic system between government and market, as well as people's communes, unitary public ownership, unified purchase and marketing of agricultural products, and household registration on the dimension of urban–rural economic relationship. After reform and opening up, China shifted its development focus from heavy industry to economic growth. The combination of this new strategy and constraints led to a market-oriented system transition that propels the government to delegate discretion and benefits and give play to the market's role in resource allocation. On the dimension of urban–rural economic relationship, this institutional change has given rise to HRS, ownership diversification, market circulation of agricultural products, and the weakening of the employment control function of household registration. Overall, China's urban–rural economic relationship is beginning to transform from the previous separation toward integration. Nevertheless, in China's market-oriented economic system transition, the adjustment of government–market relationship has been accompanied by changes inside the government and the market themselves. That is, the intragovernmental and intramarket structural features are growing more and more prominent. Two typically examples of these features are regionally decentralized authoritarianism inside the government and upstream-guided market expansion inside the market. The combination of regionally decentralized authoritarianism and upstream-guided market expansion has provided the adjustment of government–market relationship with its own characteristics. While marketization is the basic trend of economic system transition, the process and way of transforming toward a market economy has been quite Chine. This will naturally incur a change in urban–rural economic relationship and make it an overall integration but with imbalance in practice.

Note

1 Dwight H. Perkins, *China's Economic Policy and Performance*, reprinted from *The Cambridge History of China (Volume 15)*, MacFarquhar R. and Fairbank K. (eds). (1992). China Social Science Press, p.493–495.

7 Manifestation and forming mechanism of imbalanced integration of urban–rural economic relationship

Since 1978, while implementing the economic growth-oriented strategy, China has promoted the adjustment of government–market relationship at the economic level. Market-oriented reform immediately became the basic trend of the country's economic system transition. Reform at home and further opening to the outside became two evolutionary lines of national economy. Over the 40 years of reform and opening up, profound changes have also taken place in the economic system arrangements associated with urban–rural economic relationship. In particular, China's overall economic system transition started with transforming the rural management mode, namely, replacing people's commune with HRS. This transformation has not only changed the resource allocation and production efficiency inside rural areas but also altered the way of product transaction and factor docking between urban and rural areas. Under these institutional changes, China's urban–rural economic relationship has unprecedentedly integrated. The formerly separated urban–rural economic relationship began to transform toward an integrated one. However, market-oriented economic system transition has created a unique intergovernmental and intermarket structure, which has not only labeled China's market-oriented system transition with its own characteristics but also conferred the integration of its urban–rural economic relationship with an imbalanced nature. In fact, imbalanced integration marks the basic feature of China's urban–rural economic relationship under the economic growth-oriented strategy. In a sense, understanding the "hows and whys" of the imbalanced integration constitutes the core content of analyzing China's urban–rural economic relationship at the current stage. As such, people need to answer a series of questions at the academic level: how shall we define the imbalanced integration of China's urban–rural economic relationship since reform and opening up? What characterize this imbalanced integration? How is this imbalanced integration relevant to China's unique economic system arrangements? Logically speaking, only by clarifying and gasping the forming mechanism of the imbalanced integration of urban–rural economic relationship can people obtain a clearer picture of the current urban–rural economic relationship and find ideas and policy measures for subsequent improvement of urban–rural economic relationship.

7.1 Implication and manifestation of imbalanced integration of urban–rural economic relationship

7.1.1 Implication of imbalance urban–rural economic relationship

Urban–rural economic relationship is a complex concept for any developing nation, as it covers a range of dimensions—factor allocation, factor allocation efficiency, and urban–rural income and consumption gap. In a large developing country like China, the formation of urban–rural economic relationship is tightly bound with the development strategy, constraints, and the way they are combined. Its connotation is also complex, systemic, and multifaceted. In the prereform heavy industry era, China's urban–rural economic relationship was a separated one. In the post-reform economic growth era, it began to transform toward integration, but the degree of integration was quite different across different fields and different periods. Hence, China's post-reform urban–rural economic relationship can be described as an imbalanced integration. Here, "imbalanced integration" is a special form of China's urban–rural economic relationship over the course of evolution. It means that against the background of market-oriented economic system transition, urban and rural microeconomic subjects began to play the leading role in product and factor allocation. Market prices also began to function as the primary mechanism of product and factor allocation. Spontaneous economic intercourse between urban and rural areas has been enhanced both in size and frequency. Despite these changes, the concrete pathway of the adjustment of government–market relationship, especially the intragovernmental and intramarket structural feature, has also resulted in a special form of behavioral choice among urban and rural microeconomic subjects, consequently the unique characteristic of the transformation of urban–rural duality. This special form and unique characteristic has led to an imbalance of urban–rural integration across different fields and a discontinuity across different periods. Now the economic and social effects of this imbalance and discontinuity have prompted further adjustment of urban–rural economic relationship.

The above definition of imbalanced integration of urban–rural economic relationship has very rich economic implications, as reflected in the following five aspects:

1. This urban–rural economic relationship took form in the particular period of economic system transition. Imbalanced urban–rural integration of urban–rural economic relationship did not appear until reform and opening up in 1978. It differs from the previous separated urban–rural economic relationship, but is not up to the criterion of a

high-profile, high-level integration. Instead, it is a transitional from the previous separation toward a high-profile, high-level integration;

2. This urban–rural economic relationship stemmed from the complex, systemic, and multifaceted nature of urban–rural economic relationship itself. It accounts for the differentiated manifestation among different aspects of China's urban–rural economic relationship in the economic system transition era—factor allocation, factor allocation efficiency, and urban–rural income and consumption gap. The out-sync across different dimensions or inconsistency across different periods represents an important feature of the change of urban–rural economic relationship;
3. In transforming toward integration, urban–rural economic relationship also shows an imbalance, as is reflected in multiple aspects. Apart from factor allocation, factor allocation efficiency, and urban–rural income and consumption gap, the imbalance of integration is also reflected in the institutional arrangements that propels the evolution of urban–rural economic relationship. Economic system arrangements are tightly bound with the integration and imbalance of urban–rural economic relationship. As the latter is the byproduct of the choice and implementation of the former, the former should be utilized to give a systemic and in-depth explanation of the latter;
4. This urban–rural economic relationship took form when China worked to promote the adjustment of government–market relationship at the economic level in pursuit of economic growth which aimed to highlight the role of market in resource allocation. However, after reform and opening up, intragovernmental and intramarket structural features have grown more and more evident. Particular economic system arrangements have also been shaped around the structures. This has made China's economic system transition unique and led to an imbalanced integration of urban–rural economic relationship in terms of institutional arrangements and concrete performances. In this sense, imbalanced integration implies that China's urban–rural economic relationship is a "unique story", rather than a "universal story" that can be observed in the economic development of other nations;
5. Imbalanced integration of urban–rural economic relationship inevitably brings about a diverse array of economic results. Evaluation of imbalanced integration from different perspectives often results in distinctly different conclusions. Judgments regarding China's current urban–rural duality will easily vary among different people. In the temporal sense, compared with the previous separation, imbalanced integration of urban–rural economic relationship contributes positively to economic development. But compared with the subsequent high-profile, high-level integration, there still is much room for improvement. After all, China's mission to transform urban–rural duality has not been fully attained. To improve and perfect its urban–rural economic relationship in future,

China should not stay on the surface of this relationship, but should response straight to the underlying economic system factors.

7.1.2 Manifestation of imbalanced integration of urban–rural economic relationship

Compared with the planned economy era, since reform and opening up, imbalanced integration of urban–rural economic relationship has been first of all reflected by the gradual integration between the urban and rural sectors from the previous separation. This integration is reflected in the following three aspects:

1. Along with the implementation of HRS, farmers gradually became the economic subjects in rural areas on household basis. Along with the ownership diversification in urban industrial sector and the reform of SOEs, enterprises gradually became microeconomic subjects with greater economic autonomy. Whether in rural or urban China, microeconomic subjects all gained greater economic autonomy and were largely freed from the dependence on direct state economic control. Under this situation, urban and rural microeconomic subjects needed market mechanism to carry out product transaction—rural residents provide agricultural products to the urban sector, and the urban sector provide means of production and living, including industrial products and service products, to rural residents. Microeconomic subjects could trade products spontaneously according to market price signals instead of mandatory government plans. The urban and rural sectors were also tightly bound together due to product transaction. Enhanced spontaneity in product transaction suggests increased integration between urban and rural areas. As indicated by Table 7.1, from 1985 to 2012, per capita sale of agricultural and sideline products kept going up, with an increase from 123.49 kg to 529.75 kg for grain, from 4.13 kg to 22.98 kg for cotton, from 53.76 kg to 164.13 kg for vegetable, and from 16.27 kg to 30.74 kg for pork;

These changes reveal continuously improved rural households' supply capacity of agricultural products, as well as continuously enhanced commercialization and marketization degree of agricultural products. The former concerns the emancipation and development of rural productivity and the latter the economic system transition between urban and rural areas. Accompanying the enhanced commercialization and marketization of agricultural products was the increased size, scope, and frequency of product transaction between urban and rural areas.

2. Urban and rural microeconomic subjects need both product transaction and the reallocation of productive factors. Now that the economic

Table 7.1 China's per capita sale of agricultural and sideline products by rural households from 1985 to 2012

Year	*Grain*	*Cotton*	*Vegetable*	*Fruit*	*Pork*	*Egg*	*Milk*	*Aquatic product*
1985	123.49	4.13	53.76	6.78	16.27	2.21	1.02	1.74
1990	180.24	4.31	65.07	13.17	17.84	1.89	1.68	2.05
1995	179.20	4.31	79.96	24.28	24.17	3.54	1.90	2.94
2000	264.74	5.59	132.07	46.43	30.19	6.32	2.67	5.82
2001	268.04	7.05	132.94	48.21	30.86	5.96	3.65	6.53
2002	281.15	6.94	143.77	49.06	32.30	6.54	4.87	8.04
2003	294.35	16.77	147.58	48.83	29.49	7.06	7.29	7.47
2004	287.25	19.19	151.57	57.48	26.62	6.39	7.67	7.28
2005	375.79	22.06	167.93	61.62	32.19	10.52	11.27	8.54
2006	394.64	23.79	172.98	59.49	34.44	10.96	13.27	8.94
2007	394.06	24.92	169.99	66.79	27.55	10.69	14.62	9.85
2008	44.45	20.68	170.83	64.94	25.36	12.84	15.05	10.26
2009	482.93	23.56	170.84	72.78	31.70	12.91	12.66	10.72
2010	460.46	14.71	168.26	65.93	33.10	12.87	11.27	11.13
2011	481.45	19.91	174.52	60.82	29.76	9.15	10.42	9.14
2012	529.75	22.98	164.13	71.04	30.74	10.13	9.32	9.71

Source: *Chinese Statistical Yearbook* 2013.

growth-oriented strategy was implemented, to change the mode of factor allocation, the only way was to improve the fluidity of factors. To improve the efficiency of factor allocation, the only way was to change the mode of factor allocation. Only by improving the efficiency of factor allocation was it possible to realize sustainable high-speed economic growth. After 1978, along with market-oriented economic system reform, China's urban and rural microeconomic subjects are able to circulate and reallocate factors spontaneously according to market price signals. In particular, with emancipated rural productivity and relaxed urban and rural household registration, similar to the duality transformation process revealed by the Lewis-Fei-Ranic model, the nonagricultural transfer of rural labor also emerged in post-reform China. Now that the nonagricultural transfer of rural labor has become an important characteristic fact in the process of economic development, this factor flow has also tied the urban and rural sectors more tightly together. Notably, while rural labor always flows into sectors where their economic evaluation is higher, the divergence in labor evaluation is associated with the distribution of capital factors across different sectors. Hence, the nonagricultural transfer of rural labor manifests a change in the way capital and labor are combined in the urban and rural sectors. It is essentially not a matter of reallocation of individual labor factors and its economic returns;

To describe the economic integration between urban and rural areas caused by labor reallocation, the important economic term "rural migrant worker"

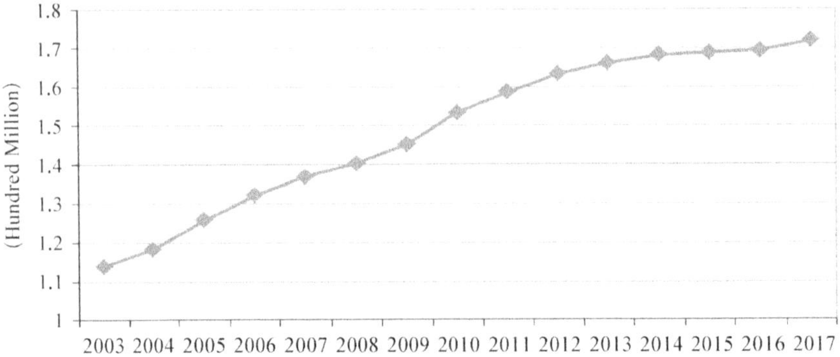

Figure 7.1 Number of outside migrant workers in China from 2003 to 2017.

Source: CEIC Data.

should be an ideal example. According to whether the employment is in the towns or villages of the place of household registration, China's rural migrant workers can be grouped as local rural migrant workers and outside rural migrant workers. The latter can serve as a metric of how labor factors are circulated and allocated between urban and rural areas. Figure 7.1 compares the number of outside rural migrant workers in China from 2003 to 2017. Over this period, the number of outside rural migrant workers increased from 114 million to 172 million. Outside rural migrant workers have already become the majority of China's rural migrant worker population. Evidently, the employment size of rural labor in the urban sector is huge. Their destinations and professions are also far ranging. Over the course of high-frequency, mass transfer of rural labor, profound changes have also taken place in the urban–rural distribution of labor. As has been discussed earlier, since reform and opening up, the share of rural employment in total employment has been declining constantly, whereas that of urban employment has been growing constantly. After 2014, the share of urban employment already exceeded 50 percent and has remained above 50 percent ever since. China's employment structure has changed from rural-dominated in the past to urban-dominated today.

3. Enhanced spontaneity of commodity and factor transaction between urban and rural areas signifies improved efficiency of factor allocation between urban and rural areas. That is, products and factors are more likely to find, between urban and rural areas, sectors where their economic evaluation is higher. Along with the improvement of factor allocation efficiency, China's GDP has recorded sustained high-speed growth, which may benefit both urban and rural microeconomic subjects. More specifically, in the temporal sense, labor productivity has been increasing among different industries both in urban and rural

China, so has resident income and consumption expenditure. By horizontal comparison, comparative labor productivity and income and consumption gap between urban and rural China have begun to step out of the previously constant high and, in some intervals, have even declined continuously, as has been revealed by our analysis on comparative labor productivity of industries and income and consumption gap earlier. Apart from these indicators, Engel coefficient, which measures resident consumption level from consumption expenditure structure, can also be used to describe urban–rural economic gap. Figure 7.2 compares the Engel coefficient level between urban and rural residents from 1981 to 2017. Throughout the investigation period, the Engel coefficient level has been on the fall both for urban and rural residents, with urban residents recording a decline from 56.66 percent to 28.64 percent, and rural residents from 59.80 percent to 31.18 percent. This implies that resident consumption expenditure in urban and rural China is becoming increasingly inclined toward development materials and enjoyment materials other than food, and this change of consumer pattern is consistent between urban and rural residents. By comparison, for some time intervals within the investigation period, namely, 1981–1984 and 2010–2017, the Engel coefficient of rural residents dropped more quickly than that of urban residents, drawing the two figures closer to each other. This signifies that the consumption structure and consumption pattern are assimilating between urban and rural residents, and urban–rural economic relationship is also remarkably integrated.

Since reform and opening up, although China's urban–rural economic relationship has been transforming from separation toward integration, this

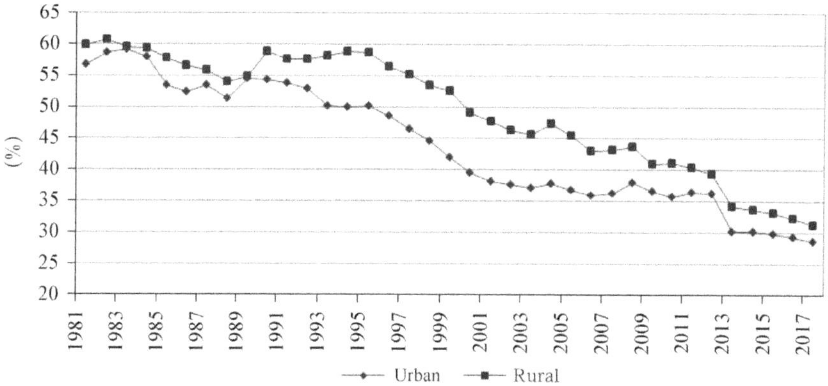

Figure 7.2 China's Engel's coefficient of urban and rural residents from 1981 to 2017.

Source: CEIC Data.

integration varies across different dimensions and different periods. The word "imbalance" portraits the complex and structural nature of the evolution of China's urban–rural economic relationship. By "imbalance", we mean the following three features:

1. The fluctuation in the temporal variation of urban–rural economic relationship. As emphasized by our concept definition earlier, in the sense of result, urban–rural factor allocation and the efficiency of this allocation are reflected by the change in urban–rural income gap and urban–rural consumption gap. For a large developing country like China, urban–rural economic gap is even more prominent than other major developing economies, and it often represents an important part of overall income gap. As such, the gradual reduction of urban–rural income gap or urban–rural consumption gap is an important signature of the integration of urban–rural economic relationship. As discussed above, since 1978, China's urban–rural income gap and consumption gap have both been fluctuated, and they have even widened over some time intervals. Although both figures have been reducing since 2009, this reduction should be investigated across a longer time span. Our analysis on Engel coefficient between urban and rural residents above also shows that, by horizontal comparison, Engel coefficient gap has not been reducing continuously over all time intervals. The fluctuation of urban–rural economic gap signifies that China's urban–rural economic relationship has not been evolving steadily along one same direction. Integration is not the only theme describing the dynamics of urban–rural economic relationship. To date, China still needs to further optimize institutional mechanisms and policy arrangements in favor of urban–rural integration;
2. The evolutionary differentiation across different dimensions of urban–rural economic relationship. In the sense of result, urban–rural economic relationship is reflected by the change of urban–rural income gap, urban–rural consumption gap and the like. Changes in these indicators are also closely associated with how public goods and social security resources are allocated between urban and rural areas. The allocation of public goods and social security resources between urban and rural areas itself will affect the income level of urban and rural residents (transfer income is one of the four sources of income for Chinese farmers). It will also affect the consumption level of urban and rural residents by affecting expectations (the supply of social security acts on consumption expenditure by affecting expectations). Over the 40 years of reform and opening up, especially after the entry into the 21st century, with sustained growth in GDP and fiscal revenue, the government's supply capacity of public goods for urban and rural areas has been enhanced remarkably in the temporal sense. The implementation of the "innovation, coordination, green, open, sharing" concepts also

signifies that even more importance is attached to equalizing the access to basic public services between urban and rural residents. By horizontal comparison, however, rural residents still lag behind their urban counterparts in access to basic education, basic medical care, and basic old-age insurance. While the employment control function of urban and rural household registration is weakening, its function of social security resource allocation is still working well.

As indicated by Table 7.2, since 2009, China's urban–rural income gap and consumption gap have both been on the fall, but the density of health workers (the number of health workers per thousand residents) in urban areas has remained higher than that in rural areas all the time, with a gap of 2.43 in 2009 and 2.66 in 2016. No noticeable convergence is observed with increasing time. The same happened to the density of certified practitioners, registered nurses, and density of beds in health institutions. This signifies that, although urban–rural income gap and consumption gap are reducing, urban–rural social duality is still prominent in China. The solidification of urban–rural social duality signifies that farmers are still an "identity". This phenomenon will act negatively on the capital formation, occupational choice, children's education of farmers, as well as amplify the economic differentiation inside rural areas after capital, technology, and knowledge have gone rural. Urban–rural social duality will eventually hamper the continued transformation of urban–rural dual economy.

3. The structural differentiation inside urban and rural areas during the evolution of urban–rural economic relationship. Since reform and opening up, the enhancement of factor flow and the adjustment of the mode factor allocation between urban and rural areas has led to a change in urban–rural income gap and consumption gap. Amid these changes, the evolution of urban–rural economic gap is inevitably accompanied by a structural change inside urban and rural areas. Regarding urban and rural areas as two "homogenized" plates is faced with increasing practical challenge. As such, even though the economic gap is narrowing between the urban and rural sectors, it is still unrealistic to directly deduce that urban–rural economic problems have been fully resolved. Instead, the analysis on urban–rural economic relationship should be extended into the structural changes inside urban and rural areas respectively.

Inside urban areas, while the transformation of urban–rural duality has been accompanied by the nonagricultural transfer of rural labor, this transfer is often an occupational change without transforming the "identity" of farmers. The term "rural migrant worker" draws a vivid picture of this inconsistency between identity transformation and occupational change. While rural migrant workers can work in nonagricultural

Table 7.2 Structural changes inside urban and rural areas and comparison of social security between urban and rural China from 2009 to 2016

Year	*Salary (yuan/a)*		*Urbanization rate (%)*		*Rural internal income (yuan)*		*Density of urban–rural health workers (person/thousand people)*	
	Migrant worker	*Urban on-the-job worker*	*Resident population*	*Registered population*	*Minimum income household*	*Maximum income household*	*Urban*	*Rural*
2009	17,004	32,736	48.34	33.77	1549.30	12319.05	7.15	2.94
2010	20,280	37,147	49.95	34.17	1869.80	14049.69	7.62	3.04
2011	24,588	42,452	51.27	34.71	2000.51	16783.07	6.68	2.66
2012	27,480	47,593	52.57	35.33	2316.21	19008.89	7.90	3.19
2013	31,308	52,388	53.73	35.93	2583.23	21272.70	9.18	3.64
2014	34,368	57,361	54.77	36.63	2768.10	23947.40	9.70	3.77
2015	36,864	63,241	56.10	39.90	3085.60	26013.90	10.21	3.90
2016	39,300	68,993	57.35	41.20	3006.50	28448.00	10.79	4.05

Source: In the salary column, salaries of farmer workers are calculated by multiplying the monthly salary of outgoing farmer workers by 12; salaries of urban on-the-job workers are the averages of on-the-job workers in urban nonprivate sector, which are sourced from CEIC Data. Urbanization rates of resident population and urbanization rates of resident population from 2009 to 2013 are sourced from CEIC database; urbanization rates of registered population from 2014 to 2016 are sourced from the statistics communiques on national economic and social development of China for individual years; internal rural incomes from 2014 to 2016 are sourced from CEIC database and those from 2014 to 2016 come from the "*Chinese Statistical Yearbook 2017*); densities of urban–rural health workers come from the "*Chinese Statistical Yearbook 2017*".

industries and can receive higher labor remunerations than agricultural income, they are not comparable to holders of an urban household register in occupational choice, wage level, and access to social security. This makes it hard for rural migrant workers to merge into the city where their new job is located. Consequently, the classic urban–rural duality addressed by development economy changes into a "new duality" local to urban China. This new duality implies that the Lewis-Fei-Ranis model is no longer able to explain the transformation pathway of China's dual economy, since it implicitly equates the job change of rural labor to their identity transformation. As indicated by Table 7.2, since 2009, although the income level of rural migrant workers has become more superior over their previous agricultural income, it has always remained inferior to the annual salaries of urban on-the-job workers. In 2009, the gap of average annual salary between urban on-the-job workers and rural migrant workers was 1.93. In 2016, this figure was 1.76. In the temporal sense, this gap has been fluctuating with no continuous, observable sign of reduction. Over the same period, the urbanization rate of registered population remained lower than that of resident population all the time. In 2009, the gap of urbanization rate between resident population and registered population was 14.57. In 2016, this figure rose to 16.15. This signifies that inside urban areas, the new duality between rural migrant workers and registered population is still very prominent.

Inside rural areas, along with the innovation of agricultural management mode, the nonagricultural transfer of rural labor, and the gradual injection of nonrural productive factors, members inside rural areas have begun to differentiate quickly over occupational choice, production mode, and factor allocation mode. Various forms of business entities—traditional home-run farm households, home farms, specialized farm cooperatives, and leading enterprises have sprouted in rural areas. Among rural residents, economic behavior and income source have also begun to diversify. Gao F. (2018c) noticed the differentiation among farmers under the country's rural revitalization strategy, and pointed out that, on the economics dimension, factor allocation mode is the right cut-in point for examining this differentiation. According to the allocation mode of land, labor, capital and other productive factors, China's farmers can be divided into five groups: traditional farmers, off-the-home farmers, off-the-land farmers, endogenous new farmers, and exogenous new farmers. In line with this differentiation, the income inequality among rural residents has also widened significantly. As indicated by Table 7.2, the income gap between maximum and minimum income households has been rising constantly. From 2009 to 2016, this gap grew from 7.95 to 9.46. Hence, regarding rural residents as an internally highly homogeneous group is facing increasing practical challenge.

To sum up, since the start of reform and opening up in 1978, along with the adjustment of government–market relationship at the economic system level, China's urban–rural economic relationship has been transforming from separation toward integration, as can be observed from the evolution of the product transaction, factor allocation, and economic gap between urban and rural areas. Yet, this integration has not proceeded with green light all the way. So far, the integration is still imbalanced, as evidenced by the temporal fluctuation of urban–rural economic gap, the dynamic differences between urban–rural economic gap and social gap, and the prominent structural feature inside urban and rural areas. Evidently, since reform and opening up, China's urban–rural economic relationship has been evolving in multiple directions, exhibiting the complex, systemic, and multifaceted nature of evolution. In theoretical research, these directions should be explained under a proper logical framework.

7.2 Forming logic of imbalanced integration of urban–rural economic relationship

Since reform and opening up, China's urban–rural economic relationship can be characterized as an imbalanced integration. As this imbalanced integration is set in the stage of market-oriented economic system transition, it should be explained in light of this local practice and against the background of system transition. As discussed earlier, based on the combination of development strategy and constraints, China's economic system change has revolved around the adjustment of government–market relationship and intended to propel the government to delegate discretion and benefits to microeconomic subjects and continuously enhance the market's role in resource allocation. Nevertheless, in a large developing country with socialist system like China, this institutional transition has not only led to changes in government-market relationship but also the emergence of intragovernmental and intramarket structural features. Intergovernmental and intermarket institutional arrangements also constitute a component of the adjustment of government–market relationship. That is, regionally decentralized authoritarianism and upstream-guided market expansion have taken form, which forces China to pick up a unique pathway to realize market-oriented reform. Based on this unique economic system transition, we can identify the forming logic of the imbalanced integration of China's urban–rural economic relationship. As illustrated by Figure 7.3, in China, as a large developing country in the process of economic system transition, the imbalanced integration of urban–rural economic relationship should be explained by considering the following basic mechanisms.

7.2.1 Basic change of government–market relationship

The relationship between government and market represents the core proposition of economic system choice. Without considering the intergovernmental and intermarket structural feature, compared with planned

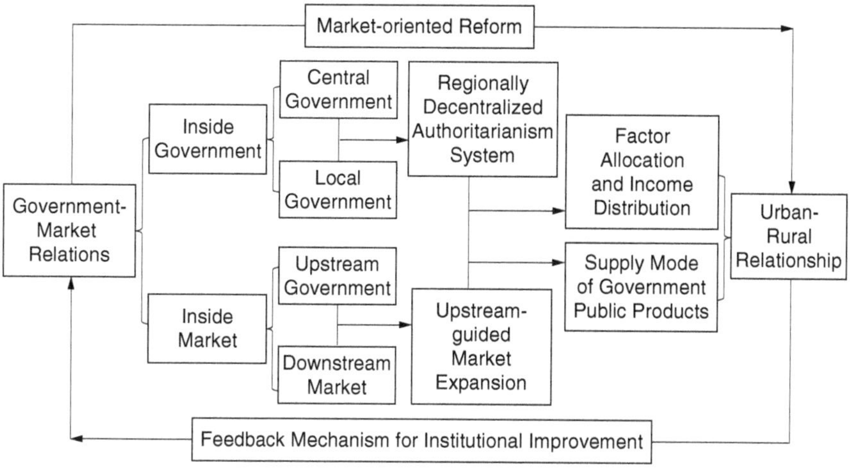

Figure 7.3 Forming logic of imbalanced integration of China's urban–rural economic relationship.

economy high-power centralization at the central government level, market economy is more able to deal with complex demand and supply information, to stimulate the economic vigor of microeconomic subjects, to cause the optimal allocation of resources and foster the emancipation and development of productivity. This economic system comparison offers an explanation as to why market-oriented reform would become a common practice among planned economies in the second half of the 20th century. Since 1978, while shifting its focus from heavy industry toward economic growth, China has also carried out economic transition from planned economy to market economy. A socialist market economy has been established as the goal of the country's economic system reform. On the dimension of government–market relationship, this transition is typically manifested by the gradual relaxation of government's economic control at all levels. The government's major economic function has switched to defining property rights and providing public goods. Microeconomic subjects mainly rely on market mechanism for commodity and resource allocation. "Market-oriented" marks the basic trend of the adjustment of government–market relationship in post-reform China.

From the perspective of urban–rural economic relationship, China's market-oriented system transition has performed excellently, too. The implementation of HRS, the marketization of agricultural product circulation system, and the gradual relaxation of urban and rural household registration discussed earlier can all serve as good evidence. Enhanced commodity and factor fluidity between urban and rural areas, on the one hand, manifests increased integration between urban and rural areas. That is, the urban and rural sectors are more tightly tied together by market mechanism. Urban and rural microeconomic subjects are able to both provide commodities to and obtain commodities from each other, bring China's urban–rural economic relationship out of the predicament of separation and hampered intercourse among microeconomic subjects. On the other hand, it also manifests the complexity of income distribution between urban and rural areas. While enhanced commodity and factor fluidity between urban and rural areas can improve economic efficiency, optimize resource allocation, and make labor remuneration play a flareout role at large, endowment disparities between urban and rural areas, and among different subjects inside urban and rural areas, also become more prominent. As individual microeconomic subjects differ in degree of market involvement and ability to profit from the market, the change of urban–rural income gap and consumption gap is also volatile, the economic gap among individual microeconomic subjects inside urban and rural areas also become apparent. Urban–rural economic gap has not been reducing constantly along one same direction. Consequently, market-oriented reform itself will bring about an integration of urban–rural economic relationship with fluctuating economic gap.

7.2.2 Intragovernmental structural feature

In economic system choice, government–market relationship usually concerns the way government and market are combined. It assumes that government is fully homogenized inside. However, in a large developing country like China, government is divided into different administrative levels, and governments at different levels are faced with differentiated goal functions and constrains. Hence, it is incorrect to look at government as a fully homogenized concept. Rather, attention should be paid to the structural feature among different levels of governments and the corresponding institutional arrangements. Since reform and opening up in 1978, China has gradually formed a regionally decentralized authoritarianism among different levels of governments. As a result, central–local economic relationship becomes an important determinant of economic and social performances. From the perspective of urban–rural economic relationship, regionally decentralized authoritarianism is associated with economic growth goals and the incompatibility between financial and administrative powers commonly facing local governments. The pursuit of economic growth to relieve fiscal revenue and expenditure pressures is the main cut-in point for understanding the behavioral logic of local governments. This intragovernmental structural feature and the intergovernmental institutional arrangement affect urban–rural economic relationship through the following two mechanisms.

One is factor allocation and income distribution. While the central government has managed to foster the delegation of economic discretion to urban and rural residents, which helps deepen the economic integration between urban and rural areas, local governments still have a hand in the allocation of particular factors (e.g., the allocation of core factors like land, capital, and important energy sources, or allocation of the upstream market) and affect the distribution of the allocation thereof (e.g., land finance, distribution of land expropriation income), which will all make a difference to the evolution of urban–rural economic relationship. Table 7.3 compares China's land transfer revenue and expenditure from 2009 to 2015. In items related to land transfer revenue and expenditure, land sales income equals to land sales revenue minus cost expenditure, and land sales income is distributed between the urban and rural sectors. In detail, expenditure for urban construction and government-subsidized housing mainly goes to the urban sector. Expenditure for rural infrastructure construction, land consolidation, and farmland protection, as well as for agricultural land development, farmland irrigation and water conservancy, and educational funds, primarily goes to the rural sector. From 2009 to 2015, the share of expenditure for urban construction in total land sales income was 50.89 percent, 59.46 percent, 59.06 percent, 51.17 percent, 47.60 percent, 45.21 percent, and 51.83 percent, respectively. The share of expenditure for government-subsidized housing was 2.85 percent, 3.66 percent, 7.03 percent, 9.47 percent, 9.10 percent, 8.46 percent and 12.09 percent, respectively. Together, they accounted for 53.74 percent, 63.12 percent, 66.09 percent, 60.64 percent, 56.70 percent, 53.66 percent, and 63.92 percent, respectively, with an average annual of 59.70 percent. In contrast, the share of expenditure for the rural sector in land sales income was 15.51 percent, 17.76 percent, 23.36 percent, 31.94 percent, 33.85 percent, 27.10 percent, and 37.10 percent, respectively, with an annual average of 26.66 percent. From these figures, we can see how land sales income is distributed between urban and rural sectors, which is still heavily tilted toward urban areas.

The other is supply of public goods. The integration of urban–rural economic relationship is closely associated with the allocation of public goods between urban and rural areas. Under regionally decentralized authoritarianism, the central government provides generalized urban and rural public goods, and this supply is dependent on national financial capacity and the adjustment of development concept. Local governments provide regional urban and rural public goods, and this supply is dependent on their own financial position and how they incentivize administrative performance. Subject to constraints on fiscal revenue and expenditure (i.e., incompatibility between financial and administrative powers) and an economic growth-oriented incentive mechanism (race for growth), local governments will often choose to allocate resources to fields more capable of showing economic growth performance or to groups more capable of exerting pressure on them. Consequently, on the local governments' allocation list of public resources, the supply of public goods related to urban and rural livelihood are often not on the top. In the allocation of urban and rural public goods, the urban sector is more advantaged as it weighs heavier in policy-making. This allocation of public goods (e.g., regional undersupply of basic social

Table 7.3 China's revenue and expenditure of land transfer from 2009 to 2015

Description	*2009*	*2010*	*2011*	*2012*	*2013*	*2014*	*2015*
Land Sales Revenue	14239.70	29397.98	33477.00	28886.31	41649.20	42940.30	33657.73
Expenditure for Land Sale Revenue	12327.10	26977.60	33172.16	28421.85	40883.91	41210.98	33727.78
Cost Expenditure	7694.21	16732.23	24053.76	22624.90	33716.36	33952.37	26844.59
• Expenditure for Compensation for Land Appropriation and Demolition	4985.67	–	15040.43	17401.60	21760.03	21216.03	20310.79
• Expenditure for Subsidizing Land-expropriated Farmers/ Resettlement of SOE Employees	1386.08	–	3503.35		3358.67	3529.96	
• Expenditure for Development Prior to Land Sale	1322.46	–	5509.98	5223.30	8580.04	9206.38	6533.90
Land Sale Income	6564.49	12665.75	9423.24	6261.41	7932.86	8987.93	6813.14
• Expenditure for Urban Construction	3340.99	7531.67	5564.8	3204.15	3776.04	4063.02	3531.53
• Expenditure for Government-Subsidized Housing	187.10	463.62	662.35	593.01	721.84	760.10	823.49
• Construction of Rural Infrastructure	433.10	1 444.90	760.45	488.08	516.75	428.90	1667.97
• Expenditure for Land Consolidation and Farmland Protection	477.56	655.98	1 067.59	1 017.17	1 424.50	1 146.72	
• Agricultural Land Development	107.25	148.66					
• Expenditure for Irrigation and Water Conservancy Funds	–	–	140.75	24.59	378.37	482.80	423.51
• Expenditure of Education Funds	–	–	232.66	269.95	365.38	377.07	436.69

Source: Based on data of the "*Management and Use of Land Transfer Income in China*" and the "*Land Transfer Revenue and Expenditure in China*" released by the Ministry of Finance for individual years. Land transfer incomes balance of land transfer income of the year deducted by cost expenditure. The land transfer income of 2013 is calculated according to the rate of variation given by the "*Land Transfer Revenue and Expenditure in China 2014*".

security for rural areas) will also make a difference to urban–rural economic relationship. Obviously, inside the government, the central government's promotion of market-oriented reform and supply of public goods can help realize the integration of urban–rural economic relationship, whereas local governments' allocation of the factors and regional public goods can easily lead to an imbalance of urban–rural economic relationship. Accordingly, the coexistence of integration and imbalance becomes an important feature describing China's current urban–rural economic relationship.

7.2.3 Intramarket structural feature

Since reform and opening up, China as a large developing country with socialist system has not been promoting market-oriented system transition at the same pace among all fields, but in a sequential, differentiated, progressive manner. Consequently, the intramarket structural feature has grown more and more prominent. Hence, it is also inappropriate to look at market in government–market relationship as fully homogenized. In particular, as China has been liberalizing the downstream market while retaining control over the upstream market (e.g., land, capital, and important energy sources), this has given rise to the unique market-oriented transition of upstream-guided market expansion. This intramarket structural feature will also make a difference to urban–rural economic relationship through two dimensions:

One is factor allocation and income distribution. In the downstream market (e.g., agricultural products, agricultural means of production, labor employment), rapid marketization has led to frequent spontaneous intercourse between urban and rural microeconomic subjects, which is conducive to increasing the integration between the urban and rural sectors. In the upstream market (e.g., land, capital, and important energy sources), in contrast, the comparatively slow marketization has repressed the economic intercourse between urban and rural areas. Overall, the market-oriented reform of factors lags behind that of products, suggesting that urban–rural factor market is commonly distorted. For example, while urban and rural residents are still discriminated by their identity, the nonagricultural transfer of rural labor and the flow of urban labor into rural areas are both exposed to institutional resistance, which will hamper the integration of urban–rural economic relationship. The uncoordinated marketization implies that there is still vast room for institutional reform and for economic efficiency improvement. It also implies that China's current urban–rural economic relationship has yet to attain a high-profile, high-level integration.

The other is supply of public goods. Since reform and opening up, China has embarked on market-oriented economic system transition, which targets establishing a socialist market economy. Nevertheless, market is not a nature-born "ingenious machine". Market mechanism works under the premise of a whole set of economic system arrangements. Particularly, the effective operation of market economy is preceded by two pairs of systems or two public goods. One is the property right system and market transaction system as the prerequisite of operation; the other is the distribution adjustment system and social protection system as the result of operation. Upstream-guided market expansion signifies that China has different property right protection and market transaction arrangements for different markets, suggesting that different microeconomic subjects may have different economic gains in market operation. In that connection, governments' distribution adjustment system and social protection system for microeconomic subjects—especially supply of basic public goods characterized by urban–rural integration—becomes very critical, but urban–rural equalization of basic public services is still "on the way". In summary, upstream-guided market expansion is a double-edged sword for the evolution of urban–rural economic relationship. China's effort to relax the downstream market and foster commodity marketization has led to an expansion in the option and an integration of economic relationship among urban and rural microeconomic subjects. Yet, the exposure of the upstream market to control and the ongoing equalization of public goods between urban and rural areas will also result in an imbalance in the integration of urban–rural economic relationship.

Government–market relationship, intergovernmental structure, and intermarket structure constitute the explanatory logic of the imbalanced integration of China's urban–rural economic relationship. In this explanatory framework, the adjustment of government–market relationship represents the main trend of the entire economic system transition. Both intergovernmental structure and intermarket structure take place under this general trend. Without market-oriented economic system transition, the intergovernmental regionally decentralized authoritarianism and intermarket upstream-guided market expansion would become water without source or a tree without roots. When the central government relied on mandatory plans to allocate resources, unified purchase and marketing and high power centralization depicted the basic feature of the relationship among different levels of governments. Product market and factor market were both subject to the strict control of government departments. Hence in the planned economy era, even though there existed intergovernmental and intermarket structural problems, they did not count much. Regionally decentralized authoritarianism and upstream-guided market expansion emerged in the context of economic system transition. However, once the intergovernmental and intermarket structural features appear, they imply that China has to take a unique road to market-oriented transition. Since reform and opening up in 1978, China has indeed transformed from planned economy to market economy. Yet, this transition is different from other countries in terms of pathway and mode. Regionally decentralized authoritarianism has distinguished China's resource allocation subjects from major developed economies. Upstream-guided market expansion has distinguished China's system transition road from the former Soviet Union and East European countries. More notably, these intergovernmental and intermarket structural features are characterized by institutional complementarity and nestification. That is, regionally decentralized authoritarianism requires local governments to have allocation over certain factors, and upstream-guide market expansion happens to provide this condition. Upstream-guided market expansion is based on the government's ability to control the system transition process, and regionally decentralized authoritarianism serves as the institutional factor to maintain the controllability of reform process.

As far as urban–rural economic relationship is concerned, whether it be adjustment of government–market relationship or intergovernmental and intermarket structural features and institutional arrangements, they all have brought about double effects on the evolution of urban–rural economic relationship. On the one hand, products and factors are reallocated between urban and rural areas according to market mechanism, which enhances the integration between urban and rural areas. On the other hand, during marketization, the allocation of public goods is affected by the behaviors of different levels of governments, as well as the interaction among different segments of the market, which led to an imbalance in the integration of urban–rural economic relationship. As can be seen, the imbalanced integration of urban–rural economic relationship is associated with the particular background of market-oriented system transition—it stemmed from the market-oriented economic system transition that China is promoting, but the pathway of this system transition is also unique. In the long run, imbalanced integration of urban–rural economic relationship signifies enhanced factor allocation efficiency and economic strength. It also signifies the continuation, accumulation, and intensification of structural problems in national economy. The former makes it feasible for China to continue to improve its urban–rural economic relationship; the latter makes it necessary for the country to do so. The coupling of these two aspects will produce a feedback to development strategy, constraints and their combination, and stimulate the continued adjustment of urban–rural economic relationship by deepening economic system reform.

7.3 Imbalanced integration of urban–rural economic relationship and its explanation: an example

Since reform and opening up, China has been pushing forward economic system transition by adjusting government–market relationship. It has also created unique intergovernmental and intermarket structural arrangements, namely, regionally decentralized authoritarianism and upstream-guided market expansion, in the course of transition. This has distinguished China's economic system transition from those of other economies. Government–market relationship, and intergovernmental and intermarket institutional arrangements have made a difference to China's urban–rural economic relationship and endowed it with the remarkable feature of imbalanced integration. In order to validate the forming mechanism of this imbalanced integration, we can use the evolution of China's urban–rural economic relationship since 2009 to exemplify the logic connection between economic system choice and imbalanced integration. As demonstrated earlier with statistical data, since 2009, China's urban–rural gap has taken a "new form", or its connotation has been changing. That is, the income gap between the urban and rural sectors has gradually changed toward a new duality inside urban areas and an income differentiation inside rural areas. With narrowing urban–rural income gap, the increasing structural contrast inside urban and rural areas is becoming a new form and new challenge for China's urban–rural inequality. Against the background of narrowing urban–rural income gap and the emergence of new duality inside urban areas and income differentiation inside rural areas, China's urban–rural duality is showing a fairly prominent "solidification". That is, rural residents are still inferior than their urban counterparts in access to basic education, basic medical care, and basic old-age insurance resources (Gao F., 2018b). In the course of these changes, the gradual narrowing of urban–rural income gap denotes an integration of urban–rural economic relationship, whereas the remarkable gap in social security between urban and rural areas, and the broadening economic gap inside urban and rural areas themselves signal an imbalance of urban–rural economic relationship. Imbalanced integration marks the basic pattern of urban–rural economic relationship in the post-2009 period, which should be explained in light of the characteristics of China's economic system transition.

Using the above forming mechanism of imbalanced integration, we can provide an explanation on the connotation transformation of China's urban–rural gap (Gao F., 2018b). Since 2009, China's economic system change has not only continued to highlight the resource allocation function of the market on the dimension of government–market relationship, the intergovernmental structural arrangement has also inherited the post-decentralization institutional framework. This institutional framework contains two important base points. One is the central government's assessment and incentive on local governments' administrative performances. Although the central government has already emphasized the scientific development concept and the development concept of "innovation, coordination, green, open, and sharing", due to the differences in the identification and displayability among individual indicators scaling the development goal, the goal functions of local governments often have to revolve around economic growth rate. "Race for growth" is still existent in the economic practices of different levels of local governments. The other is the competition among local governments within their respective administrative boundaries, for rare promotion opportunities or financial resources. Whether for political or economic incentives, local government leaders will first consider how to maximize the development goal or minimize the development cost within their jurisdiction so as to remain advantaged in the opportunity of administrative promotion or access to financial resources.

In contrast to intergovernmental structural arrangements, China's intermarket structural arrangements mainly revolve around labor and land factors, and its core is to push forward market-oriented reform through the subdivision and combination of the factor rights structure. These structural arrangements also contain two important base points. First, in the labor market, the labor reallocation between urban and rural areas is divided into two separate processes: the transfer of labor use right, and the transformation of laborers' identity right. The nonagricultural transfer of rural labor is above all the transfer of labor use right by farmers based on comparison of economic gains. The relaxed employment control function of household registration right provides the institutional condition for this transfer, although household registration still plays a remarkable role in labeling identity or allocating social security resources. Second, in the rural land market, along with the nonagricultural transfer of rural labor and the loosening of the farmer-land tie, farmers may not necessarily engage in agricultural management after obtaining land contract right. The dichotomy between collective ownership of rural land and farmers' land contract right under HRS has also been broken. Recently, China's rural land ownership has been subdivided into collective ownership, farmers' contract right, and land management right. "Three rights division" has become an important direction for China to refine HRS and press ahead rural land system change. With the "three rights division" for farmland, farmers can assign their management right, without losing their contract right, through the land transfer market, thereby allowing the social reallocation of the land within the contract term; rural collective organizations can exercise their right to expropriate land and to supervise the land contract right and management right; nonrural capital, technical, information, and other factors are more likely to flow into rural areas and combine with land factors. Evidently, the identity transformation in the labor market and the ownership in the land market represent the "upstream market" in the market structural feature. With these upstream markets still under control, farmers have the opportunity to increase their economic return by reallocating labor use right and/or land management right, namely, by activating spontaneous transaction in the downstream market.

Based on the intergovernmental and intermarket structural arrangements above, since 2009, China has continued with the previous nonagricultural transfer of rural labor. As indicated by CEIC Data statistics, as of 2017, China had a rural migrant worker population was 28,652 million, with local and outside rural migrant workers contributing 146.7 million and 171.85 million, respectively. Over the same period, rural China also saw a booming market of land management right transfer. As indicated by the NBS statistics, as of the end of 2016, 31.95 million hectares of household contracted land had been transferred, 67.89 million households had transferred out their contracted land, accounting for 29.7 percent of total household contract households. After 2009, rural labor and land transfer has made a great difference to farmers' income growth, and consequently the evolution of urban–rural income gap over this period. When rural labor is free to be transferred among different regions and different sectors, the allocation efficiency of rural land and the resulted wage income are greatly improved. When rural land management right is free to be transferred between farmer households and between farmer households and other business entities, the allocation efficiency and the resulted farmers' property income are greatly improved. Over this period, the implementation of a succession of pro-agricultural policies has also brought about higher transfer income for farmers. Coupling of these changes will definitely narrow down the income gap between the urban and rural sectors.

It is worth noting that, with regionally decentralized authoritarianism in place, local governments' race for economic growth also provided effective incentives for the reallocation of rural labor and land factors. Local governments' "race for growth" is incentive-compatible with enhanced fluidity of rural factors. For local governments, whatever the direction, the flow of rural labor will help increase the GDP by optimizing the efficiency of labor allocation. The reallocation or rural land will also propel the innovation of agricultural management, optimize the industrial structure and hence contribute to economic growth. This indicates that an active "downstream market" of rural labor and land coincides with the goal orientation of local governments. As a result, since 2009, the reallocation of factors between urban and rural China has first of all led to a narrowing in urban–rural income gap. By source of income, the per capita disposable income of urban and rural residents can be separated into wage income, net operating income, net property income, and net transfer income. According to CEIC Data statistics, from 2013 to 2017, farmers' net operating income remained higher than urban residents', with faster growth in wage income, net property income, and net transfer income. Hence, urban–rural income gaps in these three aspects are all reducing remarkably. In terms of wage income, the gap dropped from 4.5 to 4.04; in terms of property income, the gap dropped from 13.1 to 11.91; in terms of transfer income, it dropped from 2.63 to 2.51. The narrowing gap is closely associated with the reallocation of labor and land use right between urban and rural areas. At large, reduced urban–rural income gap suggests a big stride of urban–rural economic relationship from separation toward integration.

However, one point remains. The reallocation of rural labor and land use right has not solely led to a reduction in urban–rural income gap. As an addition, this reallocation is also accompanied by other two results. First, after rural labor have flown into cities, besides engaging in nonagricultural industries and receiving economic returns, they also need to integrate into the urban sector and transform their identity, yet their identity transformation is closely relevant to household registration and the underlying allocation of public goods between urban and rural areas. Without fundamentally eliminating the urban–rural separated allocation of public goods, the labor outflows from rural areas (what we call "rural migrant workers") will form a new duality with urban registered population. As demonstrated earlier, new dual economy is a derivative and characteristic fact of the transformation of China's urban–rural duality. Second, with the non-agricultural transfer of rural labor and the transfer of land management right, the "homogeneity" inside rural areas where each farmer household contracts and cultivates land has been broken. Individual farmer households are often faced with a variety of occupation and factor allocation modes to choose from. The go-rural of capital has also created a new norm of bi-directional factor flow between urban and rural areas (Luo L.J., Luo Y.Z. & Luo T., 2014). At present, "urbanization" and "counter-urbanization" of factor flow in China often takes place at the same time, although the go-rural of factors does not represent the main aspect of urban–rural factor flow. The superposition of these factors has intensified the differentiation among different rural members, broadening the income distribution gap inside rural areas. Consequently, reduced income gap between urban and rural areas is accompanied by increased income gap inside rural areas.

The new duality and the farmer differentiation inside rural areas signify that the current integration of China's urban–rural economic relationship is imbalanced. To understand these two phenomena of imbalance, the essence is to answer two questions: why, with enhanced urban–rural factor fluidity, is the allocation of public goods between urban and rural areas separated, and what does a "solidified" urban–rural dual society mean to the differentiation inside rural areas. As discussed earlier, China's market-oriented system transition has been revolved around the adjustment of government-market relationship, wherein the role of market mechanism in optimizing resource allocation has growing more and more prominent. Nevertheless, the functioning of the market itself requires the adjustment and follow-up of government functions. Government–market relationship is a matter of mutual complementation and enhancement instead of replacement. On ground of this, after the entry into the 21st century, in face of increasing challenge of imbalanced, uncoordinated, unsustainability development, the Chinese government has to work hard to equalize the basic public services between urban and rural areas. For local governments at different levels, however, their pursuit for local economic growth does not fully concur with the demand of public goods supply under urban–rural factor fluidity. For both inflows and outflows of rural labor, increased supply of social security for mobile labor signifies increased fiscal expenditure for the local government. It is difficult to carry forward residents' social security between different local governments due to level differentiation. Consequently, localized administrative management becomes contradictory with the mobile urban–rural factor allocation. Under an economic systems wherein local governments race for growth, equalized allocation of public goods between urban and rural areas is usually not intrinsically consistent with the goal pursuit of local governments, which constitutes an important driver of the "solidified" urban–rural dual society and the new duality inside urban areas.

From the objective outcome, the "solidified" dual society caused by intergovernmental feature and institutional arrangements will not only hamper urban–rural economic relationship but will also have a negative impact on China's overall goal of sustainable development and common prosperity. In the urban sector, it narrows the occupational choice and wage growth of rural transfer residents; in the rural sector, it affects the allocation efficiency and income distribution of various productive factors. As discussed earlier, inside rural China, farmers are becoming increasingly differentiated. Over time, the go-rural of capital, information, technology, knowledge, and other factors may further increase in scale as well as scope. The Central Economic Working Conference held in December 2017 explicitly noted that China must improve the institutional mechanism for urban–rural integrated development and eliminate all obstacles that hamper factors from going to the countryside". The "No. 1 Document of 2018 titled "Opinions of the CPC Central Committee and the State Council on the Implementation of the Rural Revitalization Strategy" also emphasized the need to "promote the free flow and equal exchange of urban and rural factors, promote the simultaneous development of new industrialization, informationization, urbanization, and agricultural modernization, accelerate the formation of a new form of relationship between industry and agricultural or between urban and rural areas with mutual enhancement, mutual complementation, full integration, and common prosperity". NBS statistics also show that in 2016, 309.17 hectares of household contracted cultivated land was transferred to enterprises, accounting for 9.7 percent of total transfer of household contracted cultivated land.

For local governments, the go-rural of capital and other factors can propel the innovation of agricultural management and accelerate the integration of the primary, secondary, and tertiary rural industries to become a new economic growth point, which is highly consistent with their pursuit of local economic growth and their goal of increasing fiscal revenue. However, under a "solidified" urban–rural dual society, the go-rural of capital and other non-agricultural factors is usually faced with two challenges. First, a "solidified" dual society compromises the input of public goods in rural areas and the formation of human capital for farmers, whereas the go-rural of capital and other factors has to be combined with these factors in rural areas. This signifies that the "solidified" dual society will affect the bidirectional flow of factors between urban and rural sectors due to docking difficulties. Second, even though capital and other factors can go rural and the scale is increasing, under a "solidified" dual society, rural residents, especially those operating in small scale, are not only faced with the superiority of large-scale capital management, but also the disparity in access to social security resources inside rural areas, which can further intensify the economic differentiation inside rural areas. This intensification is not solely attributable to how hard farmers work or how much share of economic resources they hold but also to the institutional disparity underpinning the access to public goods among different groups inside rural areas. While under a "solidified" urban–rural dual society, factor flow between urban and rural areas is conducive to improving the efficiency of factor allocation, the differentiation inside rural areas can also continue to increase. Right in this sense, when trying to establish a new urban–rural economic relationship, China should pay attention to farmer differentiation inside rural areas and continue to explore for an institutional mechanism in favor of the organic interconnection between small farmer households and modern agriculture.

The above analysis indicates that since the start of reform and opening up in 1978, the urban–rural economic relationship in China, as world's largest developing nation, has been breaking out of the previous separation toward an integration with imbalance. The integration is typically reflected by the enhanced spontaneous transaction of products and factors between urban and rural areas, as well as the periodically narrowing urban–rural income and consumption gap. The imbalance is reflected by the fluctuation of urban–rural income and consumption gap, the continuation of urban–rural social security gap, and the broadened income gap inside urban and rural areas. An imbalanced integration signifies the complex, systemic, and multifaceted nature of the evolution of China's urban–rural economic relationship. China's urban–rural economic relationship does not exist by itself. It is the embodiment of the overall economic system choice on the urban–rural dimension. Hence, the imbalanced integration of urban–rural economic relationship has to be explained in the context of China's market-oriented economic system transition.

Therefore, we can establish an analytical logic for imbalanced integration from the perspectives of government–market relationship, intragovernmental structure, and intramarket structure. In such a framework, government–market relationship signifies the basic direction of China's system reform; the regionally decentralized authoritarianism inside the government and the upstream-guided market expansion side the market, on the other side, denote the uniqueness of the way of the country's economic system reform. Both changes in government–market relationship and the intragovernmental and intramarket structural arrangements can affect urban–rural economic relationship in favor of integration and imbalance. The imbalanced integration of China's urban–rural economic relationship since reform and opening up is precisely the product of these economic systems. Particularly, since 2009, against the narrowing urban–rural income gap was the broadening economic gap inside urban and rural areas, and the narrowing urban–rural economic gap is not accompanied by narrowing urban–rural social security gap. This contradiction can be explained by our political economy analytical framework described earlier, especially the forming logic of imbalanced integration. In a word, after reform and opening up, government–market relationship, intragovernmental structure, and intramarket structure have indeed made a difference to the evolution of China's urban–rural economic relationship. Hence, the imbalanced integration of China's urban–rural economic relationship should be closely examined in light of these institutional characteristics.

8 Main economic effects of imbalanced integration of urban–rural economic relationship

Since the start of reform and opening up in 1978, with ongoing implementation of its economic growth-oriented strategy, China has pushed forward an economic system change. The core of this change is to form market-oriented economic system transition on the dimension of government–market relationship and to create a regionally decentralized authoritarianism and an upstream-guided market expansion in the course of this transition. These economic systems have pushed China's urban–rural economic relationship out of the previous separation toward an integration with an imbalance. For a large developing country like China, the urban and rural sectors are the pillars of national economy; urban–rural economic relationship is also a component of the whole economic system. Once in place, it will act on overall economic development by affecting the behaviors of microeconomic subjects and hence become a determinant of the country's fundamental goal of sustainable economic development and common prosperity. In terms of development performance, imbalanced integration stemmed from China's implementation of the economic growth-oriented strategy. This implementation has indeed succeeded in driving the continuous high-speed economic growth and become an important backup force for world "miracle" of GDP growth made by China. Nevertheless, imbalanced integration has also made urban–rural economic gap an important part of overall income distribution gap and acted negatively on the country's transformation of economic development mode and the high-quality economic development. In this sense, imbalanced integration of urban–rural economic relationship has already become an important presentation of China's economic structural problems. In a word, since reform and opening up, imbalanced integration of urban–rural economic relationship has brought about both achievements and challenges to China's economic development. Understanding the multiple aspects of this outcome is particularly important to subsequent exploration on the possible improvements on urban–rural economic relationship.

8.1 Contribution of urban–rural labor reallocation to economic growth

Since the start of reform and opening up in 1978, the imbalanced integration of China's urban–rural economic relationship is first of all reflected by the closer connection between the urban and rural sectors so that microeconomic subjects are free to reallocate products and factors spontaneously between urban and rural areas. Particularly, the large-scale transfer of rural labor has become an important coupler between the urban and rural sectors; factor flow can also contribute to sustainable economic growth by optimizing resource allocation. Hence, exploring the contribution of urban–rural labor transfer to China's post-reform economic growth constitutes an important proposition with practical significance. So far, China's primary industry is mainly concentrated in rural areas, while secondary and tertiary industries are mainly found in urban areas. Labor flow between urban and rural China since reform and opening up has been closely associated with the interindustrial flow of labor. That is, massive armies of rural labor have left the primary industry and entered secondary and tertiary industries in the rural sector. Hence, we can analyze the contribution of imbalanced integration of urban–rural economic relationship to China's economic growth by measuring changes in the interindustrial allocation of labor—the labor structure effect. From a methodological point of view, Hao D.M. (2006) factorized economic growth by exponential analysis and discussed the labor structure effect of China's economic growth over different periods from 1978 to 2004. Gao F. (2010) made an empirical study on the factorization and labor structure effect of economic growth among different provinces from 1978 to 2007 with provincial panel data. We can use exponential analysis in Hao D.M. (2006) to investigate the contribution of urban–rural labor reallocation to economic growth in China since 1978. This measurement method assumes that the economic growth of a particular country can be attributed to two factors: labor input and labor productivity. Let Y, L, and P stand for the GDP, labor input, and labor productivity of a country over a certain period, then we have: $Y = L \cdot P$. To express economic growth rate, we can let t_1 and t_0 stand for the report period and the base period; Y^1, L^1, $P^1$and Y^0, L^0, P^0 for the GDP, labor input, and labor productivity at time points t_1 and t_0; $\dot{Y}$, $\dot{L}$, $\dot{P}$ for the GDP growth rate, labor input growth rate, and labor productivity growth rate from t_0 to t_1, then we have:

$$\begin{aligned}\dot{Y} &= \frac{Y^1 - Y^0}{Y^0} = \frac{P^1L^1 - P^0L^0}{P^0L^0} = \frac{P^0(L^1 - L^0) + L^0(P^1 - P^0) + ((P^1 - P^0)(L^1 - L^0)}{P^0L^0} \\ &= \frac{(L^1 - L^0)}{L^0} + \frac{(P^1 - P^0)}{P^0} + \frac{(P^1 - P^0)}{P^0} \cdot \frac{(L^1 - L^0)}{L^0} = \dot{P} + \dot{L} + \dot{P} \cdot \dot{L}\end{aligned} \tag{8.1}$$

Eq. (8.1) shows that GDP growth rate is the sum of labor productivity growth rate, labor input growth rate, and the product of labor productivity growth rate and labor input growth rate. On this basis, we can analyze labor productivity growth rate and labor input growth rate separately and then factorize GDP growth rate.

In terms of labor productivity, this factor often differs from one industry to another. Let P_1, P_2, and P_3 stand for the labor productivity of the primary, secondary, and tertiary industries; Y_1, Y_2, and Y_3 for the GDP of the primary, secondary, and tertiary industries; L_1, L_2, and L_3 stand for the labor input of the primary, secondary, and tertiary industries; R_1, R_2, and R_3 for the share of labor input of the first, secondary, and tertiary industries in total labor input. Then, we can get the expression of labor productivity shown below:

$$P = \frac{Y}{L} = \frac{Y_1 + Y_2 + Y_3}{L} = \frac{Y_1}{L} + \frac{Y_2}{L} + \frac{Y_3}{L} = \frac{Y_1}{L_1}\cdot\frac{L_1}{L} + \frac{Y_2}{L_2}\cdot\frac{L_2}{L} + \frac{Y_3}{L_3}\cdot\frac{L_3}{L}$$
$$= P_1 \cdot R_1 + P_2 \cdot R_2 + P_3 \cdot R_3 \qquad (8.2)$$

Eq. (8.2) indicates that the labor productivity of a particular economy is the weighted average of the labor productivity of the three industries weighted by their respective labor input. Out of this expression, we have derived the factorization result of labor productivity growth rate from t_0 to t_1:

$$\dot{P} = \frac{P^1 - P^0}{P^0} = \frac{P_1^1 \cdot R_1^1 + P_2^1 \cdot R_2^1 + P_3^1 \cdot R_3^1 - (P_1^0 \cdot R_1^0 + P_2^0 \cdot R_2^0 + P_3^0 \cdot R_3^0)}{(P_1^0 \cdot R_1^0 + P_2^0 \cdot R_2^0 + P_3^0 \cdot R_3^0)} = \frac{P_1^0 \cdot R_1^0}{P^0}$$
$$\cdot \frac{P_1^1 \cdot R_1^1 - P_1^0 \cdot R_1^0}{P_1^0 \cdot R_1^0} + \frac{P_2^0 \cdot R_2^0}{P^0} \cdot \frac{P_2^1 \cdot R_2^1 - P_2^0 \cdot R_2^0}{P_2^0 \cdot R_2^0} + \frac{P_3^0 \cdot R_3^0}{P^0} \cdot \frac{P_3^1 \cdot R_3^1 - P_3^0 \cdot R_3^0}{P_1^0 \cdot R_1^0} = \frac{Y_1^0}{P^0 \cdot L^0}$$
$$\cdot \frac{P_1^0 (R_1^1 - R_1^0) + R_1^0 (P_1^1 - P_1^0) + (P_1^1 - P_1^0)(R_1^1 - R_1^0)}{P_1^0 \cdot R_1^0}$$
$$+ \frac{Y_2^0}{P^0 \cdot L^0} \frac{P_2^0 (R_2^1 - R_2^0) + R_2^0 (P_2^1 - P_2^0) + (P_2^1 - P_2^0)(R_2^1 - R_2^0)}{P_2^0 \cdot R_2^0} \qquad (8.3)$$
$$+ \frac{Y_3^0}{P^0 \cdot L^0} \frac{P_3^0 (R_3^1 - R_3^0) + R_3^0 (P_3^1 - P_3^0) + (P_3^1 - P_3^0)(R_3^1 - R_3^0)}{P_3^0 \cdot R_3^0}$$
$$= y_1^0 (\dot{R}_1 + \dot{P}_1 + \dot{P}_1 \dot{R}_1) + y_2^0 (\dot{R}_2 + \dot{P}_2 + \dot{P}_2 \dot{R}_2) + y_3^0 (\dot{R}_3 + \dot{P}_3 + \dot{P}_3 \dot{R}_3)$$
$$= \Sigma_{i=1}^3 (y_i^0 \dot{P}_i) + \Sigma_{i=1}^3 (y_i^0 \dot{R}_i) + \Sigma_{i=1}^3 (y_i^0 \dot{P}_i \dot{R}_i)$$

From Eq. (8.3), labor productivity growth rate can be decomposed into three parts: $\Sigma_{i=1}^3 (y_i^0 \dot{P}_i)$ is the weighted average of labor productivity growth rates weighted by the shares of GDP of the industries at the base time, which represents the overall labor productivity growth purely caused by labor productivity growth in the industries under a constant share of GDP and hence can be called pure productivity effect; $\Sigma_{i=1}^3 (y_i^0 \dot{R}_i)$ is the weighted average of the growth rates of share of labor input weighted by the share of GDP of the industries over the base period, which represents the overall labor productivity growth purely caused by change in the share of labor input of the industries under a constant share of GDP, as change in the share of labor inputs reflects the inter-industrial reallocation of labor, it can be called pure labor structure effect; $\Sigma_{i=1}^{3}(y_i^0 \dot{P}_i \dot{R}_i)$ is the weighted average of the products of labor productivity growth rates and the grow rates of share of labor input weighted by the share of GDP of the industries over the base period, which represents the overall labor productivity growth caused by the interaction of change in labor productivity and change in share of labor input of the industries, hence can be called the interaction between pure productivity effect and pure labor structure effect.

In terms of labor input, as well as labor productivity, labor input is also an important determinant of the economic growth of a particular country. Similar to the factorization of labor productivity growth rate, labor input growth rate can also be analyzed from change in labor input of the three industries. Thus, we have the following expression:

$$\begin{aligned}\dot{L} &= \frac{L^1 - L^0}{L^0} \\ &= \frac{L_1^0(\dot{L}_1 + 1) + L_2^0(\dot{L}_2 + 1) + L_3^0(\dot{L}_3 + 1) - (L_1^0 + L_2^0 + L_3^0)}{L^0} \\ &= \frac{L_1^0\dot{L}_1 + L_2^0\dot{L}_2 + L_3^0\dot{L}_3}{L^0} = \frac{L^0R_1^0\dot{L}_1 + L^0R_2^0\dot{L}_2 + L^0R_3^0\dot{L}_3}{L^0} \\ &= R_1^0\dot{L}_1 + R_2^0\dot{L}_2 + R_3^0\dot{L}_3 = \sum_{i=1}^{3} R_i^0\dot{L}_i \end{aligned} \tag{8.4}$$

If we substitute the expressions of labor productivity growth rate and labor input growth rate into the expression of GDP growth rate, then we get the factorization formula of GDP growth rate written as follows:

$$\begin{aligned}\dot{Y} &= \dot{P} + \dot{L} + \dot{P}\cdot\dot{L} = \Sigma_{i=1}^{3}(y_i^0\dot{P}_i) + \Sigma_{i=1}^{3}(y_i^0\dot{R}_i) + \Sigma_{i=1}^{3}(y_i^0\dot{P}_i\dot{R}_i) + \Sigma_{i=1}^{3}(R_i^0\dot{L}_i) \\ &+ \Sigma_{i=1}^{3}(R_i^0\dot{L}_i)\cdot[\Sigma_{i=1}^{3}(y_i^0\dot{P}_i) + \Sigma_{i=1}^{3}(y_i^0\dot{R}_i) + \Sigma_{i=1}^{3}(y_i^0\dot{P}_i\dot{R}_i)] = \Sigma_{i=1}^{3}(y_i^0\dot{P}_i) \\ &+ \Sigma_{i=1}^{3}(R_i^0\dot{L}_i) + \Sigma_{i=1}^{3}(y_i^0\dot{P}_i)\cdot\Sigma_{i=1}^{3}(R_i^0\dot{L}_i) + \Sigma_{i=1}^{3}(y_i^0\dot{R}_i) + \Sigma_{i=1}^{3}(y_i^0\dot{P}_i\dot{R}_i) \\ &+ \Sigma_{i=1}^{3}(R_i^0\dot{L}_i)\cdot\Sigma_{i=1}^{3}(y_i^0\dot{R}_i) + \Sigma_{i=1}^{3}(R_i^0\dot{L}_i)\cdot\Sigma_{i=1}^{3}(y_i^0\dot{P}_i\dot{R}_i)\end{aligned} \tag{8.5}$$

Eq. (8.5) indicates that the GDP growth rate of a particular country over a given period can be decomposed into seven parts. $\Sigma_{i=1}^{3}(y_i^0\dot{P}_i)$ is pure productivity effect; $\Sigma_{i=1}^{3}(R_i^0\dot{L}_i)$ is pure labor input effect; $\Sigma_{i=1}^{3}(y_i^0\dot{P}_i)\cdot\Sigma_{i=1}^{3}(R_i^0\dot{L}_i)$ is the interaction between pure productivity effect and pure labor input effect. All three parts are irrelevant to change in labor structure R_i. $\Sigma_{i=1}^{3}(y_i^0\dot{R}_i)$ is pure labor structure effect, which scales the degree of economic growth purely caused by the reallocation of labor among different industries under given share of GDP and labor productivity of the industries. $\Sigma_{i=1}^{3}(y_i^0\dot{P}_i\dot{R}_i)$ is the interaction between pure productivity effect and pure labor structure effect; $\Sigma_{i=1}^{3}(R_i^0 \dot{L}_i)\cdot\Sigma_{i=1}^{3}(y_i^0 \dot{R}_i)$ is the interaction between pure labor input effect and pure labor structure effect; $\Sigma_{i=1}^{3}(R_i^0 \dot{L}_i)\cdot\Sigma_{i=1}^{3}(y_i^0 \dot{P}_i \dot{R}_i)$ is the interaction among pure labor input effect, pure productivity effect, and pure labor structure effect. As $\Sigma_{i=1}^{3}(y_i^0 \dot{R}_i)$, $\Sigma_{i=1}^{3}(y_i^0 \dot{P}_i \dot{R}_i)$, $\Sigma_{i=1}^{3}(R_i^0 \dot{L}_i)\cdot\Sigma_{i=1}^{3}(y_i^0 \dot{R}_i)$, and $\Sigma_{i=1}^{3}(R_i^0 \dot{L}_i)\cdot\Sigma_{i=1}^{3}(y_i^0 \dot{P}_i \dot{R}_i)$ are all relevant to change in labor structure, these four parts can be called aggregate labor structure effect to differentiate them from the pure labor structure effect expressed by $\Sigma_{i=1}^{3}(y_i^0 \dot{R}_i)$. Based on this factorization structure, we can use $\Sigma_{i=1}^{3}(y_i^0 \dot{R}_i)/\dot{Y}$ and $\Sigma_{i=1}^{3}(y_i^0 \dot{R}_i)/\dot{P}$ to express the contribution of pure labor structure effect to GDP growth rate and to labor productivity growth rate.

According to the factorization method of GDP growth, we can examine the economic results of labor reallocation among the three industries in China from 1978 to 2017, thus finding out the contribution of imbalanced integration of urban–rural economic relationship to economic growth. All figures related to GDP, added value of the three industries, employment, and employment of three industries come from CEIC Data. To exclude the influence of price factors on GDP, we used GDP index (1978=100) to process the GDP figures and yielded GDP figures calculated based on the constant-price figures of 1978. The GDP growth rate figures were also calculated based on constant-price GDP. The labor productivity of all three industries equals to the added value of the respective industry divided by its employment. Labor productivity growth rate and labor input growth rate were calculated according to their respective original figures.

Figure 8.1 compares China's overall labor productivity and the labor productivity of three industries from 1978 to 2017. Over this period, both

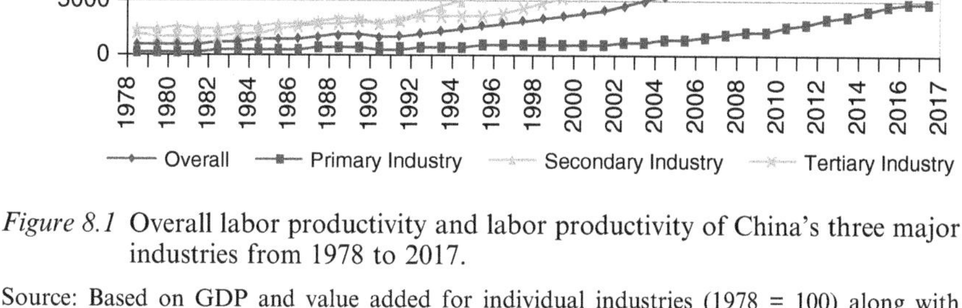

Figure 8.1 Overall labor productivity and labor productivity of China's three major industries from 1978 to 2017.

Source: Based on GDP and value added for individual industries (1978 = 100) along with employment figure within the corresponding range; original figures all come from CEIC Data.

overall labor productivity and the labor productivity of three industries increased year by year, reflecting continued improvement of labor output efficiency. Overall labor productivity rose from 916.19 yuan to 16356.58 yuan; the labor productivity of the primary industry rose from 359.65 yuan to 4799.27 yuan; the labor productivity of the secondary industry rose from 2527.23 yuan to 23541.25 yuan; and that of the tertiary industry rose from 1850.87 yuan to 18801.47 yuan. By horizontal comparison, the labor productivity of the primary industry was lower than that of the secondary and tertiary industries all the time. For example, based on the constant-price figures of 1978, in 2017, the labor productivity of the secondary and the tertiary industries was 4.91 times and 3.92 times higher than that of the primary industry. As labor productivity is generally closely relevant to economic returns, this labor productivity gap signals the intrinsic need for cross-sector flow of labor. After reform and opening up, China's market-oriented economic system reform has relaxed employment control among industries (and between urban and rural areas). This way, the flow of labor from the rural sector into the urban sector, or from the primary industry into the secondary or tertiary industry, has become a characteristic fact of national economic operation, as is evidenced by changes in the figures measuring the employment structure of the three industries, the employment structure between urban and rural areas, and urbanization rate.

According to the factorization method of GDP growth rate described above, we can measure the contribution of different factors to economic growth since reform and opening up. From 1978 to 2017, GDP rose from 367.87 billion yuan to 82.7 trillion yuan. By GDP index (1978 = 100), after excluding price factors, GDP rose from 367.87 billion yuan to 12.70 trillion yuan. As indicated by Table 8.1, from 1979 to 2017, annual growth rate of GDP was 9.54 percent, whereas annual growth rate of labor productivity was 7.75 percent and that of pure labor input effect was 1.74 percent. Obviously, between the two major drivers of GDP growth, labor productivity growth is the key driver of the country's sustained GDP growth. If we take a closer look at the labor structure effect in labor productivity growth, we will discover that from 1979 to 2017, the annual growth rate of pure labor structure effect was 1.43 percent; the annual growth rate of aggregate labor structure effect was 1.51 percent.

According to the calculation method for the contribution of labor structure effect to economic growth and to labor productivity growth, we can yield that with the investigation period from 1979 to 2017, the annual average contribution of pure labor structure effect to China's GDP growth rate was 13.31 percent and that to labor productivity growth rate was 16.12 percent. Pure labor structure effect should have contributed to both GDP growth and labor productivity growth. If cross terms of pure labor structure effect with other factors are included, the contribution of aggregate labor structure effect to GDP growth and labor productivity growth will be even more significant. On the contrary, if labor structure effect between urban

Table 8.1 China's labor structure effect and its contribution to economic growth from 1979 to 2017

Year	GDP growth rate	Labor productivity growth rate	Pure productivity effect	Pure labor input effect	Pure labor structure effect	Effect of 4 cross terms	Overall labor structure effect	Pure labor structure effect/GDP growth rate	Pure labor structure effect/labor productivity growth rate
1979	7.60	5.31	4.02	2.17	1.40	0.01	1.32	18.41	26.33
1980	7.81	4.40	2.41	3.26	1.94	0.19	2.06	24.87	44.09
1981	5.17	1.89	1.00	3.22	0.93	0.02	0.92	17.94	49.05
1982	8.93	5.16	5.10	3.59	0.07	0.18	0.06	0.77	1.34
1983	10.84	8.11	6.61	2.52	1.45	0.26	1.54	13.38	17.87
1984	15.14	10.93	6.47	3.79	4.37	0.51	4.63	28.85	39.96
1985	13.44	9.63	7.00	3.48	2.31	0.65	2.72	17.18	23.98
1986	8.94	5.95	3.64	2.82	2.23	0.24	2.37	24.97	37.54
1987	11.69	8.51	7.10	2.93	1.34	0.33	1.46	11.46	15.73
1988	11.23	8.06	7.15	2.94	0.84	0.31	0.94	7.45	10.38
1989	4.19	2.31	3.42	1.83	–1.06	0.00	–1.13	–25.37	–45.93
1990	3.91	–1.21	–11.11	17.02	–0.11	–1.89	–0.11	–2.91	1.01
1991	9.29	8.06	7.44	1.15	0.52	0.18	0.62	5.63	6.49
1992	14.22	13.07	11.07	1.01	1.74	0.40	2.03	12.24	13.31
1993	13.87	12.75	9.36	0.99	3.14	0.37	3.42	22.64	24.62
1994	13.05	11.97	9.12	0.97	2.83	0.14	2.88	21.68	23.65
1995	10.95	9.95	7.47	0.90	2.55	0.03	2.51	23.25	25.58
1996	9.93	8.52	6.45	1.30	2.01	0.17	2.09	20.21	23.56
1997	9.23	7.87	7.10	1.26	0.69	0.18	0.78	7.45	8.74
1998	7.84	6.59	6.60	1.17	–0.04	0.10	–0.01	–0.45	–0.54
1999	7.67	6.53	7.17	1.07	–0.59	0.02	–0.65	–7.74	–9.10
2000	8.49	7.45	7.64	0.97	–0.16	0.04	–0.19	–1.86	–2.12
2001	8.34	7.28	7.39	0.99	–0.12	0.08	–0.11	–1.38	–1.59

(*Continued*)

Table 8.1 (Continued)

Year	*GDP growth rate*	*Labor productivity growth rate*	*Pure productivity effect*	*Pure labor input effect*	*Pure labor structure effect*	*Effect of 4 cross terms*	*Overall labor structure effect*	*Pure labor structure effect/GDP growth rate*	*Pure labor structure effect/ labor productivity growth rate*
2002	9.13	8.41	9.00	0.66	–0.47	–0.06	–0.59	–5.13	–5.57
2003	10.04	9.36	8.04	0.62	1.21	0.16	1.32	12.06	12.93
2004	10.11	9.33	6.07	0.72	3.21	0.11	3.28	31.77	34.44
2005	11.40	10.82	7.42	0.52	3.15	0.31	3.43	27.65	29.11
2006	12.72	12.22	8.71	0.44	3.25	0.32	3.53	25.53	26.57
2007	14.23	13.71	10.75	0.46	2.83	0.20	2.98	19.89	20.64
2008	9.65	9.30	7.76	0.32	1.46	0.12	1.55	15.07	15.64
2009	9.40	9.02	7.08	0.35	1.81	0.16	1.94	19.23	20.04
2010	10.64	10.23	8.33	0.37	1.78	0.17	1.91	16.70	17.35
2011	9.54	9.08	6.79	0.41	2.20	0.13	2.30	23.08	24.23
2012	7.86	7.46	6.00	0.37	1.43	0.06	1.47	18.17	19.14
2013	7.76	7.38	5.26	0.36	2.10	0.04	2.12	27.03	28.43
2014	7.30	6.91	5.20	0.36	1.69	0.05	1.72	23.19	24.48
2015	6.90	6.63	5.65	0.26	0.89	0.11	0.98	12.85	13.38
2016	6.72	6.51	6.06	0.20	0.42	0.05	0.46	6.22	6.42
2017	6.86	6.81	6.36	0.05	0.50	–0.05	0.45	7.24	7.30
Avg.	9.54	7.75	6.26	1.74	1.43	0.11	1.51	13.31	16.12

Source: All original figures related to GDP, added value of three industries, overall employment, employment of three industries, and GDP index (1978 = 100) used in the calculation of GDP growth factorization come from CIEC Data.

and rural areas is not included, the annual growth rate of China's GDP should have dropped by at least 1.43 percentage points and that of labor productivity should have dropped by at least 1.51 percentage points. Obviously, since reform and opening up in 1978, China's GDP has sustained high-speed growth. Labor transfer between urban and rural areas, especially the non-agricultural transfer of rural labor, has changed the employment structure among different industries. This change constitutes an important driver of the country's sustained high-speed economic growth. From the perspective of promoting the economic growth-oriented strategy, the imbalanced integration of urban–rural economic relationship has indeed contributed positively to this strategic implementation.

8.2 Impact of urban–rural income gap on overall income distribution

Since reform and opening up, the imbalanced integration of urban–rural economic relationship has not only affected the degree of China's economic growth but also its income distribution. The income distribution gap among different social groups has become an important structural issue facing the country's modernization drive. As a large developing country with socialist system, the goal of China's economic development is to achieve common prosperity on the basis of emancipated and developed productivity, which is bound to involve concerns and resolutions of the income gap among different social groups. For any country, resident income gap is a concept with very rich connotations, and it can be spread from different perspectives and based on different research instruments. For example, the former includes the gap between urban and rural areas, among regions, among industries, and between labor and capital. The latter include dual contrast coefficient, variable coefficient, and Geni coefficient. For a large developing country like China, however, resident income gap is typically manifested between urban and rural areas and among different regions. In fact, urban–rural gap and regional gap constitute the core contents of resident income gap in China. One point remains: how shall we discriminate the contribution of urban–rural income gap to overall resident income gap? This is an important point for understanding the performance of imbalanced integration of urban–rural economic relationship on the distribution dimension.

In terms of research instruments, existing studies on urban–rural income gap have often relied on per capita net income data, while those on regional income gap usually rely on per capita GDP data. The use of different sets of data would make it hard to factorize between urban and rural areas and among different regions. Compared with per capita GDP, using per capita net income data would be more likely to meet the need of factorizing resident income gap. Furthermore, existing studies on the factorization of China's overall Gini coefficient are not only faced with the demerit of not internalizing regional income gap but also the challenge of being unable to provide the needed additivity and decomposability. Now that Theil index is more suitable for factorizing income inequality than Gini coefficient, it would be recommendable to hold a prudent attitude toward income gap factorization results based on Gini coefficient (Li H., 2005). Some existing studies try to decompose income gap into an urban–rural portion and a regional portion with Theil index. One problem with these attempts is that the first-order decomposition sequence of Theil index will affect income distribution judgments. If the urban–rural portion came before the regional portion, the urban–rural income inequality would be exaggerated; if the regional portion went before the urban–rural portion, the regional income inequality would be exaggerated (Wang H.L. & Xu X., 2006). Hence, using the right analytical instrument to factorize resident income gap in China and reveal the contribution of urban–rural income gap to overall resident income gap becomes an important content of explaining the economic performance of the imbalanced integration of China's urban–rural economic relationship.

From a methodological point of view, according to Shorrocks A.F. (1980), Theil first-order index can factorize income gap either between urban and rural areas or among regions, but it cannot do them both. For this reason, Akita T. (2003) and Tang D.B. & Zhang J. (2001) extended Theil index to second-order nesting, which Gao F. (2012a) used in his empirical study on the trend and intrinsic mechanism of resident income gap in China from 1978 to 2009 based on the data sets of 31 provinces. This nesting algorithm assumes that i =1, 2 as the urban and rural sectors; j =1, 2, 3 as eastern, central, and western China[1], k=1, 2, ...31 as the 31 provinces (municipalities, autonomous regions) including Beijing, Tianjin,... Xinjiang; y_{ijk} and n_{ijk} as resident income and population in sector i of region j, province k; $Y = \sum_i^2 \sum_j^3 \sum_k^{31} y_{ijk}$ and $N = \sum_i^2 \sum_j^3 \sum_k^{31} n_{ijk}$ are total income (total population), which is the sum of incomes (populations) in sector i of region j, province k. Hence, the second-order nesting form of Theil T is written as

$$T = \sum_i^2 \sum_j^3 \sum_k^{31} \left(\frac{y_{ijk}}{Y}\right) \log\left(\frac{y_{ijk}/Y}{n_{ijk}/N}\right) \tag{8.6}$$

If we let $T_{di} = \sum_j^3 \sum_k^{N_{ij}} (\frac{y_{ijk}}{Y_i}) \log(\frac{y_{ijk}/Y_i}{n_{ijk}/N_i})$, which represents the regional income gap in sector i; $T_{BS} = \sum_i^2 (\frac{Y_i}{Y}) \log(\frac{Y_i/Y}{N_i/N})$, which represents the sector (or urban–rural) gap in overall income gap, where $Y_i = \sum_j^3 \sum_k^{N_{ij}} y_{ijk}$, $N_i = \sum_j^3 \sum_k^{N_{ij}} n_{ijk}$, then Eq. (8.6) can be rewritten as

$$T = \sum_i^2 \left(\frac{Y_i}{Y}\right) T_{di} + \sum_i^2 \left(\frac{Y_i}{Y}\right) \log\left(\frac{Y_i/Y}{Y_i/N}\right) = \sum_i^2 \left(\frac{Y_i}{Y}\right) T_{di} + T_{BS} \tag{8.7}$$

Next, let $T_{ij} = \sum_k^{N_{ij}} (\frac{y_{ijk}}{Y_{ij}})\log(\frac{y_{ijk} / Y_{ij}}{n_{ijk} / N_{ij}})$, which represents the residents' intraregional income gap in sector i of region j; $T_{pi} = \sum_j^3 (\frac{Y_{ij}}{Y_i})\log(\frac{Y_{ij} / Y_i}{N_{ij} / N_i})$, which represents the residents' interregional income gap in sector i of region j, where $Y_{ij} = \sum_k^{N_{ij}} y_{ijk}$, $N_{ij} = \sum_k^{N_{ij}} n_{ijk}$, then we have

$$T_{di} = \sum_j^3 \sum_k^{N_{ij}} \left(\frac{y_{ijk}}{Y_i}\right)\log\left(\frac{y_{ijk}/Y_i}{n_{ijk}/N_i}\right) = \sum_j^3 \left(\frac{Y_{ij}}{Y_i}\right)T_{ij} + \sum_j^3 \left(\frac{Y_{ij}}{Y_i}\right)\log\left(\frac{Y_{ij}/Y_i}{N_{ij}/N_i}\right)$$

$$= \sum_j^3 \left(\frac{Y_{ij}}{Y_i}\right)T_{ij} + T_{pi} \tag{8.8}$$

Then Eq. (8.7) can be rewritten as

$$T = \sum_i^2 \left(\frac{Y_i}{Y}\right)T_{di} + T_{BS} = \sum_i^2 \left(\frac{Y_i}{Y}\right)\left[\sum_j^3 \left(\frac{Y_{ij}}{Y_i}\right)T_{ij} + T_{pi}\right] + T_{BS}$$

$$= \sum_i^2 \sum_j^3 \left(\frac{Y_{ij}}{Y_i}\right)T_{ij} + \sum_i^2 \left(\frac{Y_i}{Y}\right)T_{pi} + T_{BS} = T_{WD} + T_{BD} + T_{BS} \tag{8.9}$$

Eq. (8.9) is the second-order nested decomposition of Theil T. Obviously, the overall resident income gap scaled by Theil T can be decomposed into three parts T_{WD}, T_{BD}, and T_{BS}. Here, $T_{WD} = \sum_i^2 \sum_j^3 (\frac{Y_{ij}}{Y_i}) T_{ij}$, $T_{BD} = \sum_i^2 (\frac{Y_i}{Y}) T_{pi}$, and $T_{BS} = \sum_i^2 (\frac{Y_i}{Y})\log(\frac{Y_i / Y}{N_i / N})$ measure the intraregional, interregional, and urban–rural resident income gap, respectively. In the same way, we can yield the second-order nested decomposition of Theil L as follows:

$$L = \sum_i^2 \sum_j^3 \sum_k^{31} \left(\frac{n_{ijk}}{N}\right)\log\left(\frac{n_{ijk}/N}{y_{ijk}/Y}\right) \tag{8.10}$$

Through similar decomposition process to that of Theil L, we can eventually obtain:

$$L = \sum_i^2 \sum_j^3 \left(\frac{N_{ij}}{N}\right)L_{ij} + \sum_I^2 \left(\frac{N_i}{N}\right)L_{pi} + L_{BS} = L_{WD} + L_{BD} + L_{BS} \tag{8.11}$$

Unlike Theil T, Theil L weighs the items with share of population rather than share of income. By combining both indexes together, we can reveal how much each factor affects resident income gap. The second-order nested decomposition based on Theil index can examine the effect of both urban–rural income gap and regional income gap on overall resident income gap. In the case of Theil T, for example, T_{WD}/T, T_{BD}/T, and T_{BS}/T scale the contributions of intraregional, interregional, and urban–rural gap to overall resident income gap, respectively. In the same way, we can calculate the contributions of intraregional, interregional, and urban–rural gap to overall resident income gap in Theil L.

The above discussion provides a methodology for studying the factorization of resident income gap in China, especially the contribution of urban–rural income gap to overall resident income gap. Since the start of reform and opening up in 1978, the fluctuation of urban–rural income gap has represented an aspect of the imbalanced integration of China's urban–rural economic relationship. Hence to investigate the contribution of urban–rural income gap to overall resident income gap is essentially to explain the effect of imbalanced integration of urban–rural economic relationship on overall distribution. Considering the availability and consistency of data, we used the empirical data of China's 31 provinces (autonomous regions/municipalities, *sic passim*) from 1992 to 2016. For this period, per capital disposable income of urban residents, rural population, urban population, consumer price index of rural residents, and consumer price index of urban residents in different regions were needed. Except the consumer price index figures of urban and rural residents that come from *China Statistical Yearbook*, all other figures come from CEIC Data. After 2013, China conducted an integrated survey on the income and expenditure and living conditions of households. Hence, the rural resident income over the 2014–2016 interval is the per capita disposable income. To exclude the effect of price factors on resident income gap, we used urban and rural residents' consumer price index (1992 = 100) to reduce resident income and yielded the urban and rural resident income figures calculated at constant prices.

The calculation results can be summarized as Table 8.2 and Table 8.3. Overall resident income gap has been fluctuating across different time intervals at large. In the case of Theil T, for example, over the 1992–1994 interval, this figure rose from 0.1574 to 0.1876 and then gradually dropped to 0.1412 in 1998. Over the 1998–2003 interval, it rose again and then hovered above 0.1900 until 2009. From 2009 to 2016, the figure gradually dropped from 0.1925 to 0.1252. The same happened to Theil L, too. This suggests that since 1992, China's overall resident income gap has been fluctuating remarkably, without any sign of unidirectional increase or reduction. Notably, in overall resident income gap, different components play different roles. Neither intraregional nor interregional gap has acted as the main driver of overall gap changes, whereas urban–rural income gap has played the key role in this effect. Throughout the entire investigation period, the annual average contribution of urban–rural income gap to Theil T and Theil L was 77.28 percent and 76.05 percent, the annual average contribution of intraregional income gap was 8.14 percent and 6.99 percent and that of interregional gap was 14.58 percent and 16.96 percent, respectively. This suggests that so far, China's overall resident income gap is largely a matter

Table 8.2 Factorization of Theil T of China's resident income gap from 1992 to 2016

Year	*Absolute value*				*Contribution*			
	T	T_{WD}	T_{BD}	T_{BS}	T/T	T_{WD}/T	T_{BD}/T	T_{BS}/T
1992	0.1574	0.0187	0.0171	0.1216	100	11.88	10.84	77.28
1993	0.1797	0.0197	0.0207	0.1393	100	10.98	11.52	77.50
1994	0.1876	0.0212	0.0231	0.1433	100	11.29	12.31	76.40
1995	0.1743	0.0186	0.0271	0.1285	100	10.68	15.57	73.75
1996	0.1520	0.0175	0.0272	0.1073	100	11.49	17.93	70.59
1997	0.1435	0.0157	0.0274	0.1004	100	10.94	19.08	69.97
1998	0.1412	0.0156	0.0267	0.0989	100	11.03	18.91	70.07
1999	0.1517	0.0151	0.0264	0.1102	100	9.94	17.43	72.63
2000	0.1626	0.0142	0.0271	0.1213	100	8.75	16.66	74.59
2001	0.1740	0.0150	0.0276	0.1315	100	8.59	15.87	75.54
2002	0.1821	0.0134	0.0263	0.1424	100	7.37	14.42	78.21
2003	0.1958	0.0145	0.0273	0.1540	100	7.41	13.94	78.65
2004	0.1966	0.0150	0.0269	0.1547	100	7.63	13.67	78.70
2005	0.1980	0.0139	0.0276	0.1564	100	7.02	13.95	79.03
2006	0.1900	0.0127	0.0280	0.1583	100	6.39	14.05	79.56
2007	0.1947	0.0117	0.0259	0.1572	100	5.99	13.30	80.71
2008	0.1905	0.0108	0.0252	0.1544	100	5.68	13.24	81.08
2009	0.1925	0.0112	0.0259	0.1533	100	5.82	13.47	80.71
2010	0.1829	0.0106	0.0254	0.1468	100	5.82	13.89	80.29
2011	0.1707	0.0102	0.0245	0.1359	100	5.98	14.37	79.65
2012	0.1636	0.0096	0.0234	0.1307	100	5.85	14.28	79.87
2013	0.1498	0.0093	0.0208	0.1196	100	6.21	13.92	79.87
2014	0.1339	0.0091	0.0186	0.1062	100	6.78	13.90	79.32
2015	0.1291	0.0088	0.0181	0.1021	100	6.85	14.03	79.13
2016	0.1252	0.0089	0.0176	0.0987	100	7.11	14.08	78.81
Avg.	0.0136	0.0245	0.1310	0.1691	100	8.14	14.58	77.28

Source: Calculated by the author through second order nested decomposition of resident income gap.

of urban–rural income gap, and the change in urban–rural economic relationship plays a decisive role in the evolution of overall resident income gap. Since reform and opening up in 1978, imbalanced integration of urban–rural economic relationship has become the core determinant of the direction of overall resident income gap at the distribution level. To optimize resident income distribution, it is essential to address and ameliorate the imbalanced integration of urban–rural economic relationship.

8.3 Impact of urban–rural labor market distortion on resident consumption gap

Since reform and opening up, imbalanced integration of urban–rural economic relationship has led to changes in China's urban–rural income gap, which still represents the majority of overall resident income gap. Income

Table 8.3 Factorization of Theil L of China's resident income gap from 1992 to 2016

Year	*Absolute value*				*Contribution*			
	L	L_WD	L_BD	L_BS	*L/L*	L_WD/L	L_BD/L	L_BS/L
1992	0.1516	0.0171	0.0195	0.1149	100	11.27	12.89	75.83
1993	0.1746	0.0168	0.0246	0.1332	100	9.65	14.08	76.27
1994	0.1832	0.0169	0.0276	0.1386	100	9.24	15.08	75.69
1995	0.1729	0.0146	0.0336	0.1247	100	8.42	19.44	72.14
1996	0.1516	0.0141	0.0332	0.1043	100	9.32	21.91	68.77
1997	0.1437	0.0132	0.0327	0.0979	100	9.18	22.75	68.08
1998	0.1411	0.0128	0.0317	0.0966	100	9.06	22.49	68.45
1999	0.1530	0.0126	0.0322	0.1082	100	8.21	21.04	70.76
2000	0.1654	0.0115	0.0336	0.1204	100	6.94	20.29	72.77
2001	0.1792	0.0120	0.0351	0.1320	100	6.72	19.59	73.69
2002	0.1907	0.0112	0.0345	0.1450	100	5.86	18.11	76.04
2003	0.2071	0.0120	0.0357	0.1594	100	5.82	17.22	76.96
2004	0.2093	0.0127	0.0347	0.1620	100	6.06	16.56	77.37
2005	0.2135	0.0125	0.0351	0.1658	100	5.87	16.45	77.68
2006	0.2176	0.0119	0.0358	0.1699	100	5.47	16.46	78.08
2007	0.2150	0.0116	0.0332	0.1702	100	5.38	15.43	79.19
2008	0.2118	0.0113	0.0317	0.1688	100	5.36	14.98	79.66
2009	0.2157	0.0118	0.0325	0.1714	100	5.46	15.09	79.45
2010	0.2062	0.0113	0.0310	0.1639	100	5.47	15.04	79.49
2011	0.1933	0.0111	0.0299	0.1522	100	5.73	15.49	78.78
2012	0.1864	0.0105	0.0284	0.1474	100	5.65	15.24	79.12
2013	0.1708	0.0099	0.0261	0.1348	100	5.82	15.26	78.92
2014	0.1500	0.0093	0.0216	0.1191	100	6.21	14.38	79.40
2015	0.1451	0.0090	0.0210	0.1151	100	6.19	14.47	79.34
2016	0.1413	0.0090	0.0203	0.1120	100	6.38	14.39	79.23
Avg.	0.1796	0.0123	0.0302	0.1371	100	6.99	16.96	76.05

Source: Calculated by the author through second order nested decomposition of resident income gap.

level is an "instrument" factor affecting resident consumption status. Compared with urban–rural income gap, urban–rural consumption gap is better able to reflect the disparity between urban and rural residents in living conditions and welfare level. Since the late 1970s, while the absolute consumption expenditure of China's urban and rural residents has been growing unidirectionally, urban–rural resident consumption gap has performed differently across different time intervals. By temporal and cross-country comparison, China's urban–rural consumption gap is still at a high level. Urban–rural consumption gap concerns the transformation of duality, expansion of domestic consumption, and transition of industrial structure. "Urban–rural consumption gap not only impede China's economic growth in future but also contributes negatively to people's well-being and the construction of a harmonious society" (Xu M. & Jiang Y., 2015). Hence, it is of great practical value to explore the drivers and influencing factors of urban–rural economic relationship. On the other side, the imbalanced integration of China's urban–rural economic relationship is also reflected by the obstruction still existent against the spontaneous flow of factors between urban and rural areas. For example, while the employment control function of urban and rural household registration has been weakening, its social security resource allocation function is still working prominently. This has caused an inconsistency between occupational transition and identity transformation in the transfer of labor, as typically evidenced by the new duality—inequalities in job opportunity, wage income, and social welfare—faced by rural labor after nonagricultural transfer. The new duality implies that so far China is still suffering from labor market distortion or mismatched labor factors between urban and rural areas. The cause and effect of this distortion, consequently, becomes an important topic of theoretical research. Based on this reality, empirically investigating the effect of a distorted urban–rural labor market on resident consumption gap can be seen as another cut-in point for understanding the effect of imbalanced integration of urban–rural economic relationship.

To understand the effect of labor market distortion on urban–rural consumption gap in post-reform China, the essence is to clarify the relevance between duality transformation and system transition (Gao F. & Wang Y.N., 2016). According to the Lewis-Fei-Ranic model, we can use Figure 8.2 to describe the labor flow and welfare effects under a dual economy. Here, diagrams (a) and (b) illustrate the balance of the labor market in the rural and the urban sector, respectively, in which the horizontal axis denotes the amount of labor and the longitudinal axis the wage income. D_t and D_m are the labor marginal output line or labor demand line of the urban and the rural sector; S_t and S_m are the labor supply line of the two sectors before the flow of labor. Before cross-sector flow of labor, the wage of the rural sector, W_a, was lower while that of the urban sector, W_b, was higher. Assuming that the labor market is effective and without considering the transaction cost,

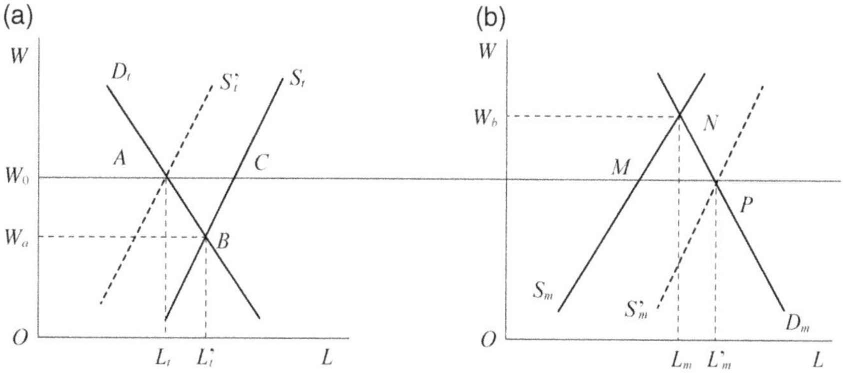

Figure 8.2 Labor flow and welfare effect under urban–rural dual economy.

this wage difference will serve as a market "signal" that induces rural labor to flow into the urban sector, which in economic practice corresponds to the nonagricultural transfer of labor and an increase in urbanization. So in diagram (a), S_t moves up left while in diagram (b) S_m moves down right. The result is that rural labor productivity or wage level continues to rise due to labor reduction, while urban labor productivity or wage level continues to fall due to labor increase. The transfer of labor has changed the labor demand and supply between the two sectors and caused a convergence of labor productivity and wage level between them. This change continues until the labor supply line of the rural sector has moved to S' and that of the urban sector has moved to W_0. At that time, the labor market equilibrium wage for both the urban and rural sectors is W_0. The amount of labor outflow from the rural sector is $L_t - L'_t$, while the amount of labor absorbed by the urban sector is $L'_m - L_m$. When the labor flow between the two sectors has led to the same labor productivity or wage level, according to the Lewis-Fei-Ranis model, the transformation of duality economy has completed for that economy. In terms of economic effect, in diagram (a), $S_{\triangle ABC}$ is the welfare increase in the rural sector caused by labor outflow and consequently wage increase; in diagram (b), $S_{\triangle ABC}$ is the welfare increase in the urban sector caused by labor inflow and consequently employment increase. Together, they constitute resource allocation efficiency improvement or economic growth level caused by labor reallocation. Obviously, under the condition of an effective labor market and in the absence of transaction cost, labor flow between the urban and rural sectors will improve the factor allocation efficiency and contribute to the emancipation and development of the whole social productivity.

In the Lewis-Fei-Ranis model, the flow of labor between urban and rural areas is the fundamental pathway for a country to resolve its dual economy. Cross-sector transfer of labor is both a process of improving factor allocation efficiency, hence increasing GDP, and a process of flattening the labor productivity and wage for laborers among different industries and sectors. One point remains the effect of intersectoral labor flow and reallocation is determined by the effectiveness of the labor market. Especially for China, as a large developing country in the process of economic system transition, the marketization of factors is still lagging behind the marketization of commodities, and labor market distortion is still a characteristic fact in the country's economic system transition, as can be clearly observed from the changes in government–market relationship and the intragovernmental and intramarket structural features discussed earlier. Given that China's market-oriented system transition is progressive in nature, even though there is a gap between the urban and rural sectors in labor productivity or wage level and rural labor objectively need to improve their own economic position through reallocation, the labor market takes a long time to perfect itself. Its institutional or noninstitutional aspects are very likely to suppress the sufficient flow of labor, hence delaying the cross-sector, cross-industrial, and cross-regional transfer of productive factors through labor market distortion. Labor market distortion is comparative to a number of "wedges" added into the nonagricultural transfer of rural labor, preventing the fulfillment of economic growth and wage flattening effects forecast by the Lewis-Fei-Ranis model.

In Figure 8.2, labor market distortion means that the up-left movement of St (and the down-right movement of S_m) is slow or intermittent, which will cause the gap between the wage of the urban sector, W_b, and the wage of the rural sector, Wa, to stay at a constant high, thus greatly constraining the wage increase for rural labor and the employment growth of the urban sector. If we introduce a perfection degree of the labor market, we will discover that the transformation of dual economy is dependent on the labor flow among different sectors, whereas labor flow is dependent on the effectiveness of the labor market. Here the key point is, after the effectiveness of the labor market, the flow of labor between the urban and rural sectors will not always take place automatically, which coincides with China's transition background of a perfecting factor market and hence differs from the assumption of a perfect factor market implied by the Lewis-Fei-Ranis model. From the perspective of the influencing mechanism, labor market distortion affects urban–rural consumption gap through the following two channels.

One is urban–rural income gap. That is, labor market distortion will contribute negatively to the transformation of dual economy, especially the convergence of urban–rural income gap. Income level is the basic variable affecting the consumption expenditure of different social groups, whereas urban–rural income gap represents an important determinant of urban–rural consumption gap. This signifies that, without considering other factors, labor market distortion will contribute negatively to the reduction of urban–rural consumption gap through income gap.

Second is the allocation of public goods or social security resources. In the Lewis-Fei-Ranis model, the nonagricultural transfer of rural labor is mainly resulted from the intersectoral wage difference, and rural labor always look for jobs with higher labor productivity or wage level. Here the implied assumption is urban and rural labor (and residents) enjoy the same level of social security without identity-based social welfare gap, and the flow of labor is purely an occupational transition targeted at improving income level. In developing countries, however, compared with their urban counterparts, rural residents are disadvantaged in policy-making and access to social security. Among discussions regarding local problems of China, many articles have noted that the residents' social security in urban and rural China is relevant to their household register or "identity"; different identities have accounted for the social security difference or dual society between urban and rural residents. Our study on post-reform urban–rural economic relationship earlier in this book also demonstrates that an important proof of the current imbalanced integration between urban and rural China is that the urban–rural allocation gap of public goods is still solidified, and the urban–rural equalization of basic public goods is still in progress.

Logically speaking, the intersectoral flow of labor will contribute positively to the reduction of dual society. The nonagricultural transfer of rural labor will allow then to "discover" through comparison the allocation gap of social security resources and rely on "voice" or on "vote-by-foot" to propel urban–rural equalization of basic services. Besides, some rural labors also have the opportunity of becoming an urban residents to gain access to better social security. In particular, household registration is small and medium Chinese cities and towns has been largely liberated now. Its social security resource allocation function is beginning to loosen. Even so, in the course of China's economic system transition, social security is till allocated mainly according to the "identity" attribute of citizens or farmers rather than the post-transfer job of rural labor. The nonagricultural transfer does make a difference to the allocation benchmark of "identity" but to a very limited extent. Inside urban areas, the allocation of public goods and social security resources also differs according to their size and level. Big cities, especially megacities, are more likely to provide more abundant basic public services for their citizens. This signifies that while reduced labor market distortion helps converge the public service and social security gap between urban and rural areas, given the importance and continuity of "identity" in social security allocation, the role of increased labor market degree in reducing urban–rural social security gap and consequently urban–rural consumption gap is not really prominent. In other words, while labor market distortion will contribute negatively to the reduction of urban–rural consumption gap through social security allocation, this contribution is insignificant as a result of the "identity" attribute of social security allocation itself.

On these grounds, it is necessary to select indicators that match the essence of concepts for empirical study. After 1992, China established the reform goal of socialist market economic system; after 2013, it tuned the statistical caliber of urban and rural resident income. Considering the availability, accuracy, and consistency of empirical data, we can use the panel data of China 31 provinces (autonomous regions/municipalities, *sic passim*) from 11,992 to 2013 for empirical study. Following is a description of the analytical indicators and data sources involved herein.

$$DS = \frac{a_a}{a_m} \times \frac{y_a}{1 - y_a} \times \frac{1 - l_a}{l_a} \times e^{(r_m - r_a)s_a} \times e^{(s_m - s_a)r_m} \tag{8.12}$$

1. Labor market distortion (*DS*). In the presence of dual economy, the economic system of a particular country is divided into two parts: the urban sector and the rural sector. As labor market distortion reflects how well labor input matches labor output in a particular sector after human capital factors are controlled, in light of Gai Q.E., Zhu X. & Shi Q.H. (2013), the degree of labor market distortion (or labor market integration) of individual regions was measured in the following form:

In Eq. (8.12), A_a and α_m are the labor substitution elasticity of the rural sector (as represented by the primary industry) and urban sector (as represented by the secondary and tertiary industries) of a province; y_a and l_a are the share of value added of the primary industry in GDP and the share of the primary industry in total labor; s_a and s_m are the years of education of labor in the two sectors; and r_a and r_m are the rate of return to education of labor in the two sectors. The higher the resulted *DS* value, the higher the degree of labor market integration, and the lower the degree of labor market distortion, and the *vice versa*. In calculating Eq. (8.12), the first thing is to determine the labor substitution elasticity of the two sectors. Consistently with Brandt L. & Zhu X. (2010), Bosworth B. & Colins S.M. (2008), α_a and α_m are set at 0.5.

In calculating the degree of labor market distortion in China, other data are also needed as the support. The share of value added of the primary industry of the 31 provinces from 1992 to 2013 is derived from the value added of the primary industry and GDP provided by CEIC Data; the share of employment of the primary industry of the 31 provinces/autonomous regions/municipalities) is based on CEIC Data figures, the statistical yearbooks of the provinces, and national economic and social development bulletins. Considering the availability of data, we used the overall average years of education of labor to scale the years of education of urban labor; the overall average years of education and the average years of education of rural labor = share of uneducated × 0 + share of primary school graduates × 6 + share of junior high school graduates × 9 + share of senior high school graduates × 12 + share of university graduates and above × 16. The share of uneducated figures come from CEIC Data and the yearbooks of individual provinces. Existing statistics do not provide the rate of return to education of urban and rural labor of individual provinces, but Liang R. (2011) made a measurement based on China Nutrition and Health Survey 1989–2009 data. Here we used the average of the figures for 1997, 2000, 2004, 2006, and 2009 from their study, namely, 0.0263 for the rural sector and 0.0477 for the urban sector, to represent the rate of return to education of the two sectors of individual provinces.

$$CG = \sum_{j=1}^{2}\left(\frac{c_j}{c}\right)\ln\left(\frac{c_j}{c}/\frac{p_j}{p}\right) = \left(\frac{c_1}{c}\right)\ln\left(\frac{c_1}{c}/\frac{p_1}{p}\right) + \left(\frac{c_2}{c}\right)\ln\left(\frac{c_2}{c}/\frac{p_2}{p}\right) \quad (8.13)$$

2. Urban– consumption gap (*CG*). As stated earlier, urban–rural consumption gap can be expressed in three forms: nominal gap, actual gap, and Theil index. Existing literature usually chooses to use per capita consumption expenditure of urban residents/per capita living expenditure of rural residents to represent urban–rural consumption gap, which neither excludes the effect of price factors nor includes changes in population structure. To include changes in urban–rural population

structure, here we scale urban–rural consumption gap in the form of Theil index. Let *CG* represent the urban–rural consumption gap of a province in a given year, then we have:

In Eq. (8.13) j =1, 2 represents the urban and rural sectors; p_j is the urban (j=1) and rural (j =2) population; $p=p_1+p_2$ is the total population; c is the urban (j = 1) and rural consumption (j =2); $c=c_1+c_2$ is the total consumption. To exclude price factors, urban consumption equals real per capita consumption expenditure of urban residents multiplied by urban population; rural consumption equals real per capita living expenditure of rural residents multiplied by rural population. Here, real per capita consumption expenditure of urban residents is the per capita consumption expenditure deflated by the urban CII index (fixed basis, 1992 = 1) of each individual province; real per capita living expenditure of rural residents is the per capita living expenditure deflated by the rural CII index (fixed basis, 1992 = 1) of that province. The urban and rural CII indexes (fixed basis, 1992 = 1) are calculated according to the urban and rural CII indexes (previous year = 100). All data related to per capita consumption expenditure of urban residents, per capita living expenditure of rural residents, urban and rural CII indexes (previous year = 100), population of urban residents, and population of rural residents of individual provinces involved in the calculation come from CEIC Data and the statistical yearbooks of Tibet and Chongqing.

$$IG = \sum_{j=1}^{2} (\frac{i_j}{i})\ln(\frac{i_j}{i}/\frac{p_j}{p}) = (\frac{i_1}{i})\ln(\frac{i_1}{i}/\frac{p_1}{p}) + (\frac{i_2}{i})\ln(\frac{i_2}{i}/\frac{p_2}{p}) \quad (8.14)$$

3. Urban–rural income gap (*IG*). The simplest measure of urban–rural income gap is per capital disposable income of urban residents/per capita disposable income of rural residents. However, similar to urban–rural consumption gap, this indicator is essentially the nominal urban–rural income gap, since it neglects both the effect of population structure on urban–rural income gap, and the effect of income source on urban–rural income gap. Hence, its expression of urban–rural income gap is defective. In existing statistics, urban and rural resident income in all Chinese provinces can be separated by source of income into wage income, operating income, property income, and transfer income, the last mainly coming from the government's or enterprises' welfare supply to laborers (or residents). According to our logical deduction earlier, labor market distortion (or degree of labor market integration) first affects the nontransfer income of urban and rural residents. Based on this understanding, here urban–rural income gap excludes residents' transfer income gap and is defined as the gap of wage income, operating income, and property income between urban and rural residents.

Similar to urban–rural consumption gap, here we still use Theil index to scale the urban–rural income gap of individual provinces. Let *IG* represent the urban–rural income gap of a province in a given year, then we have:

In Eq. (8.14), $p = p_1 + p_2$ is the total population; i is the urban (j=1) and rural (j=2) income; $i = i_1 + i_2$ is the total income. Here income is the sum of the wage income, operating income, and property income of urban and rural residents of a province. To exclude the effect of price factors, we deflated the per capita disposable income of urban residents with the urban CII index (fixed basis, 1992 = 1), and the per capita net income of rural residents with the rural CII index (fixed basis, 1992 = 1), of the related province, thus yielding the real per capita disposable income of urban residents and the real per capita net income of rural residents. To reflect the gaps of wage income, operating income, and property income between urban and rural residents of a province, we can define urban resident income = urban real per capita disposable income × (1 – share of transfer income in urban resident income), and rural resident income = real per capita net income of rural residents × (1– share of transfer income in rural resident income). All data related to per capita net disposable income of urban residents, per capita net income of rural residents, urban and rural CII indexes (previous year = 100), population of urban residents, and population of rural residents of individual provinces come from CEIC Data and the statistical yearbooks of Tibet and Chongqing. Data related to share of transfer income in urban resident income (which is expressed as share of transfer income in per capita total income of urban residents) and share of transfer income in rural resident income (which is expressed as share of transfer income in per capita net income of rural residents) of individual provinces over 1992–2013 come from "China Rural Statistical Yearbook", NBS website, and the statistical yearbooks of the respective provinces. Data of the two shares of Chongqing from 1992 and 1996 are the same as those of Sichuan.

4. Urban–rural social security gap (*SG*). Existing statistics do not provide the social security gap between urban and rural residents in China's 31 provinces from 1992 to 2013. Existing studies in this respect are usually class-wise—they focus on separate classes such as education, medical care, and old age insurance. These studies are very inspiring, but they don't seem to give an overall description of the degree of access to urban and rural social security resources and its changes. In fact, urban–rural social security gap is typically the difference between urban and rural residents in access to transfer income in their overall income. Hence, we used the transfer income comparison between urban and rural residents as the

Therefore, the transfer income comparison of urban and rural residents in each province (autonomous region, municipality) is used as the proxy variable of urban–rural social security gap, and the actual degree of this gap is measured by Theil index. In a given year, the gap between urban and rural social security in a province (autonomous region, municipality directly under the central government) is as follows:

$$SG = \sum_{j=1}^{2}\left(\frac{s_j}{s}\right)\ln\left(\frac{s_j}{s}/\frac{p_j}{p}\right) = \left(\frac{s_1}{s}\right)\ln\left(\frac{s_1}{s}/\frac{p_1}{p}\right) + \left(\frac{s_2}{s}\right)\ln\left(\frac{s_2}{s}/\frac{p_2}{p}\right) \quad (8.15)$$

Similar to the expressions of urban–rural consumption and urban–rural income gap, in Eq. (8.15), $p=p_1+p_2$ represents total population; s is the size of urban (j=1) and rural (j=2) social security; $s=s_1+s_2$ is total social security. Here the urban–rural security level of individual provinces is expressed by per capita transfer income. Again, we deflated the per capita disposable income of urban residents with the urban CII index (fixed basis, 1992 = 1) and the per capita net income of rural residents with the rural CII index (fixed basis, 1992 = 1), thus yielding the real per capita disposable income urban residents and the real per capita net income of rural residents. On this basis, we can define the urban residents' social security of a province = real per capita disposable income of urban residents × share of transfer income in urban resident income, and rural residents' social security = real per capita net income of rural residents × share of transfer income of rural resident income. Data used for calculating urban–rural social security gap come from the same sources as those used for calculating urban–rural income gap.

5. Control variables. For China as a large developing country in the stage of economic system transition, urban–rural consumption gap is not solely determined by urban–rural income gap, and or urban–rural social security gap. It is the result of the joint action of a range of factors. In addition to labor market distortion, here we will try to control the influences of the following factors on urban–rural consumption gap.

a Per capita GDP (*PY*). We deflated the per capita GDP of individual provinces with their respective per capita GDP index (1992 = 100) to yield their real per capita GDP and took their natural log. To obtain the per capita GDP index, we first converted the GNP index (previous year = 100) of individual provinces into GNP index (1992 = 100), worked out the population change index (1992 = 1) according to population size, then divided the GNP index by population change index, thereby indirectly yielding the per capita GDP index (1992 = 100) of each province. All data related to GDP index (previous = 100), population, and per capita GDP of the provinces come from CEIC Data;
b Marketization process (*MR*), which is expressed by share of number of non-SOE workers in total number of workers in individual provinces. All data related to number of workers and non-SOE workers from 1992

to 2008 come from "China Compendium of Statistics"; those from 2009 to 2013 come from the statistical yearbooks of the respective provinces;

c Opening degree (*OP*), which is expressed by share of export trade volume in GDP of individual provinces. Data related to the export trade volume from 1992 to 2013 come from CEIC Data. Export volumes have been converted into RMB according to the exchange rate to facilitate comparison with GDP;

d Infrastructure (*IN*), which is expressed by highway mileage per unit of land area in individual provinces. Data related to highway mileages from 1992 to 2013 come from CEIC Data; land area data of the provinces are based on 2011 statistics;

e Government financial capacity (*FI*), which is expressed by share of general budget expenditure in GDP. Financial expenditure data from 1992 to 2008 come from "China Compendium of Statistics"; those from 2009 to 2013 come from CEIC Data.

As deduced earlier, in the presence of urban–rural duality, labor market distortion will affect urban–rural consumption gap through the two mechanisms of urban–rural income gap and urban–rural social security gap. To test these observations, we can put forward the following model for analysis:

$$CG_{it} = \alpha + \beta_1 DS_{it} + \beta_2 PY_{it} + \beta_3 MR_{it} + \beta_4 OP_{it} + \beta_5 IN_{it} + \beta_6 FI_{it} + \varepsilon_{it} \tag{8.16}$$

In Eq. (8.16), CG_{it} is the urban–rural consumption gap of province i in time t; DS_{it}, PY_{it}, MR_{it}, OP_{it}, IN_{it}, and $FI_{it}$are the labor market distortion (degree of labor market integration), per capita GDP, marketization degree, opening degree, infrastructure, and government's financial capacity of province i in time t; β_1, β_2, β_3, β_4, β_5, and β_6 are the coefficients of these explanatory variables. While other variables are controlled, a negative β_1 means that labor market distortion will contribute negatively to urban–rural consumption gap. That is, reduced labor market distortion (as indicated by gradually increased DS_{IT} figure) will lead to reduced urban–rural consumption gap (as indicated by gradually reduced CG_{it} figure), and *vice versa*. To reveal how labor market distortion affects urban–rural consumption gap, we put forward two more models as follows for assistant analysis:

$$IG_{it} = \alpha + \beta_1 DS_{it} + \beta_2 PY_{it} + \beta_3 MR_{it} + \beta_4 OP_{it} + \beta_5 IN_{it} + \beta_6 FI_{it} + \varepsilon_{it} \tag{8.17}$$

$$SG_{it} = \alpha + \beta_1 DS_{it} + \beta_2 PY_{it} + \beta_3 MR_{it} + \beta_4 OP_{it} + \beta_5 IN_{it} + \beta_6 FI_{it} + \varepsilon_{it} \tag{8.18}$$

In Eq. (8.17), CG_{it} is the urban–rural income gap of province i in time t; in Eq. (8.18), SG_{it} is the urban–rural social security gap of province i in time t;

the meanings of the remaining variables are the same as in Eq. (8.16). When the other variables are controlled, a negative β_1 in Eq. (8.17) means that labor market distortion will contribute negatively to urban–rural income gap. In the same way, a negative β_1 in Eq. (8.18) means that labor market distortion will contribute negatively to urban–rural social security gap. Considering the dependence of resident consumption on income level and social security, a negative β_1 in both Eqs. (8.17) and (8.18) means that labor market distortion will contribute negatively to urban–rural consumption gap through income gap and social security gap.

Before applying the established econometric model for empirical study, we need to perform unit root test on the variables of Eqs. (8.16), (8.17), and (8.18) first. According to the characteristics of the related variables, all unit root testing is performed in forms containing intercept and trend terms. Methods used include Levin, Lin & Chu t *, Breitung T-stat, Im, Pesaran & Shin w-stat, ADF-Fisher Chi-square, and PP-Fisher Chi-square. Table 8.4 presents the results based on these methods and EViews7.0. The first-order difference of each and every sequence can reject the original hypothesis that includes unit root at the significance level of 1 percent, suggesting that all sequences involved in Eqs. (8.16), (8.17), and (8.18) are integrated of order 1. After the variables have passed unit root test, we need to analyze their co-integration by Pedroni, Kao, and Engle-Granger two-step method and Johansen-Fisher test, especially Pedroni's Panel v-statistic, Panel rho-statistic, Panel PP-statistic, Panel ADF-statistic, Group rho-statistic, Group PP-statistic, Group ADF-statistic for cointegration testing. Using a combination of these methods, we discover that all variables involved in Eqs. (8.16), (8.17), and (8.18) can reject the original hypothesis that excludes cointegration, suggesting that from 1992 to 2013, the CG_{it}(and IG_{it}, SG_{it}) maintained a constantly stable relationship with DS_{it}, PY_{it}, MR_{it}, OP_{it}, IN_{it}, FI_{it} for all 31 provinces of China.

After the variables have passed unit root test and cointegration test, models. Eqs. (8.16), (8.17), and (8.18) can be econometrically regressed. To further clarify the effect of labor market distortion on urban–rural consumption gap, we made a separate study on the national panel data of 31 provinces, the panel data of 11 eastern China provinces, and the panel data of 20 central and western China provinces[2]. To determine the exact form of regression equations, EViews7.0 can be used to provide the Hausman test statistical values and *P* values, as indicated by Table 8.5. All Hausman test *P* values are smaller than 0.05. Obviously, random effect model should be rejected and fixed effect model should be used. In the case of whole China, Eq. (8.16) describes the effect of labor market distortion *DS* and control variables on urban–rural consumption *CG*. As indicated by Table 8.5, the coefficient of determination of this regression equation is 0.8506, and the adjusted coefficient of determination is 0.8422, suggesting that this equation provides satisfactory regression result and *DS* and control variables possess fairly good explanatory power for *CG*. The coefficient β_1 of *DS* is –0.136 and

Table 8.4 Unit root testing of explained variables and explanatory variables in the model

Test method	*CG*	*IG*	*SG*	*DS*	*PY*	*MR*	*OP*	*IN*	*FI*
Levin, Lin& Chu t*	–18.6119 (0.000)	–10.518 (0.000)	–16.520 (0.000)	–14.212 (0.000)	–4.784 (0.000)	–11.942 (0.000)	–19.006 (0.000)	–19.285 (0.000)	–11.273 (0.000)
Breitung t-test	–9.501 (0.000)	–9.699 (0.000)	–10.588 (0.000)	–6.360 (0.000)	–2.821 (0.002)	–7.632 (0.000)	–11.091 (0.000)	–19.030 (0.000)	–7.032 (0.000)
Im, Pesaran & ShimW-stat	–12.433 (0.000)	–10.256 (0.000)	–14.501 (0.000)	–15.289 (0.000)	–5.632 (0.000)	–9.212 (0.000)	–16.561 (0.000)	–13.756 (0.000)	–11.182 (0.000)
ADF Fisher Chi-square	247.722 (0.000)	207.957 (0.000)	291.844 (0.000)	305.973 (0.000)	138.746 (0.000)	204.996 (0.000)	322.682 (0.000)	265.100 (0.000)	228.098 (0.000)
PP Fisher Chi-square	583.193 (0.000)	305.008 (0.000)	350.863 (0.000)	284.794 (0.000)	146.208 (0.000)	295.066 (0.000)	629.600 (0.000)	269.852 (0.000)	279.416 (0.000)

Note: Bracketed figures are the *P* values of related first-order difference test statistics.

Table 8.5 Regression result of the impact of urban–rural labor market distortion on resident consumption gap

Region	*National*			*East China*			*Central & West China*		
Variable	*CG*	*IG*	*SG*	*CG*	*IG*	*SG*	*CG*	*IG*	*SG*
Constant	*0.001*	*0.024*	*1.132****	*–0.048**	*0.092****	*0.56*	*0.084***	*0.072***	*1.226****
	(0.025)	*(0.025)*	*(0.116)*	*(0.028)*	*(0.024)*	*6****	*(0.038)*	*(0.037)*	*(0.175)*
						(0.129)			
DS	*–0.136****	*–0.094****	*–0.061*	*–0.061*****	*–0.005**	*–0.062*	*–0.206****	*–0.150****	*–0.058*
	(0.014)	*(0.094)*	*(0.066)*	*(0.013)*	*(0.011)*	*(0.061)*	*(0.023)*	*(0.022)*	*(0.105)*
PY	*0.023****	*0.012*****	*–0.057*****	*0.019****	*–0.009****	*–0.002*	*0.018****	*0.012***	*–0.057***
	(0.003)	*(0.003)*	*(0.015)*	*(0.004)*	*(0.033)*	*(0.017)*	*(0.005)*	*(0.005)*	*(0.024)*
MR	*–0.090****	*–0.038***	*–0.044*	*–0.093****	*0.006*	*(0.128*	*–0.068***	*–0.043*	*–0.272***
	(0.017)	*(0.017)*	*(0.080)*	*(0.017)*	*(0.015)*	*0.080)*	*(0.030)*	*(0.029)*	*(0.139)*
OP	*0.057****	*0.019**	*0.004*	*0.053****	*0.033*	*–0.048*	*0.057*	*–0.112****	*0.240*
	(0.015)	*(0.014)*	*(0.063)*	*(0.010)*	**** (0.008)*	*(0.044)*	*(0.045)*	*(0.044)*	*(0.208)*
IN	*0.019****	*0.005*	*–0.062*****	*–0.015***	*0.014***	*–0.164****	*–0.020***	*0.044*	*–0.021*
	(0.006)	*(0.006)*	*(0.028)*	*(0.007)*	*(0.006)*	*(0.030)*	*(0.008)*	*(0.008)*	*(0.038)*
FI	*–0.090****	*–0.039****	*–0.467****	*(0.022)*	*0.119****	*–0.937****	*–0.089****	*–0.031*	*–0.440****
	(0.018)	*(0.017)*	*(0.080)*	*0.047*	*(0.040)*	*(0.215)*	*(0.023)*	*(0.023)*	*(0.108)*
Region	*National*			*East China*			*Central & West China*		
Method	*Fixed*	*Fixed*	*Fixed*	*Fixed*	*Fixed*	*Fixed*	*Fixed*	*Fixed*	*Fixed*
Variable	CG	IG	SG	CG	IG	SG	CG	IG	SG
Constant	0.001	0.024	1.132***	–0.048*	0.092***	0.56	0.084**	0.072**	1.226***
	(0.025)	(0.025)	(0.116)	(0.028)	(0.024)	6***	(0.038)	(0.037)	(0.175)
						(0.129)			
DS	–0.136***	–0.094***	–0.061	–0.061****	–0.005*	–0.062	–0.206***	–0.150***	–0.058
	(0.014)	(0.094)	(0.066)	(0.013)	(0.011)	(0.061)	(0.023)	(0.022)	(0.105)
PY	0.023***	0.012****	–0.057****	0.019***	–0.009***	–0.002	0.018***	0.012**	–0.057**
	(0.003)	(0.003)	(0.015)	(0.004)	(0.033)	(0.017)	(0.005)	(0.005)	(0.024)
MR	–0.090***	–0.038**	–0.044	–0.093***	0.006	(0.128	–0.068**	–0.043	–0.272**
	(0.017)	(0.017)	(0.080)	(0.017)	(0.015)	0.080)	(0.030)	(0.029)	(0.139)

OP	0.057*** (0.015)	0.019* (0.014)	0.004 (0.063)	0.053*** (0.010)	0.033 *** (0.008)	–0.048 (0.044)	0.057 (0.045)	–0.112*** (0.044)	0.240 (0.208)
IN	0.019*** (0.006)	0.005 (0.006)	–0.062**** (0.028)	–0.015** (0.007)	0.014** (0.006)	–0.164*** (0.030)	–0.020** (0.008)	0.044 (0.008)	–0.021 (0.038)
FI	–0.090*** (0.018)	–0.039*** (0.017)	–0.467*** (0.080)	(0.022) 0.047	0.119*** (0.040)	–0.937*** (0.215)	–0.089*** (0.023)	–0.031 (0.023)	–0.440*** (0.108)
Method	Fixed	Fixed	Fixed	Fixed	Fixed	Fixed	Fixed	Fixed	Fixed
Hausman test	109.51 (0.000)	102.95 (0.000)	69.58 (0.000)	72.24 (0.000)	26.82 (0.000)	22.05 (0.001)	31.86 (0.000)	34.06 (0.000)	26.31 (0.000)
R^J	0.8506	0.8786	0.7874	0.8817	0.8616	0.8803	0.7741	0.8433	0.6691
Adjusted R2	0.8422	0.8718	0.7755	0.8733	0.8518	0.8718	0.7604	0.8338	0.6491
F Value	101.99	129.62	66.35	104.79	87.58	103.44	56.73	89.11	33.49
Observed Value	682	682	682	242	242	242	440	440	440

Note: ① Bracketed figures corresponding to the regression coefficient are the standard errors; ② Bracketed figures corresponding to Hausman test are the *P* values; ③ ***, **, and * represent significance at the level of 1, 5, and 10 percent.

can pass the 1 percent statistical significance test, suggesting that labor market distortion (or degree of labor market integration) is positively (or negatively) related to urban–rural consumption gap. A reduction of labor market distortion by 1 unit, or an increase of degree of labor market distortion by 1 unit, will lead to a reduction of urban–rural consumption gap by 0.136 unit. In terms of the control variables, β_2 is 0.023, β_4 is 0.057, and β_5 is 0.019. That is, an increase of per capita GDP, opening degree, and infrastructure by 1 unit will lead to an increase of urban–rural consumption gap by 0.023, 0.057, and 0.019 unit, respectively. These three variables are positively related to *CG*, suggesting that the "development bonus" brought by China's economic growth, opening to the outside world, and infrastructure construction is distributed unevenly between urban and rural areas. β_3 and β_6 are both –0.090. That is, an increase of marketization degree and of government financial capacity by 1 unit will lead to a reduction of urban–rural consumption gap by 0.090 unit. This suggests that China's market-oriented system transition and enhanced government financial capacity have boosted the transformation of dual economy through improved resource allocation efficiency and refined public goods allocation.

In the case of eastern China and central and western China, in the Eq. (8.16) of eastern China, the coefficient of determination and adjusted coefficient of determination are 0.8817 and 0.8733 respectively; those in the Eq. (8.16) of central and western China are 0.7741 and 0.7604, respectively. For both regions, the results of the other control variables are very close to those of whole China, with coefficient β_1 of *DS* at –0.061 and –0.206, against suggesting that labor market distortion contributes negatively to their respective urban–rural consumption gap. That is, a reduction of degree of labor market distortion by 1 unit will lead to a reduction of urban–rural consumption gap by 0.061 unit and 0.206 unit for eastern China and central and western China, respectively. Labor market distortion affects urban consumption gap even more significantly in central and western China possibly because eastern China has a higher degree of labor market integration and hence there is smaller possibility to reduce urban–rural consumption gap through labor market integration. Besides, central and western China has more abundant rural labor resources, but its urban sector is less able to create job opportunities than that of eastern China. This results in even greater labor market distortion and consequently greater influence on urban–rural consumption gap, or, in other words, urban–rural consumption gap is more sensitive to the degree of labor market integration in central and western China. Despite the difference in effect between different regions, however, the conclusion of empirical analysis is consistent. That is, whether for whole China or for the two parts of China, labor market distortion contributes negatively to urban–rural consumption gap, and increased degree of labor market integration constitutes an important channel for reducing urban–rural consumption gap. This signifies that the imbalanced integration of China's urban–rural economic relationship since reform and opening up, especially the labor market distortion caused by household registration, hampered the reduction of urban–rural consumption gap and the sustained transformation of dual economy.

In the process of economic system transition, labor market distortion will contribute negatively to urban–rural consumption gap. To clarify how this effect works, we can use models Eqs. (8.17) and (8.18) for empirical study. In the case of whole China, the coefficient of determination and adjusted coefficient of determination of the regression equation of Eq. (8.17) are 0.8786 and 0.8718, respectively. Labor market distortion *DS* and other control variables have high explanatory power for urban–rural income gap *IG*. The coefficient β_1 of *DS* is –0.094 and can pass the 1 percent significance test. Obviously, a reduction of degree of labor market distortion by 1 unit or an increase of degree of labor market integration by 1 unit will lead to a reduction of urban–rural income gap by 0.094 unit. The signs of control variables are the same as the regression result of Eq. (8.16), except only that the coefficient β_5 of *IN* becomes insignificant. The coefficient of determination and adjusted coefficient of determination of Eq. (8.18) are 0.7874 and 0.7755, respectively. The explanatory variables are also more convincing for the explained variable *SG*. The coefficient β_1 of *DS* is –0.061 but cannot pass the significance test, suggesting that reduced degree of labor market distortion theoretically can reduce urban–rural social security gap. However, as currently China's social security is allocated mainly according to "household register" or "identity", increased degree of labor market integration cannot significantly lead to a convergence in urban–rural security gap. In the case of eastern China, the coefficient β_1 of *DS* in Eq. (8.17) is –0.005 and can pass the 10 percent significance test; the coefficient β_1 of *DS* in Eq. (8.18) is –0.062 but cannot pass the significance test, suggesting that in eastern China, labor market distortion contributes negatively to urban–rural income gap and this contribution is now very modest due to high degree of labor market integration. Labor market distortion does not act on urban–rural social security gap very remarkably. In the case of central and western China, the coefficient β_1 of *DS* in Eq. (8.17) is –0.150 and can pass the 1 percent significance test; the coefficient β_1 of *DS* in Eq. (8.18) is –0.058 and cannot pass the significance test. Obviously, in central and western China, reduced degree of labor market distortion can lead to significant reduction of urban–rural income gap, but cannot lead to significant reduction of urban–rural social security gap

Both national and regional panel data indicate that reduced degree of labor market distortion (or increased degree of labor market integration) will lead to significant reduction of China's urban–rural income gap, but will not lead to significant convergence of the country's urban–rural social security gap; the negative effect of labor market distortion on urban–rural consumption gap (and urban–rural income gap) is particularly prominent in central and western China. This conclusion confirms our theoretical deduction earlier in this book that in the process of post-reform economic development, China's urban–rural income gap and urban–rural social security gap are the core variables accounting for the change of urban–rural consumption gap. Currently, China's labor market distortion affects urban–rural consumption gap mainly through income gap, and it does not affect urban–rural consumption gap significantly through social security gap. Labor market distortion and its effect on urban–rural consumption gap is mainly reflected by the adverse effect of imbalanced integration of urban–rural economic relationship on realizing the country's goal of sustainable economic development and common prosperity.

In a word, since the start of reform and opening up in 1978, China's urban–rural economic relationship has been basically characterized by imbalanced integration. This means that the country's urban–rural economic relationship has moved from the previous separation toward integration. It also means that within this integration there is currently an imbalance across different fields and periods and therefore China is now in a transitional stage toward high-profile, high-level integration. This imbalance integration of urban–rural economic relationship results from changes in government–market relationship, the intragovernmental and intramarket structural feature, and the corresponding institutional arrangements under the implementation of the economic growth-oriented strategy. Once formed, these economic system arrangements will affect the behavioral choice of microeconomic subjects. For example, urban and rural residents are free to carry out product transaction and factor flow according to price signals. In particular, the nonagricultural flow of rural labor has become an important bridge linking urban–rural economic relationship, although this flow is also accompanied by new duality inside urban areas and labor market distortion.

The behavioral choice of microeconomic subjects will also bring about the corresponding economic results. Compared with the urban–rural separation in the planned economy era, imbalanced integration of urban–rural economic relationship has, first of all, driven China's economic growth by improving the resource allocation efficiency. Urban–rural labor reallocation or labor structure effect should have constituted an important driver of China's high-speed economic growth. However, imbalanced integration of urban–rural economic relationship has also come hand in hand with the change of economic gap among different social groups. So far, urban–rural income gap is still the major part of the resident income gap in China. To adjust its resident income distribution, China has to respond and resolve the key factor of urban–rural income distribution. Besides, imbalanced integration signals the existence of labor market distortion between urban and rural China, which acts on urban–rural consumption gap by affecting urban–rural income gap and urban–rural social security gap. Increased degree of urban–rural labor market integration will lead to further reduction of urban–rural consumption gap. In short, over the 40 years of reform and opening up, the imbalanced integration of China's urban–rural economic relationship has supported the high-speed GDP growth, but has also exacerbated the structural problem in its economic system. It is an important cause of the imbalanced, uncoordinated development of national economy. Naturally, the implementation performance of imbalanced integration of urban–rural economic relationship will also change the country's economic development strategy and constraints. In particular, concerns about economic structural problems intrinsically calls for continued improvement of urban–rural economic relationship.

Notes

1 Eastern China include 11 provinces (municipalities): Liaoning, Beijing, Shanghai, Tianjin, Hebei, Shandong, Zhejiang, Jiangsu, Fujian, Hainan, and Guangdong; central China includes 8 provinces: Henan, Anhui, Hubei, Hunan, Jiangxi, Shanxi, Jilin, and Heilongjiang; western China includes 12 provinces (autonomous regions/municipalities: Chongqing, Sichuan, Gansu, Shaanxi, Ningxia, Yunnan, Guangxi, Guizhou, Tibet, Xinjiang, Inner Mongolia, and Qinghai.

2 Eastern China includes 11 provinces (municipalities): Beijing, Tianjin, Hebei, Liaoning, Shanghai, Jiangsu, Zhejiang, Fujian, Shandong, Guangdong, and Hainan; central and western China includes 20 provinces (autonomous regions/municipalities): Shanxi, Jilin, Heilongjiang, Anhui, Jiangxi, Henan, Hubei, Hunan, Inner Mongolia, Guangxi, Chongqing, Sichuan, Guizhou, Yunnan, Tibet, Shaanxi, Gansu, Qinghai, Ningxia, and Xinjiang.

9 Collaborative integration: China's urban–rural economic relationship in the new era

In 1978, China launched the historical process of market-oriented reform and integration into the global economy. Since reform and opening up, the sustained high-speed GDP growth has been accompanied by the evolution of urban–rural economic relationship, namely, the change from separation toward imbalanced integration. For a large developing country in the stage of system transition, imbalanced integration of urban–rural economic relationship is the product of development strategy, constraints, and their combination. If we say a separated urban–rural economic relationship served the heavy industry first strategy, then an imbalanced integration of urban–rural economic relationship is the intrinsic product of economic growth-oriented strategy. From the practical results, imbalanced integration of urban–rural economic relationship has indeed driven the sustained fast GDP growth. Both urban and rural resident income and consumption have been increasing in the temporal sense, although the resulted labor market distortion and urban–rural income distribution gap have also exacerbated the structural problems of economy at the same time, preventing urban and rural residents from sharing the fruit of high-speed growth in a relatively equal manner. After emancipating and developing productivity, China is still faced with the mission of fulfilling its goal of sustainable development and common prosperity. In short, to accompany the imbalanced integration of urban–rural economic relationship, China's post-reform national economy has featured the double performance of high-speed economic growth and outstanding structural problems.

The dual development performance has pushed China's economy up into a new stage and brought it into a new era. This will inevitably cause a dynamic change in economic development strategy, constraints, and their combination. In 2002, the report to the Sixteenth National Congress of the CPC called on holding a "scientific outlook on development". In 2015, the Fifth Plenary Session of the Eighteenth CPC Central Committee proposed implementing the five development concepts of "innovation, coordination, green, openness, and sharing". In 2017, the report to the Nineteenth National Congress of the CPC explicitly noted that socialism with Chinese characteristics has entered a new era, China's main social contradiction has transformed and its economy has switched into a high-quality development stage. These statements signify that at the particular point of time when reform is entering its fortieth anniversary, China's economic development strategy has also undergone major adjustments. Shifting from economic growth to coordinated development has become an important direction of economic development in the new era. This shift is bound to lead to continued advancement of economic system change, and economic system reform will extend to farther and broader fields. Accordingly, urban–rural economic relationship also needs to move gradually from imbalanced integration toward coordinated integration.

9.1 Proposal and constraints of overall coordinated development strategy

Since reform and opening up, China has established and implemented an economic growth-oriented development strategy and thus promoted the market-oriented economic system transition. At the economic system level, government–market relationship has changed from the previous high government control to the decentralization of powers and transfer of profits to microeconomic subjects. The role of market in optimizing resource allocation has become increasingly prominent. In the process of market-oriented transition, the intragovernmental and intramarket structural feature has been emerged, resulting in a regionally decentralized authoritarianism inside the government and an upstream-guided market expansion inside the market. These institutional arrangements have affected the behavioral choice of microeconomic subjects and given rise to outstanding imbalanced integration of urban–rural economic relationship. The superposition and interaction of imbalanced integration of urban–rural economic relationship with other factors—such as increased openness degree, progress in science and technology, accumulation of material and human capital—has propelled the sustained fast GDP growth and significantly improved the country's productivity from the level at the beginning of reform and opening up. Table 9.1 compares China's GDP and per capita GDP from 1978 to 2017. Over the 40 years of reform and opening up, China's GDP has increased from 367.9 billion yuan to 82.7122 trillion yuan, and its per capita GDP has increased from 385 yuan to 59660 yuan, recording an average annual growth rate of 9.59 percent for GDP and 8.55 percent for per capita GDP, respectively. Assuming a base value of 100 for 1978, in 2017, the GDP index and per capita GDP index are as high as 3452.1 and 2380.8. Obviously, the sustained high-speed GDP growth represents an important characteristic factor of China's modernization drive over the 40 years of reform and opening. In the temporal sense, the economic growth over the 40 years of reform and opening up is the fastest and the greatest throughout the history of China.

Table 9.1 China's GDP and per capita GDP growths from 1978 to 2017

Year	*GDP (billion yuan)*	*Per capita GDP (yuan)*	*GDP Index (previous year=100)*	*Per capita GDP Index (Previous year=100)*	*GDP Index (1978=100)*	*Per capita GDP Index (1978=100)*
1978	367.9	385.0	111.7	110.2	100.0	100.0
1979	410.0	423.0	107.6	106.2	107.6	106.2
1980	458.8	468.0	107.8	106.5	116.0	113.1
1981	493.6	497.0	105.1	103.8	122.0	117.3
1982	537.3	533.0	109.0	107.4	132.9	126.0
1983	602.1	588.0	110.8	109.2	147.3	137.6
1984	727.9	702.0	115.2	113.7	169.6	156.4
1985	909.9	866.0	113.4	111.9	192.4	175.1
1986	1 037.6	973.0	108.9	107.3	209.6	187.9
1987	1 217.5	1 123.0	111.7	109.9	234.1	206.5
1988	1518.0	1 378.0	111.2	109.4	260.4	226.0
1989	1 718.0	1 536.0	104.2	102.6	271.3	231.9
1990	1 887.3	1 663.0	103.9	102.4	281.9	237.5
1991	2 200.6	1 912.0	109.3	107.8	308.1	256.0
1992	2 719.5	2 334.0	114.2	112.8	351.9	288.8
1993	3 567.3	3 027.0	113.9	112.6	400.7	325.1
1994	4 863.7	4 081.0	113.0	111.8	453.0	363.4
1995	6 134.0	5 091.0	111.0	109.8	502.6	398.9
1996	7 181.4	5 898.0	109.9	108.8	552.5	433.9
1997	7 971.5	6 481.0	109.2	108.1	603.5	469.1
1998	8 519.6	6 860.0	107.8	106.8	650.8	501.1
1999	9 056.4	7 229.0	107.7	106.7	700.7	534.8
2000	10 028.0	7 942.0	108.5	107.6	760.2	575.7
2001	11 086.3	8 717.0	108.3	107.6	823.6	619.1
2002	12 171.7	9 506.0	109.1	108.4	898.8	671.2
2003	13 742.2	10 666.0	110.0	109.4	989.0	734.0
2004	16 184.0	12 487.0	110.1	109.5	1 089.0	803.4
2005	18 731.9	14 368.0	111.4	110.7	1 213.1	889.7
2006	21 943.8	16 738.0	112.7	112.1	1 367.4	997.3
2007	27 023.2	20 505.0	114.2	113.6	1 562.0	1 133.3
2008	31951.6	24 121.0	109.7	109.1	1 712.8	1 236.3
2009	34 908.1	26 222.0	109.4	108.9	1 873.8	1 345.8
2010	41 303.0	30 876.0	110.6	110.1	2 073.1	1 481.8
2011	48 930.1	36 403.0	109.5	109.0	2 270.8	1615.4
2012	54 036.7	40 007.0	107.9	107.3	2 449.2	1 733.8
2013	59 524.4	43 852.0	107.8	107.2	2 639.2	1 859.1
2014	64 397.4	47 203.0	107.3	106.8	2 831.8	1 984.7
2015	68 905.2	50 251.0	106.9	106.4	3 027.2	2 110.9
2016	74 358.6	53 935.0	106.7	106.1	3 230.6	2 240.6
2017	82 712.2	59 660.0	106.9	106.3	3 452.1	2 380.8

Source: CEIC Data.

More notably, by cross-country comparison, over the 40 years of reform and opening up, China's high-speed economic growth can also be called a world "miracle". In the history of the human economic development, it is rare and even unprecedented for a large developing country with a population of nearly 1.4 billion to sustain an annual average growth of nearly 10 percent in 40 years. As a large developing country with socialist system, China has indeed displayed its comparative advantage over other countries in emancipating and developing productivity since reform and opening up. Under the macro background of economic globalization, the sustained high-speed growth has significantly enhanced the nation's economic strength, comprehensive national strength, and international influence. China's share in world GDP has been rising constantly and is catching up with or even overtaking other major developed countries.

Figure 9.1 compares the shares of China, the United States, and Japan in world GDP. At the current dollar prices, from 1978 to 2017, China's GDP increased from 149541 billion yuan to 12.24 trillion yuan, and its share in world GDP increased from 1.75 percent to 15.17 percent. In contrast to China's sustained high-speed economic growth, after the mid-1990s, Japan's share in world GDP has been falling continuously. In 2017, Japan's share in world GDP already dropped to 6.04 percent. In 2010, China already surpassed Japan as world's second largest economy with GDP next only to the United States. Besides Japan, within the investigation period, China's GDP was also catching up with the United States. The Unites States' share in world GDP showed a gradual decline with fluctuation, especially after the entry into the 21st century. In 1978 and 2017, the United States' share in

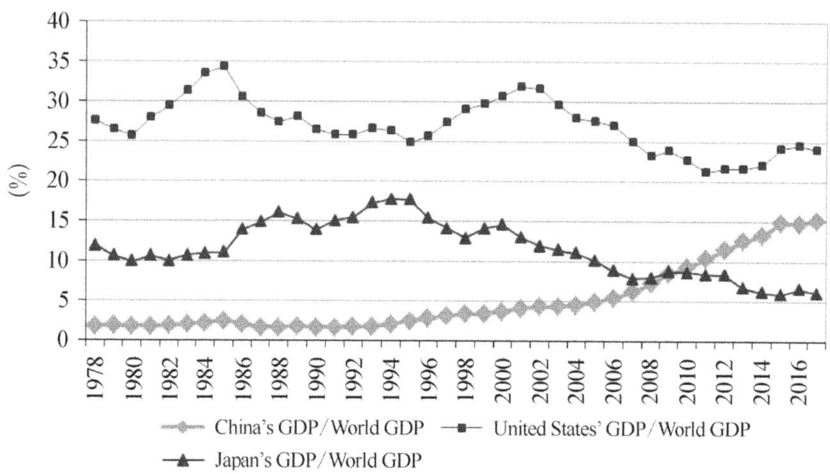

Figure 9.1 China's share in world GDP compared with the United States and Japan from 1978 to 2017.

Source: All original figures needed for calculation come from World Bank Data.

world GDP was 27.59 percent and 24.03 percent, respectively, while China's share in United States' GDP rose from 6.35 percent to 63.11 percent.

Accompanying the sustained high-speed GDP growth is the growth of total population in post-reform China, but at a much slower pace than GDP. As a result, China's per capita GDP has been increasing constantly and catching up quickly with other major economies. At the current dollar prices, from 1978 to 2017, China's per capita GDP increased from 156.40 dollars to 8826.99 dollars; its share in world per capita GDP rose from 7.85 percent to 82.38 percent, its share in the United States' GDP rose from 1.48 percent to 14.83 percent, and that in Japan rose from 1.77 percent to 22.97 percent. While China is still a developing country so far, its per capita GDP qualifies under the upper-middle-income countries criterion defined by the United Nations. These figures clearly demonstrate that China's sustained high-speed growth over the 40 years of reform and opening up is dramatic in the world, too. It has profoundly changed the country's own economic position and economic connection with the outside world.

The sustained high-speed GDP growth signifies that China's economic growth-oriented strategy has achieved remarkable performance. Nevertheless, the post-reform high-speed aggregate growth is not the only theme of China's economy. In fact, against the sustained high-speed aggregate growth is the succession of structural problems confronting China's national economy. High-speed aggregate growth and outstanding structural problems constitute the "two surfaces of a coin". Theoretically speaking, the national economy of any country is composed of different parts, and the sustainable development of economy is dependent on the relative balance among these different parts. Of course this balance is not attained by means of mandatory government plans, but the collaboration between market mechanism and government function in imbalanced, uncoordinated development exists among these parts, accumulation and exacerbation of structural problems will pose a major challenge to the long-term development of economy. Since the start of reform and opening up in 1978, along with market-oriented economic system transition, China's national economy has displayed structural problems in many aspects, such as demand structure, industrial structure, input structure, and the tension between economic growth and ecological environment. In response to these structural problems, after raising the proposition of thoroughly implementing the scientific outlook on development, the report to the Seventeenth National Congress of the CPC specifically noted that the scientific outlook on development takes development as its paramount essence, human-oriented as its core, full harmony and sustainability as its basic requirement, and overall planning and coordination as its fundamental method with a view to coordinating among urban and rural development, regional development, economic and social development, man-nature harmony, domestic development and opening to the outside world.

In national economic statistics, demand structure is a cut-in point for understanding the economic development of a particular country. Keynes' demand management theory and policy choice in macroeconomics are right based on demand structure. Hence, we can describe the structural problems of China's economic system with respect to demand structure since reform and opening up as an example. As indicated by Table 9.2, on expenditure basis, China's GDP can be decomposed into final consumption expenditure, gross capital formation, net export of goods and services. Among them, final consumption expenditure can be further decomposed into resident consumption expenditure and government consumption expenditure; resident consumption expenditure can be further decomposed into urban resident consumption expenditure and rural resident consumption expenditure. Since reform and opening up in 1978, China's expenditure-based GDP has displayed at least three features. First, in terms of expenditure-based GDP, final consumption expenditure and gross capital formation are the principal part of GDP, but the share of the former has been falling while that of the latter has been rising. From 1978 to 2010, the share of final consumption expenditure (final consumption expenditure/GDP) dropped from 61.44 percent to 48.45 percent, while that of gross capital formation rose from 38.87 percent to 47.8 percent. After 2010, under supply-side structural reform, the share of final consumption expenditure began to rise but has not reached the level at the beginning of reform and opening up. Second, in terms of final consumption, government consumption and resident consumption constitute the two components of final consumption expenditure. Throughout the investigation period, the share of government consumption (government consumption expenditure/GDP) has remained very stable, with its value fluctuating between 13 and 15 percent all the time, whereas that of resident consumption (resident consumption expenditure/GDP) has been falling for a long time. For example, from 1978 to 2010, the share of resident consumption dropped from 48.40 percent to 35.56 percent, a decrease of nearly 13 percentage points. After 2010, this figure gradually went up and reached 39.10 percent in 2017, but is still incomparable to the level in 1978 when reform and opening up first started. Third, in terms of resident consumption, urban resident consumption and rural resident consumption constitute the two components of resident consumption expenditure. In China, the change of share of these two components has been unidirectional. That is, the share of urban resident consumption (urban resident consumption expenditure/GDP) has been rising while that of rural resident consumption (rural resident consumption expenditure/GDP) has been falling. In 2017, the share of urban resident consumption and of rural resident consumption was 30.70 percent and 8.41 percent, respectively. The change of the share of urban and rural resident consumption is closely associated with urbanization. Notably, the share of rural resident consumption has been falling at a far greater speed than that of rural population. By registered population, in 2017, the share of rural residents in total population was 57.65 percent, yet the share of their consumption was a merely 21.50 percent, suggesting that the pervasive low consumption of the vast

Table 9.2 Shares of different parts of China's expenditure-based GDP from 1978 to 2017 (%)

Year	*Final Consumption Expenditure*					*Gross Capital Formation*	*Net Export of Goods & Services*
	Final Consumption Expenditure	*Government Consumption Expenditure*	*Resident Consumption Expenditure*	*Urban Resident Consumption*	*Rural Resident Consumption*		
1978	61.44	13.04	48.40	18.35	30.06	38.87	–0.31
1979	63.22	13.84	49.38	18.62	30.76	37.27	–0.49
1980	64.85	13.77	51.08	20.15	30.92	35.48	–0.32
1981	66.11	13.11	53.00	20.52	32.49	33.54	0.34
1982	65.89	13.06	52.84	19.35	33.49	32.43	1.68
1983	66.78	13.80	52.99	19.68	33.30	32.38	0.84
1984	65.13	14.90	50.23	19.58	30.65	34.85	0.02
1985	64.46	14.06	50.41	20.05	30.36	39.54	–4.00
1986	64.23	13.69	50.54	20.82	29.72	38.21	–2.44
1987	62.13	12.94	49.19	20.95	28.24	37.78	0.09
1988	61.46	12.33	49.13	22.05	27.08	39.53	–0.99
1989	63.56	12.99	50.57	22.54	28.02	37.51	–1.07
1990	62.94	13.46	49.48	22.0	27.49	34.38	2.68
1991	61.54	13.87	47.66	22.47	25.19	35.67	2.79
1992	59.36	14.31	45.04	23.29	21.76	39.63	1.01
1993	57.93	14.21	43.72	24.22	19.50	43.96	–1.89
1994	57.91	13.98	43.93	25.14	18.79	40.79	1.30
1995	58.82	13.20	45.62	26.87	18.75	39.56	1.62
1996	59.76	13.07	46.68	27.05	19.63	38.22	2.02
1997	59.37	13.60	45.77	27.07	18.70	36.20	4.44
1998	60.20	14.78	45.41	28.01	17.40	35.56	4.25
1999	62.34	16.19	46.15	29.84	16.31	34.86	2.79
2000	63.30	16.58	46.72	31.20	15.52	34.33	2.37
2001	61.61	16.03	45.58	30.93	14.65	36.30	2.09

2002	60.57	15.53	45.04	31.12	13.91	36.90	2.53
2003	57.49	14.58	42.90	30.05	12.85	40.37	2.14
2004	54.74	13.82	40.92	29.10	11.82	42.6	2.60
2005	53.62	13.86	39.77	28.71	11.05	40.98	5.40
2006	51.86	13.84	38.03	27.79	10.23	40.61	7.53
2007	50.14	13.41	36.73	27.31	9.42	41.24	8.62
2008	49.22	13.17	36.05	27.04	9.01	43.21	7.57
2009	49.37	13.17	36.20	27.4	8.76	46.3	4.30
2010	48.45	12.89	35.56	27.38	8.18	47.8	3.67
2011	49.59	13.27	36.32	27.87	8.45	48.01	2.40
2012	50.11	13.42	36.70	28.34	8.36	47.18	2.71
2013	50.31	13.50	36.81	28.53	8.28	47.25	2.44
2014	50.73	13.25	37.48	29.08	8.40	46.77	2.50
2015	51.82	13.77	38.05	29.59	8.46	44.75	3.43
2016	53.63	14.28	39.35	30.73	8.63	44.14	2.22
2017	53.62	14.52	39.10	30.70	8.41	44.41	1.97

Source: CEIC Data.

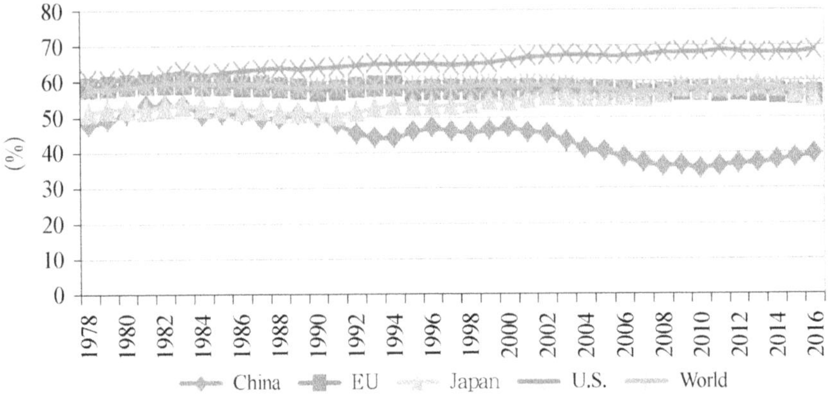

Figure 9.2 China's share of household consumption expenditure compared with the world and major economies from 1978 to 2016.

Source: World Bank Data.

rural population is the core reason explaining the declining resident consumption rate. From the demand structure point of view, China's consumption rate, resident consumption rate, and rural resident consumption rate have been declining remarkably. This structural problem has greatly brought serious adverse results to the sustainable development and policy choice of domestic economy.

To obtain a clearer understanding of the structural feature of China's economic development since reform and opening up, we can make a cross-country data comparison to reflect the structural changes between China and the world and other major economies. As illustrated by Figure 9.2, according to World Bank statistics, from 1978 to 2016, the share of resident consumption (resident consumption expenditure/GDP) of the world and the EU was very stable, with the world recording 57.98 percent and 58.29 percent, and the EU 58.40 percent and 56.08 percent. Over the same period, the United States and Japan even showed a small increase, with the United States recording an increase from 60.52 percent to 68.64 percent, and Japan from 51.32 percent to 55.69 percent. In contrast to the world and other major economies, China displayed a gradual decline. In 1978 and 2016, China's share of resident consumption expenditure was 47.82 percent and 39.46 percent. Its decline was particularly noticeable over the 1990–2020 period, when it dropped constantly from 49.99 percent to 35.36 percent, with a decrease of nearly 15 percent. After 2010, China's share of resident consumption expenditure began to climb up slowly, yet its figure has not reached the level in 1978 when reform and opening up first started and lags far behind the world and major developed countries, although China is different from major developed countries in terms of development level and development stage. Hence, it is inappropriate to directly compare the share of resident consumption expenditure of a given year. However, it is still valuable to observe the consumption expenditure changes among different countries across a longer run (1978–2016). More importantly, after reform and opening up, China's GDP and per capita GDP have been catching up with or even surpassed the world and major developed countries. Its per capita GDP also qualifies under the upper-and-middle income countries criterion defined by the international organization. As such, the demand structure, especially the share of resident consumption expenditure of major developed countries, is of referential significance to China. The cross-country comparison shows that in the global context, the decline in share of resident consumption expenditure in China's demand structure is remarkable. Its change has a striking difference from the world and major developed countries.

It won't be hard to see that since the start of reform and opening up in 1978, driven by the imbalanced integration of urban–rural economic relationship and other factors, China's economy has featured high-speed growth accompanied by outstanding structural problems. This situation not only signifies that the economic growth-oriented strategy has achieved remarkable results but also implies that China's economy is increasingly challenged by a series of structural problems. Reform and opening up has brought China into a new era and new stage, and it is yelling for immediate adaptive adjustment of the country's economic development strategy. In fact, after the entry into the 21st century, China already noticed a series of structural problems in the process of economic development, and of the challenges posed by imbalanced, uncoordinated, unsustainable development problems in the economic system. Its policy texts also began to straighten out the previous economic growth-oriented strategy. For example, in October 2003, the Third Plenary Session of the Sixteenth CPC Central Committee put forward the innovation of development outlook, namely, to implement a new development outlook with overall planning and coordination as the value orientation. This signified that the country's development strategy has shifted from economic growth to coordinated development (Gao F., 2016b). In October 2007, the report to the Seventeenth National Congress of the CPC raised the idea of a scientific outlook on development. It explained that a scientific outlook on development was proposed because in the new century and new stage, China's development had displayed a series of new periodical features which, at the economic level, typically consisted of a series of structural problems, such as how to narrow urban–rural and interregional development gap and achieve the coordinated economic and social development. These policy texts imply that China was beginning to realize the structural problems behind its economic growth-oriented strategy and to take actions to resolve these problems. Promoting the coordination among different parts of economy was placed in a more importance position.

This idea has been continued in the policy texts that followed. Particularly, the Eighteenth National Congress of the CPC in 2012 marked the start of accelerated adjustment of economic development strategy. In October 2015, the Fifth Plenary Session of the Eighteenth CPC Central Committee called on solving development problems, cultivating development advantages, and firmly establishing and implementing the development concept of "innovation, coordination, green, openness, sharing". The new development concept signifies that coordinated development has replaced the economic growth-oriented strategy even more greatly. In the transition of China's post-reform development strategy, the Nineteenth National Congress of the CPC in 2017 undoubtedly played a crucial role. The report to the Nineteenth National Congress of the CPC declared that socialism with Chinese characteristics has entered a new era and noted that China's main social contradiction has transformed into the contradiction between people's increasing needs for a better life and imbalanced and inadequate development. It also emphasized that China's economy has shifted from a high-speed growth stage to a high-quality development stage, and it is therefore necessary to implement new development concepts in the economic domain and build a modern economic system. The substantial emancipation and development of social productivity, and the sustained high-speed GDP growth, have changed the "backward social production" in China's previous main social contradiction. The constant accumulation and exacerbation of structural problems in different fields, especially economy, has highlighted the "imbalanced, inadequate development" of the country's current main social contradiction.

Consistent with the redirection of development strategy, at the practical and operational level, China began to promote the formation of an indicator system, policy system, standard system, statistics system, performance evaluation, and government performance assessment that support high-quality development, to create and refine the institutional environment. A typical example was the 2016 provincial green development index and public satisfaction statistics jointly released by the NBS, National Development & Reform Commission, Ministry of Environmental Protection, and Organization Department of the CPC Central Committee. Highlighting the challenges of imbalanced development in the main social contradiction, shifting to high-quality development in economic development positioning, stressing the five development concepts in economic development pathway, and underlining the collaboration of economic growth with other fields in development performance assessment–these signaled a true second transition of China's economic development strategy since the founding of the PRC. That is, the country has shifted its development focus from economic growth to coordinated development in the new era.

Notably, at a point of time when reform and opening is advancing into the 40th year, the redirection of China's development strategy from economic growth to coordinated development does not mean that its previous strategic choice was "wrong". Development strategies must be understood in light of the particular practical background underlying these strategies. Any development strategy derives from a particular temporal and spatial background. Both the heavy industry first strategy and the economic growth-oriented strategy have served the core problems facing China in different periods. Both of them constitute important links for China as a large developing socialist country to fulfill its goal of sustainable development and common prosperity. It is therefore against the logic of historical evolution to criticize or blame the previous development strategy from the current development stage. In fact, the coordinated development strategy is not only temporally successive from the economic growth-oriented strategy, but also logically associated with it. The institutional arrangement under the economic growth-oriented strategy have placed GDP growth in the paramount position, leading to imbalanced, uncoordinated, unsustainable economic development. To solve these problems, China has to make a change in development outlook, development concept, and development strategy, and the transformation of main social contradiction has to regard imbalanced, inadequate development as the main bottleneck to modernization. The economic growth-oriented strategy has effectively emancipated and developed social productivity and greatly enhanced the country's economic strength and comprehensive national strength. This provides China with more solid material foundation to solve the series of structural problems in national economy and to fundamentally change the backward social production facing the transformation of main social contradiction.

Evidently, at the entry into a new era, the formal establishment and actual implementation of a coordinated development strategy has its particular practical logic. It is a succession and an improvement of the previous development strategy. Notably, the formal establishment of the coordinated development strategy does not necessarily mean the realization of this strategy. The switch of the previous development strategy toward the new one is always accompanied by the systemic transition involving continuous changes among different components of national economy. This signifies that it will take a long time for China's economic development to truly become coordinated. In practice, China is facing a series of constraints in implementing the coordinated development strategy. The structural problems confronting China's economy are not unitary but polynary. They exist between urban and rural areas, among regions and industries. These structural problems are usually interwoven and nested with each other, making it even more difficult to effectively resolve the imbalanced, uncoordinated, and unsustainable development problems.

Although China has made outstanding achievements in economic growth over the 40 years of reform and opening up, so far it is still a developing country with world's largest population. Its per capita GDP and per capita income of urban and rural residents are still far behind those of developed countries, which means that China still needs to maintain quick economic growth. Therefore, how to balance quick economic growth against coordinated development has become a new challenge that China has to face up and respond to in its current economic development. More notably, over the 40 years of reform and opening up, China has formed the corresponding institutional arrangements and incentives across different fields based on the economic growth-oriented strategy. The "race for growth", in particular, still exerts practical influence to the behavioral choice of many local governments. This means that the "path dependence" of the current institutional arrangements will work to hamper the implementation of the coordinated development strategy. In a word, over the 40 years of reform and opening up, while promoting the economic growth-oriented strategy, China has formed a particular set of institutional arrangements on the dimension of government–market relationship, intragovernmental structure, and intramarket structure, which have affected the behavioral choice of urban and rural microeconomic subjects, and resulted in the imbalanced integration of urban–rural economic relationship. Obviously, the existing economic system has both spurred China's economic growth and exacerbated its structural problems on the economic dimension. This development performance has caused a change in the previous development strategy, constraints, and their combination, which is bound to lead to constant change in the economic system, thus driving the country's urban–rural economic relationship to transform from imbalanced integration toward collaborative integration.

9.2 Connotation and realization conditions of collaborative integration of urban–rural economic relationship

As China shifts its development focus from economic growth to coordinated development, its urban–rural economic relationship has begun to change, too. In the presence of the still prominent urban–rural duality, the change of urban–rural economic relationship should be seen as an important part of the realization of China's coordinated development strategy. In terms of its evolutionary direction, the imbalanced integration of urban–rural economic relationship since reform and opening up should be redirected to collaborative integration. Here integration still emphasizes the substantial flow of products and factors between urban and rural areas, while collaboration pays more attention to the balance and complementarity among different components of urban–rural factor allocation. It is both a rectification on the previous integrated urban–rural economic relationship with imbalance, as well as a response to the country's pursuit to build a moderately prosperous society in all respects and a socialist modern economy.

Compared with imbalanced integration, collaborative integration of urban–rural economic relationship is a higher-profile, higher-level integration. It covers at least the following connotations. First, the urban and rural sectors should have higher fluidity and reallocation efficiency of commodities and factors, so as to optimize resource allocation continuously, thus stimulating the fast growth of China's economy. In particular, productive factors should turn from the previous unidirectional flow in rural areas to the subsequent bidirectional flow between urban and rural areas. The inflow of capital, technology, information, and other productive factors into rural areas should be addressed as an important part of urban–rural integration. From the factor flow point of view, simultaneous occurrence of "urbanization" and "counter-urbanization" should become a new norm of economic connection between the urban and rural sectors, which responds to the factor allocation mode in the concept of urban–rural economic relationship. Second, the growth resulted from efficient factor allocation should be shared between urban and rural areas more equally. That is, urban and rural residents should be able to share the fruits of economic development in a relatively equal manner. Their income and consumption gap should be converged continuously. Urban–rural equalization in basic public services should also be advanced at a higher speed. Converged urban–rural income gap, consumption gap, and social security gap are a response to the distribution of factor allocation results in the concept of urban–rural economic relationship. Third, in addition to emphasizing the economic connection between the urban and rural sectors, urban–rural economic relationship should also include concerns related to the internal structural problems of the urban and rural sectors. As time goes on, especially with the further enhancement of factor fluidity between urban and rural areas, the new duality inside the urban sector and farmer differentiation inside the rural sector are very likely to continue and even intensify.

Against this background, China's urban–rural economic relationship in the new era not only includes the transformation of urban–rural duality but not the resolution of the internal structural problems of the urban and rural sectors, which understands urban–rural economic relationship in a broader and more dynamic context. Based on these multiple connotations, it is easy to see that collaborative integration of urban–rural economic relationship is an intrinsic product of China's coordinated development strategy. That is, for a large developing country with socialist system like China to implement the coordinated development strategy, it is important to cause urban–rural economic relationship to transform from imbalanced integration to collaborative integration, and to support the smooth implementation of the new development strategy in the formation and construction of new urban–rural economic relationship.

Collaborative integration, in essence, is a new pattern urban–rural economic integration or a new form of urban–rural economic relationship formed in China's economic system under the general background of a coordinated development strategy. This new pattern or new form is relative to the previous imbalanced integration. It rectifies the imbalance confronting the integration of urban–rural economic relationship: temporal fluctuation of urban–rural economic gap, variational difference between urban–rural economic gap and social gap, and the emergence of urban and rural internal features. Based on the multiple connotations described above, we can put forward the measurement indicators for collaborative integration of urban–rural economic relationship. Considering that different indicators reveal different dimensions of collaborative integration, it is necessary to apply a comprehensive indicator system to measure collaborative integration. This comprehensive measurement indicator system should at least include the following contents: degree of labor market integration between urban and rural areas; degree of commercialization of urban and rural products, especially agricultural products; degree of inflow of urban capital factors into rural areas; degree of convergence between urban and rural areas in informatization, degree of convergence between urban and rural areas in labor productivity; reduction of urban–rural income gap and consumption gap; degree of equalization between urban and rural areas in allocation of basic public goods; degree of reduction of rural poverty incidence; degree of integration of rural industries and increase of value added; and degree of improvement of total factor productivity of rural industries. Given that urban–rural factor flow is inevitably accompanied by the change of urban–rural spatial structure, collaborative integration of China's urban–rural economic relationship also implies that governments at all levels can provide the appropriate infrastructure and public services according to the population aggregation between, and inside, urban and rural areas. In a nutshell, collaborative integration does not mean that urban and rural areas will become fully homogeneous. It means that between these two sectors, and among the individual components of these sectors themselves, the institutional obstacles on product and factor flow can be eliminated, thus creating a new economic interaction that merges different sectors or components into one another. Urban and rural residents will also be able to enjoy increasingly equalized living conditions and welfare.

However, one point remains. China's urban–rural economic relationship cannot transform from imbalanced integration to collaborative integration by itself. Imbalanced integration came into being under a particular development strategy and based on a series of institutional conditions. Even when the development strategy has changed substantively, collaborative integration of urban–rural economic relationship will still rigidly rely on a series of economic system conditions. Similar to the previous period, these economic system conditions are also preceded by changes government–market relationship, intragovernmental structure, and intramarket structure. Yet the connotation and orientation of these changes are significantly different from the previous economic growth-oriented period. More specifically:

1 Between government and market, to achieve collaborative integration of urban–rural economic relationship, China needs to continue to advance market-oriented reform so as to cause the market to play a more decisive role in urban–rural resource allocation, and microeconomic subjects to have greater choice and smaller transaction cost in urban–rural resource allocation. In addition to continuously

decentralizing powers to urban and rural microeconomic subjects, governments at all levels should also enhance the supply of public goods through function transformation, thus providing institutional support for the market mechanism to play its role. This includes defining and protecting property rights, strengthening urban and rural infrastructure construction, and promoting the equalization basic services between urban and rural areas. As discussed earlier, currently, China's factor marketization is lagging behind commodity marketization, and factor market distortion exists between urban and rural areas. These shortfalls mean that there is still room for further deepening the market-oriented economic system reform, and the role of the market in optimizing resource allocation still needs to be further highlighted and released. In a nutshell, the main line of government–market relationship is to make the market play a decisive role in the allocation of resources and give better play to the role of the government, which is the key proposition for China's to deepen economic system reform at the current time.

2 Inside the government, since reform and opening up, China has seen increasing intragovernmental structural feature. Over time, China has gradually formed a regionally decentralized authoritarianism among different levels of governments, which, while accelerating economic growth, has also exacerbated the structural problems in economic system. To achieve collaborative integration of urban–rural economic relationship, China has to improve this economic system arrangement among different levels of governments. That is, it should, while retaining the central government's economic governance and macroeconomic control, refine the financial management and incentive of local governments to enhance the coupling of economic development goals among different levels of governments, cause local governments to turn from "race for growth" toward "race for coordination", "race for innovation", and "race for people's livelihood", and cause deepening economic system reform and high-quality development to become the consensus and unanimous action among different levels of governments. In particular, for collaborative integration of urban–rural economic relationship, market-oriented reformation means reduced discretion for local governments over the allocation of core factors (especially land factors); equalization of basic public services between urban and rural areas means increased responsibility for local governments for financial expenditure. Hence, intergovernmental economic system reform should consider local governments' willingness and ability to promote the change of urban–rural economic relationship.

3 Inside the market, over the 40 years of reform and opening up, China's market-oriented system transition has featured progressive advancement, and marketization has not been pushed forward at the same pace among all different fields. As far of the intramarket structural feature is concerned, since 1978, China has formed an upstream-guided market

expansion inside the market. Compared with planned economy, this market-oriented transition has expanded the economic autonomy of microeconomic subjects and spurred the high-speed economic growth on the basis of improved resource allocation efficiency. Nevertheless, the marketization process has been highly different among different fields. Its mutual nesting with intergovernmental institutional arrangements has further exacerbated the economic structural problems. The previous imbalanced integration of urban–rural economic relationship is tightly bound with this intermarket structural feature. With urban–rural economic relationship moving toward collaborative integration, China has to rectify the marketization gap among different fields and eliminate the obstacles on the market-based allocation of land, capital, and labor factors between urban and rural areas. Particularly, it should gradually reduce the coverage and strength of government control over the upstream market, place the focus of deepening economic system reform in accelerating the marketization of factors, and switch governments' influence on economic operation to macro control and the supply of public goods.

In a nutshell, collaborative integration of China's urban–rural economic relationship in the new era is preceded by the change of government–market relationship, intragovernmental structure, and intramarket structure. The new combination of development strategy and constraints also means that China needs to promote a change in these fields so as to provide institutional environment for the new development strategy and for the behavioral choice of microeconomic subjects. We can describe the effects of government–market relationship, and intragovernmental structure, and intramarket structure on the evolution of urban–rural economic relationship from the change of rural land property system as an example. We chose rural land property right system as an analytical case because rural land property right system represents an important determinant of the behavioral choice of urban and rural residents, especially rural residents. At present, the relaxed control of rural land property right system—such as the implementation of "three rights division" on cultivated land—also affects the reallocation of urban factors. That is, it provides a pulling force for the inflow of productive forces like capital, information, and technology from the urban sector into the rural sector. The simultaneous occurrence of "urbanization" and "counter-urbanization" also provides the precondition for the change of rural land property right system.

Since 1949, China's property right system of rural cultivated land has changed many times. To understand these changes, we should consider the characteristics of government-market relationship; the intra-governmental and intra-market institutional arrangements have provided the tractive and supporting force for these changes (Gao F., 2018d). From 1949 to 1953, China formed a rural land property right system of farmer monopoly. Here farmer monopoly means that under the land reform oriented at "land to the tiller", farmers monopolized full land property rights including the right to own, use, dispose of, and profit from land. In the early days of the PRC, when China needed to restore national economy in a context where agriculture and farmers represented the majority of national economy, it had to place emancipating agricultural productivity in the first place of economic order restoration. The emancipation of agricultural productivity was based on giving farmers full land property right and thus stimulating farmers' agricultural production vitality. The "Land Reform Act of the People's Republic of China" adopted and enacted in 1950 explicitly stipulated that the former land ownership system of feudal exploitation by the landlord class and implement a land ownership system of farmers.

In terms of intra-governmental and intra-market structural feature, the inter-governmental and inter-market institutional arrangements in that period allowed the rural land property right system of farmer monopoly to be effectively realized. For, after the victory of the War of Liberation and the Anti-Japanese War, China's central government had strict control over local governments, and local governments were highly dependent on and obedient to the authority of the central government. That is, the goal and behavioral difference among different levels of governments were insignificant, and government could be seen as a highly homogeneous concept. Moreover, the Chinese government had relaxed control over both the upstream core factor market and the downstream general factor market and commodity market at that time, as evidenced by the fact that farmers owned land ownership and rural land could be traded freely. The inter-governmental consistency in action and inter-market full autonomy guaranteed the effective implementation of "land to the tiller"; farmers released their investment momentum and management vitality by acquiring full land property right. This greatly improved the agricultural production efficiency and emancipated agricultural productivity over that period.

After 1953, China's heavy industry first strategy began to conflict with the constraints of capital shortage and labor abundance at that time. To solve this conflict, the land property right system of farmer monopoly also changed to a land property right system of collective monopoly. Under the background of agricultural collective movement and socialist transformation, people's communes owned the ownership and management right of rural land in the form of collective. Rural surplus was allowed to flow into the industrial sector according to the country's development strategy orientation and became important capital sources for pushing forward the heavy industry first strategy. In terms of intra-governmental and intramarket institutional arrangements, from 1953 to 1978, on the inter-governmental dimensions, central government's strict control over local governments was continued. Unified collection and allocation of financial resources represented an important intergovernmental economic system arrangement over that period. Under a planned economy with high power centralization when local governments often played the role of an "executor" of the mandatory plans of the central government, such strict control guaranteed the consistency between the central and local governments in economic action. On the inter-market dimension, the previous full relaxation changed to full control. Under a planned economy with high power centralization when both the upstream core factor market and the downstream general factor and commodity market were under strict control, it was actually impossible for microeconomic subjects to carry out factor flow and commodity exchange according to price signals. These intergovernmental and intermarket institutional arrangements allowed the rural land property right system of collective monopoly to be fully executed. As a result, the rural land system reform strongly supported the development of heavy industry and the establishment of an independent industrial system, but it also brought national economy to the verge of collapse by suppressing the production efficiency of microeconomic subjects, and caused China's urban–rural economic relationship to display a distinct feature of separation.

In the late 1970s, China put forward the idea of centering around economic construction and highlighted the significance of emancipating and developing productivity. Its development strategy also shifted from heavy industry to economic growth. Nevertheless, this transformation was constrained by the dominance of farmers and rural employment and the persistently low efficiency of agricultural production. In view of this reality, China changed the former rural land property right system of collective monopoly into a rural land property right system of two rights separation, and people's communes into HRS. In this rural system change, rural collectives still owned land ownership to reflect the continuity of the previous rural land property right system; farmers had the right to contract and management land in units of households to reflect a reform to the previous rural land property right system. This change was intended to motivate the economic vitality of farmers by liberalizing the contracted management right of rural land without altering collective ownership, thus providing the power engine for increasing agricultural investment and developing agricultural productivity.

The rural land property right system with two rights separation conferred farmers with the contracted management right of land in units of households, but this right was subject to limitations on term and scope. It had an underlying hypothesis that the relationship between farmers and rural land was stable, namely, farmers who contracted land at the legal level were those who managed the land at the operational level. From the intra-governmental and intra-market institutional arrangements, while China began to decentralize powers to local governments after 1978, the core economic system, especially with respect to finance and taxation, was still at a transitional stage. The central government still maintained strict control over local governments. Local governments' economic autonomy was quite limited. Inside the market, on the contrary, the upstream market was still under control, but the downstream market was being liberalized, as evidenced by the cancellation of unified purchase and marketing of agricultural products and the development of commodity markets. These inter-governmental and inter-market institutional arrangements allowed the land property right system with two rights separation to be effectively promoted in practice. In 1983, contracting production or work households already accounted for the absolute majority of total number of rural production brigades. In contrast to people's communes, the land property right system with two rights separation conferred farmers with the autonomy of land management, and farmers' management efforts were directly tied with their own economic gains. This created a powerful driving force for significantly improving agricultural productivity.

Over the 1978–1993 period, China formed a rural land property right system with two rights separation; over the 1994–2013 period, this system evolved into a rural land property right system with two rights disintegration. Two rights disintegration means that inside rural land ownership, local governments were involved in the exercise of rural collectives' land ownership, while inside rural land management right, there were cases where a land contractor was unnecessarily the land user due to labor transfer. The reason was that after the mid-1990, China was still implementing the economic growth-oriented strategy, whereas rural labor was beginning to flow across industries, regions, and sectors. Such a situation called for an adjustment to the previous rural land property right system, in a way that allowed farmers to transfer land use right by leasing, exchange, transfer, stock cooperation or other means within the term of contract without changing collective ownership and farmers' contracting, so as to reallocate land between contractors and other agricultural business entities.

From the perspective of policy texts, the "Several Policy Measures regarding the Current Agricultural and Rural Economic Development" issued by the CPC Central Committee and the State Council in November 1993 decided that "after the expiry of the original contract term of cultivated land, it will be extended for another 30 years without change". It also noted that "to the extent of upholding collective ownership of land and without changing the land use, subject to the consent of the contractee, the use right of land may be transferred on paid basis according to law". This means that China was relaxing the previous strict rule that a land contractor must be the land user. After 1994, the inter-governmental and inter-market institutional arrangements also changed remarkably, especially the implementation of a financial power decentralization reform on the inter-governmental dimension. This way, the central government decentralized economic powers to local governments, and local governments had the momentum to maximize their own interests by affecting factor allocation. In terms of rural land property right system, local governments could participate in the decision making regarding the allocation of land ownership by affecting rural collectives. It could also improve the economic growth within their jurisdictions by encouraging the transfer of the contracted management right. Of rural land. Land transfer income also occupied a distinguished position in local fiscal revenues. In the meantime, on the inter-market dimension, the upstream market was still under control while the downstream market was being liberalized. Upstream market control means that governments still had a strong influence on the allocation of core factors, especially with respect to the conversion of rural land into urban land, which relied on the local government to expropriate and supply the land. In the downstream market, in contrast, the reallocation around the contracted management right of rural land was unprecedentedly developed thanks to the transfer of rural labor.

The rural land property right system with two rights disintegration adapted to urban–rural factor transfer and contributed to the reallocation of rural land among different groups. Yet its implementation was greeted by the following challenges. First, the contractors held the full contracted management right of the land, but the transfer usually involved only part of this right. Two rights disintegration could not reflect the difference between farmers' contracting and transfer rights. Second, local governments often played a prominent role in the allocation of rural land factors, as typically reflected by the "land finance" practice. In fact, the role of local governments in rural land allocation already became an important driver of urban–rural economic imbalance in the new era. Third, with the change of development strategy and constraints, there was an intrinsic need to adjust the rural land property right system with two rights disintegration. Since the Eighteenth National Congress of the CPC, China's development strategy has shifted from emancipating and developing productivity to emphasizing coordinated economic development, as evidenced by the establishment of the development concepts of "innovation, coordination, openness, green, sharing". The report to the Nineteenth National Congress of the CPC declared that the socialism with Chinese characteristics has entered a new era, and highlighted concern about imbalanced, inadequate development in main social contradiction. The report signals the formal redirection of development strategy from economic growth to coordinated development, marking another important adjustment of development strategy following reform and opening up. This combination of development strategy and constraints calls for adjusting the country's rural land system from time to time to form a new momentum and new mechanism in favor of the integrated development of urban and rural China in the new era.

In view of this situation, since 2014, China has taken "three rights division" as the basic direction of rural land property system reform in the new era. The core of "three rights division" is to decompose farmers' contracted management right into contracting right and management right, so as to allow diversified choices for farmers, social allocation of land and bidirectional flow of factors between urban and rural areas, and to form a better balance between improving rural economic efficiency and stabilizing social order. "Three rights division" not only represents a continuation of the previous rural land property right system, since it emphasizes the land ownership by collectives like both the "two rights separation" and "two rights disintegration"; it also represents a reform to the previous rural land property right system, since it covers two rights concepts of contracting right and management right, and emphasizes that these rights can produce a new form of combination through land transfer. From the perspective of policy text, in 2014, the "No.1 Document" of the Central Committee proposed for the first time that the country should "to the extent of bringing into effect the collective ownership of rural land, stabilize farmers' contracting right, liberalize land management right, and allow the use of the management right of contracted land as a mortgage to finance from financial institutions". This marked the escalation of "three rights division" of rural land from guiding ideology into actual operation. "Three rights division" consequently became the basic direction of rural land property right system reform in the new historical era, and another institutional innovation of rural reform following HRS.

In terms of intra-governmental and intra-market institutional arrangements, "three rights division" is both a continuation of and a reform to the previous rural land property right system. "Three rights division" emphasizes the need to bring into effect the collective ownership of rural land, since collective ownership is the prerequisite for stabilizing contracting right and liberalizing management right. Rural land ownership is generally exercised by collective organizations such as "two village boards" (village party branch and village committee), which are both economic organizations and administrative ones. In a way, they are an extension of administrative hierarchy in rural areas. On ground of this, the execution of land ownership not only depends on the interrelation between individual villagers and collective organizations, but also on the interrelation between local governments and collective organizations. From the connotation of "three rights division", to bring into effect collective ownership means to enhance the consistency between the central government and local governments. That is, the central government will weaken local governments' actual influence on land allocation by deepening financial system reform and administrative incentive reform, which constitutes a reform to the previous intergovernmental institutional arrangement. Furthermore, "three rights division" emphasizes the need to activate land management right, since the decomposition of contracted management right into contracting right and management right can well accommodate the rural social practice where the land contractor is unnecessarily the land manager, allow the social allocation of rural land through the transfer of management right, thus expanding farmers' occupational choice and income channel, and improving the fluidity and allocation efficiency of land factors. Here the key point is to, while regulating the upstream market of land (e.g., land ownership), further activate the downstream market of land by allowing the flow and transaction of management right among different subjects and make the land transfer price the core variable reflecting the relative scarcity of the downstream market. The liberalization of the downstream market also means that the bidirectional flow of capital, labor, and other factors between urban and rural areas is enhanced, the inflow of productive factors like capital,

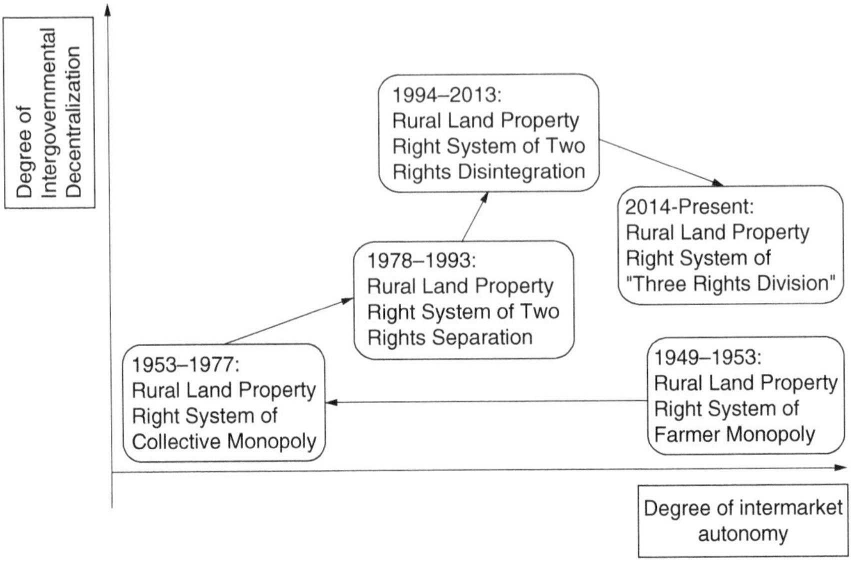

Figure 9.3 Evolution of China's rural land property right system since 1949.

Source: Gao F. (2018d).

technology, and information into rural areas can be supported by the land system, and microeconomic subjects enjoy greater autonomy to allocate factors between urban and rural areas.

Based on the intragovernmental and intramarket institutional arrangements, we can look at the consistency of economic behavior between the central and local governments as the longitudinal axis, and the autonomy of microeconomic subjects between the upstream and downstream markets as the horizontal axis, so as to understand the evolution of China's rural land property right system and the formation of "three rights division" on the economic history dimension. As illustrated by Figure 9.3, since 1949, China's intergovernmental power decentralization has displayed a weak–strong–weak profile, whereas its intermarket autonomy has shown just the opposite picture. Accordingly, the country's rural land property right system has evolved from farmer monopoly, collective monopoly, two rights separation, two rights disintegration, and "three rights division". Over the course of this evolution, "three rights division" has largely been embedded in the combination of development strategy and constraints, and the process of intergovernmental and intermarket institutional change. It features an economic transition of China's continued progressive reform according to practice. "Three rights division" is path-dependent. That is, it is a continuation of the collective ownership of land ownership and combination between unification and separation in the previous system. At the same time, it is also a continuous reform. That is, it continues farmers' economic rights and interests of land by retaining contracting right and reflects the more effective allocation of rural land inside rural and urban areas by activating management right.

On the whole, "three rights division" is to, without changing the collective ownership of land, release the vitality of land allocation by way of subdividing and enhancing the tradability of property right, which means that a new rural land property right structure has formed in rural China. Given that rural land is also partly responsible for social security, and it can usually serve as a membership right for farmers in the community, "three rights division" is intended to, without touching farmers' contracting right, improve the allocation efficiency of rural land through the transfer of management right, and guarantee that in the process of urbanization, farmers are still protected with a "safety valve" if they choose to retreat to rural areas. This finds a new balance between improving the economic efficiency and giving play to the social security function of land. During intragovernmental and intramarket institutional evolution, the change of China's rural land property right system from two rights separation, two rights disintegration to "three rights division" was a spontaneous evolution. Continued progressive change could not have given rise to other forms of rural land property right system. This evolution not only reflects the interconnection between intragovernmental or intramarket institutional arrangements and land property right system. It also reflects the dynamic change of China's urban–rural economic relationship from separation to imbalanced integration and further to collaborative integration from the perspective of land system.

9.3 Policy options for realizing collaborative integration of urban–rural economic relationship

Following the heavy industry first and economic growth-led development strategies implemented over the past years since the founding of the People's Republic of China, the country has now formally switched to a coordinated development strategy, which represents a second key adjustment of its economic development strategy at a particular milestone where reform and opening-up has been advanced for 40 years. To match this, the country's urban–rural economic relationship, after decades of separation and imbalanced integration, is also waiting to be redirected toward a new landscape of collaborative integration. Compared with imbalanced integration, collaborative integration relates to a higher profile and a higher level of integration of urban–rural economic relationship. Indeed, collaborative integration of urban–rural economic relationship constitutes an important part of achieving the coordinated development strategy. Today, when our socialism with Chinese characteristics has entered a new era, collaborative integration of urban–rural economic relationship should not only be emphasized as a concept but also be put into action as a practice. As to the implementation conditions, after 40 years of reform and opening-up, China is better prepared for collaborative integration of urban–rural economic relationship than at the beginning of reform and opening-up and even than in the beginning of the 21st century.

In terms of development concept, collaborative integration of urban–rural economic relationship can only be introduced and implemented against a background of transforming the development concept. In fact, it is closely connected with China's need to liberate and develop productivity and consequently realize the goal of sustainability and common prosperity as a socialist country. Now China has boosted the transformation of the development concept, as reflected by the introduction of the scientific outlook on development and the five concepts for development, the transformation of main social contradiction and reorientation of economic development, and the goal-setting to basically achieve modernization and become a great modern country. China's economy is turning from a stage of high-speed growth into a stage of high-quality development. Here, high-quality development implies a higher level of coordination, balance, and sustainability of the national economy. In the goal-setting to basically achieve modernization and become a great modern country, the degree to which common prosperity is achieved for individual social groups is a critical element. At a special time when reform and opening-up is celebrating its fortieth anniversary, the change in the development concept is promoting us to switch from an economic growth-led strategy to a coordinated development one. This offers the ideological basis for the collaborative integration of urban–rural economic relationship.

In terms of material conditions, after 40 years of reform and opening-up, China's economic growth-led development strategy has achieved remarkable performances, as reflected by the world "miracle" made by our continued rapid GDP growths and the substantially greater economic strength, overall national strength, and international influence of the country as a whole. From a temporal point of view, Chinese urban and rural residents are finding their income level, consumption expenditure, and social welfare improvement procedure greatly improved. Indeed, they are already benefiting from a better social and economic position thanks to the market system transition, although the degree of this improvement may still vary considerably among different social groups. The financial resource mobilization capacity of the entire country is also growing rapidly–from 1978 to 2017, China's fiscal revenue already increased from 113.226 billion yuan to 17.26 trillion yuan, providing solid material basis for collaborative integration of urban–rural economic relationship. Frankly, no collaborative integration of urban–rural economic relationship would ever be truly realized in a context of backward social productivity and universal material shortage.

In terms of economic architecture, collaborative integration of urban–rural economic relationship signifies enhanced fluidity of urban–rural products and factors, as well as sustained reduction of urban–rural income divide and consumption divide, down to a level at least equal to or lower than that in the mid-1980s. Reduction of economic divide is viable only against a backdrop of changed urban–rural population structure. In fact, after 40 years of reform and opening-up, China's ongoing industrialization and urbanization have kept its agriculture and rural areas under constant "sector shrinkage". China itself has now turned from relying on agricultural output, agricultural employment and rural population as the subject to relying on non-agricultural output, non-agricultural employment and urban population as the subject. Furthermore, targeted poverty alleviation and elimination endeavors aimed at rural areas have also made remarkable achievements. At the current rural poverty standard, from 1990 to 2016, China's incidence of rural poverty had dropped sharply from 73.5 percent to 4.5 percent. Above changes in economic architecture also provides supporting conditions for redirecting the country's urban–rural economic relationship from imbalanced integration to collaborative integration.

In terms of technical means, collaborative integration of urban–rural economic relationship should be preceded by improved efficiency of commodity and factor allocation between (and within) urban and rural areas, whereas the cost for interconnecting market information makes a significant difference to this allocation efficiency. In that connection, since the implementation of the reform and opening-up, especially since the beginning of the 21st century, China's information technology has gained rapid development and wide application. Table 9.3 compares the numbers of Internet

Table 9.3 Number of Internet users and rate of Internet popularization in China from 2006 to 2017

Year	*Number of Internet Users (million)*				*Internet Popularization Rate (%)*		
	National	*Internet Users with Mobile Phone Access*	*Urban*	*Rural*	*National*	*Urban*	*Rural*
2006	137.00	17.00	113.89	23.11	10.42	19.54	3.16
2007	210.01	50.40	157.39	52.62	15.89	25.96	7.36
2008	298.17	117.60	213.57	84.60	22.45	34.22	12.02
2009	384.00	233.44	277.20	106.81	28.77	42.97	15.49
2010	457.30	302.73	332.46	124.84	34.10	49.64	18.60
2011	513.10	355.58	377.10	136.00	38.08	54.59	20.71
2012	564.00	419.97	408.34	155.67	41.65	57.37	24.24
2013	617.58	500.06	440.95	176.63	45.39	60.31	28.05
2014	648.75	556.78	470.34	178.41	47.43	62.78	28.84
2015	688.26	619.81	492.79	195.47	50.07	63.90	32.39
2016	731.25	695.42	530.90	200.40	52.89	66.95	33.98
2017	771.98	752.65	563.55	208.43	55.53	69.28	36.15

Source: The rate of Internet popularization figures is calculated according to the number of Internet users/population figures. The national (urban and rural) number of Internet users figures come from CEIC Data.

users and the Internet penetration rates across the period from 2006 to 2017. Since 2006, China has witnessed a steep rise in the number of Internet users and the Internet penetration rate. During this period, the number of Internet users in China skyrocketed from 137 million to 771.98 million, with the number of mobile Internet users climbing from 17 million to 752.65 million. Mobile terminals have already become the principal part for the development and application of Internet technology in China at this stage. Over the same period of time, the national, urban, and rural Internet penetration rates had risen from 10.42 percent, 19.54 percent, and 3.16 percent to 55.53 percent, 69.28 percent, and 36.15 percent, respectively. The rise in the Internet penetration rate and the wide application of mobile terminal technologies imply a drastic reduction in the information acquisition cost for urban and rural microeconomic subjects; the reduction in transaction cost will contribute to more frequent, more extensive economic interactions between (and within) urban and rural areas. This suggests that the promotion of information technology provides favorable technical conditions for collaborative integration of China's urban–rural economic relationship.

In a nutshell, in a general context of the transition of the development strategy from economic growth led to coordinated development, redirecting the country's urban–rural economic relationship from imbalanced integration to collaborative integration is both necessary and feasible. How to straighten up the formation mechanism of imbalanced integration and consolidate the implementation conditions for collaborative integration through economic institutional changes based on government–market relationship and the intragovernmental and intramarket structural characteristic forthwith becomes the core to this redirection. On grounds of the foregoing theoretical and empirical studies, if China is to realize collaborative integration of urban–rural economic relationship now, an important thing to do is to continue to deepen economic institutional reform, and rely on sustained economic institutional changes to bring to reality collaborative integration of urban–rural economic relationship. In practice, economic institutional changes are usually attained through a series of economic policies. These policies serve as the fuel for transforming from imbalanced integration to collaborative integration.

Logically speaking, policies matching collaborative integration of urban–rural economic relationship should have the following characteristics: First, systematic. That is, imbalanced integration of urban–rural economic relationship is not a single, separate problem. Specifically, the imbalance in urban–rural factor allocation is manifested in multiple aspects; the fluctuations in urban–rural income divide and consumption divide are also entangled with each other. The multiaspects of imbalance also imply that, instead of relying on one single policy, we have to combine a number of policies to realize the anticipated goal, and rely on systematic policies to resolve the systematic problems in the current urban–rural economic relationship. Second, institutional. That is, imbalanced integration of urban–rural economic relationship derives from a series of economic systems. Redirecting the development strategy to coordinated development does provide economic basis for economic institutional changes, yet this strategic redirection does not naturally equal instant changes on institutional dimensions such as government–market relationship. Collaborative integration of urban–rural economic relationship has to address "institutional complementation". That is, the formulation of urban–rural economic policies should be considered from the perspective of deepening economic institutional reform instead of simply relying on the "blood transfusion" of government financial resources to achieve short-lived urban–rural economic balance. Third, differential. China is a developing nation that implements socialist system. Different areas usually vary distinctly in economic development stage. The manifestation form and concrete causes of their urban–rural economic relationship may differ from one another, too. Overall, the transformation of urban–rural dual economy in the eastern part of the country is proceeding ahead of that in the central and western parts. The intersectoral factor flow between urban and rural areas there is also more active than in the central and western parts. Hence, to realize collaborative integration of urban–rural economic relationship, we not only need to launch national, universal economic policies but also motivate governments of different areas to explore economic policies suitable for their respective local particularities. Adjusting measures to local conditions and timing is also a critical benchmark for implementing policies related to urban–rural economic relationship. Fourth, feasible. That is, collaborative integration of urban–rural economic relationship is not simply a theoretic issue concerning urban–rural relational changes. It is also a practical issue closely related to the current national conditions, especially the institutional evolution, of the country. To advance the urban–rural relational evolution, we cannot adopt options that are theoretically perfect but practically inoperable. Instead, those theoretically less perfect but practically more operable ones are desirable. In an overpopulated and oversized developing country like China, if we are to effectively realize collaborative integration of urban–rural economic relationship, giving full play to the accumulation effect of policies and continuously promoting their refinement is of fatal importance.

Based on the coordinated development strategy and the country's socioeconomic development momentum, since the beginning of the 21st century, especially over the most recent years, China has implemented a series of policy changes around urban–rural economic relationship. For instance, from 2004 to 2018, China has issued a consecutive series of central government's "No.1 Documents" themed around resolving agricultural, farmer, and rural area issues. In 2002, China explicitly proposed that governments at all levels should actively guide the farmers to build a new rural cooperative medical care scheme focusing on comprehensive arrangement for serious diseases. Its essence is to form a rural medical care mutual assistance system focusing on comprehensive arrangement for serious diseases with funds pooled from individuals, collectives, and government. In 2009, China began to implement pilot projects for the new rural old-age insurance system. Different from the former financial practice of relying on the self-savings of farmers, this new rural endowment system emphasizes the responsibility of the state for ensuring that the elderly are provided for properly. These efforts register a big step for China toward ensuring equal access to public services between urban and rural residents. Besides, China's product and factor circulation channels between urban and rural areas have also been continuously broadened. Particularly, its urban and rural household registration reform has stepped up into a higher dimension and a broader range. For instance, in July 2014, the State Council issued the "Opinions on Further Promotion of Reform of the Household Registration System", which explicitly stated that the country will further adjust the household registration policy, unify the urban and rural household registration, and fully implement the residence permit system. By 2020, we will basically establish a new household registration system that adapts to building a moderately prosperous society in all respects, effectively supports social administration and public services, guarantees citizens' rights in accordance with the law, and is people-oriented, scientific, efficient, standardized and orderly, and strive to achieve the settlement of about 100 million agricultural transfer population and other permanent residents in cities and towns. As stated above, urban and rural household registration stemmed out of the planned economy period carries the dual functions of regulating employment and allocating social security resources. Since the implementation of reform and opening-up, the employment regulation function of household registration has been weakening. If the new household registration system is to be effectively attained in 2020, this will mean that the social security resource allocation function of household registration is also stepping down from the stage of history.

In the realization of collaborative integration of urban–rural economic relationship, the Report of the Nineteenth National Congress of the CPC plays an undisputedly critical role, not only because this report noted that the main contradiction in the Chinese society has changed and its economic development stage has transitioned but also because this report put forward the proposition of implementing the strategy for rural vitalization in building a modern economic system. The rural vitalization strategy is an overall disposition made by China around rural reform and development in the background of the new era. It emphasizes the multiple tasks such as priority development of agriculture and rural areas, modernization of agriculture and rural areas, and prosperity of industries, the deepening of the reform of land property rights system, and the cultivation and expansion of new-type rural business entities. Hence, it constitutes a response to agricultural and rural development and urban–rural economic relational changes from a systems perspective based on the current economic architectural changes. Further, the central government's "No.1 Document" of 2018 gives top priority to implementing the rural vitalization strategy as the mainline. It emphasizes that implementing the rural vitalization strategy is the internal need for resolving the imbalanced, inadequate development in China, and the inevitable requirement for realizing the goal of sustainable economy and common prosperity. It also emphasizes that implementing the rural vitalization strategy should be based on establishing and improving the institutional mechanism and policy system for urban–rural integrated development as the starting point and foothold. In summary, after entering the 21st century, the mainline of China's implementation of urban–rural economic policies has been exceptionally clear. That is, to redirect imbalanced integration to collaborative integration and ensure that this redirection serves the coordinated development strategy. Besides, the basic foothold of these policies is to further highlight the government's resource preferences toward agriculture, rural area and farmers while activating the market mechanism, which reflects a response to the institutional reform mainline of continuously adjusting government–market relationship.

The problem, however, lies in the reality that collaborative integration of urban–rural economic relationship is a system engineering effort, and the previous imbalanced integration still poses a "path dependence" effect in practice. Hence, how well the existing economic policies are implemented still takes quite some time to observe. More importantly, as collaborative integration of urban–rural economic relationship involves more than one subject, we have to consider the participation motives and incentive compatibility among different subjects. The previous imbalanced integration was the product of government–market relationship and intragovernmental and intramarket structural characteristics and institutional arrangements. Hence, as a correction of and a transcendence beyond imbalanced integration, collaborative integration of urban–rural economic relationship has to respond to the needs of policies changes in these areas. On the dimension of government–market relationship, its core is to truly demonstrate and cause the play of, the decisive role of the market in resources allocation, and give better play to the role of government. Here, government and market are not a simple substitution of the scope of roles, but a functional complementation and mutual enhancement based on the coordinated development strategy. Outside government–market relationship, refining the intragovernmental and intramarket institutional arrangements should precede the implementation of collaborative integration. In other words, in a context where China is deepening market-oriented system transition, a "market-driven plus government-compensated policy" is a policy option for China to realize collaborative integration of urban–rural economic relationship. Government–market relationship, intragovernmental and intramarket institutional changes, and the incentive compatibility among participants play a supporting role for policy implementation. On these grounds, the collaborative integration of urban–rural economic relationship in the context of the current times should start with a combination of the following policies (Gao F., 2018e). These policies can well match the "systematic, institutional, differential, and feasible" principles. They can also support China in achieving sustained improvement of urban–rural relationship in the background of the country's coordinated development strategy.

1 Improve the efficiency of rural factor allocation by deepening land system reform. To realize collaborative integration of urban–rural economic relationship, the first thing to do is to continue to improve the efficiency of commodity and factor allocation. In advancing the refinement of urban–rural economic relationship, China should place raising the marketization degree of urban–rural factors and continuing to ease government regulation on top of its agenda. In the background of a new era, China's efforts in deepening market-oriented reform on urban–rural factors are typically manifested in the area of rural land factors. This is mainly because: "Land is the basic means of production for agriculture, an important life guarantee for farmers, and the root for maintaining the harmony and stability of the rural society" (Song H.Y., 2018). The rural land system and ownership structure hold the balance to rural economic development. Since the implementation of reform and opening-up, China's rural economic reform has been closely tied with land system reform. Given that rural land is still shouldering the social security function for farmers, providing a "safety valve" and a "buffer zone" for farmers' fluidity between urban and rural areas and that the dominance of public ownership of the means of production is still the basic feature of China's economic system, private or state ownership of rural land is not an option for the country's current land ownership system reform. China's rural areas should, on the basis of upholding the collective ownership of land, give farmers more choices by stabilizing their land contracting rights and liberalizing their land management rights. They should also economize the transaction cost among micro-economic subjects by developing land circulation market and interconnecting land circulation information and push the "three rights division" reform of rural arable land to a higher dimension and a broader range. The extension of land contract relationship for another 30 years after the expiration of the second round of contract precisely reflects this system reform orientation.

By virtue of these system reforms, after contracting the land, farmers may either use it directly or circulate its operating rights to others, or assign its contracting rights and operating rights to a collective organization. This market-oriented revolution is a second "decentralization of power and transfer of profits" for farmers under the new architecture. It is important to releasing rural labor, introducing external capital, and promoting rural business mode innovation. Given that the "three rights division" of land involves multiple stakeholders, when implementing "three rights division" of rural land, China should vigorously resolve the incentive compatibility among different stakeholders. Only when all land stakeholders are benefited and improved from institutional changes is it able to smoothly push forward the land ownership system evolution of "three rights division". Emphatically, in addition to extensively promoting the "three rights division" of arable land, China should also actively implement "three rights division" (the division of ownership, entitlement, and use rights) pilot projects for rural homestead, which may include social or market allocation of homestead by individual farmers, or "resources to assets, funds to stocks, farmers to shareholders" operations by collective organizations to improve the efficiency of factor allocation. Fundamentally, the "three rights division" reform of rural arable land and homestead is to rely on the subdivision of the land ownership system to push forward the marketization of land factors and to improve the efficiency of urban–rural factor allocation.

2 Refine the mode of urban–rural factor exchange by virtue of sustained institutional changes. Since the implementation of reform and opening-up, the integration of China's urban–rural economic relationship has relied on the improvement of urban–rural product and factor fluidity as the prerequisite and the ability of microeconomic subjects to spontaneously allocate factors as a critical condition. In the background of the new era, collaborative integration of China's urban–rural economic rely even more on substantial factor fluidity and optimal allocation between and within urban and rural areas as a prerequisite. Since 1978, there have been unidirectional outflows of rural labor, land and capital. This fluidity has helped improve the efficiency of factor allocation and boosted economic growth. But between urban and rural areas, there also exists a distorted factor market, and the income distribution after factor reallocation is also more biased toward urban areas. The distribution of land assignment income between urban and rural areas demonstrated earlier serves as an obvious evidence.

In a context of implementing the coordinated development strategy, toward factor fluidity caused by price factors, China should not render forced intervention with government power. Nor should we forcefully confine rural factors to rural areas only, or forcefully require urban factors to go rural. Instead, we should try to refine the mode of urban–rural factor exchange by correcting the economic system of universal nature. We should deepen land requisition system reform. Rural land provides farmers with both means of production and social security. Hence, we should raise the compensation standard for land-lost farmers using both agricultural output and social security resources as the criteria and ensure that land requisition income is more biased toward areas ensuring equal access to public services between urban and rural residents. We should speed up pushing rural collective land for commercial construction into the land market. Land increment income should be distributed to "first guarantee the legitimate rights and interests of the disadvantaged land-lost farmers and ensure that the state and the related investors also receive the necessary compensation or reward, too" (Jian X.H., 2015). We should improve the factor rate of return of rural economy by virtue of land circulation, management innovation, and industrial function expansion to attract high-quality farmers back to the countryside and become new occupational farmers and attract high-quality urban talents to come into the countryside and become new "farmers" (Research Group at the Department of Rural Economic System & Operation & Management of Ministry of Agriculture, 2016). We should make the best use of the relative stability of rural communities, allow and encourage rural cooperative financial institutions to develop and expand, push capital downward to the countryside under the premises of setting up a negative list of rural investment so that rural economy will become an important area for financial development to serve real economy, and encourage rural business subjects to use "Internet + " and other information technologies to bring down the transaction cost for factor interconnection.

3 Speed up urban–rural equalization of basic public services. In the new era, China needs to fulfill the development concepts of "innovation, coordination, green, openness, sharing", and to push its economy from high-speed growth toward high-quality development. Moreover, the identity-based urban–rural gap of social security resources has already dragged down urban–rural integration, as evidenced by the new duality problem in the process of urbanization. To solve these problems, China has to face up to its urban–rural gap in access to public goods and social security, address narrowing dual society as an important content of establishing a new form of urban–rural relationship, and extend the integrated development between the urban and rural sectors from converging income gap to equalizing basic public service.

This equalization of basic public services can be achieved through two channels. First is to effectively strengthen the integration of rural population into urban areas. With economic growth and enhanced financial capacity, China needs to gradually lower the threshold for settling down in cities of different sizes and levels after careful classification. In particular, small and medium-sized cities with more effective population size and lower integration cost should quickly lift household register barriers, allow more rural population to work in urban areas and eventually integrate into urban life, and turn the out-sync between occupational transition and identity transformation into consistency between occupational transition and identity transformation. Second is to practically upgrade the supply of rural social security. That is, in addition to sustain the healthy development of urbanization, China should also strengthen the supply of public goods like medical care, basic old age insurance, and basic education for rural residents, provide more development opportunities for rural residents, increase the human capital of rural residents, reduce the "gold content" gap between urban and rural household registers, and make the supply of social security an inclusive underpinning mechanism that can fit in with the population flow pattern.

4 Improve the efficiency of rural economy by innovating the production management and organization mode. To achieve collaborative integration of urban–rural economic relationship in the new era, China has to effectively activate the intrinsic capacity of rural economy, and meet people's growing need for a better life. Hence the rural sector needs to provide diversified products and services. It also needs to extend the previous in-production link into the pre- and post-production segments, and to organize moderate scale management to increase the return on factors and market bargaining power. Besides, the expansion of urban–rural factor flow and reallocation channels will also cause urban capital and other productive factors to flow into the rural sector. All these factors signify the continuous change of rural production management and organization mode.

Since reform and opening up, China has replaced people's communes with HRS and profoundly reformed the rural production management and organization mode. This double-layer management system combining unification and separation has greatly promoted the emancipation and development of rural productivity. In the new era, China needs to further change its rural production management and organization mode. In this regard, China needs to, while adhering to HRS, activate land use right to reform the combination of rural factors. The government can consummate the rural land transfer market and improve the information matching degree in land allocation to spur the reallocation of land factors. The government can provide land, fiscal, financial, and industrial policy guidance to cause rural management to improve the integration of the three industries while ensuring food security and form new momentum of rural management on the basis of extended industrial chain, improved value chain, and expanded industrial function. In addition, the government should also consummate a screening and training mechanism targeting at professional farmers, so as to improve the human capital content of rural practitioners through education and training, quickly form a large team of professional farmers that are professionally skillful, sensitive to market variation, and capable of factor integration. It should provide an integrated service system for new business entities, such as large specialized households, family farms, farmers' co-operatives, and leading agricultural enterprises, causes the formation of a new pattern of functional complementation and interest sharing between these business entities and small farmer households, and resolve the broadening income gap inside rural areas by virtue of interest sharing between small farmer households and through the guidance of land, finance,

finance and industrial policies, the government can promote rural management to improve the degree of integration of the three industries on the basis of ensuring food security and form a new driving force for rural management on the basis of extending the industrial chain, improving the value chain and expanding the industrial functions. In addition, the government should improve the screening and training mechanism for professional farmers, improve the human capital content of rural practitioners through education and training, and form a large number of professional farmers with professional skills, sensitive to market changes and the ability to integrate elements as soon as possible, agricultural leading enterprises and other new business entities provide a comprehensive service system, which promotes the new business entities and small farmers to form a new pattern of complementary functions and benefit sharing. We should rely on the benefit sharing mechanism between small farmers and modern agricultural business entities to solve the problem of widening income gap in rural areas.

5 Improve the collimation of rural economic policies according to the classification and collaboration criterion. The implementation of a coordinated development strategy means the continuous reform of the economic system. That is, China needs to achieve institutional change amid the continuous adjustment of government-market relationship, thus affecting the behavioral choice and decision-making pattern of microeconomic subjects. This institutional change is also the intrinsic need for achieving collaborative integration of urban–rural economic relationship. As institutional changes rely on economic policies as the carrier, given the internal differentiation among farmers and the differentiated rural development across different regions of a large country, it is particularly important to improve the collimation, pertinence, and effectiveness of rural economic policies. To improve the collimation of rural economic policies, it is necessary to classify the target and object against which the policy is to be implemented, and to create an overall institutional reform effect through the collaboration among different policies.

Significant gaps of economic development exist among different regions of China. Therefore, it is important to, in addition to the given basic rural economic system, allow different regions to innovate rural economic system according to their own local characteristics, activate the enthusiasm of governments at different levels for exploring rural policies, encourage different regions carry out horizontal rural policy learning and extension, and avoid forcing the national-scale implementation of a regional policy by administrative power. Particularly, eastern China regions may encounter a number of problems involved in the refinement of urban–rural economic relationship earlier than others due to their high development level, such as metropolitan modern agriculture, integration of the three industries in rural areas, improvement of rural total factor productivity, and formation of rural professional labor. Practices, experiences, and lessons learned should be summarized to give play to the referential and enlightening functions of the urban–rural integrated development in these regions for the other parts of China. Besides, gaps also exist among farmers in respect of occupation, income, consumption, and factor allocation. Therefore, rural economic policies should first of all identify their core targets and implementation objects. They should discriminate policies targeting small farmer households, large specialized households, family farms, and specialized cooperatives; discriminate policies supporting grain yield increase, farmer income increase, and urban–rural equalization of basic public services; discriminate policies for stimulating market vitality, for targeted poverty alleviation, and for reducing gaps among farmers. This way, the overall implementation effect of rural policies will be improved on the basis of classification and enhanced collaboration.

6 Deepen the economic system reform at different levels of governments based on the incentive compatibility criterion. In the new era, collaborative integration of urban–rural economic relationship not only involves the adjustment of government-market relationship. It also involves intra-governmental and intra-market structural adjustment and institutional change. The latter constitutes the most unique part of the economic system transition of China as a large developing country at the institutional level. Land property right system reform and urban–rural factor exchange means that market-oriented reform is going deeper, and that factor marketization is coinciding with commodity marketization. This is an adjustment of government-market relationship, as well as an adjustment of the intra-governmental and intra-market institutional arrangements. In terms of inter-governmental institutional arrangements, after the mid-1990s, China's inter-governmental power decentralization reform has given rise to a set of economic system arrangements between the central government and local governments, and among individual local governments. These arrangements have both led to local governments' "race for growth", thus spurring the high-speed GDP growth, and caused local governments to intervene in factor allocation, thus exacerbating the economic structural problems.

At present, to achieve a collaborative integration-oriented urban–rural economic relationship and robustly promote the rural revitalization strategy and other major deployments, China has to address the interaction of political and social factors with economic activities and understand the evolutionary logic of its urban–rural economic relationship. Hence, it is necessary to decompose urban–rural integrated development into the objective functions of different levels of local governments to form a local government performance indicator system, evaluation system, evaluation system, assessment system, and incentive system that match the collaborative integration of urban and rural areas. Besides, national financial management reform should be deepened to truly resolve the imbalance between financial power and administrative power commonly facing local governments, cause local governments at different levels to further lift their market control with clearly defined rights and responsibilities and relative balance of payments. By changing the economic system arrangements of the central government and local governments different levels, a new pattern of rights-responsibility symmetry will be created in governments at different levels and lay a solid intergovernmental institutional foundation for collaborative integration of urban–rural economic relationship.

10 Conclusions and prospects

From a global perspective, urban–rural duality is common among developing nations, causing the transformation of duality an important mission facing the modernization drive of these countries. Development economics has also formed the dual economy theory represented by the Lewis-Fei-Ranis model. As the largest developing country in the world, China has also been troubled by urban–rural duality all the time since the late 1940s. Over time, China's urban–rural duality has displayed differentiated features and behaviors across different periods of time. Dynamic evolution of urban–rural duality constitutes a characteristic fact of China's economic development. Given this practical background, it becomes an important topic to explain the evolutionary mechanism of China's urban–rural economic relationship across a long time span, which has a positive significance to both the extension of existing dual economy theories and the raising of policy recommendations concerning the urban–rural coordinated development in China. From a political economy perspective, this book makes a systematic analysis on the typical "development" issue of dual economy and traces the evolutionary trajectory of China's urban–rural economic relationship since the founding of the PRC with the descriptions "separation", "imbalanced integration", and "collaborative integration". This reflects a positive response to this major topic. It also showcases the profound influence of the 40 years of reform and opening up on China's economy and society from the urban–rural economic relationship dimension.

In development economics, the Lewis-Fei-Ranis model, a classic model for explaining dual economy problems, has wide influence on understanding the urban–rural structural changes in developing nations. The model assumes that urban–rural duality stemmed from the endowment disparities between the urban and rural sectors, and a perfect factor market and the transfer of rural labor in an economy constitute the core driver of structural transformation. Nevertheless, these implied assumptions do not fully agree with China's practical background. Since the founding of the PRC in 1949, China has always been a large developing country with socialist system. After the late 1970s, China embarked on the great course of reform and opening up, marking a transition from planned economy toward market economy and from closed economy to open economy. Market-oriented economic system transition is an important target of China's modernization drive since reform and opening up.

This signifies that China's economic development has been revolving around a fundamental proposition all the time. That is, how shall a large developing country with socialist system realize its goal of sustainable development and common prosperity? China's economic development features three keywords: socialist system, a large developing country, and economic system transition of a large developing country. These keywords not only mean that China needs to realize a higher goal (the pursuit of sustainable development and common prosperity is contained in China's socialist system) against tougher conditions (a large developing country with population and geographical sizes rarely found elsewhere in the world). It also means that so far China is still in the process of market-oriented transition. A perfecting market, rather than a perfect market, depicts the real picture of China's national economic operation.

On ground of this, to understand China's urban–rural economic relationship, we have to draw inspirations from existing research literature, and put forward a more convincing analytical framework based on local practice. From the political economy perspective, this book holds that China's urban–rural economic relationship should be understood by setting it into the country's overall economic development, by addressing the social realities of socialist system, a large developing country, and economic system transition, and by addressing the interaction chain among development strategy and constraints, choice of economic system, behavior of microeconomic subjects, and performance of economic development (transformation of urban–rural economic structure). Among all these interactions, the combination of development strategy and constraint is always subject to the fundamental proposition of how a large developing country with socialist system shall realize its goal of sustainable development and common prosperity. However, the social practice in response to this topic has been proceeding by stage and by step. That is, development strategy, constraints, and their combination have differed across different periods of time. Over each period, the combination of development strategy and constraints will give rise to the corresponding economic system, which will typically revolve around government–market relationship. However, in a large developing country like China where structural features exist inside both the government and the market, the economic system is bound to break the government–market dichotomy and to encompass rules or institutional arrangements targeting the intragovernmental and intramarket structural features.

In a nutshell, China's local characteristics determine that its economic system covers both the main line of economic operation mechanism and the intragovernmental and intramarket structural arrangements typical of a large developing country, which have served as the driver for realizing a development strategy against particular constraints. However, after it is chosen and implemented, the economic system will definitely affect the behavioral choice of microeconomic subjects by means such as defining property rights and transaction order. This choice will result in corresponding economic results or development performances, primarily urban–rural duality and its transformation, which in turn further leads to dynamic changes in urban–rural economic relationship by affecting development strategy and constraints. The above analytical framework of urban–rural economic relationship is different from the Lewis-Fei-Ranis model in that it attempts to derive the influence of economic system and its changes on China's urban–rural economic relationship based on China's local characteristics. Hence, it understands China's urban–rural economic relationship from "political economy of development" instead of solely from the perspective of development economics.

Based on the political economy analytical framework, this book places its research in a long time period spanning from the founding of the PRC in 1949 up to the present day and discusses the basic characteristics and changes of China's urban–rural economic relationship across different time intervals over this period. In a large developing country with socialist system like China, it is impossible to realize the goal of sustainable economic development and common prosperity overnight. It is bound to be a stage-by-stage, progressive process. In the early years of the PRC, when the country was faced with a complex environment and multiple challenges both at home and abroad, China chose a heavy industry first strategy at the economic level, which conflicted with the adverse endowments (capital shortage and labor abundance) at that time. Hence, all economic systems revolved around resolving this conflict. That is, the economic systems resulted from the combination of development strategy and constraints. On the dimension of urban–rural economic relationship, China gradually formed people's communes in rural areas and unitary public ownership in urban areas, unified purchase and marketing of agricultural products, and urban and rural household registration. All these systems were intended to allow the government (especially the central government) to maintain strict control over urban–rural allocation of products and factors through mandatory plans, so as to provide capita sources for the development of heavy industry and at the same time avoid "diluting" the capital of the industrial sector on account of labor flow.

During this period, due to the implementation of planned economy with high-power centralization and strict control of the central government, the differentiation among different levels of governments and different markets was almost negligible. That is, government–market relationship made up the whole content of economic system arrangements. Such institutional arrangements had wide influence on the behavioral choice of urban and rural microeconomic subjects. Urban and rural residents even had no opportunity to allocate products and factors spontaneously according to economic benefit calculations. As a result of these economic systems, from the founding of the PRC up to the late 1970s, China managed to form an independent and fairly complete industrial system against the extremely unfavorable initial conditions. Yet, its entire national economy was on the verge of collapse due to low efficiency of resource allocation. As far as urban–rural economic relationship is concerned, as microeconomic subjects in the urban and rural sectors had no chance to carry out product transaction and factor allocation, and their gaps of labor productivity, income and consumption were all constantly high, separation represented the basic feature of China's urban–rural economic relationship over that period.

Over a long time after the founding of the PRC, the institutional arrangements serving the heavy industry first strategy had brought about the double results of spurring national industrialization but suppressing economic efficiency. Over time, the accumulation of these results greatly changed the strategic goal and constraints of the early days of the PRC. From 1978, China's development strategy began to shift from heavy industry to economic growth. Constraining it was the influence of prolonged planned economy and the national reality that rural population and rural employment made up the nation's majority. In view of this new combination of development strategy and constraints, China decided to rely on adjusting government–market relationship to push forward economic system reform. Its mainline was to cause the government to relax its economic control over microeconomic subjects and continuously highlight the role of market in resource allocation. Using market mechanism to improve the efficiency of resource allocation, thus realizing high-speed economic growth reflects the similarity of China's economic development to that of the other countries. Accordingly, reform and opening up became the key choice of China's economy and society since the late 1970s.

Nevertheless, as a large developing country with socialist system, China began to see its intragovernmental and intramarket structural features, namely, regionally decentralized authoritarianism and upstream-guided market expansion. This shows that China's market-oriented system transition is different from that of other economies. That is, China is unique in terms of the pathway and mode of market-oriented system transition. Under the above economic systems, the behavioral choice of China's microeconomic subjects is bound to produce the corresponding results. That is, China's GDP has created a world "miracle" of growth, yet this miracle has been accompanied by the continuous accumulation and exacerbation of structural problems in the economic domain. As far as urban–rural economic relationship is concerned, the above economic systems have led to enlarged room for microeconomic subjects to allocate resources between urban and rural areas, continuously improved efficiency of resource allocation, greatly emancipated and developed social productivity, and constantly increased income and consumption for urban and rural residents in time series. In the meantime, changes of China's urban–rural income gap and consumption gap have also been fluctuating, and the reduction of urban–rural income gap has not been accompanied by synchronous reduction of social security gap. This signifies that since the implementation of reform and opening up in 1978, China's urban–rural economic relationship has moved out of the previous separation into a new pattern of overall integration with some imbalance.

After the entry into the new century, especially since the Eighteenth National Congress of the CPC in 2012, China began to promote the adaptive adjustment of development concepts. Its development strategy also shifted from economic growth to coordinated development. The report to the Nineteenth National Congress of the CPC explicitly declared that the socialism with Chinese characteristics has entered a new era and clearly noted that the main social contradiction has transformed and the social development period has changed, signaling that China has formally established a coordinated development strategy at the economic level. Nevertheless, the coordinated development strategy is faced with the institutional constraints that agree with an economic growth-oriented strategy. A system capable of ensuring high-speed economic growth is unnecessarily one capable of naturally supporting coordinated development. The change of the combination of development strategy and constraints signifies an adaptive adjustment of the economic system. As such, to promote a coordinated development strategy, China has to deepen economic system reform. To this end, China not only needs to make the market play a decisive role in the allocation of resources but also deepen reform to improve the intragovernmental and intramarket institutional arrangements, namely, to optimize regionally decentralized authoritarianism and upstream-guided market expansion, so that the behavioral choice of microeconomic subjects will better accord with the coordinated development strategy.

As far as urban–rural economic relationship is concerned, under the coordinated development strategy, China is bound to push its urban–rural economic relationship from imbalanced integration toward collaborative integration. Here collaborative integration covers improved urban–rural factor fluidity and allocation efficiency, reduced urban–rural income gap and consumption gap, increased degree of urban–rural equalization of basic public services, as well as optimized structure among different parts of economy against the differentiation inside urban and rural areas. In terms of the realization mechanism, collaborative integration needs to refine policy arrangements by taking systemic, institutional, differentiated, and workable actions to speed up urban–rural factor marketization, reduce urban–rural market transaction cost, increase urban–rural equalization of basic public services, and form the intrinsic momentum for local governments. In a nutshell, a "market driven + government compensated combination policy" is the policy choice for China to realize collaborative integration of urban–rural economic relationship. Government–market relationship, intragovernmental and intramarket institutional change, and incentive compatibility among participants play a supporting role in the implementation of the policy.

Obviously, this book uses a political economy analytical framework to explain the evolutionary logic of China's urban–rural economic relationship. The theoretical implication of this research is the Lewis-Fei-Ranis model is an important ideological source for understanding China's urban–rural duality, but we cannot directly derive the forming and evolutionary logic of China's urban–rural economic relationship from this model. The exploration of China's urban–rural economic relationship since the founding of the PRC should be rooted in the local characteristics of China—socialist system, a large developing country, and economic system transition, and identify from these characteristics the core concepts for understanding duality and the connections among the concepts. In the theoretical construction concerning China's urban–rural economic relationship, we have to note three key points:

First, in a large developing country with socialist system like China, there is no such a thing as a separate urban–rural economic relationship problem. Any urban–rural economic relationship problems is the concrete manifestation of the major proposition of development strategy in the urban and rural sectors. Hence, to understand the evolutionary logic of China's urban–rural economic relationship, we need to place it in a larger spectrum, namely, to insert it into the whole economic and social system of China. Only in this way can we accurately explain how such an urban–rural economic relationship came into being and why it has evolved in this manner.

Second, while China's urban–rural economic relationship is the product of the behavioral choice of microeconomic subjects, the behavioral choice of microeconomic subjects not only results from differentiated individual characteristics but also from common institutional conditions. Hence, it is particularly important to understand the formation and evolution of China's urban–rural economic relationship in different periods, and how these economic systems have affected microeconomic subjects. To explain the evolution of urban–rural economic relationship, we have to answer how these economic systems formed and how they changed.

Third, for a large developing country with socialist system like China, to discuss economic systems, we not only need to analyze government–market relationship but also the intragovernmental and intramarket structural features. We should not take it for granted that government and market are intrinsically highly homogeneous concepts. Instead, we should break through government–market dichotomy to prove into the internal characteristics of the two concepts. The change of government–market relationship reflects the generality of the change of government–market relationship, whereas intragovernmental and intramarket structural features reflect the particularity of the change of China's economic system. In particular, since reform and opening up, regionally decentralized authoritarianism and upstream-guided market expansion have constituted the most distinctive part of China's economic system. To understand urban–rural economic relationship, we have to derive the generality and particularity of this institutional change. Evidently, political economy is effective in understanding China's economic development problems, it is important to explain China's urban–rural economic relationship from the perspective of "political economics of development", and the proposition of establishing a socialist political economy with Chinese characteristics does have its practical basis.

From a practical point of view, after the founding of the PRC, especially over the 40 years of reform and opening up, China has been committed to promoting an unprecedented economic structural change in human history. Promoting industrialization and urbanization in a large populous country with a population of nearly 1.4 billion is a major event with unparalleled size and far-reaching influence. However, compared with other economies, China's industrialization and urbanization pathway has some similarities, such as the nonagricultural transfer of rural labor, as well as differences, such as "rural migrant workers" in the flow of rural labor. This means that China's urban–rural economic relationship has been accompanied by its local characteristics like socialist system, a large developing country, and economic system transition. Therefore, it is largely an embodiment of a "China story". As demonstrated earlier, across a longer time span, China's urban–rural economic relationship has been serving such a fundamental proposition. That is, how shall a large developing country with socialist system realize its goal of sustainable development and common prosperity? Guided by this fundamental proposition, China has formed differentiated development strategies and constraints over different periods of time. Institutional arrangements and the resulted urban–rural economic relationship are the products of implementing these development strategies. The heavy industry first strategy in the planned economy era was accompanied by separated urban–rural economic relationship. This suggests that China's urban–rural duality is not solely a matter of resource endowments. It is also a natter of development strategic choice. At the beginning of reform and opening up 40 years ago, China chose an economic growth-oriented strategy. Its implementation has greatly emancipated and developed social productivity, but has also resulted in an imbalanced integration of urban–rural economic relationship. This suggests that China's urban–rural dual economy has not been transforming at the same pace among all dimensions, and this imbalance is the byproduct of high-speed economic growth.

The differentiated performance of China's urban–rural economic relationship among different periods does not mean that the previous institutional choice was "wrong". It merely matched the development strategy and constraints of a particular period. Hence, we cannot use the subsequent development level and strategic choice to criticize the previous economic system choice and the corresponding urban–rural economic relationship. At a point of time when the socialism with Chinese characteristics is entering a new era, China's economic growth-oriented strategy formally switched to coordinated development strategy. Its main social contradiction also requires the country to emphatically respond to the problem of imbalanced, inadequate development. This inevitably calls for an upgrade of urban–rural economic relationship from imbalanced integration to collaborative integration. Similar to the previous evolution of development strategy and urban–rural economic relationship, shifting the development focus from economic growth to coordinated development also represents an important step toward the realizing of the fundamental proposition. The core of this change is also to promote a series of economic system changes. That is, realizing the adjustment of government–market relationship and intragovernmental and intramarket structure and deepening economic system reform play a key role in achieving collaborative integration of China's urban–rural economic relationship.

By combining these theoretical implications with practical directions, we can yield the characteristics and evolutionary roadmap of China's urban–rural economic relationship over different periods of time. As indicated by Table 10.1, since the founding of the PRC, in order to realize the fundamental goal of sustainable economic development and common prosperity, China has undergone three different stages, over which it has formed differentiated institutional arrangements and urban–rural economic relationship, and economic theories closely associated with these practical changes.

From 1953 to 1997, China's primary goal in the economic domain was to rebuild the order of national economy. To this end, it established a heavy industry first strategy. To match this development strategy, particular economic system arrangements were formed in government–market relationship, inside the government, and inside the market. The theoretical basis guiding these institutional arrangements was the Soviet political economy. As a result, separation between the urban and rural sector became the feature of the country's urban–rural economic relationship. From 1978 to 2012, China's primary goal in the economic domain was to promote sustained high-speed economic growth. To this end, its development strategy began to turn from heavy industry to economic growth. To effectively implement this development strategy, a set of economic system arrangements were formed in government–market relationship, inside the government, and inside the market. During this period, intragovernmental and intramarket structural features gradually became prominent. The theoretical basis guiding this institutional change is comprehensive. It includes both an introduction and extension of neoclassic economics in China, as well as an innovation and development of political economy in China. After 2012, in addition to high-speed economic growth, China became more inclined toward the goal of sustainable development and common prosperity. Its development strategy also gradually switched toward coordinated development. The report to the Nineteenth National Congress of the CPC can be seen as the official establishment and implementation of this development strategy. This change of development strategy inevitably leads to a change of government–market

Table 10.1 Theoretical and policy implications of China's urban–rural economic relationship during different periods of time

Item	*1949–1977*	*1978–2012*	*After 2012*
Main Objective	To reestablish economic order	High-speed economic growth	Sustainable development & common prosperity
Development strategy	Heavy industry priority	Economic growth oriented	Coordinated development
Institutional feature	Planned economy	Market-oriented transition	To deepen economic system reform
Intergovernmental system	Central-local full consistency	Politically centralized, economically decentralized	Right & responsibility coupling among different levels of governments
Intermarket system	Full control upstream and downstream	Upstream controlled, downstream liberalized	Reform progress coincidence between upstream & downstream markets
Theory	Dominated by the Soviet political economy	Extension of neoclassic economics and development of political economy	Socialist political economy with Chinese characteristics
Urban–rural economic relationship	Separation	Imbalanced integration	Collaborative integration

relationship and intragovernmental and intramarket structure. That is, China needs to deepen economic system reform: besides fully releasing market vitality, it also needs to improve the coupling degree of economic goals among different levels of governments, and the matching degree of marketization process among different markets. In this period, China should, on the basis of continuously accumulating practical elements, form a logic-reasoning political economy with Chinese characteristics, which is to become the main theoretical basis guiding China's economic construction. Only with the support of this institutional change and the guidance of local theories can China's urban–rural economic relationship change from imbalanced integration to collaborative integration.

In a word, this book provides an explanation of the evolution of China's urban–rural economic relationship from separation to integration from the perspective of political economy. Relative to the dual economy theory of development economics, this explanation is more of a marginal improvement that better matches the local practice of China. It addresses government–market relationship and intragovernmental and intramarket structural features at the theoretical level. In particular, it explains the uniqueness of China's economic system transition from intragovernmental structure and intramarket structure. The uniqueness of economic system and the multifaceted nature of economic performance provide important support for establishing a political economy with Chinese characteristics. The exploration and formation of a political economy with Chinese characteristics is a major proposition. Around this major proposition, subsequent research should identify the characteristic facts of China's economic development so as to form core propositions and develop an intrinsically logically consistent theoretic system according to these propositions. This theoretic system will exhibit the diversity and abundance of economic development theory. It will reflect the contribution of China's economic development practice to the development of economic theory and provide referential blueprint for the economic development, especially the transformation of urban–rural economic relationship, of other large developing countries.

From a practical point of view, this book explains the evolutionary mechanism of China's urban–rural economic relationship since the founding of the PRC, especially over the 40 years of reform and opening up, from the perspective of political economy. Yet, this explanation of mechanism is more of a framework. Its analysis and argumentation of mechanism is more reflected at the logical level. Subsequent research could use this framework to further examine a number of subdivisions of the topic of urban–rural economic relationship. For example, in a large developing country with socialist system like China, how can local governments at different levels maintain their economic autonomy and at the same time remain consistent with the fundamental goal established by the central government? How to set local governments' incentives that match the coordinated development strategy in the new era? How to determine the appropriate extent to which urban–rural income gap and urban–rural consumption gap are to be reduced? How to effectively link up new agricultural business entities with small farmer households in the bidirectional flow of factors between urban and rural areas? How to smoothly transfer public goods between urban and rural areas and among individual regions amid universal population flow? How to resolve the current economic differentiation inside urban and rural areas in a sustainable manner? How to match improved urban–rural factor fluidity with localized social governance of different local governments? Evidently, our research herein reveals part, instead of all, of the grand issue of China's urban–rural economic relationship. Subsequent research of China's urban–rural economic relationship based on the interface between political economy and development economics, or "political economy of development", could be greeted by a range of themes and "practical riddles". Research around these themes not only constitutes an extension and support for our research herein, it also constitutes the theoretical sources for China to effectively implement economic policies for the new urban–rural economic relationship. We have good reason to believe that, with sustained economic development in China and continuously improved theoretical research, China's urban–rural economic relationship is bound to change from imbalanced integration to collaborative integration.

Afterword

In 1978, China embarked on the great cause of overall reform and opening up with the reform of rural management system as the cut-in point. Ever since reform and opening up, extensive and profound changes have taken place in the country's economic and social architecture. This year marks the very time of the fortieth anniversary of reform and opening up. To commemorate this milestone, it is necessary to explore the evolutionary trajectory and internal logic of different segments of China's economy, so as to gain an insight into, and catch hold of, the "road leading to future" by looking back on and reviewing the "road bringing us here". As the largest developing country in the world, China has featured a prominent urban–rural duality so far. Therefore, it is important and necessary to make a systematic explanation on the evolution of China's urban–rural economic relationship. The evolutionary mechanism of China's urban–rural economic relationship should be understood across a long-time span. That is, the situations after 1949 and before reform and opening up should be included into consideration, so as to analyze the "story behind" the evolution of China's urban–rural economic relationship. In this book, the author attempts to explain the evolutionary trajectory and change mechanism of China's urban–rural economic relationship after the founding of the PRC, especially over the 40 years of reform and opening up based on literature review, under a political economy analytical framework specifically designed for local characteristics, and then put forward the possible development trend of, and policy choice for, the development of China's urban–rural economic relationship in the new era in a logically consistent manner. Obviously, this book forms a response to the grand topic of commemorating the fortieth anniversary of reform and opening up on the dimension of theoretical exploration.

In the existing development economics, the Lewis-Fei-Ranis model represents the classic theory that describes and explains the urban–rural duality in developing economies. However, the dual economy theory also implies important hypotheses, such as a dual economy originates from urban–rural endowment gap, the capital-labor ratio is constant, and the urban–rural factor market is perfect, which do not totally agree with the economic practice of China. This book emphasizes that, since the founding of the PRC, China as a large developing country with socialist system has been faced with the fundamental proposition of realizing the goal of sustainable growth and common prosperity. In response to this proposition, in 1978, China initiated a market-oriented economic system transition. Socialist system, a large developing country, and economic system transition have constituted the social background of China's economic development. Based on this background, there has been an interaction chain among development strategy and constraints, choice of economic system, behavior of microeconomic subjects, and performance of economic development (transformation of urban–rural economic relationship). Within this interaction chain, choice of economic system plays a critical role in urban–rural economic relationship, but choice of economic system itself derives from the way national development strategy is combined with constraints. When there is a change in the development strategy and constraints, and the way of their combination, urban–rural economic relationship is bound to change as an outcome of adjustments of the economic system and the change of the behavior of microeconomic subjects. Notably, in China, the choice of economic system revolves around government–market relationship, whereas structural features exist inside the government and the market themselves. Hence, related inter-governmental and inter-market rules also constitute an important part of China's economic system. Obviously, this book does not seek to analyze China's urban–rural duality based on the Lewis-Fei-Ranis model. Instead, it puts forward concepts based on local characteristics and builds an analytical framework for China's urban–rural economic relationship from the perspective of political economy.

Based on this political economy analytical framework, the book examines the evolution of China's urban–rural economic relationship over different periods of time since the founding of the PRC. It points out that before 1978, the system arrangements resulted from the combination of the heavy industry first strategy and constraints led to separated urban–rural economic relationship, which in turn gave rise to the double results of accelerated industrialization with low economic efficiency, and imbalanced development between urban and rural areas. Consequently, after 1978, China began to shift its development focus to economic growth. The new combination of development strategy and constraints has resulted in unique government–market relationship and intra-governmental and intra-market institutional arrangements. Between the government and the market is the market-oriented economic system transition. Inside the government and the market are regionally decentralized authoritarianism and upstream-guided market expansion. The implementation of these systems has prompted sustained high-speed GDP growth. On the dimension of urban–rural economic relationship, these institutional arrangements have resulted in an overall integration but with imbalance. In fact, imbalanced integration well describes China's urban–rural economic relationship since reform and opening up. At present, China is switching from economic growth to coordinated development. This new combination of strategy and constraints implies that the country's urban–rural economic relationship is transforming from an imbalanced integration to a collaborative one. To achieve collaborative integration of urban–rural economic relationship in the new era, China needs to reform its economic system continuously, namely, to make the market play a decisive role in the allocation of resources and give better play to the role of the government. Furthermore, to achieve collaborative integration, it should also address the perfection of its intergovernmental and intermarket economic systems and highlight participation constraints and incentive compatibility constraints for related stakeholders as the base point for implementing policies in favor of the collaborative integration of urban–rural economic relationship.

Obviously, based on a localized political economy analytical framework, this book tries to make a systematic explanation on the evolutionary mechanism of China's urban–rural economic relationship across a long time span. This effort does not only reflect a positive response to China's continuous effort to transform its urban–rural economic relationship but it also reflects a positive response to the construction of a political economy of socialism with Chinese characteristics. The research of this book reveals that behind the evolution of China's urban–rural economic relationship is the change of development strategies, constraints, and economic system arrangements. Urban–rural economic relationship is set in the context of China's overall modernization process, and it changes dynamically with the adjustment of the macroeconomic architecture. While 40 years of reform and opening up has brought about profound changes in urban–rural economic relationship, in the context of the new era, it is imperative to transform this relationship from an imbalanced integration to a collaborative one. In terms of the research topic herein, my focus has been on the political economy analysis of urban–rural economic relationship all the time, and this book represents an outcome of my contemplation on China's urban–rural duality. It may contain something distinctive and innovative relative to existing literature, but may also contain something that needs further extension and improvement. Particularly, as mentioned in Chapter 10, "Conclusions and Prospects", in the context of the new era, China is facing the great mission of constructing a new form of urban–rural relationship. China's urban–rural duality is showing new features, new problems, and new challenges over the course of transformation, too. This signifies that there are still many unsolved riddles in the research of China's urban–rural economic relationship, and it is still necessary for me and other researchers to respond to this practical reality through theoretical innovation.

The writing and publication of this book have benefited from the great practice of the 40 years of reform and opening up in China, which has allowed the different dimensions of the country's urban–rural economic relationship to become evident enough for observation and analysis across a long time span. Without the rich social practice of the 40 years of reform and opening up, the research herein and the writing of this book would become water without source or a tree without a root. The practice of the 40 years of reform and opening up has also offered more favorable conditions for social science workers to carry out studies. The research herein is funded by the Major Project of the National Social Science Foundation (project no. 17ZDA066), the Key Project of the National Social Science Foundation (project no. 17AJL010), the Projects of the "Dawn Program" of Shanghai (project no. 16SG06), and Type I Summit Program of Theoretical Economics of Fudan University. I owe my research herein to Professor Zhang Huiming, Professor Li Huizhong, Professor Shi Lei, Professor Ma Tao, Professor Yan Fashan, Professor Jiao Bifang, Professor Li Jieming, Professor Meng Jie, Professor Wang Lixin, Professor Wang Dihai, and Professor Chen Shuo of School of Economics, Fudan University, for their kind correction and help, and to my postgraduate students Wang Yanan, Tang Tao, Wu Xiaoli, Meng Shuo, Xu Xiaoxi, Li Bin, Zou Lisha, and Mao Jiarui for the extensive work they did in collating and processing data. I also want to thank Mr. Xu Huiping, Mr. Cen Pinjie, and Mr. Fang Yichao of Fudan University Press for their strong support during the publication of this book and the energy and time they employed in editing and publishing this book. Thank you all again!

Bibliography

Akita T. (2003). Decomposing Regional Income Inequality in China and Indonesia Using Two-Stage Nested Theil Decomposition Method, *The Annals of Regional Science*, (37): 55–77.

Bai Y.X. (2012). Chinese Perspective on the Urban-rural duality: Formation, Development, Path, *Academic Monthly*, 2012 (5): 67–76.

Bardhan P., Udry C. (1999). *Development Microeconomics*, New York: Oxford University Press.

Bengs, C. (2004). Urban-rural Relations in Europe, In Collections of Inter-regional Conference on Strategies for Enhancing Urban-rural Linkages Approach to Development and Promotion of Local Economic Development. http://www.upo-palnning.Org/detail.Asp? articleID=129.

Bo Y.B. (1991). *A Review of Certain Major Policies and Events* (Vol. 1, p. 290). Central Party School Press.

Bo Y.B. (1999). *A Review of Certain Major Policies and Events (Volume 1)*, Beijing: Central Party School Press.

Boeke J.B. (1953). *Economics and Economic Policy of Dual Societies as Exemplified by Indonesia*, New York: Institute of Pacific relationship.

Bosker M., Brakman S., Garretsen H., Schramm M. (2012). Relaxing Hukou: Increased Labor fluidity and China's Economic Geography, *Journal of Urban Economics*, 72(2): 252–266.

Bosworth B., Collins S.M. (2008). Accounting for Growth Comparing China and India, *Journal of Economic Perspectives*, 22: 45–66.

Bourguignon F., Morrison C. (1998). Inequality and Development: The Role of Dualism, *Journal of Development Economics*, 57: 233–257.

Brandt L., Rawski T.G. (2009). *China's Great Economic Transformation*, Shanghai: Gezhi Publishing House.

Brandt L., Zhu X. (2010). Accounting for China's Growth, University of Toronto, Working Paper, No.394

Brookfield H. (2008). Family Farms Are Still Around: Time to Invert the Old Agrarian Question, *Geography Compass*, 2(1): 108–126.

Cai F. (2003). Rural Urban Income Gap and Critical Point of Institutional Change, *Social Sciences in China*, 2003 (5): 93–111.

Cai F. (2010). Demographic Transition, Demographic Dividend and Lewis Turning Point in China, *Economic Research Journal*, 2010 (4): 4–13.

Cai F. (2006). Economic Analysis on Industry Back-nurturing Agriculture and Cities Supporting Countryside, *Chinese Rural Economy*, 2006 (1): 11–17.

Cai F. (2008). *Lewis Turning Point: A Coming New State of China's Economic Development*, Beijing: Social Sciences Academic Press.

Cai F. (2008). Thirty Years of Rural Reform in China: An Analysis from the Perspective of Institutional Economics, *Social Sciences in China*, (6): 99–110.

Cai F., Du Y. Wang M.Y. (2003). *Political Economics Analysis of Labor Migrating*, Shanghai: Shanghai SDX Joint Publishing Company.

Cai F., Lin Y.M. (2003). *Chinese Economy: Reform and Development*, Beijing: China Financial & Economic Publishing House.

Cai F., Wang M. (2008). A Counterfactual Analysis on Unlimited Surplus Labor in Rural China, *China & World Economy*, 16(1): 51–65.

Cai F., Yang T. (2000). Political Economics on Urban-rural Income Inequality, *Social Sciences in China*, 2000(4): 11–22, 204.

Cao K.H., Birchenall J.A. (2013). Agricultural Productivity, Structural Change, and Economic Growth in Post-reform China, *Journal of Development Economics*, 104(3): 165–180.

Chang H., Dong X., Macphail F. (2011). Labor Migration and Time Use Patterns of the Left-behind Children and Elderly in Rural China, *The World Development*, 29(12): 2199–2210.

Chang J.X., Zhao H.T. (2016). The Impact of Work Unit's Ownership on Wage Differentials between the Labor of Urban and Rural Household Registration, *China Economic Quarterly*, 15 (2): 627–646.

Chaplin H., Davidova S., Gorton M. (2004). Agricultural Adjustment and the Diversification of Farm Households and Corporate Farms in Central Europe, *Journal of Rural Studies*, 20(1): 61–77.

Chavas J.P. (2001). Structural Change in Agricultural Production: Economics, Technology and Policy, *Handbook of Agricultural Economics*, 1: 268–269.

Chen B.K., Lin Y.F. (2013). Development Strategy, Urbanization and Urban-rural Inequality, *Social Sciences in China*, 2013(4): 81–102.

Chen B.K. (2012). Income Inequality and Consumption Demand: Theory and Evidence from China, *Nankai Economic Studies*, 2012(1): 33–49.

Chen B.K., Lin Y.F. (2010). Heavy Industry-oriented Development Strategy, Urbanization and Urban-rural Inequality, *Nankai Economic Studies*, 2010 (1): 3–18.

Chen B.K., Zhang P.F., Yang R.D. (2010). Government Educational Expenditure, Human Capital Investment and Urban-rural Gap in China, *Management World*, 2010(1): 36–43.

Chen F. (2013). The Urban-rural Relationship: A Foreign Literature Review, *Chinese Rural Economy*, 2013(6): 80–89.

Chen S., Chen X., Xu J. (2016). Impacts of Climate Change on Agriculture: Evidence from China, *Journal of Environmental Economics and Management*, 76(3): 105–124.

Chen S., Xu J.T., Zhang H.P. (2016). Impacts of Climate Change on Food Production in China: Evidence from County-level Panel data, *Chinese Rural Economy*, 2016(5): 2–15.

Chen X.J., Yu X.H. (2011). Research and Review on Urban-rural integration of Public Goods Supply, *Economic Perspectives*, 2011 (12): 89–92.

Chen Y.S., Zhang Y. (2015). The Inequality Effect and Social Integration in Urbanization, *Social Sciences in China*, 2015(6): 78–95.
Chen Z.S., Gao Y.H. (2015). Scale Measurement of Public Economy in China and Potential of Deepening the Mixed Economy Reform, *Comparative Economic & Social Systems*, 2015(1): 17–32.
Cheng Y.H. (2006). Calculation and Decomposition of the Overall Gini Coefficient in Dual Economies, *Economic Research Journal*, 2006(1): 109–120.
Cheng Y.H. (2007). Evolution of and Decomposition Analysis on Overall Gini Coefficient in China after Reform, *Social Sciences in China*, 2007(4): 45–60.
Chernina E., Dower P.C., Markevich A. (2014). Property Rights, Land Liquidity, and Internal Migration, *Journal of Development Economics*, 110: 191–215.
Chiodi V., Jaimovich E. (2012). Montes-Rojas G. Migration, Remittances and Capital Accumulation: Evidence from Rural Mexico, *Journal of Development Studies*, 48(8): 1139–1155.
Chun-Chung Au, Henderson J.V. (2006). How Migration Restrictions Limit Agglomeration and Productivity in China, *Journal of Development and Economics*, 80(2): 350–388.
Demurger S., Gurgand M., Li S., Yue X.M. (2009). Migrants as Second-class Workers in Urban China? A Decomposition Analysis, *Journal of Comparative Economics*, 37(4): 610–628.
Demurger S., Li S., Yang J. (2012). Earnings Differentials between the Public and Private Sectors in China: Exploring Changes for urban Local Residents in the 2000s", *China Economic Review*, 23(1): 138–153.
Ding H.F., Liu X.Y. (2017). Spatio-temporal Evolution of Urbanization and Urban-rural Income Disparity, *Economic Geography*, 2017 (4): 32–41.
Dong X.L., Xu H. (2012). Chinese Rural Financial Exclusion and Its Influencing Factors Empirical Analysis: Based on the Distribution Network of Financial Institutions in Rural Areas, *Journal of Financial Research*, 2012(9): 115–126.
Ellis F. (2006). *Peasant Economics Farm Households and Agrarian Development*, Shanghai: Shanghai People's Publishing House.
Fan G., Lu Y. (2013). Economic Developing Stage and National Saving Expansion: Extend by the Lewis' Dual Economic Model, *Economic Research Journal*, 2013(3): 19–29.
Fan S., Gulati A., Thorat S. (2008). Investment, Subsidies and Pro-poor Growth in Rural India, *Agricultural Economics*, 39(2): 163–170.
Fang F.Q. (2009). A Study of Inadequate Consumer Demand among Chinese Residents—Based on Data for Urban and Rural Areas in Different Provinces, *Social Sciences in China*, 2009 (2): 68–82.
Fei J.C.H., Ranis G. (1964). *Development of the Labor Surplus Economy: Theory and Policy*, Homewood, IL: Richard D. Irwin.
Fei J.C.H., Ranis G. (1999). *Growth and Development from an Evolutionary Perspective*, Cambridge, Mass.: Blackwell Publishers.
Fields G.S. (2005). A Welfare Economic Analysis of Labor Market Policies in the Harris-Todaro Model, *Journal of Development Economics*, 76: 127–146.
Fu M.H., Qi C.J. (2016). Element Endowment, Technical Progress Bias and Agricultural Total Element Productivity Growth: Based on Comparative Study of 28 Countries, *Chinese Rural Economy*, 2016 (12): 76–90.

Gai Q.E., Zhu X., Shi Q.H. (2014). Impact of Labor Transfer on China's Agricultural Production, *China Economic Quarterly*, 2014(3): 1147–1170.

Gai Q.E., Zhu X., Shi Q.H. (2013). Labor Market Distortion, Structural Change and Labor Productivity in China, *Economic Research Journal*, 2013 (5): 87–97.

Gao F. (2010). Factor Decomposition and Labor Structure Effect of Economic Growth in China's Provinces: 1978-2007, *The Journal of Quantitative & Technical Economics*, 2010(7): 21–37.

Gao F. (2012a). Factor Decomposition of Urban Residents Income Gap Variation: Trend and Explanation, *Economic Science*, 2012(3): 7–19.

Gao F. (2012b). *The Transformation of the Urban-rural Dual Economy in China: Theoretical Interpretation and Empirical Analysis*, Shanghai: Shanghai SDX Joint Publishing Company.

Gao F. (2014a). The Inflection Point of China's Urban and Rural Consumption and Its Economic Growth, *Statistical Research*, 2014 (12): 43–48.

Gao F. (2014b). Share of Labor Remuneration, Urban-rural Income Distribution and Chinese Household Consumption, *Academic Monthly*, (11): 40–49.

Gao F. (2015). Evolution Trend and Internal Mechanism of Regional Total Factor Productivity in Chinese Agriculture, *The Journal of Quantitative & Technical Economics*, 2015 (5): 3–19.

Gao F. (2016a). *Theoretical Research and Empirical Analysis on the Exchange Relationship between Urban and Rural Factors in China*, Shanghai: Shanghai People's Publishing House.

Gao F. (2016b). *Socialist Political Economics with Chinese Characteristics*, Shanghai: Fudan University Press, 2016.

Gao F. (2016c). The Return of Political Economy and the Selection Logic of China's Economic Doctrine, *China Review of Political Economy*, (5): 158–182.

Gao F. (2018a). Generality, Heterogeneity of China's Economic Development and Its Implication, *Academic Monthly*, (6): 57–66.

Gao F. (2018b). Connotation Transformation of Urban-rural Disparity in China and Its Political Economic Interpretation, *Journal of Northwest University (Philosophy & Social Sciences Edition)*, (4): 7–18.

Gao F. (2018c). Peasant Differentiation and Its Extended Meaning from the Perspective of China's Rural Revitalization Strategy, *Journal of Fudan University (Social Sciences Edition)*, (5): 149–158.

Gao F. (2018d). Formation Logic and Implementation of the "Three Rights Separation" for Agrarian Land in China, *The Economists*, (4): 86–95.

Gao F. (2018e). Forty Years of Rural Economic Reform in China: Implementation Logic and Development Trend, *Qiushi Monthly*, (5): 11–21.

Gao F., Wang Y.N. (2016). Labor Market Distribution and Urban-rural Consumption Gap: An Empirical Study on Provincial Panel Data, *Qiushi Monthly*, (12): 75–85.

Graeub B.E. *et al.* (2016). The State of Family Farms in the World, *World Development*, 87(11): 1–15.

Gray C.I., Bilsborrow R.E. (2014). Consequences of Out-Migration for Land Use in Rural Ecuador, *Land Use Policy*, 36: 182–191.

Gu Y.K., Xu Y.J. (2004). Study on the Evaluating Index of the Urban-rural Integration, *Zhejiang Social Sciences*, (6): 95–99.

Guo J.X. (2005). Human Capital, the Birth Rate and the Narrowing of the Urban-rural Income Gap, *Social Sciences in China*, (3): 27–37.

Guo Q.H. (2013). Functional Positioning Institutional Supply for Growth of New Agricultural Business Entities, *Chinese Rural Economy*, (4): 4–11.

Gu S.Z., Li Z.Y. (1998). Institutional Analysis of China's Bottom up Urbanization, *Social Sciences in China*, (2): 60–70.

Han C.H. (2017). Individual Farmers and Scale Farming: Reviews of the Theoretics of the Family Farm, *Economic Research Journal*, (7): 184–199.

Han H.B., Zhang L. (2015). The Threshold Effect of Agricultural Informatization on the Agricultural TFP Growth, *Chinese Rural Economy*, (8): 11–21.

Han J. (2009). Sixty Years of Urban-rural Relation Evolution in China: Retrospect and Prospect, *Reform*, (11): 5–14.

Hao D.M. (2006). The Analysis of Effect of Labor Structure Based on Index Method, *Statistical Research*, (6): 69–72.

Hao D.M. (2016). The Contribution of Rural Labor Forces Transfer to the Growth of China's National Economy, *Chinese Rural Economy*, (9): 44–57.

Hayami Y., Ruttan V.W. (1985). *Agricultural Development—An International Perspective*, Baltimore, Maryland: The John Hopkins University Press.

Hayashi F., Prescott C.E. (2008). The Depressing Effects of Agricultural Institutions on the Prewar Japanese Economy, *The Journal of Political Economy*, 116(4): 573–632.

He Z.X., Qu R.X. (2015). The Agricultural Policy Financial Supply and Financial Repression: Evidence Based on the Data from 147 Counties of China, *Journal of Financial Research*, (2): 148–159.

Hertel T., Fan Z. (2004). Labor Market Distortions, Rural-urban Inequality and the Opening of China's Economy, World Bank Policy Research Working Paper3455, November 2004.

Hong Y.X., Chen W. (2003). Urbanization and Integration of Urban and Rural Area, *Economic Theory and Economic Management*, (4): 5–11.

Hong Z. (2011). Is the Reform of New Rural Financial Institutions Feasible? *Economic Research Journal*, (2): 44–58.

Hsieh C.T., Klenow P.J. (2009). Misallocation and manufacture TEP in China and India, *The Quarterly Journal of Economics*, 124(4): 1403–1448.

Huang J.K., Gao L.L., Ji X.Q., Rozelle S. (2012). *Rural Land Tenure, Transfer and Investment in China*, Shanghai: Gezhi Publishing House.

Islam N., Yokota K. (2008). Lewis Growth Model and China's Industrialization, *Asian Economic Journal*, 22(4): 359–396.

Jian X.H. (2015). Some Widely Debated Issues of the Rural Reform and Development in China, *Academic Monthly*, (7): 33–41.

Jiang C., Si D.K., Su Z.W. (2016). Research on the Dynamic Fluctuation and Influence Factors of Urban-rural Income Gap in China, *The Journal of Quantitative & Technical Economics*, (2): 41–57.

Jiang Y.M., Xian R.S., Zhang X.L. (2015). Reflection on Marx and Engels' Thoughts about Urban-rural Economic relationship, *China Review of Political Economy*, 2015(4): 102–117.

Jiao B.F., Lin D., Peng J.N. (2011). The New Construction and Application of the Estimation System of Urban and Rural Integration, *Fudan Journal (Social Sciences Edition)*, (4): 75–83.

Jin S.Q., Deininger K. (2009). Land Rental Markets in the Process of Rural Structural Transformation: Productivity and Equity Impacts from China, *Journal of Comparative Economics*, 37: 629–646.

Just D.R. (2011). Calibrating the Wealth Effects of Decoupled Payments: Does Decreasing Absolute Risk Aversion Matter? *Journal of Econometrics*, 162(1): 25–34.

Kanbur R., Zhang X.B. (1999). Which Regional Inequality? The Evolution of Rural-urban and Inland-coastal Inequality in China from 1983 to 1995, *Journal of Comparative Economics*, 27: 686–701.

Kanwar S. (2006). Relative Profitability, Supply Shifters and Dynamic Output Responses in a Developing Economy, *Journal of Policy Modeling*, 28(1): 67–88.

Knight J., Li S. (2005). Wages, Firm Profitability and Labor Market Segmentation in Urban China, *China Economic Review*, 16(3): 205–228.

Knight J., Song L. Huaibin J. (1999). Chinese Rural Migrants in Urban Enterprises: Three Perspectives, *Journal of Development Studies*, 35(3): 73–104.

Kong X.Z. (2014). Status and Top Level Design of New Agricultural business entities, *Reform*, (5):32-34.

Krueger A., Maurice S., Alberto A. (1992). *The Political Economy of Agricultural Pricing Policy* (Vol. 5). Baltimore, Maryland: The Johns Hopkins University Press.

Kumbhakar S.C., Christopher F.P. (2009). The Effects of Match University and Bargaining on Labor Market Outcomes: Evidence from Buryer and Seller Specific Estimates, *Journal of Productivity Analysis*, 31(1): 1–14.

Kwan F. (2009). Agricultural Labor and the Incidence of Surplus Labor: Experience from China during Reform, *Journal of Chinese Economic and Business Studies*, 7(8): 341–361.

Lardy, N.R. (1992). Economic Recovery and the First Five-year Plan. In R. MacFarquhar and J.K. Fairbank (Eds.), *The Cambridge History of China Vol. 14: The People's Republic, Part 1,The Emergence of Revolutionary China, 1949–1965* (p. 131). China Social Sciences Press.

Lewis A. (1954). Economic Development with Unlimited Supplies of Labor, *The Manchester School*, 22(2): 139–191.

Li C.L. (2014). The Changing Trend of Educational Inequality in China (1940-2010): Reexamining the Urban-rural Gap on Educational Opportunity, *Sociological Research*, (2): 65–89.

Li D., Tang X.M. (2013). Economic Volatility with Unlimited Labor Supply in China, *The Quarterly Journal of Economics*, (3): 823–846.

Li, H. (2005). Discussion on Decomposition Analysis of Gini Coefficient, *The Journal of Quantitative & Technical Economics*, (3): 127–135.

Li H., Kung J. (2015). Fiscal Incentives and Policy Choices of Local Governments: Evidence from China, *Journal of Development Economics*, 116: 89–104.

Li J.Y. (2016). Effect Evaluation of Agricultural Subsidies Policy: Incentive Effect and Wealth Effect, *Chinese Rural Economy*, (12): 17–32.

Li J.Y., Li H. (2016). Urban-rural Income Gap and Consumption Structure: A Study Based on Relative Income Hypothesis, *The Journal of Quantitative & Technical Economics*, (8): 97–112.

Li M., Shao T. Liu S.Y. (2014). International Experience of Integration of Urban and Rural Areas and Ins Enlightenment to China, *Chinese Rural Economy*, (6): 83–96.

Li Y.Y., Zhong X.M. (2012). Fiscal Policy and the Marginal propensity of Rural and Urban Residents to Consume, *Social Sciences in China*, (12): 63–81.

Li S., Sicular T. (2014). The Distribution of Household Income in China: Inequality, Poverty and Politics, *The China Quarterly*, 217: 1–41.

Li Y., Yin J.F. (2007). Anatomy of High Saving Rate of China, *Economic Research Journal*, (6): 14–26.

Liang R. (2011). The Difference between Urban and Rural Education Returns and Income Gap in China, *Contemporary Economic Science*, 33 (6): 64–71, 124.

Liang Q., Chen Q.Y., Wang R.Y. (2013). Household Registration Reform, Labor fluidity and Optimization of the Urban Hierarchy, *Social Sciences in China*, (12): 36–59.

Liao Z.J., Guo X.M. (2015). Logic and Direction of the Agricultural Operation Organizational System Evolution in China: An analytical Framework for Industrial Chain Integration, *Chinese Rural Economy*, (2): 13–21.

Lin G. (2014). Historical Changes of the Urban-rural Relationship in China and the Contemporary Issues, *China Rural Survey*, (5): 2–12.

Lin Y.F., Cai F., Li Z. (2012). *The Chinese Miracle: Development Strategy and Economic Reform (enlarged edition)*, Shanghai: Shanghai SDX Joint Publishing Company, Shanghai People's Publishing House.

Lin Y.F., Chen B.J. (2009). Development Strategy and Urban-rural Consumption Inequality, *Zhejiang Social Sciences*, (4): 10–16.

Lin Y.F., Liu M.X. (2003). Growth Convergence and Income Distribution in China, *The Journal of World Economy*, (8): 3–14.

Lin Y.F., Yu M.J. (2009). The Political Economy of Price Scissors in China: Theoretical Model and Empirical Evidence, *Economic Research Journal*, (1): 42–56.

Ling C., Zhang A.Q. (2012). Preventive Saving of Urban and Rural Residents in China: Theory and Evidence, *Management World*, (11): 20–27.

Lipton M. (1977). *Why Poor People Stay Poor: Urban Bias in World Development*, Cambridge, MA: Harvard University Press.

Liu G.C. (2017). The Effect of Financial Structure on Urban-rural Income Gap Viewed through Economic Growth and Urbanization, *Finance & Trade Economics*, (6): 98–114.

Liu G.X. (2017). On Marx and Engels' Institutional Ideology of Urban and Rural Development, *Social Sciences Front*, (6): 248–251.

Liu H.M., Zhang Z.J., Wang K.Q. (2012). Analysis of Influencing Factors for Urban-rural Integration in China, *Chinese Rural Economy*, (8): 4–15.

Liu H.P., Li Y., Zhang G.Q. (2015). Research on Explicit and Implicit Factors Affecting Urban and Rural Consumption Duality—Based on Quantile Regression and Decomposition of CHFS Data of 2011, *West Forum*, (5): 1–11.

Liu J., Li S. (2013). Variation of Consumption Inequality in China. In S.L.H., Sato, T.L. Shi (Eds.), *Analysis on Movement of Income Gap in China—Research on Income Distribution of Chinese Residents IV*. Beijing: People's Press.

Liu W., Cai Z.Z. (2018). How to Look at the Reality that China is Still a Developing Country? *Management World*, (9): 1–15.

Liu X.L. (2008). Decomposition of Income Disparity in China: 1995–2006, *Economic Science*, (3): 5–19.

Liu X.L. (2017). Research of China's Experience in Utilizing Medical Insurance and Medical Service Level for Urban and Rural Residents, *World Economics*, (3): 169–192.

Liu Z. (2005). Institution and Inequality: The Hukou System in China, *Journal of Comparative Economics*, 33(1): 133–157.

Long H.M., Ling L., Tan C.P., Wang, Z.P. (2015). Research on the Regional Differences of Income Gap between China's Urban and Rural Areas: Based on Regional Data, *Journal of Financial Research*, (3): 83–96.

Lu M., Chen Z. (2004). Urbanization, Urban-based Economic Policies and Urban-rural Inequality, *Economic Research Journal*, (6): 50–58.

Lu M., Chen Z. (2009). Why Land and Registration System Need Combining Reform —A Theoretical and Empirical Review on China's City and Regional Development, *Academic Monthly*, (9): 78–84.

Lu M., Wan G. (2014). Urbanization and Urban Systems in the People's Republic of China: Research Findings and Policy Recommendations, *Journal of Economic Surveys*, 28(4): 671–685.

Lu X.Y. (2000). New Situation and New Tasks of New Stage of Rural Development, *Chinese Rural Economy*, (6): 4–13.

Lu X.Y. (2002). *Three Rural Issues: Study on Agricultural, Village and Farm*, Beijing: Social Science Academic Press.

Lu Y.L. (2008). Does Hukou Still Matter? The Household Registration System and Its Impact on Social Stratification and fluidity in China, *Social Sciences in China*, 2008(1): 149–162.

Lu Z.Y. (2016). The Welfare Effects from the Development of the New Agricultural Entities, *The Journal of Quantitative & Technical Economics*, (6): 41–58.

Luo L., Luo Y., LuoT. (2014). A Confirmatory Study on China's Two-way Urban-Rural Integration – Based on the Survey Data of Huairou District, Beijing. M*anagement World*, (11): 60–69, 79.

Luo X., Zhu P.F., Xiang G.D. (2014). An Empirical Study on China's Urbanization Path under Urban-rural Integration, *The Journal of Quantitative & Technical Economics*, (10): 21–36.

Luo Y.M., Fan L.M. (2015). The Role of Land in Growth of Farmers' Income: Protection or Obstacle? *Economic Research Journal*, (8): 146–161.

Luo Y.M., Fan L.M. (2014). Spatial Characteristics of the Income Increase Effect of Rural Human Capital in China, *Management World*, (9): 58–76.

Lyu W., Chu D.Y. (2011). Study on Urban-rural Income Gap and Economic Growth, *Economic Information*, (12): 30–36.

Lyu W., Gao F. (2013). Urbanization, Citizenization and Urban-rural Income Gap Comparison and Selection of Citizenization Measures, *Finance & Trade Economics*, (12): 38–46.

Ma J.L., Chen Y.F., Qian X.P. (2012). Climate factors, intermediate input and Corn Yield Growth: Empirical Analysis Based on Multilevel Modeling at Rural Household Level in Hebei, *Chinese Rural Economy*, (11): 11–20.

MacFarquhar R. and Fairbank K. (Eds). (1992a). The Cambridge History of China (Volume 14). Beijing: China Social Science Press.

MacFarquhar R. and Fairbank K. (Eds). (1992b). The Cambridge History of China (Volume 15). Beijing: China Social Science Press.

Mao P.H., Xu J. (2015). Farmland System, Land Management Right Transfer and Farmers' Income Growth, *Management World*, (5): 63–74.

Mao X.F., Liu J. (2011). Has China Reached the Lewis Turning Point? *Journal of Financial Research*, (8): 1–14.

Meng F.Q., Deng B.G. (2014). Household Registration Discrimination in Labor Market and Urban-rural Wage Inequality: Analysis Based on Quantile Regression and Decomposition, *Chinese Rural Economy*, (6): 56–65.

Meng X., Bai N. (2008). How Much have Wages of Unskilled Workers in China Increased? *China: Linking Market for Growth* (pp. 151–175). Canberra: Asia Pacific Press.

Meng X., Zhang J. (2001). The Two-tier Labor Markets in Urban China, *Journal of Comparative Economics*, 29(3): 485–504.

Meyer B., Sullivan J. (2013). Consumption and Income Inequality and the Great Recession, *American Economic Review*, 103(2): 178–183.

Meyer B., Sullivan J. (2011). Further Results on Measuring the Well-being of the Poor using Income and Consumption, *Canadian Journal of Economics*, 44(1): 52–87.

Naughton B. (2010). *The Chinese Economy: Transitions and Growth*, Shanghai: Shanghai People's Publishing House.

Ni G.H., Cai F. (2015). What Is the Proper Land Management Scale Really Needed by Farmers? *Economic Research Journal*, (3): 159–171.

Ning G.J., Li R. (2016). An Analysis on Differences in Citizenship Attainment for Rural to Urban Migrants with Different Migration Scopes, *Chinese Journal of Population Science*, (4): 37–47.

Niu J.L. (2013). Migration and Its Impact on the Differences in Health between Rural and Urban Residents in China, *Social Sciences in China*, (2): 46–63.

North D.C. (1994). *Structure and Change in Economic History*, Shanghai: Shanghai SDX Joint Publishing Company, Shanghai People's Publishing House.

Ouyang Z.G. (2014). Does the Promotion of Urban-rural Economic Integration Hinder the Expansion of Urban-rural Income Gap? *The Journal of World Economy*, (2): 116–135.

Overbeek G., Terluin I. (2006). *Rural Areas under Urban Pressure: Case Studies of Rural-urban Relationships across Europe*, The Hague: Agricultural Economics Research Institute.

Pan W.X. (2010). The Consumption Behavior Differences between Urban and Rural Residents and Policy Implications, *Statistical Research*, (8): 66–73.

Pan Y., Du X.M. (2010). Labor fluidity, Industrialization Process and Regional Economic Growth, *The Journal of Quantitative & Technical Economics*, (5): 34–48.

Parman J. (2012). Good School Make Good Neighbors: Human Capital Spillovers in Early 20th Century Agriculture, *Exploration in Economic History*, 49: 316–334.

Peng D.Y., Chen W.Y. (2014). Research on Income Distribution Based on Theil Index of Consumption Gap, *Journal of Zhongnan University of Finance and Economics*, (2): 30–37.

Piketty T., Yang L., Zucman G. (2017). Capital Accumulation, Private Property and Rising Inequality in China, 1978–2015, NBER Working Paper 23368.

Qian L., Ye J.T. (2017). Effect of Key Factor Marketization on the Reduction of Urban-rural Income Gap: An Empirical Analysis Based on Provincial Panel Data, *Journal of China Agricultural University*, (7): 210–220.

Qu F.T., Tian G.M. (2011). Urban-rural Coordination and Reform of Rural Collective Land Right System, *Management World*, (6): 34–46.

Ranis G., Fei J.C.H. (1961). A Theory of Economic Development, *American Economic Review*, 51(4): 533–565.

Ravallion M., Chen S. (2007). China's (Uneven) progress against Poverty, *Journal of Development Economy*, 82(1): 1–42.

Research Group of Department of Rural Economic System and Management of Ministry of Agriculture. (2016). Survey on the Development of New Farmers in the Background of Agricultural Supply Side Structural Reform, *Chinese Rural Economy*, (4): 2–11.

Research Group of Rural Department of the Development Research Center of the State Council. (2014). From Urban-rural duality to Urban-rural Integration, *Management World*, (9): 1–12.

Rozelle S., Taylor J.E., Brauw A. (1999). Migration, Remittances and Agricultural Productivity in China, *American Economic Review*, 89(2): 287–291.

Shi L., Gao F. (2006). Regional Economic Gap: An Empirical Study Based on Economic Structure Transformation, *Management World*, (5): 35–44.

Shi Z.F. (2013). *Ultranormal Growth: Chinese Economy 1970-2049*, Shanghai: Shanghai People's Publishing House.

Shi Z.L., Yang Y.Y. (2011). Impact and Policy Implication of Off-farm Work on Rural Labor Force Capability Development, *Management World*, (12): 40–54.

Shifa A.B. (2013). The Dual Policy in the Dual Economy—The Political Economy of Urban Bias in Dictatorial Regimes, *Journal of Development Economics*, 105(1): 77–85.

Shorrocks A.F. (1990). The Class of Additively Decomposable Inequality Measures, *Econometrica*, 48(3): 613–625.

Song H.Y. (2018). Forty Years of Rural Reform in China: Retrospect and Consideration, *Journal of Nanjing Agricultural University (Social Science Edition)*, (3): 1–11.

Song H.Y. (2004). Adjusting the Urban-rural Relationship: International Experiences and Their Implications for China, *Comparative Economic and Social Systems*, (3): 88–91.

Su F., Fang L. (2016). Regional Differences of Rural Financial Exclusion in China: Insufficient Supply or Insufficient Demand? *Management World*, (9): 70–83.

Su L.J., He Y.F., Jin S.N. (2006). Integrative Study of Panel Data on Urban-rural Resident Consumption and Income Relationship in China, *The Journal of World Economy*, (5): 65–72.

Sun J., Zhang Q.C. (2012). Empirical Analysis on Imbalanced Urban-rural Financial Development and Urban-rural Income Gap, *World Economic Papers*, (3): 108–120.

Sun N.H., Du Y., Hong Y.M. (2009). The Distortion of the Labor Market, the Difference in Its Efficiency, and the Income Disparity between Peasants and Town People, *Management World*, (9): 44–52.

Sun W.H., Fang X.Q. (2014). Different Roads of Urban-rural Relation Evolution: Comparison and Enlightenment, *Jiangsu Social Sciences*, (2): 92–97.

Sun W.K., Bai C.E., Xie P.C. (2011). The Effect on Rural Labor fluidity from Registration System Reform in China, *Economic Research Journal*, (1): 28–41.

Sun X.Z. (2016). Advancing Legislative Research into the Operational Model of Farmland Subject to Division of Three Rights, *Social Sciences in China*, (7): 145–163.

Tang D., Zhang J. (2011). Kuznets Process of China's Economic Growth, Urbanization and Income Distribution: Theory and Experience . *World Economic Review*, (5): 15–34.

The Central Party Literature Press. (1993). *Selected Important Articles Since the Founding of China* (Vol. 4, pp. 706–707). The Central Party Literature Press.

Veenhuizen R. Van. (2006). Cities Farming for the Future: Urban Agriculture for Green and Productive Cities, RUAF Foundation, IDRC and HRR.

Vollrath D. (2009). How Important are Dual Economy Effects for Aggregate Productivity? *Journal of Development Economics*, 88(2): 325–334.

Walley J., Zhang S.M. (2007). A Numerical Simulation Analysis of Labor fluidity (Hukou) Restrictions in China, *Journal of Development Economics*, 83(2): 392–410.

Wan H.Y., Li S. (2013). The Effects of Household Registration System Discrimination on Urban-rural Inequality in China, *Economic Research Journal*, (9): 43–55.

Wang D.W. (2009). The Lewis Turning Point in China: Signs and Implications, *Population Research*, (2): 32–35.

Wang D.W., He Y.P. (2005). The Nature, Dimension and Implications of Rural-urban Disparity in China, *China Rural Survey*, (3): 25–37.

Wang H., Xu X. (2006). Income Inequality: Between Regions or Between Urban and Rural Areas, *Management World*, (11): 41–50.

Wang J., Zhong X.H. (2011). Has the Lewis Turning Point Arrived in China?—Theoretical Analysis and International Experience, *Social Sciences in China*, (5): 22–37.

Wang J.N., Zhang Q.L. (2005). The Basic Characteristics and Development Trend of Income Gap between Urban Residents and Rural Residents, *Statistical Research*, (3): 37–39.

Wang O., Yang J. (2014). Impact of Agricultural Subsidies on Food Production in China, *Chinese Rural Economy*, (5): 20–28.

Wang R. (2006). The Analysis of Factors Resulting in Change of Income Difference between Rural and Urban Residents of China: Also To Discuss the Applicability of Hypothesis of Down "U", *Statistical Research*, (4): 14–19.

Wang W.T. (2009). Urbanization Process and Urban-rural Basic Public Service Equalization, *Finance & Trade Economics*, (2): 40–45.

Wang X.H., Wen T. (2015). The Evolution of Differences about Consumption Behavior and Consumption Structure between Urban and Rural Residents, *The Journal of Quantitative & Technical Economics*, (10): 90–107.

Wang X.L., Fan G., Yu J.W. (2017). *Marketization Index of China's Provinces*, Beijing: Social Science Academic Press.

Wang Y.F. (2012). The Estimation of Income Distribution in Urban and Rural China, *The Journal of Quantitative & Technical Economics*, (6): 61–73.

Wang Y.M., Yao X.G., Zhou M.H. (2013). Rural Laborer Outflow, Regional Disparity and Food Production, *Management World*, (11): 67–76.

Wei H.K. (2016). Urban-rural Integration in the New Normal and Its Promotion Strategy, *Chinese Rural Economy*, (1): 2–16.

Wen G., Xiong J. (2014). The Hukou and Land Tenure System as Two Middle Income Traps—the Case of Modern China, *Frontiers of Economics in China*, 9(3): 438–459.

Wen Y. (2016). *Great Industrial Revolution of China*, Beijing: Tsinghua University Press.

Winters P., et al. (2009). Assets, Activities and Rural Income Generation: Evidence from a Multicounty Analysis, *World Development*, 37(9): 1435–1452.

Wu D., Huo X.X. (2010). Empirical Study on Consumption Gap and Income Gap Interaction between Urban and Rural Residence: Evidence from VEC Model, *Journal of Agrotechnical Economics*, (8): 101–106.

Wu H.J., He L.X., Zhang Z.G. (2014). Effects of Demographic Age Structure on Urban-rural Residents' Consumption Disparity in China, *The Journal of Quantitative & Technical Economics*, (2): 3–19.

Wu L. (2000). A Beyond-the-limit Tough Choice: On the Institutional Choice of Agricultural Modernization in China in 1949–1998, *Researches in Chinese Economic History*, (2): 87–98.

Wu L. (2007). Historic Analysis of Urban-rural Relations in 1949–2006, *Researches in Chinese Economic History*, (1): 23–31.

Wu X.M., Perloff J.M. (2005). China's Income Distribution, 1985–2001, *Review of Economics and Statistics*, 87(4): 763–775.

Wu Y.P. (2017). *A Political Explanation of Economic Growth*, Beijing: SDX Joint Publishing Company.

Wu Y.X. (2013). Inequality of Educational Opportunities between Urban and Rural Residents in China and Its Evolution, *Social Sciences in China*, (3): 4–21.

Xiao W., Xiao L.Z. (2013). Agricultural Technical Progress, Food Production Increase and Farmers' Income Growth in a Dual Economy, *Chinese Rural Economy*, (6): 4–13.

Xie Z.F., Zhang W. (2015). China's Economic Growth and Fiscal Decentralization: Analysis Based on a Panel Data after Tax System Reforming, *The Quarterly Journal of Economics*, (2): 435–452.

Xin X.F., Qin F. (2011). Decomposition of Agricultural Labor Productivity Growth and its Regional Disparity in China, *China Agricultural Economic Review*, 3(1): 92–100.

Xing C.B., Jia S.Y., Li S. (2013). Regional Distribution of the Return to Education for Rural-to-Urban Migrants and Its Impact on Migration, *Economic Research Journal*, (11): 114–126.

Xu C.G. (2001). The Fundamental Institutions of China's Reforms and Development, *Journal of Economic Literature*, 49(4): 1076–1151.

Xu F. (2015). Spatio-temporal Evolution of Urban-rural Income Disparity, *Shanghai Journal of Economics*, (10): 114–120.

Xu M., Jiang Y. (2015). Can China's Industrial Structure Upgrading Narrow the Gap between Urban and Rural Consumption? *The Journal of Quantitative & Technical Economics*, (3): 3–21.

Xu Q., Tian S.C., Xu Z.G., Shao T. (2008). Rural Land System, Land Fragmentation and Farmers' Income Inequality, *Economic Research Journal*, (2): 83–92.

Xu Z.Y., Guo Z.C., Jing L.B. (2014). The Turning Point for Urban-rural Consumption Gap in China—Segmental Quantitative Detection Incorporating Scrolling Dummy Variables, *Economic Information*, (6): 32–49.

Yang D.T. (2004). Education and Allocative Efficiency: Household Income Growth during Rural Reforms in China, *Journal of Development Economics*, 74: 137–162.

Yang J.D. (2013). The Evolution Trend and Causes of Consumption Inequality in China, *Finance & Trade Economics*, (4): 111–120.

Yang N., Ma C.X. (2014). The Dynamic Inverted U Effect of Financial Development on the Urban-rural Income Gap and the Forecast of Its Dropping Point, *Journal of Financial Research*, (11): 175–190.

Yao Y.J. (2005). Financial Development, Urbanization and Urban-rural Income Gap in China—Co-integration Analysis and Granger Causality Test, *China Rural Survey*, (12): 2–8.

Ye C., Chen M.X. (2008). Review about the Theoretical Evolvement of Rural-urban relationship, (1): 34–39.

Yin H.P., Liu Y.L. (2016). Rural Laborers' Remaining in Rural, Rural-urban Migration or Returning to Rural during Urbanization Process, *Chinese Journal of Population Sciences*, (4): 26–36.

Yu C.L. (2011). Fiscal Decentralization, Public Goods Supply and Urban-rural Income Inequality in China, *Economic Issues in China*, (5): 36–45.

Yu Y.X., Zhang P. (2011). A Discussion on Lewis Turning Point of China under the Framework of Lewis Model, *World Economic Papers*, (6): 32–45.

Zhang G.T., Jiang J., Chen Y. (2010). The Impact of Chinese Rural Surplus Labor Transfer on Economic Growth, *China Industrial Economy*, (10): 15–23.

Zhang L., Li S., Darity Jr. W.A., Sharpe R.S. (2014). Analysis of Household Registration Discrimination in China's Labor Market, *Management World*, (11): 35–46.

Zhang L.J., Li Q., Luo R.F., Liu C.F., Rozelle S. (2005). The Investment in Public Goods and the Regional Distribution in Rural China, *Chinese Rural Economy*, (11): 73–81.

Zhang L.J., Shen Y. (2007). The Analysis of Three Major Effects of Financial Development on the Urban - rural Income Gap, *The Journal of Quantitative & Technical Economics*, (2): 73–81.

Zhang L.Y. (2007). The Analysis and Policy Research on Consumption Difference between Urban and Rural Areas under the Dualistic, *China Soft Science*, (2): 11–16.

Zhang M.L. (2014). Analysis on Rural Homestead Transfer Mode and Institutional Selection, *Reform of Economic System*, (3): 85–89.

Zhang R.L. (2003). Urban-rural Relationship in China and Its Social Changes, *Social Science Front Bimonthly*, (3): 241–244.

Zhang T. (2003). Fluctuation and Causal Analysis of China's Income Gap: 1985-2012, *The Journal of Quantitative & Technical Economics*, (3): 3–22.

Zhang W.J., Fang Z.R., Huang J.X. (2015). Disparity between Urban and Rural Areas in China: A Business Cycle Perspective, *The Quarterly Journal of Economics*, (2): 651–676.

Zhang X., Liu X.G., Fan G. (2014). Rural Labor Migration and Household Saving Rate: The Perspective of Discrepancy in Income and Social Security, *Economic Research Journal*, (4): 130–142.

Zhao Y., Jiang H.C. (2007). Supply of Main Rural Public Goods from Farmers' Perspective: Evidence from 32 Administrative Villages in 11 Counties (Cities) of Shandong, *Chinese Rural Economy*, (5): 52–62.

Zheng G., Ye Y.M. (2009). The Stage of Chinese Urban-rural Relation and Its Development Model, *Journal of Renmin University of China*, (6): 87–92.

Zheng Y.G. (2010). Establishing New Types of Industry-Agriculture and Urban-Rural Relations: Aims and Policies, *Teaching and Research*, (4): 5–14.

Zhong C.P., Chen S.P., Xu C.S. (2013). Structural Transform, Factor Pricing and Farmers' Action: Theoretical and Empirical Evidence for Agricultural Subsidies, *Journal of Financial Research*, (5): 167–180.

Zhou D.M. (2009), Technical Progress, Technical Efficiency, and Productivity Growth of China's Agriculture, *The Journal of Quantitative & Technical Economics*, (12): 70–82.

Zhou J., Yang X.Z. (2009), China's Rural Consumption Behavior Changes and Rural-Urban Mechanism, *Economic Research Journal*, 2009(1): 83–95.

Zhou W., Zhao F., Yang F., Li L. (2017). Land Transfer, Reform of Household Registration System and Urbanization in China: Theoretical and Simulation Test, *Economic Research Journal*, 2017(6): 185–199.

Zhou X.G. (2017). *The Institutional Logic of Governance in China: An Organization Approach*, Beijing: SDX Joint Publishing Company.

Zhou Y.B. (2009). Urbanization, Urban-Rural Income Gap and Overall Income Inequality in China: An Empirical Test of the Inverse-U Hypothesis, *The Quarterly Journal of Economics*, 2009(3): 1239–1256.

Zhou Z., Ma Q.C., Kong X.Z. (2016). Quantitative Study on the Contribution of Agricultural Mechanization to Rural Labor Transfer, *Journal of Agrotechnical Economics*, 2016(2): 52–62.

Zhu J.L., Li Z.L. (2016). Hukou System Reform, Individuals Flows and Regional Disparities: Based on the Intertemporal Model of Heterogeneous Individuals Flows, *The Quarterly Journal of Economics*, 2016(2): 797–816.

Zhu X., Shi Q.H., Gai Q.E. (2011). Misallocation and TFP in Rural China, *Economic Research Journal*, 2011(5): 86–98.

Zhu X.K., Luo C. (2011). Theoretical Logic and Sinicization of the Consumption Function: A Survey of Literature, *Economic Research Journal*, 2011(1): 140–153.

Zou H., Li A.L., Yu K.Z. (2013). Measurement, Birth Cohort Decomposition and Formation Mechanism of Consumption Inequality: Discussion with Income Inequality, *The Quarterly Journal of Economics*, 2013(4): 1231–1254.

Index

Note: Page numbers in *Italic* refer to figures; and in **bold** refer to tables

For Product Safety Concerns and Information please contact our EU representative GPSR@taylorandfrancis.com
Taylor & Francis Verlag GmbH, Kaufingerstraße 24, 80331 München, Germany

www.ingramcontent.com/pod-product-compliance
Ingram Content Group UK Ltd.
Pitfield, Milton Keynes, MK11 3LW, UK
UKHW021031021026
476168UK00012BA/1395
9781032029283